*The Cultural Nature
of Human Development*

THE *Cultural* NATURE

Barbara Rogoff

O F *Human Development*

OXFORD
UNIVERSITY PRESS

2003

OXFORD

UNIVERSITY PRESS

Oxford   New York

Auckland   Bangkok   Buenos Aires   Capetown   Chennai
Dar es Salaam   Delhi   Hong Kong   Istanbul   Karachi   Kolkata
Kuala Lumpur   Madrid   Melbourne   Mexico City   Mumbai   Nairobi
São Paulo   Shanghai   Taipei   Tokyo   Toronto

Library of Congress Cataloging-in-Publication Data
Rogoff, Barbara.
The cultural nature of human development / Barbara Rogoff.
    p.   cm.
Includes bibliographical references and index.
ISBN 978-0-19-513133-8
1. Socialization.   2. Child development.   3. Cognition and culture.
4. Developmental psychology.   I. Title.
HM686 .R64 2003
305.231 — dc21   2002010393

20   19   18

Printed in the United States of America
on acid-free paper

For Salem, Luisa, Valerie, and David

with appreciation for their companionship

and support all along the way.

ACKNOWLEDGMENTS

I deeply appreciate the wisdom, support, and challenges of Beatrice Whiting, Lois and Ben Paul, Mike Cole, Sylvia Scribner, Shep White, Jerry Kagan, Roy Malpass, Marta Navichoc Cotuc, Encarnación Perez, Pablo Cox Bixcul, and the children and parents of San Pedro, who opened my eyes to patterns of culture and how to think about them.

I am grateful to the insightful discussions and questions of Cathy Angelillo, Krystal Bellinger, Rosy Chang, Pablo Chavajay, Erica Coy, Julie Holloway, Afsaneh Kalantari, Ed Lopez, Eugene Matusov, Rebeca Mejía Arauz, Behnosh Najafi, Emily Parodi, Ari Taub, Araceli Valle, and my graduate and undergraduate students who helped me develop these ideas. I especially appreciate the suggestions of Debi Bolter, Maricela Correa-Chávez, Sally Duensing, Shari Ellis, Ray Gibbs, Giyoo Hatano, Carol Lee, Elizabeth Magarian, Ruth Paradise, Keiko Takahashi, Catherine Cooper, Marty Chemers, and Wendy Williams and the valuable assistance of Karrie André and Cindy White. The editorial advice of Jonathan Cobb, Elizabeth Knoll, Joan Bossert, and several anonymous reviewers greatly improved the book. I greatly appreciate the donors and UCSC colleagues who created the UCSC Foundation chair in psychology that supports my work.

CONTENTS

The Cultural Nature
of Human Development

I

Orienting Concepts
and Ways of Understanding
the Cultural Nature of Human Development

Human development is a cultural process. As a biological species, humans are defined in terms of our cultural participation. We are prepared by both our cultural and biological heritage to use language and other cultural tools and to learn from each other. Using such means as language and literacy, we can collectively remember events that we have not personally experienced —becoming involved vicariously in other people's experience over many generations.

Being human involves constraints and possibilities stemming from long histories of human practices. At the same time, each generation continues to revise and adapt its human cultural and biological heritage in the face of current circumstances.

My aim in this book is to contribute to the understanding of cultural patterns of human development by examining the regularities that make sense of differences and similarities in communities' practices and traditions. In referring to cultural processes, I want to draw attention to the configurations of routine ways of doing things in any community's approach to living. I focus on people's participation in their communities' cultural practices and traditions, rather than equating culture with the nationality or ethnicity of individuals.

For understanding cultural aspects of human development, a primary goal of this book is to develop the stance that *people develop as participants in cultural communities. Their development can be understood only in light of the cultural practices and circumstances of their communities—which also change.*

To date, the study of human development has been based largely on research and theory coming from middle-class communities in Europe and North America. Such research and theory often have been assumed to generalize to all people. Indeed, many researchers make conclusions from work done in a single group in overly general terms, claiming that "*the child* does such-and-so" rather than "these children did such-and-so."

For example, a great deal of research has attempted to determine at what age one should expect "the child" to be capable of certain skills. For the most part, the claims have been generic regarding the age at which children enter a stage or should be capable of a certain skill.

A cultural approach notes that different cultural communities may expect children to engage in activities at vastly different times in childhood, and may regard "timetables" of development in other communities as surprising or even dangerous. Consider these questions of when children can begin to do certain things, and reports of cultural variations in when they do:

When does children's intellectual development permit them to be responsible for others? When can they be trusted to take care of an infant?

In middle-class U.S. families, children are often not regarded as capable of caring for themselves or tending another child until perhaps age 10 (or later in some regions). In the U.K., it is an offense to leave a child under age 14 years without adult supervision (Subbotsky, 1995). However, in many other communities around the world, children begin to take on responsibility for tending other children at ages 5–7 (Rogoff et al., 1975; see figure 1.1), and in some places even younger children begin to assume this responsibility. For example, among the Kwara'ae of Oceania,

> Three year olds are skilled workers in the gardens and household, excellent caregivers of their younger siblings, and accomplished at social interaction. Although young children also have time to play, many of the functions of play seem to be met by work. For both adults and children, work is accompanied by singing, joking, verbal play and entertaining conversation. Instead of playing with dolls, children care for real babies. In addition to working in the family gardens, young children have their own garden plots. The latter may seem like play, but by three or four years of age many children are taking produce they have grown themselves to the market to sell, thereby making a significant and valued contribution to the family income. (Watson-Gegeo, 1990, p. 87)

FIGURE 1.1

This 6-year-old Mayan (Guatemalan) girl is a skilled caregiver for her baby cousin.

When do children's judgment and coordination allow them to handle sharp knives safely?

Although U.S. middle-class adults often do not trust children below about age 5 with knives, among the Efe of the Democratic Republic of Congo, infants routinely use machetes safely (Wilkie, personal communication, 1989; see figure 1.2). Likewise, Fore (New Guinea) infants handle knives and fire safely by the time they are able to walk (Sorenson, 1979). Aka parents of Central Africa teach 8- to 10-month-old infants how to throw small spears and use small pointed digging sticks and miniature axes with sharp metal blades:

> Training for autonomy begins in infancy. Infants are allowed to crawl or walk to whatever they want in camp and allowed to use knives, machetes, digging sticks, and clay pots around camp. Only if an infant begins to crawl into a fire or hits another child do parents or others interfere with the infant's activity. It was not unusual, for instance, to see an eight month old with a six-inch knife chopping the branch frame of its family's house. By three or four years of age children can cook themselves a meal on the fire, and by ten years of age Aka children know enough subsistence skills to live in the forest alone if need be. (Hewlett, 1991, p. 34)

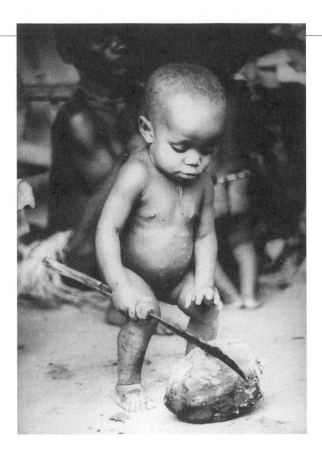

FIGURE 1.2

An Efe baby of 11 months skillfully cuts a fruit with a machete, under the watchful eye of a relative (in the Ituri Forest of the Democratic Republic of Congo).

So, at what age do children develop responsibility for others or sufficient skill and judgment to handle dangerous implements? "Ah! Of course, it depends," readers may say, after making some guesses based on their own cultural experience.

Indeed. It depends.

Variations in expectations for children make sense once we take into account different circumstances and traditions. They make sense in the context of differences in what is involved in preparing "a meal" or "tending" a baby, what sources of support and danger are common, who else is nearby, what the roles of local adults are and how they live, what institutions people use to organize their lives, and what goals the community has for development to mature functioning in those institutions and cultural practices.

Whether the activity is an everyday chore or participation in a test or a laboratory experiment, people's performance depends in large part on the circumstances that are routine in their community and on the cultural practices they are used to. What they do depends in important ways on the cultural meaning given to the events and the social and institutional supports provided in their communities for learning and carrying out specific roles in the activities.

Cultural research has aided scholars in examining theories based on observations in European and European American communities for their applicability in other circumstances. Some of this work has provided crucial counterexamples demonstrating limitations or challenging basic assumptions of a theory that was assumed to apply to all people everywhere. Examples are Bronislaw Malinowski's (1927) research questioning the Oedipal complex in Sigmund Freud's theory and cross-cultural tests of cognitive development that led Jean Piaget to drop his claim that adolescents universally reach a "formal operational" stage of being able to systematically test hypotheses (1972; see Dasen & Heron, 1981).

The importance of understanding cultural processes has become clear in recent years. This has been spurred by demographic changes throughout North America and Europe, which bring everyone more in contact with cultural traditions differing from their own. Scholars now recognize that understanding cultural aspects of human development is important for resolving pressing practical problems as well as for progress in understanding the nature of human development in worldwide terms. Cultural research is necessary to move beyond overgeneralizations that assume that human development everywhere functions in the same ways as in researchers' own communities, and to be able to account for both similarities and differences across communities.

Understanding regularities in the cultural nature of human development is a primary aim of this book. Observations made in Bora Bora or Cincinnati can form interesting cultural portraits and reveal intriguing differences in custom, but more important, they can help us to discern regularities in the diverse patterns of human development in different communities.

Looking for Cultural Regularities

Beyond demonstrating that "culture matters," my aim in this book is to integrate the available ideas and research to contribute to a greater understanding of *how* culture matters in human development. What regularities can help us make sense of the cultural aspects of human development? To understand the processes that characterize the dynamic development of individual people as well as their changing cultural communities, we need to identify regularities that make sense of the variations across communities as well as the impressive commonalities across our human species. Although research on cultural aspects of human development is still relatively sparse, it is time to go beyond saying "It depends" to articulate patterns in the variations and similarities of cultural practices.

The process of looking across cultural traditions can help us become aware of cultural regularities in our own as well as other people's lives, no matter which communities are most familiar to us. Cultural research can help us understand cultural aspects of our own lives that we take for granted as natural, as well as those that surprise us elsewhere.

For example, the importance given to paying attention to chronological age and age of developmental achievements is unquestioned by many who study human development. However, questions about age of transitions are themselves based on a cultural perspective. They fit with cultural institutions that use elapsed time since birth as a measure of development.

One Set of Patterns: Children's Age-Grading and Segregation from Community Endeavors or Participation in Mature Activities

It was not until the last half of the 1800s in the United States and some other nations that age became a criterion for ordering lives, and this intensified in the early 1900s (Chudacoff, 1989). With the rise of industrialization and efforts to systematize human services such as education and medical care, age became a measure of development and a criterion for sorting people. Specialized institutions were designed around age groups. Developmental psychology and pediatrics began at this time, along with old-age institutions and age-graded schools.

Before then in the United States (and still, in many places), people rarely knew their age, and students advanced in their education as they learned. Both expert and popular writing in the United States rarely referred to specific ages, although of course infancy, childhood, and adulthood were distinguished. Over the past century and a half, the cultural concept of age and associated practices relying on age-grading have come to play a central, though often unnoticed role in ordering lives in some cultural communities — those of almost all contemporary readers of this book.

Age-grading accompanied the increasing segregation of children from the full range of activities in their community as school became compulsory and industrialization separated workplace from home. Instead of joining with the adult world, young children became more engaged in specialized child-focused institutions and practices, preparing children for later entry into the community.

I argue that child-focused settings and ways in which middle-class parents now interact with their children are closely connected with age-grading and segregation of children. Child-focused settings and middle-class child-rearing practices are also prominent in developmental psychology, connecting with ideas about stages of life, thinking and learning processes, motivation, relations with peers and parents, disciplinary practices at home and school, competition and cooperation. I examine these cultural regularities throughout this book, as they are crucial to understanding development in many communities.

An alternative pattern involves integration of children in the everyday activities of their communities. This pattern involves very different concepts and cultural practices in human development (Rogoff, Paradise, Mejía Arauz, Correa-Chávez, & Angelillo, 2003). The opportunities to observe and pitch in allow children to learn through keen attention to ongoing activities, rather than relying on lessons out of the context of using the knowledge and skills taught. In this pattern, children's relationships often involve multiparty collaboration in groups rather than interactions with one person at a time. I examine these and related regularities throughout this book.

Other Patterns

Because cultural research is still quite new, the work of figuring out what regularities can make sense of the similarities and variations across communities is not yet very far along. However, there are several other areas that appear to involve important regularities in cultural practices.

One set of regularities has to do with a pattern in which human relations are assumed to require hierarchical organization, with someone in charge who controls the others. An alternative pattern is more horizontal in structure, with individuals being responsible together to the group. In this pattern, individuals are not controlled by others—individual autonomy of decision making is respected—but individuals are also expected to coordinate with the group direction. As I discuss in later chapters, issues of cultural differences in sleeping arrangements, discipline, cooperation, gender roles, moral development, and forms of assistance in learning all connect with this set of patterns.

Other patterns have to do with strategies for managing survival. Infant and adult mortality issues, shortage or abundance of food and other resources, and settled living or nomadic life seem to connect with cultural similarities and variations in infant care and attachment, family roles, stages and goals of development, children's responsibilities, gender roles, cooperation and competition, and intellectual priorities.

I develop these suggestions of patterns of regularity and some others throughout the book. Although the search for regularities in cultural systems has barely begun, it has great promise for helping us understand the surprising as well as the taken-for-granted ways of cultural communities worldwide, including one's own.

To look for cultural patterns, it is important to examine how we can think about the roles of cultural processes and individual development. In the first three chapters, I focus on how we can conceptualize the interrelated roles of individual and cultural processes. In the next section of this chapter, I introduce some important orienting concepts for how we can think about the roles of cultural processes in human development.

Orienting Concepts for Understanding Cultural Processes

The orienting concepts for understanding cultural processes that I develop in this book stem from the sociocultural (or cultural-historical) perspective. This approach has become prominent in recent decades in the study of how cultural practices relate to the development of ways of thinking, remembering, reasoning, and solving problems (Rogoff & Chavajay, 1995). Lev Vygotsky, a leader of this approach from early in the twentieth century, pointed out that children in all communities are cultural participants, living in a particular community at a specific time in history. Vygotsky (1987) argued that rather than trying to "reveal the eternal child," the goal is to discover "the historical child."

Understanding development from a sociocultural-historical perspective requires examination of the cultural nature of everyday life. This includes studying people's use and transformation of cultural tools and technologies and their involvement in cultural traditions in the structures and institutions of family life and community practices.

A coherent understanding of the cultural, historical nature of human development is emerging from an interdisciplinary approach involving psychology, anthropology, history, sociolinguistics, education, sociology, and other fields. It builds on a variety of traditions of research, including participant observation of everyday life from an anthropological perspective, psychological research in naturalistic or constrained "laboratory" situations, historical accounts, and fine-grained analyses of videotaped events. Together, the research and scholarly traditions across fields are sparking a new conception of human development as a cultural process.

To understand regularities in the variations and similarities of cultural processes of human development across widespread communities it is important to examine how we think about cultural processes and their relation to individual development. What do we mean by cultural processes? How do people come to understand their own as well as others' cultural practices and traditions? How can we think about the ways that individuals both participate in and contribute to cultural processes? How do we approach understanding the relation among cultural communities and how cultural communities themselves transform?

This section outlines what I call *orienting concepts* for understanding cultural processes. These are concepts to guide thinking about how cultural processes contribute to human development.

The *overarching orienting concept* for understanding cultural processes is my version of the sociocultural-historical perspective:

> *Humans develop through their changing participation in the socio-cultural activities of their communities, which also change.*

This overarching orienting concept provides the basis for the other orienting concepts for understanding cultural processes:

- *Culture isn't just what **other** people do.* It is common for people to think of themselves as having no culture ("Who, me? I don't have an accent") or to take for granted the circumstances of their historical period, unless they have contact with several cultural communities. Broad cultural experience gives us the opportunity to see the extent of cultural processes in everyday human activities and development, which relate to the technologies we use and our institutional and community values and traditions. The practices of researchers, students, journalists, and professors are cultural, as are the practices of oral historians, midwives, and shamans.

- *Understanding one's own cultural heritage, as well as other cultural communities, requires taking the perspective of people of contrasting backgrounds.* The most difficult cultural processes to examine are the ones that are based on confident and unquestioned assumptions stemming from one's own community's practices. Cultural processes surround all of us and often involve subtle, tacit, taken-for-granted events and ways of doing things that require open eyes, ears, and minds to notice and understand. (Children are very alert to learning from these taken-for-granted ways of doing things.)

- *Cultural practices fit together and are connected.* Each needs to be understood in relation to other aspects of the cultural approach. Cultural processes involve multifaceted relations among many aspects of community functioning; they are not just a collection of variables that operate independently. Rather, they vary together in patterned ways. Cultural processes have a coherence beyond "elements" such as economic resources, family size, modernization, and urbanization. It is impossible to reduce differences between communities to a single variable or two (or even a dozen or two); to do so would destroy the coherence among the constellations of features that make it useful to refer to cultural processes. What is done one way in one community may be done another way in another community, with the same effect, and a practice done the same way in both communities may serve different ends. An understanding of how cultural practices fit together is essential.

Cultural communities continue to change, as do individuals. A community's history and relations with other communities are part of cultural processes. In addition, variations among members of communities are to be expected, because individuals connect in various ways with other communities and experiences. Variation across and within communities is a resource for humanity, allowing us to be prepared for varied and unknowable futures.

There is not likely to be One Best Way. Understanding different cultural practices does not require determining which *one* way is "right" (which does not mean that *all* ways are fine). With an understanding of what is done in different circumstances, we can be open to possibilities that do not necessarily exclude each other. Learning from other communities does not require giving up one's own ways. It does require suspending one's own assumptions temporarily to consider others and carefully separating efforts to understand cultural phenomena from efforts to judge their value. It is essential to make some guesses as to what the patterns are, while continually testing and open-mindedly revising one's guesses. *There is **always** more to learn.*

The rest of this chapter examines how we can move beyond the inevitable assumptions that we each bring from our own experience, to expand our understanding of human development to encompass other cultural approaches. This process involves building on local perspectives to develop more informed ideas about regular patterns, by:

- Moving beyond ethnocentrism to consider different perspectives
- Considering diverse goals of development
- Recognizing the value of the knowledge of both insiders and outsiders of specific cultural communities
- Systematically and open-mindedly revising our inevitably local understandings so that they become more encompassing

The next two chapters take up related questions of ways to conceive of the relation between individual and cultural processes, the relation of culture and biology (arguing that humans are biologically cultural), and how to think about participation in changing cultural communities.

The remaining chapters examine regularities in the cultural nature of such aspects of development as children's relations with other children and with parents, the development of thinking and remembering and reading skills, gender roles, and ways that communities arrange for children to learn. The research literature that I draw on in these chapters is wide-ranging, involving methods from psychology, anthropology, history, sociolinguistics, education, sociology, and related fields. The different research methods enhance each other, helping us gain broader and deeper views of the cultural nature of human development. In choosing which research to include, I emphasize investigations that appear to be based on some close involvement with everyday life in the communities studied, to facilitate understanding phenomena as they play out.

The book's concluding chapter focuses on the continually changing nature of cultural traditions as well as of people's involvement in and creation of them. The chapter focuses particularly on changes related to Western schooling—increasingly pervasive in the lives of children and adults worldwide—to examine dynamic cultural processes that build new ways as well as building on cultural traditions.

Moving Beyond Initial Assumptions

It would hardly be fish who discovered the existence of water.
—Kluckhohn, 1949, p. 11

Like the fish that is unaware of water until it has left the water, people often take their own community's ways of doing things for granted. Engaging with people whose practices differ from those of one's own community can make one aware of aspects of human functioning that are not noticeable until they are missing or differently arranged (LeVine, 1966). "The most valuable part of comparative work in another culture [is] the chance to be shaken by it, and the experience of struggling to understand it" (Goldberg, 1977, p. 239).

People who have immersed themselves in communities other than their own frequently experience "culture shock." Their new setting works in ways that conflict with what they have always assumed, and it may be unsettling to reflect on their own cultural ways as an option rather than the "natural" way. An essay on culture shock illustrates this notion by describing discoveries of assumptions by travelers from the Northern Hemisphere:

Assumptions are the things you don't know you're making, which is why it is so disorienting the first time you take the plug out of a washbasin in Australia and see the water spiraling down the hole the other way around. The very laws of physics are telling you how far you are from home.

In New Zealand even the telephone dials are numbered anti-clockwise. This has nothing to do with the laws of physics—they just do it differently there. The shock is that it had never occurred to you that there was any other way of doing it. In fact, you had never even thought about it at all, and suddenly here it is—different. The ground slips. (Adams & Carwardine, 1990, p. 141)

Even without being *immersed* in another cultural system, comparisons of cultural ways may create discomfort among people who have never before considered the assumptions of their own cultural practices. Many individuals feel that their own community's ways are being questioned when they begin to learn about the diverse ways of other groups.

An indigenous American author pointed out that comparisons of cultural ways—necessary to achieve understanding of cultural processes—can be experienced as an uncomfortable challenge by people who are used to only one cultural system:

Such contrasts and comparisons tend to polarize people, making them feel either attacked or excluded, because all of us tend to think of comparisons as judgmental. . . . Comparisons are inevitable and so too is the important cultural bias that all of us foster as part of our heritage. (Highwater, 1995, p. 214)

One of my aims in this book is to separate value judgments from understanding of the various ways that cultural processes function in human development. The need to avoid jumping to conclusions about the appropriateness of other people's ways has become quite clear in cultural research, and is the topic of the next section.

Suspending judgment is also often needed for understanding one's own cultural ways. People sometimes assume that respect for other ways implies criticism of or problems with their own familiar ways. Therefore, I want to stress that the aim is to understand the patterns of different cultural communities, *separating understanding of the patterns from judgments of their value.* If judgments of value are necessary, as they often are, they will thereby be much better informed if they are suspended long enough to gain some understanding of the patterns involved in one's own familiar ways as well as in the sometimes surprising ways of other communities.

Beyond Ethnocentrism and Deficit Models

People often view the practices of other communities as barbaric. They assume that their community's perspective on reality is the only proper or sensible or civilized one (Berger & Luckmann, 1966; Campbell & LeVine, 1961; Jahoda & Krewer, 1997). For example, the ancient Greeks facilitated their own cultural identity by devaluing people with different languages, customs, and conceptions of human nature (Riegel, 1973). Indeed, the word *barbarous* derives from the Greek term for "foreign," "rude," and "ignorant" (Skeat, 1974; it is also the derivation of the name Barbara!). The term barbarian was applied to neighboring tribes who spoke languages unintelligible to the Greeks, who heard only "bar-bar" when they spoke:

> Beyond the civilizational core areas lay the lands of the barbarians, clad in skins, rude in manner, gluttonous, unpredictable, and aggressive in disposition, unwilling to submit to law, rule, and religious guidance . . . not quite human because they did not live in cities, where the only true and beautiful life could be lived, and because they appeared to lack articulate language. They were *barbaraphonoi*, bar-bar-speakers [Homer, *Iliad* 2.867], and in Aristotle's view this made them natural slaves and outcasts. (Wolf, 1994, p. 2)

To impose a value judgment from one's own community on the cultural practices of another—without understanding how those practices make sense in that community—is ethnocentric. *Ethnocentrism involves making judgments that another cultural community's ways are immoral, unwise, or inappropriate based on one's own cultural background without taking into account the meaning and circumstances of events in that community.* Another community's practices and beliefs are evaluated as inferior without considering their origins, meaning, and functions from the perspective of that community. It is a question of prejudging without appropriate knowledge.

For example, it is common to regard good parenting in terms deriving from the practices of one's own cultural community. Carolyn Edwards characterized contemporary middle-class North American child-rearing values (of parents and child-rearing experts) in the following terms:

> Hierarchy is anathema, bigger children emphatically should not be allowed to dominate smaller ones, verbal reasoning and negotiation should prevail, children should always be presented choices, and physical punishment is seen as the first step to child abuse. All of the ideas woven together represent a meaning system. (1994, p. 6)

Edwards pointed out that in other communities, not all components of this meaning system are found. If a Kenyan mother says, "Stop doing that or I will beat you," it does not mean the same thing as if the statement came from a middle-class European American mother. In an environment in which people need a certain physical and mental toughness to thrive (for heavy physical work, preparedness for warfare, long marches with cycles of hunger), the occasional use of physical discipline has a very different meaning than in an environment where physical comfort is often taken for granted. In contrast, a Kenyan mother would not consider withholding food from her children as punishment: "To her, what American mothers do (in the best interests of their children), namely, restrict children's food intake and deprive them of delicious, available, wanted food, would be terrible, unthinkable, the next thing to child abuse!" (pp. 6–7). Viewed from outside each system of meaning, both sets of practices might be judged as inappropriate, whereas from within each system they make sense.

From the 1700s, scholars have oscillated between the *deficit model*—that "savages" are without reason and social order—and a *romantic view* of the "noble savage" living in a harmonious natural state unspoiled by the constraints of society (Jahoda & Krewer, 1997). Both of these extremes treat people of cultural communities other than those of the observer as alien, to be reviled (or pitied) on the one hand, or to be wistfully revered on the other.

These models are still with us. An illustration of the deficit model appears in a report based on *one week* of fieldwork among the Yolngu, an Aboriginal community in Australia, which concluded:

> Humans can continue to exist at very low levels of cognitive development. All they have to do is reproduce. The Yolngu are, self evidently to me, not a terribly advanced group.
>
> But there is not much question that Euro-American culture is vastly superior in its flexibility, tolerance for variety, scientific thought and interest in emergent possibilities from *any* primitive society extant. (Hippler, quoted and critiqued by Reser, 1982, p. 403)

For many years, researchers have compared U.S. people of color with European American people using a deficit model in which European American skills and upbringing have been considered "normal." Variations in other communities have been considered aberrations or deficits, and intervention programs have been designed to compensate for the children's "cultural deprivation." (See discussions of these issues in Cole & Bruner, 1971; Cole & Means, 1981; Deyhle & Swisher, 1997; García Coll, Lamberty, Jenkins, McAdoo, Crnic, Wasik, & García, 1996; Hays & Mindel, 1973; Hilliard & Vaughn-Scott, 1982; Howard & Scott, 1981; McLoyd & Randolph, 1985; McShane & Berry, 1986; Moreno, 1991; Ogbu, 1982; Valentine, 1971.)

> Children and adolescents of color have often been portrayed as "problems" which we dissect and analyze using the purportedly objective and dispassionate tools of our trade. . . . With a white sample serving as the "control," [the research] proceeds to conducting comparative analyses. . . . Beginning with the assumption of a problem, we search for differences, which, when found, serve as proof that the problem exists. (Cauce & Gonzales, 1993, p. 8)

Separating Value Judgments from Explanations

To understand development, it is helpful to separate value judgments from observations of events. It is important to examine the meaning and function of events for the local cultural framework and goals, conscientiously avoiding the *arbitrary* imposition of one's own values on another group.

Interpreting the activity of people without regard for *their* meaning system and goals renders observations meaningless. We need to understand the coherence of what people from different communities *do*, rather than simply determining that some other group of people do *not* do what "we" do, or do not do it as well or in the way that we do it, or jumping to conclusions that their practices are barbaric.

Reducing ethnocentrism does not require avoidance of (informed) value judgments or efforts to make changes. It does not require us to give up our own ways to become like people in another community, nor imply a need to protect communities from change. If we can get beyond the idea that *one* way is necessarily best, we can consider the possibilities of other ways, seeking to understand how they work and respecting them in their time and place. This does not imply that *all* ways are fine—many community practices are objectionable. My point is that value judgments should be well informed.

Ordinary people are constantly making decisions that impact others; if they come from different communities it is essential for judgment *to be informed* by the meaning of people's actions within their own community's goals and practices. A tragic example of the consequences of ethnocentric misunderstanding—making uninformed judgments—is provided in an account of the medical ordeal of a Hmong child in California, when the assumptions and communication patterns of the U.S. health system were incompatible with those of the family and their familiar community (Fadiman, 1997). The unquestioned cultural assumptions of the health workers contributed to the deteriorating care of the child.

The diversity of cultural ways within a nation and around the world is a resource for the creativity and future of humanity. As with the importance of supporting species diversity for the continued adaptation of life to changing circumstances, the diversity of cultural ways is a resource protecting humanity from rigidity of practices that could jeopardize the species in the future (see Cajete, 1994). We are unable to foresee the issues that humanity must face in the future, so we cannot be certain that any one way of approaching human issues will continue to be effective. Within the practices and worldviews of different communities are ideas and practices that may be important for dealing with the challenges ahead. A uniform human culture would limit the possibilities for effectively addressing future needs. Just as the cure for some dread disease may lie in a concoction made with leaves in a rain forest, the knowledge and skills of a small community far away (or next door) may provide a solution to other ills of the present or future. Although bureaucracies are challenged by variety and comfortable with uniformity, life and learning rely on the presence of diverse improvisations.

Diverse Goals of Development

Key to moving beyond one's own system of assumptions is recognizing that goals of human development—what is regarded as mature or desirable—vary considerably according to the cultural traditions and circumstances of different communities.

Theories and research in human development commonly reveal an assumption that development proceeds (and should proceed) toward a unique desirable endpoint of maturity. Almost all of the well-known "grand theories" of development have specified a single developmental trajectory, moving toward a pinnacle that resembles the values of the theorist's own community or indeed of the theorist's own life course. For example, theorists who are extremely literate and have spent many years in school often regard literacy and Euro-American school ways of thinking and acting as central to the goals of successful development, and even as defining "higher" cultural evolution of whole societies.

Ideas of Linear Cultural Evolution

The idea that societies develop along a dimension from primitive to "us" has long plagued thinking regarding cultural processes. A clear example appears in a letter to a friend that Thomas Jefferson wrote in the early 1800s:

Let a philosophic observer commence a journey from the savages of the Rocky Mountains, eastwardly towards our sea-coast. These he would observe in the earliest stage of association living under no law but that of nature, subsisting and covering themselves with the flesh and skins of wild beasts. He would next find those on our frontiers in the pastoral state, raising domestic animals to supply the defects of hunting. Then succeed our own semi-barbarous citizens, the pioneers of the advance of civilization, and so in his progress he would meet the gradual shades of improving man until he would reach his, as yet, most improved state in our seaport towns. This, in fact, is equivalent to a survey, in time, of the progress of man from the infancy of creation to the present day. (Pearce, quoted in Adams, 1996, p. 41)

The assumption that societal evolution progresses toward increasing differentiation of social life—from the "backward" simplicity of "primitive" peoples—is the legacy of the intellectual thought of the late 1800s and early 1900s (Cole, 1996; Jahoda, 2000; Shore, 1996). For example, in 1877, cultural evolutionist Lewis Henry Morgan proposed seven stages of human progress: lower savagery, middle savagery, upper savagery, lower barbarism, middle barbarism, upper barbarism, and civilization. Societies were placed on the scale according to a variety of attributes. Especially important to his idea of the path to civilization were monogamy and the nuclear family, agriculture, and private property as the basis of economic and social organization (Adams, 1996).

The scholarly elaboration of the idea of linear cultural evolution occurred during the same era that the disciplines of psychology, anthropology, sociology, and history arose, subdividing the topics of the broader inquiry. As Michael Cole (1996) noted, it was also the period in which large bureaucratic structures were growing to handle education (in schools) and economic activity (in factories and industrial organizations). Also during this time, European influence was at its peak in Africa, Asia, and South America; in North America, large influxes of immigrants from Europe inundated the growing cities, fleeing poverty in their homelands and joining rural Americans seeking the promises of U.S. cities.

The European-based system of formal "Western" schooling was seen as a key tool for civilizing those who had not yet "progressed to this stage." Politicians spoke of school as a way to hasten the evolutionary process (Adams, 1996). In the words of U.S. Commissioner of Education William Torrey Harris in the 1890s:

But shall we say to the tribal people that they shall not come to these higher things unless they pass through all the intermediate stages, or can we teach them directly these higher things, and save them from the slow progress of the ages? In the light of Christian civilization we say there is a method of rapid progress. Education has become of great potency in our hands, and we believe that we can now vicariously save them very much that the white race has had to go through. Look at feudalism. Look at the village community stage. . . . We have had our tribulation with them. But we say to lower races: we can help you out of these things. We can help you avoid the imperfect stages that follow them on the way to our level. Give us your children and we will educate them in the Kindergarten and in the schools. We will give them letters, and make them acquainted with the printed page. (quoted in Adams, 1996, p. 43)

The assumption that societies develop along one dimension from primitive to advanced survived into the second half of the 1900s (Cole, 1996; see also Latouche, 1996). When, after World War II, the United Nations planned economic and political "development" for newly independent colonial empires, the goal was to make them more "developed" (in a unidirectional sense, like earlier attempts to make them more "civilized"). Formal schooling was a key tool. Schooling modeled on European or North American schools spread throughout the former colonial empires to "raise" people out of poverty and ignorance and bring them into "modern" ways.

Moving Beyond Assumptions of a Single Goal of Human Development

Assumptions based on one's own life about what is desirable for human development have been very difficult for researchers and theorists to detect because of their similarity of backgrounds (being, until recently, almost exclusively highly schooled men from Europe and North America). As Ulric Neisser pointed out, self-centered definitions of intelligence form the basis of intelligence tests:

Academic people are among the stoutest defenders of the notion of intelligence . . . the tests seem so obviously valid to us who are members of the academic community. . . . There is no doubt that Academic Intelligence is really important for the kind of work that we do. We readily slip into believing that it is important for *every* kind of significant work. . . . Thus, academic people are in the position of having focused their professional activities around a particular personal quality, as instantiated in a certain set of skills. We have then gone on to *define* the quality in terms of this skill set, and ended by asserting that persons who lack these special skills are unintelligent altogether. (1976, p. 138)

FIGURE 1.3

Eastern European Jewish teacher and young students examining a religious text.

Forays of researchers and theorists outside their own cultural communities and growing communication among individuals raised with more than one community's traditions have helped the field move beyond these ethnocentric assumptions. Research and theory now pay closer attention to the ways that distinct community goals relate to ideals for the development of children (see Super & Harkness, 1997).

For example, cultural research has drawn attention to variations in the relevance of literacy and preliteracy skills in different communities. In a community in which literacy is key to communication and economic success in adulthood, preschoolers may need to learn to distinguish between the colors and shapes of small ink marks. However, if literacy is not central in a community's practices, young children's skill in detecting variations in ink squiggles might have little import.

Similarly, if literacy serves important religious functions, adults may impress its importance on young children (see figure 1.3). For example, in Jewish communities of early twentieth-century Europe, a boy's first day at school involved a major ceremony that communicated the holiness and attractiveness of studying (Wozniak, 1993). The boy's father would carry him to school covered by a prayer shawl so that he would not see anything unholy along the way, and at school the rabbi would write the alphabet in honey on a slate while other adults showered the boy with candies, telling him that angels threw them down so that he would want to study.

School-like ways of speaking are valued in some communities but not others, and children become skilled in using the narrative style valued in their community (Minami & McCabe, 1995; Mistry, 1993a; Scollon & Scollon, 1981; Wolf & Heath, 1992). For example, the narrative style used in "sharing time" (show-and-tell) by African American children often involves developing themes in connected episodes, whereas the narrative style used by European American children may employ tightly structured accounts centered on a single topic, which more closely resemble the literate styles that U.S. teachers aim to foster (Michaels & Cazden, 1986). When presented with narratives from which information regarding children's group membership was removed, European American adults judged the European American children's style as more skillful and indicating a greater chance of success in reading. In contrast, African American adults found the African American children's narratives to be better formed and indicating language skill and likelihood of success in reading. The adults' judgments reflected their appreciation of the children's use of shared cultural scripts that specify what is interesting to tell and how to structure it (Michaels & Cazden, 1986).

A focus on literacy or on the discourse styles promoted in schools may not hold such importance in some cultural settings, where it may be more important for young children to learn to attend to the nuances of weather patterns or of social cues of people around them, to use words cleverly to joust, or to understand the relation between human and supernatural events. The reply of the Indians of the Five Nations to an invitation in 1744 by the commissioners from Virginia to send boys to William and Mary College illustrates the differences in their goals:

> You who are wise must know, that different nations have different conceptions of things; and you will therefore not take it amiss, if our ideas of this kind of education happen not to be the same with yours. We have had some experience of it: several of our young people were formerly brought up at the colleges of the northern provinces; they were instructed in all your sciences; but when they came back to us . . . [they were] ignorant of every means of living in the woods . . . neither fit for hunters, warriors, or counsellors; they were totally good for nothing. We are, however, not the less obliged by your kind offer . . . and to show our grateful sense of it, if the gentlemen of Virginia will send us a dozen of their sons, we will take great care of their education, instruct them in all we know, and make *men* of them. (quoted in Drake, 1834)

A more contemporary example of differences in goals comes from West African mothers who had recently immigrated to Paris. They criticized the French use of toys to get infants to learn something for the future as tiring out the babies, and preferred to just let babies play without fatiguing them (Rabain Jamin, 1994). Part of their criticism also related to a concern that such focus on objects may lead to impoverished communication and isolation (in much the same way that a U.S. middle-class parent might express concern about the negative impact of video games). These African mothers seemed to prioritize social intelligence over technological intelligence (Rabain Jamin, 1994). They more often responded to their 10- to 15-month-old infants' social action and were less responsive to the infants' initiatives regarding objects than were French mothers. The African mothers often structured interaction with their infants around other people, whereas the French mothers often focused interaction on exploration of inanimate objects (see also Seymour, 1999). When interactions did focus on objects, the African mothers stressed the social functions of the objects, such as enhancement of social relationships through sharing, rather than object use or action schemes.

Prioritization of social relationships also occurs in Appalachian communities in the United States, where commitments to other people frequently take precedence over completion of schooling. When hard times arise for family members or neighbors, Appalachian youth often leave junior high or high school to help hold things together (Timm & Borman, 1997). Social solidarity is valued above individual accomplishment. The pull of kin and neighbors generally prevails, and has for generations.

In each community, human development is guided by local goals, which prioritize learning to function within the community's cultural institutions and technologies. Adults prioritize the adult roles and practices of their communities, or of the communities they foresee in the future, and the personal characteristics regarded as befitting mature roles (Ogbu, 1982). (Of course, different groups may benefit from learning from each other, and often people participate in more than one cultural community—topics taken up later in this book.)

Although cultural variation in goals of development needs to be recognized, this does not mean that each community has a unique set of values and goals. There are regularities among the variations. My point is that the idea of a *single* desirable "outcome" of development needs to be discarded as ethnocentric.

Indeed, the idea of an "outcome" of development comes from a particular way of viewing childhood: as *preparation* for life. It may relate to the separation of children from the important activities of their community, which has occurred since industrialization in some societies (discussed in later chapters). The treatment of childhood as a time of preparation for life differs from ways of communities in which children *participate* in the local mature activities, not segregated from adult life and placed in specialized preparatory settings such as schools.

To learn from and about communities other than our own, we need to go beyond the ethnocentric assumptions from which we each begin. Often, the first and most difficult step is to recognize that our original views are generally a function of our own cultural experience, rather than the only right or possible way. This can be an uncomfortable realization, because people sometimes assume that a respectful understanding of others' ways implies criticism of their own ways. A learning attitude, with suspended judgment of one's own as well as others' ways, is necessary for coming to understand how people both at home and elsewhere function in their local traditions and circumstances and for developing a general understanding of human development, with universal features built on local variations. The prospects of learning in cultural research are enhanced by communication between insiders and outsiders of particular communities, which I address in the next section.

Learning through Insider/Outsider Communication

To move our understanding of human development beyond assumptions and include the perspective of other communities, communication between community "insiders" and "outsiders" is essential. It is not a matter of which perspective is correct—both have an angle on the phenomena that helps to build understanding.

However, social science discussions often question whether the insider's or the outsider's perspective should be taken as representing the truth (see Clifford, 1988; LeVine, 1966). Arguments involve whether insiders or outsiders of particular communities have exclusive access to understanding, or whether the views of insiders or of outsiders are more trustworthy (Merton, 1972; Paul, 1953; Wilson, 1974).

Some have even argued that, given the variety of perspectives, there is no such thing as truth, so we should give up the effort to understand social life. But this view seems too pessimistic to me. If we adopted it, we would be paralyzed not only in social science research but in daily life, where such understanding is constantly required.

The argument that only members of a community have access to the real meaning of events in that community, so outsiders' opinions should be discarded, runs into difficulty when one notes the great variations in opinions among members of a community and the difficulties in determining who is qualified to represent the group. In addition, members of a community often have difficulty noticing their own practices because they take their own ways for granted, like the fish not being aware of the water.

Furthermore, as I discuss more fully in Chapter 3, individuals often participate simultaneously in several different communities. Increasingly, the boundaries between inside and outside are blurred as people spend time in various communities (see Clifford, 1997; Walker, 2001). For example, people of Mexican descent living in what is now the United States are not entirely outsiders to European American communities; the practices and policies of the two communities interrelate. Similarly, an anthropologist who spends 10 or 50 years working in a community participates in some manner and gains some local understanding. Youngsters who grow up in a family with several cultural heritages, as is increasingly common, have some insider and some outsider understandings of each of their communities. Overlaps across communities also come from the media, daily contacts, and shared endeavors—collaborative, complementary, or contested (see figure 1.4).

Hence, it is often a simplification to refer to individuals as being "in" or

FIGURE 1.4

Leonor, Virginia, and Angelica Lozano (left to right), seated around the family's first television in their home, about 1953 (Mexican American).

"out" of particular communities; many communities do not have strict boundaries or homogeneity that clearly allow determination of what it takes to be "in" or "out" of them. (In Chapter 3, I argue that we need to go beyond thinking solely of *membership* in a single static group and instead focus on people's *participation* in cultural practices of dynamically related communities whose salience to participants may vary.)

To come to a greater understanding of human functioning, people familiar with different communities need to combine their varied observations. What is referred to as "truth" is simply our current agreement on what seems to be a useful way to understand things; it is always under revision. These revisions of understanding build on constructive exchanges between people with different perspectives. Progress in understanding, then, is a matter of continually attempting to make sense of the different perspectives, taking into account the backgrounds and positions of the viewers.

Differences in perspective are necessary for seeing and for understanding. Visual perception requires imperceptible movements of the eyes relative to the image. If the image moves in coordination with the eye movements, the resulting uniformity of position makes it so the image cannot be seen. Likewise, if we close one eye and thus lose the second viewpoint supplied by binocular vision, our depth perception is dramatically reduced. In the same way, both people with intense identification within a community (insiders) and those with little contact in a community (outsiders) run into difficulties in making and interpreting observations. However, working together, insiders and outsiders can contribute to a more edifying account than either perspective would allow by itself.

Outsiders' Position

In seeking to understand a community's practices, outsiders encounter difficulties due to people's reactions to their presence (fear, interest, politeness) as well as their own unfamiliarity with the local web of meaning of events. Outsiders are newcomers to the meaning system, with limited understanding of how practices fit together and how they have developed from prior events. At the same time, they are faced with the assumptions of community members who invariably attempt to figure out what the outsider's role is in the community, using their everyday categories of how to treat the newcomer.

The outsider's identity is not neutral; it allows access to only some situations and elicits specific reactions when the outsider is present. For example, among the Zinacantecos, a Mayan group in Mexico, Berry Brazelton (1977) noted fear of observers among both adults and infants in his study of infant development: "We were automatically endowed with 'the evil eye' . . . the effects of stranger anxiety in the baby were powerfully re-inforced by his parents' constant anxiety about our presence. We were un-able to relate to babies after nine months of age because the effect was so powerful" (p. 174).

On the other hand, an observer may elicit interest and hospitality, which may be more comfortable but also becomes a part of the events ob-served. Ruth Munroe and Lee Munroe (1971) reported that in Logoli house-holds in Africa, as soon as an observer arrived to study everyday caregiving practices with infants, the infant was readied for display. The Logoli moth-ers were very cooperative, picking up their infants and bringing them to the observer for inspection. Under such circumstances, observations would have to be interpreted as an aspect of a public greeting. Similarly, Mary Ainsworth (1977) reported that she was categorized as a visitor among the Ganda of Uganda; the mothers insisted that she observe during the after-noon, a time generally allocated to leisure and entertaining visitors.

In a study in four different communities, parents varied in their per-ception of the purpose of a home visit interview and observation of mother-toddler interactions (Rogoff, Mistry, Göncü, & Mosier, 1993). In some communities, parents saw it as a friendly visit of an acquaintance interested in child development and skills; in others, it was a pleasant social obligation to help the local schoolteacher or the researcher by answering questions or an opportunity to show off their children's skills and newest clothes. With humor in her voice, one Turkish woman asked the researcher, who had grown up locally but studied abroad, "This is an international contest . . . Isn't it?"

Issues of how to interpret observations are connected with restrictions in outsiders' access. For example:

> Among Hausa mothers, the custom is not to show affection for their infants in public. Now those psychologists who are concerned with nurturance and dependency will go astray on their frequency counts if they do not realize this. A casual [observer] is likely to witness only public interaction; only when much further inquiry is made is the ab-sence of the event put into its proper perspective. (Price-Williams, 1975, p. 17)

There are only a few situations in which the presence of outside ob-servers does not transform ongoing events into public ones: if the event is already public, if their presence is undetected, or if they are so familiar that their presence goes without note. Of course, their presence as a familiar member of a household would require interpretation in that light, just as the presence of other familiar people would be necessary to consider in in-terpreting the scene.

Insiders' Position

The issues faced by both insiders and outsiders have to do with the fact that people are always functioning in a sociocultural context. One's interpretation of the situation is necessarily that of a person from a particular time and constellation of background experiences. And if one's presence is detected in a situation, one is a participant. There is no escape from interpretation and social presentation.

Differences in how people act when they think they are being observed or not illustrate how the simple presence of an observer (or a video camera) influences behavior. For example, U.S. middle-class mothers varied their interactions with their toddlers when they thought they were being observed in a research study (video equipment was conspicuously running) versus when they thought they were simply waiting in an observation room (repairs were "being made" on the video equipment, but observers watched from behind a one-way mirror). The mothers' behavior when they thought they were being observed reflected middle-class U.S. concepts of "good mothering" (Graves & Glick, 1978). The amount of speech to their children doubled, and they used more indirect requests, engaged in more naming and action routines, and asked more questions than when they thought they were not being observed.

Insiders also may have limited access to situations on the basis of their social identity. For example, their family's standing in the community and their personal reputation are not matters that are easily suspended. When entering others' homes, insiders carry with them the roles that they and their family customarily play. It may be difficult for people of one gender to enter situations that are customary for the other gender without arousing suspicions. A person's marital status often makes a difference in the situations and manner in which he or she engages with other people. For example, it could be complicated for a local young man to interview a family if he used to be a suitor of one of the daughters in the family, or if the grandfather in the family long ago was accused of cheating the young man's grandfather out of some property. An insider, like an outsider, has far from a neutral position in the community.

In addition, an insider in a relatively homogeneous community is unlikely to have reflected on or even noticed phenomena that would be of interest to an outsider. As was mentioned in the section on ethnocentrism, people with experience in only one community often assume that the way things are done in their own community is the only reasonable way. This is such a deep assumption that we are often unaware of our own practices unless we have the opportunity to see that others do things differently. Even if contrasting practices have raised insiders' awareness of their own practices, they still may interpret them in ways that fit with unquestioned assumptions:

> We rarely recognize the extent in which our conscious estimates of what is worthwhile and what is not, are due to standards of which we are not conscious at all. But in general it may be said that the things which we take for granted without inquiry or reflection are just the things which determine our conscious thinking and decide our conclusions. And these habitudes which lie below the level of reflection are just those which have been formed in the constant give and take of relationship with others. (Dewey, 1916, p. 22)

The next section examines how varying interpretations can be used and then modified in the effort to reach more satisfactory accounts of human development in different cultural communities. Understanding across cultural groups requires adopting

> a mode of encounter that I call learning for self-transformation: that is, to place oneself and the other in a privileged space of learning, where the desire [is] not just to acquire "information" or to "represent," but to recognize and welcome transformation in the inner self through the encounter. While Geertz claims that it's not necessary (or even possible) to adopt the other's world view in order to understand it . . . I also think that authentic understanding must be grounded in the sense of genuine humility that being a learner requires: the sense that what's going on with the other has, perhaps, some lessons for me. (Hoffman, 1997, p. 17)

Moving between Local and Global Understandings

Researchers working as outsiders to the community they are studying have grappled with how they can make inferences based on what they observe. (The concepts cultural researchers have developed are important for any research in which an investigator is attempting to make sense of people different from themselves, including work with people of an age or gender different from the researcher's.) The dilemma is that for research to be valuable, it needs both to reflect the phenomena from a perspective that makes sense locally and to go beyond simply presenting the details of a particular locale. The issue is one of effectively combining depth of understanding of the people and settings studied and going beyond the particularities to make a more general statement about the phenomena. Two approaches to move from local to more global understandings are discussed next. The first distinguishes rounds of interpretation that seek open-minded improvement of understanding. The second considers the role of meaning in attempts to compare "similar" situations across communities.

Revising Understanding in Derived Etic Approaches

The process of carefully testing assumptions and open-mindedly revising one's understanding in the light of new information is essential for learning about cultural ways. The distinctions offered by John Berry (1969; 1999) among *emic, imposed etic,* and *derived etic* approaches to cultural research are useful for thinking about this process of revision.

In an *emic* approach, an investigator attempts to represent cultural insiders' perspective on a particular community, usually by means of extensive observation and participation in the activities of the community. Emic research produces in-depth analyses of one community and can often be useful as such.

The imposed and derived etic approaches attempt to generalize or compare beyond one group and differ in their sensitivity to emic information. The imposed etic approach can be seen as a preliminary step on the way to a more adequate derived etic understanding.

In an *imposed etic* approach, an investigator makes general statements about human functioning across communities based on imposing a culturally inappropriate understanding. This involves uncritically applying theory, assumptions, and measures from research or everyday life from the researcher's own community. The ideas and procedures are not sufficiently adapted to the community or phenomenon being studied, and although the researcher may "get data," the results are not interpreted in a way that is sufficiently congruent with the situation in the community being studied.

For example, an imposed etic approach could involve administering questionnaires, coding behavior, or testing people without considering the need to modify the procedures or their interpretation to fit the perspective of the research participants. An imposed etic approach proceeds without sufficient evidence that the phenomenon is being interpreted as the researcher assumes. Even when a researcher is interested in studying something that seems very concrete and involves very little inference (such as whether people are touching), some understanding of local practices and meanings is necessary to decide when and where to observe and how to interpret the behavior (for example, whether to consider touching as evidence of stimulation or sensitivity to an infant). Mary Ainsworth critiqued the use of preconceived variables in imposed etic research: "Let us not blind ourselves to the unusual features of the unfamiliar society by limiting ourselves to variables or to procedures based on the familiar society—our own" (1977, p. 145).

In a *derived etic* approach, the researcher adapts ways of questioning, observing, and interpreting to fit the perspective of the participants. The resulting research is informed by emic approaches in each group studied and by seeking to understand the meaning of phenomena to the research participants.

Cultural researchers usually aspire to use both the emic and the derived etic approaches. They seek to understand the communities studied, adapt procedures and interpretations in light of what they learn, and modify theories to reflect the similarities and variations sensitively observed. The derived etic approach is essential to discerning cultural patterns in the variety of human practices and traditions.

It may be helpful to think of the starting point of any attempt to understand something new as stemming from an imposed etic approach. We all start with what we know already. If this is informed by emic observations accompanied by efforts to move beyond the starting assumptions, we may move closer to derived etic understanding. But derived etic understanding is a continually moving target: The new understanding becomes the current imposed etic understanding that forms the starting point of the next line of study, in a process of continual refinement and revision.

Because observations can never be freed from the observers' assumptions, interests, and perspective, some scholars conclude that there should be no attempt to understand cross-community regularities of phenomena. However, with sensitive observation and interpretation, we can come to a more satisfactory understanding of the phenomena that interest us, which can help guide our actions with each other. That this process of learning never ends is not a reason to avoid it.

Indeed, the process of trying to understand other people is essential for daily functioning as well as for scholarly work. The different perspectives brought to bear on interpreting phenomena by different observers are of interest in their own right, particularly now that research participants in many parts of the world contribute to the design and interpretation of research, not just responding to the questionnaires or tests of foreign visitors.

Research on issues of culture inherently requires an effort to examine the meaning of one system in terms of another. Some research is explicitly comparative across cultural communities. But even in emic research, in which the aim is to describe the ways of a cultural community in its own terms, a description that makes sense to people within the community needs to be stated in terms that also make sense outside the system. Often, descriptions are in a language different from that of the community members, whether the shift is from one national language to another or from folk terms to academic terms. All languages refer to concepts of local importance in ways somewhat different from others, reflecting cultural concepts in the effort to communicate. Therefore, the issue of "translation"—and consideration of the meaning and comparability of situations and ideas across communities—is inescapable.

The Meaning of the "Same" Situation across Communities

An issue for any comparison or discussion across communities is the similarity of meaning or the comparability of the situations observed (Cole & Means, 1981). Simply ensuring that the same categories of people are present or the same instructions used does not ensure comparability, because the meaning of the particular cast of characters or instructions is likely to vary across communities.

For example, in collecting data with American and Micronesian caregivers and infants, researchers had a difficult choice. They could examine caregiver-infant interactions in the most prevalent social context in which caregivers and infants are found in each community: The American caregivers and children were usually alone with each other; the Micronesian caregivers and infants were usually in the presence of a group. Or they could hold social context constant in the two communities (Sostek et al., 1981). The researchers decided to observe in both circumstances and compare the findings; they found that the social context of their observations differentiated caregiver-infant interaction in each community.

Following identical procedures in two communities, such as limiting observations to times that mothers and infants are alone together, clearly does not ensure comparability of observations. Studies examining mother-infant interaction across communities need to reflect the varying prevalence of this situation. For example, several decades ago in a study in the United States, 92% of mothers usually or always cared for their infants, whereas in an East African agricultural society, 38% of mothers were the usual caregivers (Leiderman & Leiderman, 1974). A study that compared mother-child interactions in these two cultural communities would need to interpret the findings in the light of the different purposes and prevalence of mother-child interaction in each.

In addition to considering who is present, comparisons need to attend to what people are doing together, for what purposes, and how their activity fits with the practices and traditions of their community. Inevitably, the meaning of what is observed must be considered.

Serious doubts have been raised as to whether situations are ever strictly comparable in cross-cultural research, as the idea of comparability may assume that everything except the aspect of interest is held constant. In an evaluation of personality research, Rick Shweder (1979) concluded that situations cannot be comparable across cultural communities:

> To talk of personality differences one must observe behavior differences in equivalent situations. . . . The crucial question then becomes, How are we to decide that the differential responses we observe are in fact differential responses to an equivalent set of stimuli. . . . *With respect to which particular descriptive components must stimuli (situations, contexts, environments) be shown to be equivalent?* . . . A situation (environment, context, setting) is more than its physical properties as defined by an outside observer. . . . It is a situated activity defined in part by its goal *from the point of view of the actor.* "What any rational person would do under the circumstances" depends upon what the person is trying to accomplish. (pp. 282–284)

Shweder argued that because local norms for the appropriate means of reaching a goal must be written into the very definition of the behavioral situation, "two actors are in 'comparable' or 'equivalent' situations *only to the extent that they are members of the same culture!"* (p. 285).

Perhaps the most crucial issue in the question of comparability is deciding how to interpret what is observed. It cannot be assumed that the same behavior has identical meaning in different communities. For example, native Hawaiian children were observed to make fewer verbal requests for help than Caucasian children in Hawaiian classrooms (Gallimore, Boggs, & Jordan, 1974; cited in Price-Williams, 1975). However, before concluding that this group was making fewer requests for assistance, the researchers considered the possibility that the children made requests for assistance differently. Indeed, they discovered that the Hawaiian children were requesting assistance nonverbally: steadily watching the teacher from a distance or approaching, standing nearby, or briefly touching her. These nonverbal requests may be directly related to the cultural background of the children, in which verbal requests for help from adults are considered inappropriate but nonverbal requests are acceptable.

Identical behavior may have different connotations and functions in different communities (Frijda & Jahoda, 1966). Some researchers have proposed that phenomena be compared in terms of what people are trying to accomplish rather than in terms of specific behaviors. Robert Sears (1961) argued for distinguishing goals or motives (such as help seeking in the Hawaiian study) from instrumental means used to reach the goals (such as whether children request assistance verbally or nonverbally). In his view, although instrumental means vary across communities, goals themselves may be considered transcultural. John Berry proposed that aspects of behavior be compared "only when they can be shown to be *functionally equivalent*, in the sense that the aspect of behavior in question is an attempted solution" to a recurrent problem shared by the different groups (1969, p. 122; see figure 1.5).

A focus on the function (or purpose or goal) of people's behavior facilitates understanding how different ways of doing things may be used to accomplish similar goals, or how similar ways of doing things may serve different goals. Although all cultural communities address issues that are common to human development worldwide, due to our specieswide cultural and biological heritage, different communities may apply similar means to different goals and different means to similar goals.

The next two chapters focus in more depth on how we can conceive of the cultural nature of human development. They examine the idea that human development is biologically cultural and discuss ways of thinking

FIGURE 1.5

John Collier and Malcolm Collier suggested that family mealtimes could provide a basis for comparisons that would help define relationships within families in different communities. The first picture shows an evening meal in a home in Vicos, Peru; the second shows supper in a Spanish American home in New Mexico; the third picture shows breakfast in the home of an advertising executive's family in Connecticut.

about similarities and differences across cultural communities in how people learn and develop. They discuss concepts to relate individual and cultural processes, expanding on the overarching orienting concept: that humans develop through their changing participation in the sociocultural activities of their communities, which also change.

2

Development as
Transformation of Participation
in Cultural Activities

Some decades ago, psychologists interested in how cultural processes contributed to human thinking were puzzled by what they observed. Their puzzlement came from trying to make sense of the everyday lives of the people they visited by using the prevailing concepts of human development and culture. Many of these researchers began to search for more useful ways to think about the relation of culture and individual functioning.

In this chapter, I discuss why then-current ideas of the relation between individual and cultural processes made these researchers' observations puzzling. A key issue was that "the individual" was assumed to be separate from the world, equipped with basic, general characteristics that might be secondarily "influenced" by culture. An accompanying problem was that "culture" was often thought of as a static collection of characteristics. After examining these assumptions, I discuss the cultural-historical theory that helped to resolve the researchers' puzzle, focusing on my own version of it. In my view, human development is a process in which people transform through their ongoing participation in cultural activities, which in turn contribute to changes in their cultural communities across generations.

Together, Chapters 2 and 3 argue for conceiving of people and cultural communities as mutually creating each other. Chapter 2 focuses on concepts for relating cultural processes to the development of individuals. Chapter 3 addresses the companion issue of how we can think of cultural communities as changing with the contributions of successive generations of people.

A Logical Puzzle for Researchers

North American and European cross-cultural psychologists of the 1960s and 1970s brought tests of children's cognitive development from the United States and Europe to foreign places. These tests were often derived from Jean Piaget's stage theory or were tests of classification, logic, and memory.

The aim was to use measures of thinking that bore little obvious relation to people's everyday lives, to examine their ability independent of their background experience. So researchers asked people to say whether quantities of water changed when poured into different-shaped beakers, to sort unfamiliar figures into categories, to solve logic problems that could only be solved with the stated premises rather than using real-world knowledge, and to remember lists of nonsense syllables or unrelated words.

The idea was that people's "true" competence, which was assumed to underlie their everyday performances, could be discerned using novel problems that no one had been taught how to solve. People's level of competence was regarded as a general personal characteristic underlying widely different aspects of their behavior without variation across situations. The tests sought to determine general stages of thinking or general ability to classify, think logically, and remember. Some individuals (or groups) were expected to be at "higher" stages or to have better classification, logical, and memory abilities—in general—than other people. Cross-cultural research was used to examine, under widely varying circumstances, what environmental factors produced greater "competence."

The puzzle was that the same people who performed poorly on the researchers' tests showed impressive skill in reasoning or remembering (or other cognitive skills that the tests were supposed to measure) outside of the test situation. For example, Michael Cole noted that in a community in which people had great difficulty with mathematical tests, great skill was apparent in the marketplace and other local settings: "On taxi-buses I was often outbargained by the cabbies, who seemed to have no difficulty calculating miles, road quality, quality of the car's tires, number of passengers, and distance" (1996, p. 74).

With the assumption that cognition is a general competence characterizing individuals across situations, such unevenness of performance was puzzling. To try to resolve the difference in apparent "ability" across situations, researchers first tried making the content and format of the tests more familiar, to find "truer" measures of underlying competence. Researchers also tried parceling competence into smaller "domains," such as biological knowledge and physical knowledge or verbal and nonverbal skills, so that the discrepancies across situations were not as great. (This remains an active approach in the field of cognitive development.)

Researchers also began to notice that although the tests were not supposed to relate to specific aspects of people's experience, there were links between performance on the tests and the extent of experience with Western schools and literacy. It was tempting to conclude that school or literacy makes people smarter, but the researchers' everyday observations challenged that interpretation. Instead, researchers such as Sylvia Scribner and Michael Cole and their colleagues began to study the specific connections between performance on tests and experience in school. (In Chapter 7, on culture and thinking, I focus in more detail on this research and the findings.)

An Example: "We always speak only of what we see"

An example of a logical problem will serve to illustrate the connection between schooling and test performance. A common test of logical thinking is the syllogism, like those employed during the 1930s by Alexander Luria. In Luria's study, an interviewer presented the following syllogism to Central Asian adults varying in literacy and schooling:

> In the Far North, where there is snow, all bears are white. Novaya Zemlya is in the Far North and there is always snow there. What color are the bears there?

Luria reported that when asked to make inferences on the basis of the premises of syllogisms, literate interviewees solved the problems in the desired manner. However, many nonliterate interviewees did not. Here is the response of a nonliterate Central Asian peasant who did not treat the syllogism as though the premises constituted a logical relation allowing an inference:

> "We always speak only of what we see; we don't talk about what we haven't seen."
>
> [The interviewer probes:] But what do my words imply? [The syllogism is repeated.]
>
> "Well, it's like this: our tsar isn't like yours, and yours isn't like ours. Your words can be answered only by someone who was there, and if a person wasn't there he can't say anything on the basis of your words."

[The interviewer continues:] But on the basis of my words—in the North, where there is always snow, the bears are white, can you gather what kind of bears there are in Novaya Zemlya?

"If a man was sixty or eighty and had seen a white bear and had told about it, he could be believed, but I've never seen one and hence I can't say. That's my last word. Those who saw can tell, and those who didn't see can't say anything!" (At this point a younger man volunteered, "From your words it means that bears there are white.")

[Interviewer:] Well, which of you is right?

"What the cock knows how to do, he does. What I know, I say, and nothing beyond that!" (1976, pp. 108–109)

This peasant and the interviewer disagreed about what kind of evidence is acceptable as truth. The peasant insisted on firsthand knowledge, perhaps trusting the word of a reliable, experienced person. But the interviewer tried to induce the peasant to play a game involving examination of the truth value of the words alone. The nonliterate peasant argued that because he had not personally seen the event, he did not have adequate evidence, and implied that he did not think that the interviewer had adequate evidence either. When the schooled young man made a conclusion on the basis of the unverified premises stated in the problem, the nonliterate man implied that the younger man had no business jumping to conclusions.

Like this peasant, many other nonliterate interviewees refused to accept that the major premise is a "given" and protested that they "could only judge what they had seen" or "didn't want to lie." (This pattern has been replicated in other places by Cole, Gay, Glick, & Sharp, 1971; Fobih, 1979; Scribner, 1975, 1977; Sharp, Cole, & Lave, 1979; and Tulviste, 1991.) If nonliterate interviewees were not required to state the conclusion, but were asked instead to evaluate whether the hypothetical premises and a conclusion stated by the researcher fit logically, then they were willing to consider such problems as self-contained logical units (Cole et al., 1971).

The argument of the nonliterate peasant studied by Luria shows quite abstract reasoning regarding what one can use as evidence. Indeed, Luria noted that nonliterate people's reasoning and deduction followed the rules when dealing with immediate practical experience; they made excellent judgments and drew the implied conclusions. Their unwillingness to treat syllogisms as logical problems is not a failure to think hypothetically. An interviewee explained his reasoning for not answering a hypothetical question: "If you know a person, if a question comes up about him, you are able to answer" (Scribner, 1975, 1977). He reasoned hypothetically in denying the possibility of reasoning hypothetically about information of which he had no experience.

Syllogisms represent a specialized language genre that becomes easier to handle with practice with this specialized form of problem (Scribner, 1977). In school, people may become familiar with this genre through experience with story problems in which the answer must be derived from the statements in the problem. Students are supposed not to question the truth of the premises but to answer on the basis of the stated "facts."

Being willing to accept a premise that one cannot verify, and reasoning from there, is characteristic of schooling and literacy. This commonly used test of logical "ability" thus reflects rather specific training in a language format that researchers are likely to take for granted, as highly schooled individuals themselves. The puzzles questioned assumptions of generality.

Researchers Questioning Assumptions

Cultural researchers sought alternative ways to think about the relationship of individual development and cultural processes. The assumption that the characteristics of both children and cultures were general seemed to be part of the problem.

The researchers became suspicious of the idea that children progress through monolithic, general stages of development. They noted that people's ways of thinking and of relating to other people are in fact not broadly applied in varying circumstances.

Researchers also noticed similar shortcomings in treating culture as a monolithic entity. The effect of being a "member of a culture" had been assumed to be uniform across both the members and the situations in which they functioned. For example, whole cultural groups were sometimes characterized as oral, complex, or interdependent (in different research traditions). When researchers saw that members of a community often differed from each other on such dimensions and that the dimensions seemed to apply more in some circumstances than others, this called into question the whole business of trying to discern the "essence" of a culture.

Currently, scholars think about the relation of individual development and cultural processes in a variety of ways that try to look more specifically at individual and cultural attributes. Our understanding has benefited from attempts to make more fine-grained analyses of individual characteristics, domains of thinking, and cultural attributes.

However, I believe that some of the problems that remain require rethinking our basic ideas about the relation between individuals and cultural communities. I argue against the still common approach of treating individuals as entities separate from cultural processes, existing independently of their cultural communities. Such approaches look for how "culture" exerts "influence" on the otherwise generic "child."

The remainder of this chapter focuses on how we can conceptualize human development as a cultural process in which all children develop as participants in their cultural communities. First I present several approaches that have been quite influential and helpful: the work of Mead, the Whitings, and Bronfenbrenner. Then I argue that we can solve some problems by discarding the often unspoken assumption that individual and culture are separate entities, with the characteristics of culture "influencing" the characteristics of individuals.

Many researchers, including myself, have found the cultural-historical theory proposed by Lev Vygotsky to be quite helpful, and in recent decades many scholars have built on his theory. Vygotsky's influential book *Mind in Society* (1978) was introduced to the English-speaking world by some of the same researchers (including Cole and Scribner) who struggled with the puzzle of people's varied performance on cognitive tests and everyday cognitive activities. Vygotsky's theory helped connect individuals' thinking with cultural traditions such as schooling and literacy.

In the last part of this chapter, I describe my approach, which builds on the prior work. I conceive of development as transformation of people's participation in ongoing sociocultural activities, which themselves change with the involvement of individuals in successive generations.

Concepts Relating Cultural and Individual Development

Margaret Mead's pioneering work demonstrated how passing moments of shared activity, which may or may not have explicit lessons for children, are the material of development. Her careful observations of filmed everyday events, long before the introduction of portable videotape technology, helped to reveal cultural aspects of individual acts and interactions. Several related lines of investigation have provided models to help researchers think about the relation of individual development and cultural processes.

Two key approaches, Whiting and Whiting's psycho-cultural model and Bronfenbrenner's ecological system, will serve the purpose of describing how the relationship has been conceptualized. Several other current approaches, including cultural-historical perspectives, build on the work of these pioneers. In this section, I describe some of the ideas offered by these models. They have provided key concepts and sparked pathbreaking research. However, I want to raise a concern that the ways the models have diagrammed the relation between the individual and the world lead us, perhaps unintentionally, to a limiting view of individual and cultural processes—as separate entities. My concern is relevant to most diagrams relating individual and cultural processes throughout the social sciences.

Whiting and Whiting's Psycho-Cultural Model

Beatrice Whiting and John Whiting (1975) provided a "psycho-cultural model" of the relations between the development of individuals and features of their immediate environments, social partners, and institutional and cultural systems and values. This perspective stresses that understanding human development requires detailed understanding of the situations in which people develop—the immediate situations as well as the less immediate cultural processes in which children and their partners (and their ancestors) participate.

The Whitings urged a deeper understanding of cultural processes than is often the case in studies that simply relate children's development to broad categories such as culture, social class, and gender. Beatrice Whiting (1976) pressed scholars to "unpackage" these variables rather than treating them as broad packages of unanalyzed "independent variables." She emphasized that the cast of characters and settings in which children act are extremely influential in determining their course of development.

Whiting and Whiting's model (see figure 2.1) presented human devel-

FIGURE 2.1

Whiting and Whiting's model for psycho-cultural research (1975).

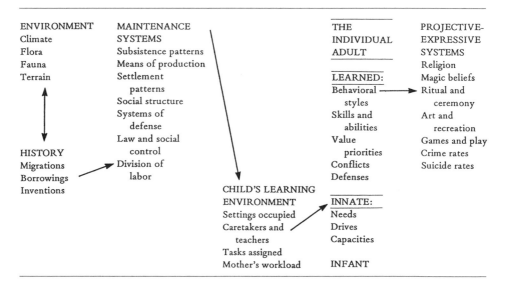

opment as the product of a chain of social and cultural circumstances surrounding the child. The chain began with the environment (including the climate, flora and fauna, and terrain) and led to the history (including migrations, borrowings, and inventions). This in turn led to the group's maintenance systems (subsistence patterns, means of production, settlement patterns, social structure, systems of defense, law and social control, and division of labor). This led to the child's learning environment, which consisted of their routine settings, caretakers and teachers, tasks assigned, and mother's workload. Then the chain arrived at the individual, including the innate needs, drives, and capacities of the infant as well as learned behavioral styles, skills, value priorities, conflicts, and defenses.

The Whitings' model contained a set of assumptions regarding the underlying direction of causality, with arrows leading from the environment and history to the child's learning environment to the individual's development. Whiting and Whiting (1975) assumed that maintenance systems determine to a large extent the learning environment in which a child grows up, and the learning environment influences the child's behavior and development.

These assumptions provided Whiting and Whiting and their research team with a framework that allowed important advances in understanding culture and child development in their landmark *Six Cultures Study* (1975). Their focus on the child's learning environment produced key research findings in the study of the cultural aspects of human development. My own work has been heavily influenced by the Whitings' ideas, and their research can be seen throughout this book.

However, the form of their diagram carries implicit assumptions that tend to constrain how we think about the relation of individuals and cultural practices, in unintended ways. The categories composing the chain are treated as independent entities, and the arrows indicate that one entity causes the next. Thus individual and cultural processes are treated "as if" they exist independently of each other, with individual characteristics created by cultural characteristics.

Bronfenbrenner's Ecological System

Urie Bronfenbrenner's ecological perspective has also contributed important ideas and research on cultural aspects of human development. Bronfenbrenner's model takes a different form from that of Whiting and Whiting, but it raises similar questions about treating individual and cultural processes as separate entities.

Bronfenbrenner stressed the interactions of a changing organism in a changing environment. In his view, the environment is composed of one's immediate settings as well as the social and cultural contexts of relations among different settings, such as home, school, and workplace. Bronfenbrenner was interested in specifying the properties and conditions of the social and physical environments that foster or undermine development within people's "ecological niches." He defined the ecology of human development as involving

> the progressive, mutual accommodation between an active, growing human being and the changing properties of the immediate settings in which the developing person lives, as this process is affected by relations between these settings, and by the larger contexts in which the settings are embedded. (1979, p. 21)

Although this definition states that the person and the settings are mutually involved, elsewhere individuals are treated as products of their immediate settings and "larger" contexts. Bronfenbrenner described his ecological system as being composed of concentric circles, like Russian nesting dolls in which a small figure nests inside a larger one inside a still larger one, and so on (see figure 2.2a).

Like the diagram in Figure 2.1 of categories connected by arrows, Bronfenbrenner's proposal of concentric circles carries the same implicit assumptions about the relation of individual and cultural processes: Individual and "larger" contexts are conceived as existing separately, definable independ-

FIGURE 2.2A

Bronfenbrenner likened his ecological system to Russian nesting dolls.

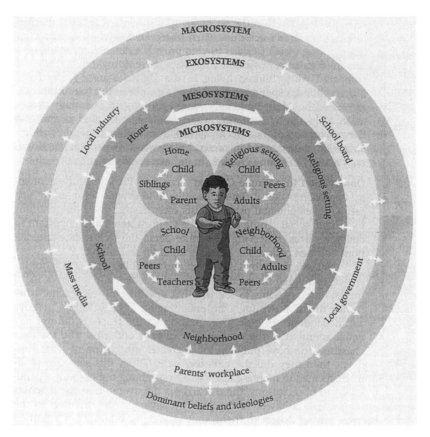

FIGURE 2.2B

Bronfenbrenner's nested ecological system as interpreted in Michael and Sheila Cole's 1996 textbook.

ently of each other, related in a hierarchical fashion as the "larger" contexts affect the "smaller" ones, which in turn affect the developing person.

In Bronfenbrenner's system, the smallest, central circle is closest to the individual's immediate experiences (see figure 2.2b). Outer circles refer to settings that exert an influence less directly (through their impact on others), without the individual's direct participation in them. The system is divided into four aspects of the ecology in which individuals function: microsystems, mesosystems, exosystems, and macrosystems. Although I am concerned with how the four systems relate, Bronfenbrenner's articulation of each of these systems is a valuable contribution:

Microsystems, according to Bronfenbrenner, are the individual's immediate experiences—the settings containing the child and others, such as home and school. One of the basic units at the level of microsystems is the dyad (that is, the pair); dyads in turn relate to larger interpersonal structures such as triads (three-person systems, such as mother-father-baby). Even in the most immediate settings, individuals and dyads are crucially dependent on third parties and larger groups.

Mesosystems, in Bronfenbrenner's approach, are the relations among the microsystems in which an individual is involved, for example, the complementary or conflicting practices of home and school. Mesosystems involve relations between and among systems—two or three or more in relation. Bronfenbrenner made the very important point that any one setting (such as the home) involves relations with others (such as school or a religious institution). He emphasized the overlaps and communication between settings and information in each setting about the other. The analysis of mesosystems gives importance to questions such as whether a young person enters a new situation (such as school or camp) alone or in the company of familiar companions, and whether the young person and companions have advance information about the new setting before they enter. Bronfenbrenner stressed the importance of ecological transitions as people shift roles or settings (for example, with the arrival of a new sibling, entry into school, graduating, finding a job, and marrying).

Exosystems relate the microsystems in which children are involved to settings in which children do not directly participate, such as parents' workplaces if children do not go there. Although children's immediate environments, in which they participate directly, are especially potent in influencing their development, Bronfenbrenner argued that settings that children do not experience directly are also very influential. He referred especially to the role of parents' work and the community's organization: Whether parents can perform effectively within the family depends on the demands, stresses, and supports of the workplace and extended family. The direct impact on children of parents' child-rearing roles is influenced by such indirect factors as flexibility of parents' work schedules, adequacy of child care arrangements, the help of friends and family, the quality of health and social services, and neighborhood safety. Aspects as removed as public policies affect all these factors and are part of the exosystem of human development.

Macrosystems are the ideology and organization of pervasive social institutions of the culture or subculture. Referring to macrosystems, Bronfenbrenner stated:

> Within any culture or subculture, settings of a given kind—such as homes, streets, or offices—tend to be very much alike, whereas be-

tween cultures they are distinctly different. It is as if within each society or subculture there existed a blueprint for the organization of every type of setting. Furthermore, the blueprint can be changed, with the result that the structure of the settings in a society can become markedly altered and produce corresponding changes in behavior and development. (1979, p. 4)

Bronfenbrenner's approach makes several key contributions; in particular, it emphasizes studying the relations among the multiple settings in which children and their families are directly and indirectly involved. The idea of examining how children and families make transitions among their different ecological settings is also extremely important. Nonetheless, the separation into nested systems constrains ideas of the relations between individual and cultural processes.

Descendents

The ideas and research of the Whitings and Bronfenbrenner have provided very important guidance for the whole field of work on culture and human development. My own research and ideas are direct descendents from this family of work, intermarried with cultural-historical ideas.

Several other approaches, influenced by the ideas of the Whitings, Bronfenbrenner, and others, focus on *ecological niches* as a way of thinking about the relation of individuals and communities. Tom Weisner, Ron Gallimore, and Cathie Jordan (1988) emphasized important features of children's daily routines for understanding cultural influences:

The personnel who are available and interacting with children
The motivations of the people involved
Cultural "scripts" used by people to guide the way they do things
The type and frequency of tasks and activities in daily routines
The cultural goals and beliefs of the people involved

Charles Super and Sara Harkness (1997) focused on the relations among children's dispositions and three subsystems of the developmental niche:

The physical and social settings in which the child lives
The culturally regulated customs of child care and child rearing
The psychology of the caregivers (including parental beliefs regarding the nature and needs of children, goals for rearing, and shared understandings about effective rearing techniques)

Issues in Diagramming the Relation
of Individual and Cultural Processes

In textbooks and scholarly treatises in a number of social science fields, the relation between individual and cultural processes is still commonly diagrammed using entities connected by arrows or contained in concentric circles (like figures 2.1 and 2.2).

These ways of sketching ideas are so familiar that social scientists may not question the assumptions they embody. Visual tools for communicating theoretical ideas constrain our ideas, often without our noticing the constraints. I think it is important to revise the diagrams to be able to represent the idea that cultural and personal processes create each other.

Boxes-and-arrows or nested-circles diagrams constrain our concepts by separating person and culture into stand-alone entities, with culture *influencing* the person (or, in some models, with the two entities interacting). Figures 2.1 and 2.2 portray the individual as separate from the environment (and therefore "subject" to its influences). The separation appears in the unidirectional causal chains between prior and later variables in the Whitings' model and in the hierarchical nesting of the inner system, dependent on those outside it, in Bronfenbrenner's ecological theory.

Behavior (or thought) is often treated as the "outcome" of independent cultural variables. The "influence" of culture on individuals has frequently been studied by "measuring" some characteristics of culture (such as the complexity of social organization in the society) and some characteristics of individuals (such as personality characteristics or measures of intelligence), and then correlating them. This contrasts with approaches that examine the contributions of individuals and cultural practices as they function together in mutually defining processes.

Diagrams separating the individual and the world are so pervasive in the social sciences that we have difficulty finding other ways to represent our ideas. The Whitings and Bronfenbrenner may not themselves have been tightly wedded to the ideas that I suggest are implied by the forms of the diagrams. In a later work, Whiting and Edwards (1988) referred less to causal chains than in the 1975 work in examining associations between gender differences and the company children keep, though still with an aim of determining how settings influence individual development. Similarly, Bronfenbrenner's nesting-doll image was accompanied by the statement that individuals and their settings are related through progressive, mutual accommodation.

Because I am interested in visual representations as tools for thought, I am seeking other ways to portray the mutual relationship of culture and human development, avoiding the idea that either occurs alone (without the contributions of the other) or that one produces the other. After describing the ways that sociocultural-historical theory treats the relation of individual and cultural processes, I provide some diagrams to portray development as a process of changing participation in sociocultural activities.

Sociocultural-Historical Theory

Many researchers interested in culture and development found in the writings of Lev Vygotsky and his colleagues a theory that laid the groundwork to help integrate individual development in social, cultural, and historical context. In contrast to theories of development that focus on the individual and the social or cultural context as separate entities (adding or multiplying one and the other), the cultural-historical approach assumes that individual development must be understood in, and cannot be separated from, its social and cultural-historical context.[1] According to Vygotsky's theory, the efforts of individuals are not separate from the kinds of activities in which they engage and the kinds of institutions of which they are a part.

Vygotsky focused on cognitive skills and their reliance on cultural inventions such as literacy, mathematics, mnemonic skills, and approaches to problem solving and reasoning (Laboratory of Comparative Human Cognition, 1983; Vygotsky, 1978; Wertsch, 1979). In this view, thinking involves learning to use symbolic and material cultural tools in ways that are specific to their use. This was exemplified by work demonstrating that experience with literacy promoted particular skills in its use, rather than promoting general cognitive advances (Scribner & Cole, 1981).

Vygotsky argued that children learn to use the tools for thinking provided by culture through their interactions with more skilled partners in the *zone of proximal development.* Through engaging with others in complex thinking that makes use of cultural tools of thought, children become able to carry out such thinking independently, transforming the cultural tools of thought to their own purposes. Interactions in the zone of proximal development allow children to participate in activities that would be impossible

---

[1]This approach is referred to interchangeably as the sociocultural, sociohistorical, or cultural-historical approach. Active scholarly work continues to examine and extend the early twentieth-century insights of Vygotsky, Luria, Leont'ev, and other Soviet scholars such as Bakhtin and Ilyenkov. See especially Bakhurst, 1995; Cole, 1995, 1996; Kozulin, 1990; van der Veer & Valsiner, 1991; Wertsch, 1991, 1998.

for them alone, using cultural tools that themselves must be adapted to the specific activity at hand.
.Cultural tools thus are both inherited and transformed by successive generations. Culture is not static; it is formed from the efforts of people working together, using and adapting material and symbolic tools provided by predecessors and in the process creating new ones.

Development over the life span is inherently involved with historical developments of both the species and cultural communities, developments that occur in everyday moment-by-moment learning opportunities. Development occurs in different time frames—at the pace of species change, community historical change, individual lifetimes, and individual learning moments (Scribner, 1985; Wertsch, 1985). These four developmental levels, at different grains of analysis, provide a helpful way of thinking about the mutually constituting nature of cultural and biological processes and the changing nature of culture, discussed in more depth in the next chapter.

Scholars are working on a coherent family of sociocultural-historical research programs and theories inspired by Vygotskian cultural-historical theory, along with related ideas emerging from several other theoretical traditions (see Goodnow, 1993; Rogoff & Chavajay, 1995). The theory of John Dewey (1916) also complements Vygotskian ideas and has helped a number of sociocultural scholars to further develop these ideas. In addition, work on communication in everyday lives in different communities has contributed important concepts for thinking about individual and cultural aspects of development (Erickson & Mohatt, 1982; Goodwin, 1990; Heath, 1983, 1989a, 1991; Mehan, 1979; Miller, 1982; Ochs, 1988, 1996; Rogoff et al., 1993; Schieffelin, 1991; Watson-Gegeo & Gegeo, 1986b).

The related proposals for sociocultural theory represent a general agreement that individual development constitutes and is constituted by social and cultural-historical activities and practices. In the emerging sociocultural perspective, culture is not an entity that *influences* individuals. Instead, people contribute to the creation of cultural processes and cultural processes contribute to the creation of people. Thus, individual and cultural processes are *mutually constituting* rather than defined separately from each other.[2]

---

[2]Related though heterogeneous sociocultural proposals include the work of Bruner, 1990; Cole, 1990, 1996; Engeström, 1990; Goodnow, 1990; Heath, 1983; Hutchins, 1991; John-Steiner, 1985; Laboratory of Comparative Human Cognition, 1983; Lave & Wenger, 1991; Miller & Goodnow, 1995; Ochs, 1988, 1996; Rogoff, 1990, 1998; Schieffelin, 1991; Scribner, 1985, 1997; Serpell, 1993; Shweder, 1991; Shweder, Goodnow, Hatano, LeVine, Markus, & Miller, 1998; Valsiner, 1987, 1994, 2000; Wenger, 1999; Wertsch, 1991. (See also the journals *Mind, Culture, and Activity* and *Culture & Psychology*.) Although my version of the sociocultural perspective has a great deal in common with other versions, there are also important differences that are beyond the scope of this overview.

Development as Transformation of Participation in Sociocultural Activity

In my own work, I emphasize that human development is a process of *people's changing participation in sociocultural activities of their communities.* People contribute to the processes involved in sociocultural activities at the same time that they inherit practices invented by others (Rogoff, 1990, 1998).

Rather than individual development being influenced by (and influencing) culture, from my perspective, people develop as they participate in and contribute to cultural activities that themselves develop with the involvement of people in successive generations. People of each generation, as they engage in sociocultural endeavors with other people, make use of and extend cultural tools and practices inherited from previous generations. As people develop through their shared use of cultural tools and practices, they simultaneously contribute to the transformation of cultural tools, practices, and institutions.

To clarify these ideas, I have been developing a series of images that aim to move beyond boxes-and-arrows and nested-circles ways of portraying cultural influences. In Figure 2.3a–g, I offer images of a sociocultural "transformation of participation perspective" in which personal, interpersonal, and cultural aspects of human activity are conceived as different analytic views of ongoing, mutually constituted processes.

In the next chapter I discuss in more depth what I mean by cultural communities. For examining the images in Figure 2.3, it may be sufficient to note that in my view, cultural processes are not the same as membership in national or ethnic groups, and that individuals are often participants in more than one community's cultural practices, traditions, and institutions.

FIGURE 2.3A

This image portrays the object of study that has been traditional in developmental psychology: the *solitary individual*. Information about relations with other people and the purpose and setting of the activity is removed. When I ask people to guess what this child is doing, their speculations are hesitant and vague: "Thinking?" "Being punished?" "Reading?"

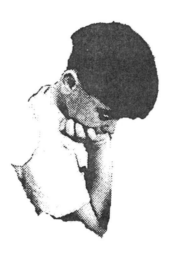

FIGURE 2.3B

Of course, the roles of other people—parents, peers, teachers, and so on—
are recognized as relevant. This image portrays how social relations have often
been investigated—by studying "the child" apart from other people, who are
studied separately even when they are engaging in the same event. Then the
"*social influences*" are examined through correlating the characteristics or
actions of the separate entities.[3] (Sometimes, analyses include bidirectional
arrows to try to include an effect of the active child on the other people.)
When I ask people to make further guesses about what the child is doing,
given information about "social influences," their hypotheses are not much
more specific than for the solitary individual in Figure 2.3a.

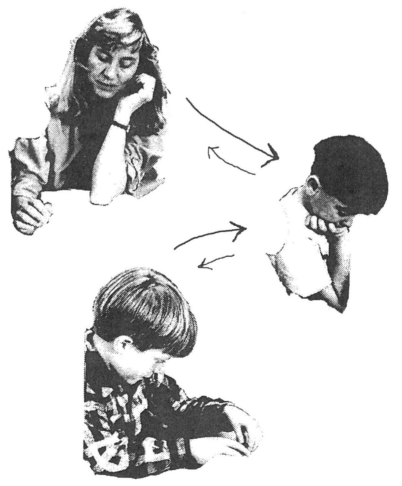

[3]Vygotskian scholars complain that frequently Vygotsky's idea of the zone of proximal development is reduced to this sort of analysis of social influences, overlooking his emphasis on cultural processes.

FIGURE 2.3C

This figure, like the two previous, is based on the boxes-with-arrows diagrams of the relation of culture and human development. When "*cultural influences*" are added (represented by the book and the cupboard), the child remains separate from them, "subject" to the effects of cultural characteristics. The individual and the rest are taken apart from each other, analyzed without regard for what they are doing together in sociocultural activities. With this portrayal of "cultural influences" information, people's guesses about what this child is doing are still not very specific, though some become more certain that the child is reading.

FIGURE 2.3D

This image focuses on the same child from the *transformation-of-participation perspective*. The child is foregrounded, with information about him as an *individual as the focus of analysis*. At the same time, interpersonal and cultural-institutional information is available in the background. A general sense of interpersonal and cultural-institutional information is necessary to understand what this child is doing, although it does not need to be attended to in the same detail as the child's efforts. When I show people this image, their guesses about what the child is doing become much more specific: "Playing a game . . . Oh, it's Scrabble . . . He's thinking about his next turn . . . It's in a classroom . . ."

FIGURE 2.3E

If, instead of wanting to study the development of that particular child, we were interested in the relationships among that child and the people beside him, we could focus on what they are doing together. This would involve an *interpersonal focus of analysis*. We would be interested in knowing that the three people are playing Scrabble as a spelling activity organized by the adult; the adult is a parent volunteer helping this child check a word in the dictionary under her elbow while his classmate works on a word for his own next turn; and they are engaging in a friendly form of competition, helping each other as they play.

The fact that this is in a classroom setting matters, but we would not be analyzing in detail how such an activity fits with the culture of this school or this community (for that, see figure 2.3f). A general sense of individual and cultural information is important as background, to understand what the people are doing.

Together, the interpersonal, personal, and cultural-institutional aspects of the event constitute the activity. No aspect exists or can be studied in isolation from the others. An observer's relative focus on one or the other aspect can be changed, but they do not exist apart from each other. Analysis of interpersonal arrangements could not occur without background understanding of community processes (such as the historical and cultural roles and changing practices of schools and families). At the same time, analysis requires some attention to personal processes (such as efforts to learn through observation and participation in ongoing activities).

The hand holding the analytic lens is also important, indicating that we, as observers or researchers, construct the focus of analysis. *The focus of analysis stems from what we as observers choose to examine*—in the case of Figure 2.3e, the relationships among these three people. It is a particular view of the event and focuses on some information as more important to us, keeping other information less distinct, as background. It is usually necessary to foreground some aspects of phenomena and background others simply because no one can study everything at once. However, the distinctions between what is in the foreground and what is in the background lie in our analysis and are not assumed to be separate entities in reality. (In contrast, the boxes-and-arrows and nested-circles approaches often treat the diagrammed entities as existing separately in reality.)

FIGURE 2.3F

Some studies (or some lines of investigation, or some disciplines) need a *cultural-institutional focus of analysis*, backgrounding the details regarding the particular people and their relations with each other. In this scene, we might be interested in studying such cultural-institutional processes as how this particular school has developed practices in which parent volunteers are routinely in the classroom, helping children learn by devising "fun educational" activities; how the community of this school revises its practices as new generations of families join in; and how the practices in this school connect with the culture and history of schooling in other innovative schools as well as in traditional schools and with national and educational policies (such an analysis is available in Rogoff, Goodman Turkanis, & Bartlett, 2001; Rogoff, 1994).

With the focus of Figure 2.3f, we see a glimpse of a moving picture involving the history of the activities and the transformations toward the future in which people and their communities engage.

FIGURE 2.3G

This figure portrays a problem that sometimes occurs if researchers recognize the importance of culture but leave out the equally important role of *the people who constitute cultural activities*. This figure is as difficult to understand as Figure 2.3a. It does not make sense to try to study cultural processes without considering the contributions of the people involved, keeping them in the background of a focus on cultural, institutional community processes.

I believe that this approach will facilitate progress in coordinating information across studies and across disciplines to develop more complete understanding of the phenomena that interest us. Keeping our focus of analysis informed by background information makes it easier to align the understanding gained across studies or disciplines that employ different focuses. Instead of being competing ways to examine phenomena, each focus informs the others.

Although I concentrate in this book on questions of personal, interpersonal, and cultural processes, biological aspects of the activity shown in Figure 2.3d–f could be the focus of analysis in other related research. For example, studies could focus on neuronal, hormonal, or genetic processes, with personal, interpersonal, and cultural information in the background. In this way, biological, sociocultural, and individual aspects of human functioning can all be seen as contributing to the overall process, rather than as rivals, trying to cut each other out of the picture. (In the next chapter, I discuss the relation of biological and cultural processes.)

Key to my approach is an emphasis on the *processes* involved in human activity. The static nature of Figure 2.3d–f does not capture this well, however; the medium of the printed page constrains the representation of dynamic processes. If you can imagine the image as a glance at a moment in a moving picture, it would do more justice to the idea of the dynamic and mutually constituting nature of individual, interpersonal, and cultural-institutional processes.

The next chapter examines concepts for thinking about cultural processes. The ways that scholars and policymakers have often thought of culture are tied to the separation of individual and culture in the box-and-arrow or nesting-circles diagrams. Culture has been treated as an outside "influence" on individual characteristics, often thought of as providing a flavor to otherwise vanilla individuals. As I explain in the next chapter, from my transformation-of-participation view, all people participate in continually changing cultural communities. Individuals and generations shape practices, traditions, and institutions at the same time that they build on what they inherit in their moment in history.

3

Individuals, Generations, and Dynamic Cultural Communities

Each of us lives out our species nature only in a specific local manifestation . . .
our cultural and historical peculiarity is an essential part of that nature.
—*Shore, 1988, p. 19*

Scholars and census takers alike struggle with how to think about the relation of individuals and cultural communities. This chapter focuses on how we can conceive of cultural processes and communities if we consider development to be a process of changing participation in dynamic cultural communities.

Two major challenges in trying to characterize people's cultural heritage are the focus of this chapter. The first challenge is moving beyond a pair of long-standing related dichotomies: cultural versus biological heritage and similarities versus differences. The second challenge is how to think of cultural processes as dynamic properties of overlapping human communities rather than treating culture as a static social address carried by individuals.

Humans Are Biologically Cultural

The well-known nature/nurture debate places culture and biology in opposition. Proponents argue that if something is cultural, it is not biological, and if something is biological, it is not cultural. In particular, psychologists have spent a long time trying to figure out what percentage of a person's characteristics is biological and what percentage is cultural or environmental. This artificial separation treats biology and culture as independent entities rather than viewing humans as biologically cultural.

63

The nature/nurture debate often attributes differences between communities to culture and similarities to biology. The debate sometimes assumes that basic human processes (such as learning language) exist in a culture-free biological form, and then contact with a particular culture induces superficial variations (such as which particular language a person speaks).

However, it is false to assume that universals are biological and variations are cultural. All humans have a great deal in common due to the biological *and* cultural heritage that we share as a species: We all walk on two legs, communicate with language, need protection as infants, organize in groups, and use tools. Our shared ecological constraints, such as regular day-night cycles, often lead to common adaptations (biological and cultural). Each of us also varies because of differences in our biological *and* cultural circumstances, yielding different visual acuity, strength, family arrangements, means of making a living, and familiarity with specific languages. Similarities and differences across communities do not divide phenomena into biological and cultural.

The defining features of the human species—such as using language and passing on inventions and adaptations to subsequent generations—are our cultural heritage. Part of our species' biological heritage is wide flexibility as well as similarities in cultural arrangements that characterize different human communities (see Heath, 1989a; Ochs, 1996).

Cultural differences are generally variations on themes of universal import, with differing emphasis or value placed on particular practices rather than all-or-none differences. For example, children's ways of learning vary across communities, such as in formal schooling, apprenticeships, or helping on the farm. At the same time, however, all children learn from observation and participation in *some* kind of community activities.

Accounting for cultural aspects of both widespread and diverse human practices will enable our understanding of the regularities within the diverse patterns that characterize human functioning. Breast-feeding provides a good example of widespread as well as diverse practices. Before baby bottles, nursing was practically essential to human survival—and virtually universal (Trevathan & McKenna, 1994). At the same time, communities vary widely in how long nursing continues. In a study in Kansas City, researchers found that the older a baby is when nursing stops, the greater the associated distress (Sears & Wise, 1950, reported in Whiting & Child, 1953). However, by worldwide standards, Kansas City babies were weaned very early; only 5 out of 70 children were still nursing at the age of 7 months. In a worldwide sample of 52 societies, the age at weaning ranged from 6 months to 5½ years, with a median of 2½ years (Whiting & Child, 1953). With the worldwide sample, as with the Kansas City study, the older the baby was, up to age 13 to 18 months, the more distress accompanied weaning. But after this peak, weaning became easier with age; older children frequently weaned themselves. The worldwide variety in weaning practices led to a more comprehensive view of regularities in the relation between age and distress at weaning.

To understand development, it is essential to figure out *in what ways* human development in different communities is alike, and in what ways it differs. We can leave behind the unproductive either/or thinking that asks whether human development is more similar *or* different across communities and whether culture *or* biology has more effect. The either/or questions are as pointless as asking whether people rely more on their right leg or their left leg for walking. I consider biological aspects to function in concert with cultural aspects.

Vygotsky provided a useful framework for thinking about the integrated, dynamic nature of individual, cultural, and species development. He proposed the study of four interrelated levels of development involving the individual and the environment in different time frames: microgenetic, ontogenetic, phylogenetic, and cultural-historical development (Scribner, 1985; Wertsch, 1985; Zinchenko, 1985). Developmental psychologists traditionally deal with *ontogenetic development*, which occurs in the time frame of the individual life span, such as across the years of childhood. This is merely a different time frame from the other three developmental levels. *Phylogenetic development* is the slowly changing species history that leaves a legacy for the individual in the form of genes, transforming over centuries or millennia. *Cultural historical development* changes across decades and centuries, leaving a legacy for individuals in the form of symbolic and material technologies (such as literacy, number systems, and computers) as well as value systems, scripts, and norms. *Microgenetic development* is the moment-to-moment learning of individuals in particular contexts, built on the individual's genetic and cultural-historical background.

These levels of analysis of development are inseparable: The efforts of individuals constitute cultural practices that further organize individuals' development. Similarly, human biological development works together with the cultural institutions and practices that characterize humanity. Development over the life course takes place within both the course of cultural history and the course of phylogenetic history.

Human development necessarily builds on the historical endowment with which humans are born both as members of their species and as members of their communities. Thus, it is a false dichotomy to focus on "nature" and "nurture" as separable influences on human development. Babies enter the world equipped with patterns of action as well as preferences and biases in learning, based on their individual and specieswide genes and prenatal experience. They also come equipped with caregivers who structure their biological and social worlds in ways deriving from their own and their ancestors' phylogenetic and cultural history (Hatano & Inagaki, 2000; Rogoff, 1990; Trevathan & McKenna, 1994).

At the same time, of course, new generations transform cultural institutions and practices and contribute to biological evolution. Birth itself involves cultural practices surrounding labor and delivery, such as the use of drugs for the mother, variations in her position (squatting, lying), and the kind of support she receives (alone or with other people, in a hospital or outdoors). The obstetric techniques of a community, such as drugs and herbal remedies, cesarean section and external version, are cultural inventions (see figure 3.1).

Such cultural inventions may shape the biological characteristics of the species (and biological changes also contribute to cultural practices). For example, cesarean sections are often performed to save infants whose heads are too big for their mothers' birth canals. Survival of such infants passes on genes for large heads and, over generations, might allow evolution of larger heads among human populations with access to cesarean sections. The cesarean section is one of many cultural technologies that contribute to the

FIGURE 3.1

An Armenian family gathered at the bedside of a mother and newborn infant.

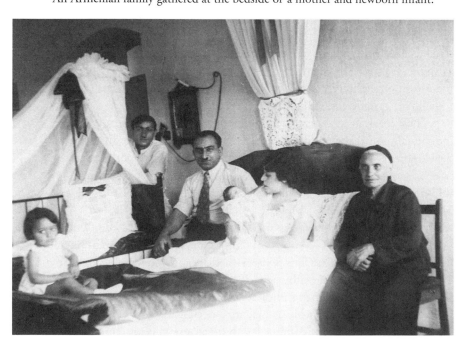

nature of the human species and the nature of our descendants. The biological changes that could result from such cultural practices may in turn contribute to changing cultural possibilities. Thus biological and cultural processes continually operate in tandem. ———> woven

Infant breathing also illustrates how cultural and biological processes function together. Around the world, there are differences in whether children sleep with other people and in whether infants are expected to sleep for long stretches (as in the U.S. the developmental goal for infants to sleep for eight uninterrupted hours by 4 to 6 months of age). In some communities, infants wake and feed about every four hours around the clock for at least the first eight months of life (Super, 1981; Super & Harkness, 1982). They often sleep with their mother and nurse on demand, with minimal disturbance of adult sleep. Mothers continue to sleep as their child nurses, or waken to feed and be sociable with the infant and others and then go back to sleep. In such arrangements, there is little parental motivation to enforce "sleeping through the night."

Some researchers speculate that encouraging infants to sleep all night may strain their immature neurological system to maintain itself over this long sleep period (McKenna, 1986; Trevathan & McKenna, 1994). In middle-class European American communities, babies are not only expected to sleep long stretches but are usually required to do it alone (Morelli, Rogoff, Oppenheim, & Goldsmith, 1992). Some research suggests that if infants sleep beside somebody rather than alone, their breathing may be supported by following the regular breathing pattern of the person beside them. Cultural differences in infant sleeping arrangements (sleeping eight hours at a stretch, alone, or following "expert" advice to place babies on their back to sleep) might have an impact on whether some vulnerable infants keep breathing or suffer Sudden Infant Death Syndrome (McKenna & Mosko, 1993; Trevathan & McKenna, 1994). In any case, cultural practices are clearly connected with biological processes from the beginning of life.

Two lines of research in human development illustrate especially well the mutually constituting nature of biological and cultural processes. One is infants' preparation to learn from other people, and another is explanations of gender differences. In both of these, discussed next, we can recognize cultural as well as biological roles in specieswide regularities as well as common patterns in the differences among communities.

Prepared Learning by Infants and Young Children

Infants are born ready to learn the ways of those around them. In either/or thinking, some scholars downplay the extent to which infants are born prepared to learn human ways, preferring to credit development to the environment. However, inheritance from thousands of years of human history provides each new generation with genes and inborn processes that prepare them for joining human life. Such inheritance contributes to infants' readiness to learn to balance on two feet, to use objects as tools, and to attract the care of adults. It probably underlies observations across cultural communities of close similarities in the sequence and timing of some infant developmental milestones and in the onset of smiling and distress over separation from an attachment figure (Gewirtz, 1965; Goldberg, 1972; Konner, 1972; Super, 1981).

Human infants are prepared to learn language, a skill they have inherited from their ancestors. The stages of language learning appear in a constant order across a large variety of communities (Bowerman, 1981; Slobin, 1973). Infants' preparation to learn language includes a propensity to learn from cultural processes, which have also been inherited from ancestors (by means of contact between the generations, not just genes).

Human learning is facilitated by an especially long infancy compared with many other animal species. Many other species are born able to do things that humans cannot, such as walking and feeding themselves. Long infancy may be responsible for our flexibility as a species in learning to use language and other cultural inventions. In this protracted early human development, children can flexibly learn the ways of any community: "Humans are born with a self-regulating strategy for getting knowledge by human negotiation and co-operative action. . . . Thus socialisation is as natural, innate or 'biological' for a human brain as breathing or walking" (Trevarthen, 1988, p. 39).

In fact, humans learn from their cultural community even before birth. Experience as a fetus allows newborns to recognize many aspects of their prenatal life. They recognize their own mother's voice; they distinguish unfamiliar from familiar stories that they heard repeatedly in their last weeks before birth (whether spoken by their mother or by another woman); and they even discriminate between an unfamiliar language and their "mother tongue" (Cooper & Aslin, 1989; DeCasper & Fifer, 1980; DeCasper & Spence, 1986; Mehler et al., 1988).

Infants' rapid language development relies on both their ability to detect language distinctions and their experience with the distinctions used in the language they hear (Jusczyk, 1997; Werker & Desjardins, 1995). Over the first year, their sensitivity declines for distinctions between sounds that they seldom hear, as they tune their ear and their vocalizations to common features of the language that surrounds them. Around the world, infants' babbling has the same sounds—the sounds of all languages—up through about 6 months of age. But sometime between 6 months and 1 year of age, children specialize in their mother tongue—they start dropping out the sounds that are not used in the language around them. For example, in Spanish, the letter "b" and the letter "v" are often heard as the same, without the auditory boundary between the "b" and the "v" as in English. Small babies in a Spanish-speaking environment initially distinguish between what English speakers call "b" and "v," but as the babies get older, that distinction drops out; "volleyball" sounds the same as "bolleyvall."

The origins of infants' predisposition to attend to language distinctions have likely arisen through both biological and sociocultural processes across the history of the human species. Undoubtedly, our ancestors experimented with ways to communicate during common efforts to survive. Those who succeeded were likely to have passed on both their genes and their practices to the next generations, contributing to this key biologically cultural feature of our species.

Language learning is also supported by biological and cultural features of human life that give infants opportunities to hear their native language and to begin to communicate with those who use it. Healthy human infants appear to come equipped with ways of achieving proximity to and involvement with other members of society, such as imitating others and protesting being left alone. Infants' efforts appear similar to those appropriate for anyone learning in an unfamiliar cultural setting: stay near trusted guides, watch their activities and get involved when possible, and attend to any instruction the guides provide.

Infants' efforts are accompanied by biological and cultural features of caregiver-child relationships and cultural practices that encourage involvement of children in the activities of their community. Whether or not they regard themselves as explicitly teaching young children, caregivers routinely model mature performance during joint endeavors, adjust their interaction, and structure children's environments and activities in ways that support local forms of learning (Rogoff, 1990).

Throughout childhood, children increasingly participate in and begin to manage the cultural activities that surround them, with the guidance of caregivers and companions (Fortes, 1938/1970). They learn the skills and practices of their community by engaging with others who may contribute to structuring the process to be learned, provide guidance during joint activity, and help adjust participation according to proficiency (see figure 3.2). For example, Mayan mothers from Guatemala assist their daughters in learning to weave by segmenting the process into steps, providing guidance in the context of joint participation, and adjusting the daughter's participation in weaving according to her increasing skill and interest (Rogoff, 1986). Similar processes occur in weaving in Mexico and tailoring in Liberia (Greenfield, 1984; Greenfield & Lave, 1982).

Children everywhere learn skills in the context of their use and with

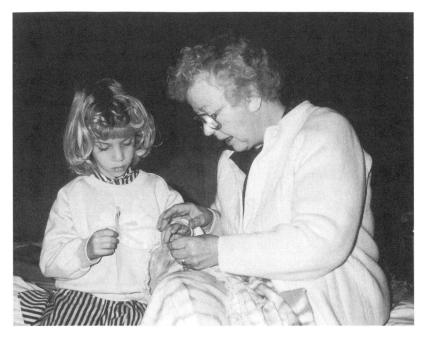

FIGURE 3.2

A European American middle-class 6-year-old learns to sew with the aid and pointers provided by her grandmother, an expert seamstress.

the aid of those around them. This is how toddlers in India learn at an early age to distinguish the use of their right and left hands (a difficult distinction for many older children in other communities). The right hand is the "clean" hand used for eating and the left one is the "dirty" hand used for cleaning oneself after defecation:

> If a child did not learn to eat with the right hand by participation and observation, a mother or older sister would manipulate the right hand and restrain the left until the child understood and did what was required. One of the earliest lessons taught a child of one-and-a-half to two years of age was to distinguish between the right and left hand and their distinctly separate usages. . . . Although we judged that the Indian style of eating required considerable manipulative skill, we observed a girl, not quite two, tear her chapati solely with her right hand and pick up her vegetable with the piece of chapati held in the right hand. (Freed & Freed, 1981, p. 60)

Similarly, European American caregivers often help infants attend to what the caregivers want them to see. If infants appear not to understand a pointing gesture, the mothers may help by touching the indicated object (Lempers, 1979). With infants as young as 3 months, these mothers attempt to achieve joint attention by following their infant's direction of gaze or by putting an object between themselves and their baby and shaking the object (Bruner, 1983; Schaffer, 1984).

Local versions of these sorts of interpersonal supports for learning are provided by a long biological and cultural history. In our species, each generation comes prepared to learn to participate in the practices and traditions of their elders, aided by shared engagement in valued and routine cultural activities. This may account for children's rapid development as participants in the practices and understandings of their community—whether learning to weave or to read, tend livestock or young children, do schoolwork, or behave according to the specific gender roles prescribed in their community. The biologically cultural nature of human development is also well illustrated by gender role development.

Where Do Gender Differences Come From?

Active debate swarms around the question of whether gender differences are biologically inevitable or culturally malleable. From the discussion above, it should be clear that I favor a view that gender differences are based on both biological and cultural heritage. Information about biological as well as cultural contributions to the patterns we observe, and about cultural similarities as well as variations, can aid us in deciding whether the observed patterns are ones that we want to continue.

The two common accounts of gender role differences, often assumed to be competing explanations, both contribute to the discussion. The biological account argues that humans and other animals are biologically prepared for gender differences, especially through their differing reproductive roles. This is often treated as being in opposition to gender role "training" that occurs through instruction and experience with a gender-structured world (Draper, 1985; Eagly & Wood, 1999). The two views are often treated in an either/or manner, with strong feelings about allegiance to one "side" or the other, in an unfortunate oversimplification (see also Miller & Keller, 2000).

Biological Preparation of Gender Roles

The biological preparation argument holds that male and female procreation involve very different reproductive strategies, which extend to many other aspects of life. According to this perspective, a major motive of animal (including human) behavior is the drive to ensure survival of one's own genes. Gender differences would stem from the fact that women have to invest heavily in each child to reproduce their genes, whereas men need invest little time and effort.

To get one child who is liable to grow up and keep on reproducing, women spend nine months pregnant, two to three years nursing (in historical worldwide averages), and more years protecting and teaching the child to be able to survive. In contrast, men can father as many children as women will allow them access to do, with very little time invested. Men can help to ensure that their genes survive by assisting women in raising the children, providing resources and protection. Such assistance is sometimes a condition for allowing men the opportunity to procreate. A creation story told among the Navajo illustrates these aspects of the biological preparation argument:

> Áltsé hastiin the First Man became a great hunter in the fourth world. So he was able to provide his wife Áltsé asdzáá the First Woman with plenty to eat. . . . Now one day he brought home a fine, fleshy deer. His wife boiled some of it, and together they had themselves a hearty meal. When she had finished eating, Áltsé asdzáá the First Woman wiped her greasy hands on her sheath. She belched deeply. And she had this to say:
>
> "Thank you shijóózh my vagina," she said, "Thank you for that delicious dinner."
>
> To which Áltsé hastiin the First Man replied this way: "Why do you say that?" he replied. "Why not thank me? Was it not I who killed the deer whose flesh you have just feasted on? Was it not I who carried it here for you to eat? Was it not I who skinned it? Who made it ready for you to boil? Is nijóózh your vagina the great hunter, that you should thank it and not me?"
>
> To which Áltsé asdzáá offered this answer: "As a matter of fact, she is," offered she. "In a manner of speaking it is jóósh the vagina who hunts. Were it not for jóósh you would not have killed that deer. Were it not for her you would not have carried it here. You would not have skinned it. You lazy men would do nothing around here were it not for jóósh. In truth jóósh the vagina does all the work around here." (Zolbrod, 1984, pp. 58–59, brought to my attention by Deyhle & Margonis, 1995)

According to the biological preparation argument, one difficulty for men attempting to assist in raising their children is that men cannot be sure that a child is theirs. (In contrast, women do know that a child is theirs.) To invest in a particular child, so the argument goes, men want some assurance of their fatherhood. This is used to account for the double standard for virginity and sexual activity.

At the same time, females control access to the males' ability to contribute genes to the next generation. To gain access, males may need to engage in deeds of daring or convince females that they can provide greater resources and protection than other males. This, in the biological preparation argument, accounts for competition among males and greater unevenness of skills among males than females.

Explanations of how gender differences arise are quite controversial. Many heated arguments are based on peoples' views of how things *should* be as well as on observations of existing gender differences. Although the biological preparation argument and the gender role training argument are often put in opposition, they need not be. Indeed, it is difficult to imagine that they do not operate in concert in some way.

Gender Role Training

The gender role training view argues that children develop the distinctive gender roles of their community from models presented in daily life and the encouragement or discouragement of gender-related activities (see figure 3.3).

An example of discouragement of gender-"inappropriate" activity is the commonly observed restriction of U.S. girls' level of activity through requirements to stay clean and protect pretty clothes. Girls in a number of

FIGURE 3.3

A little one attempts to assume the position of gender role models, Sarasota, FL, ca. 1950.

FIGURE 3.4

Gender information is pervasive in the everyday arrangements of children and families, as can be seen in this portrait in 19th-century France, by Pierre-Auguste Renoir. Madame Georges Charpentier was the wife of a prominent publisher. Her daughter sits on the family dog and her son, Paul, sits beside her, dressed in girl's clothing because he is not yet 5 years old.

societies receive more training for proper social behavior than do boys (Whiting & Edwards, 1988; see figure 3.4). A nursery rhyme from Latin America illustrates this type of sex role training:

Chiquita Bonita	Pretty Little Girl
Soy chiquita, soy bonita.	I am small, I am pretty.
Soy la perla de mamá.	I am my mother's pearl.
Si me ensucio el vestido,	If I soil my dress,
Garrotazos me dará.	She will beat me.

(Griego, Bucks, Gilbert, & Kimball, 1981, p. 6)

Gender differences appear to be nurtured by differences in the tasks usually assigned girls and boys. Beatrice Whiting emphasized that the way children learn to treat other people is aligned with the cast of characters with whom they routinely engage, especially with the gender and age of their companions:

> The power of parents and other agents of socialization is in their assignment of children to specific settings. Whether it is caring for an infant sibling, working around the house in the company of adult females, working on the farm with adults and siblings, playing outside with neighborhood children, hunting with adult males, or attending school with age mates, the daily assignment of a child to one or another of these settings has important consequences on the development of habits of interpersonal behavior, consequences that may not be recognized by the socializers who make the assignments. (1980, p. 111)

In the *Six Cultures* study, Whiting and Whiting (1975) and their colleagues observed the interactions of children who were in the company of older, same-age, and younger children. Those who commonly spent time with younger children generally behaved in a more nurturant fashion. In the varying cultural communities that Beatrice Whiting and Carolyn Edwards (1973, 1988) studied, nurturance of the older girls appeared to be related to the fact that they were far more likely to be assigned infant care than were boys. Girls of all ages were assigned chores near or inside the home, requiring compliance to their mother, whereas boys were allowed to play or work farther from home and in the company of peers. In addition, girls were assigned chores at a younger age than boys.

The impact of assignment to infant care was examined in a Luo community in Kenya (Ember, 1973). Luo mothers usually assigned girls and boys chores that were culturally defined as gender-appropriate. However, the absence of an older sister in some homes required boys to do some of the female chores. Luo boys who were assigned female work in the home, especially infant care, were less aggressive and more prosocial than boys who did not have these task assignments. Moreover, the nurturance of Luo boys with experience tending infants generalized to their interactions with other individuals.

Children look for regularities in behavior based on salient categories in their community. Gender is invariably a salient category (Whiting & Edwards, 1988). Children themselves are often more conservative about gender differences than are the adults around them. They look for rules, and if they think they have found one, they are more narrow about its application than their elders, often overlooking examples to the contrary. For example, when one of my daughters was about 2, we watched a show on TV where two geologists dressed in suits were speaking. My daughter asked who they were,

Interesting

and I told her they were professors. She said, "They can't be professors, they're mans." She knew one professor, who was a woman, so she inferred that no men could be professors. She had developed a rule and applied it strictly.

Gender information surrounds children, providing the opportunity for them to learn about their community's gender roles from parents, siblings and peers, and teachers and from other sources such as television, books, and other media. For example, many children's books and television shows in the United States give stereotyped views of what boys and men do and what girls and women do: Women characters often have stereotypically female occupations; the protagonists are generally male; if women or girls are present they tend to be in the background; and males have the adventures (Spicher & Hudak, 1997).

Subtle information about gender in young children's daily lives may be especially likely to be accepted because it is taken for granted. Lee Munroe and Ruth Munroe (1997) suggested that patterns that are perceived without conscious awareness or without being pointed out are especially likely to be regarded subsequently as preferable and more pleasant. They predicted that for this reason, gender roles would be quite resilient and slow to change.

Thus, the gender role training argument notes that information about gender role expectations is pervasive and is not just in the form of purposeful lessons or regulations but is conveyed also in differential treatment of boys and girls, men and women. This argument prioritizes the social and cultural contributions to children's development of gender roles. (Chapter 5 takes a closer look at patterns of gender roles in different cultural communities. The aim here is simply to argue that gender roles can be seen as simultaneously biologically and culturally formed; we do not need to treat biology and culture as competing forces.)

We can look at biological preparation and social learning of gender roles as involving the same processes viewed in different time frames. In Vygotsky's terms, evolutionary (biological) preparedness of gender roles involves *phylogenetic* development, and social learning of gender roles involves *microgenetic* and *ontogenetic* development of the current era's gender roles during the time frame of *cultural-historical development*. Biological preparation is thus a record of the customs and arrangements that developed from the distant past of the species. At the same time, individuals learn their part in (and revise) the customs and practices of their community's current and recent gender role distributions and societal structure.

From a sociocultural perspective, studying biological and cultural processes as they *together* contribute to changing human practices across generations will improve understanding of the preparedness of infants to learn, the origins of gender differences, and other aspects of human development. A generational approach is also central to making progress in how we think about the relation of individual cultural participation and changing cultural communities, as I argue in the next section.

Participation in Dynamic Cultural Communities

When identifying people's connections with communities, there is a widespread tendency to use a single category, often ethnic or racial, to categorize an individual. This results in the "box problem": Which box on a questionnaire do you check as your ethnic identity? Individuals categorized in the same box are assumed to be mostly alike and to differ in essential ways from individuals categorized in other boxes. (Discussions of the issues surrounding the use of ethnicity and nationality as discrete categories appear in Ferdman, 2000; Gjerde & Onishi, 2000; Hoffman, 1997; Nagel, 1994; Phinney, 1996; Rogoff & Angelillo, 2002; Verdery, 1994; Waldron, 1996; and Wolf, 1994, 1997.)

In the next section, I discuss the problem of treating culture primarily as a category of individual identity. I suggest instead that cultural processes can be thought of as practices and traditions of dynamically related cultural communities in which individuals participate and to which they contribute across generations. I then consider the unique case of middle-class European American communities, in which people are often unaware of their own cultural participation. Then I explore a way of thinking about communities across generations, as new generations carry on and revise the cultural practices of those who raised them.

Culture as a Categorical Property of Individuals versus a Process of Participation in Dynamically Related Cultural Communities

People's cultural participation is often discussed in terms of cultural or ethnic "identity," asking Who are you? or What are you? This categorization approach is based on the idea that cultural aspects of individual lives are fixed in "social address" categories such as race, ethnicity, and socioeconomic class.[1] Such social addresses are important for the study of how people categorize themselves and other individuals, but equating them with culture is problematic in ways that I discuss in this section.

[1]With the prevailing focus on individual classification, ethnic or "cultural" identity is sometimes viewed as an individual biological inheritance. Although some individual features connected with one's ancestors' community membership can be genetically inherited by individuals—such as nose shape, hair texture, salt metabolism, and propensity for certain diseases—these markers are far from central to the examination of cultural processes (see Wolf, 1994).

Instead of using a categorical approach to thinking about culture, I prefer to focus on people's involvement in their communities, to address the dynamic, generative nature of both individual lives and community practices. With cultural participation as the focus, the question for examining an individual's cultural involvement becomes What cultural practices are familiar to you? or What cultural practices have you made use of? For examining communities' cultural practices, the question becomes What ways of doing things are customary? or What sorts of everyday approaches do people usually expect? Cultural practices—such as home language(s), religion, government and legal systems, ways of teaching and learning, gender roles, skills with specific tools and technologies, and attitudes toward other groups —are central to both individual and community functioning as people build on and contribute to community cultural traditions.

Moving from considering culture as "social address" boxes or identity categories to an examination of participation in cultural communities would solve some problems that currently perplex us. Conceptualizing culture as a categorical variable of individual identity creates issues of variability within groups, overlapping involvements in different communities, and the complexities of subdividing categorization systems.

Problems of variability, overlap, and subgroups
in categorical approaches to culture

Identity categories often focus on one's ancestral nation (or continent!), overlooking important variations within nations. However, the closer one looks, the more likely one is to discern differences within groups. This is more likely with groups one knows intimately:

> If one is "Asian American" one is very much aware of the numerous ways in which internal differences are profound and consequential. Thus, Japanese Americans know the important distinctions between the generations and their attitudes toward assimilation in America (Issei, Nisei, Sansei, and now Yonsei, with patterned and different views about intermarriage, voting, assimilation, etc.). Chinese Americans see important differences between Chinese from Taiwan and Hong Kong, Southeast Asia and the Mainland, San Francisco and Walnut Creek, first or second generation, and so on. Similarly, Koreans, Filipinos, Laotians, Cambodian, and Vietnamese also note internal variations amongst themselves.
>
> While Asian Americans are sensitive to their own internal differences, they are likely to hold stereotypical views of the homogeneous character of "others," collapsing gentiles and Jews, working-class Irish

Catholics and upper-middle class Episcopalians as "white." Similarly, Blacks make astute internal distinctions between the street-wise urban and those who grew up in suburban settings with professional parents, those from a second generation who migrated from the south, and those from old-line southern elite families, between nationalist and assimilationist, etc. But these same African Americans who see internal differences in their own group [may] see "Asians" as a single, collapsed category. (Institute for the Study of Social Change, 1991, p. 12)

The splitting of groups into subgroups can go on ad infinitum, "down" to the level of the individual. Many scholars therefore worry that attending to cultural differences will unduly complicate social scientists' efforts to develop general statements about human functioning. However, this worry stems from the "box" approach to culture. Psychologists often assume that more boxes are needed in order to examine the role of national origins, religious convictions, generations since immigration, regional differences, and so on. They argue that the boxes need to be subdivided (into "subcultures") to be able to cross each of these with the others to examine their independent and interacting effects. However, the boxes and subboxes would eventually be so numerous that the whole endeavor would collapse under its own weight.

This issue dissolves if we move from thinking of culture as consisting of separate categories or factors, and instead describe individuals' participation in cultural communities. Our description can refer to national origins, religious convictions, generations since immigration, regional differences, and so on. But the features would not be regarded as separate categorical factors (even if such simplification may be handy in our data analyses; see Rogoff & Angelillo, 2002). Rather, cultural features can be treated as interdependent aspects of a multifaceted pattern.

For example, instead of describing a community using the intersection of supposedly independent categories such as nationality, race, social class, and so on, we could give a more fluid description that places each of these aspects in the historical context of the others. In this way, we might describe a Mayan Indian community in Guatemala as one where, for several centuries, most families depended on subsistence agriculture and recently have added cash crops and merchant and professional occupations and begun to send their children to Western schools.

For some research, concepts of ethnicity, social class, and personal identity are essential. Indeed, boxing disparate traditions together under a common label (e.g., Latino, African American, Asian) in public policy and everyday life *creates* a reality based on these identity categories (Barth, 1994;

Correa-Chávez, personal communication, November 2000). For example, people classed in the same boxes by law or custom come to share a common treatment and history, even if the classification system clusters people with widely disparate backgrounds.

However, if social science were to *equate* culture with the intersection of such categories, we would have destroyed the concept of culture. Such an approach would exclude the dynamic examination of the historical nature of people's participation in changing and overlapping cultural communities.

Cultural Communities

Thinking about cultural *communities* is central to my proposal to shift from an emphasis on categorical identity as a property of individuals. It helps us focus on people's participation in cultural processes that form the common practices of particular communities.

The question of what a community is has become especially important in recent years. Unfortunately, many people use the term "community" to refer simply to a collection of individuals with some single identifying characteristic. It means little more to say "the community of bicycle riders" than to say "bicycle riders" or to say "the smoking community" rather than "smokers." In my view, communities are not simply a collection of individuals sharing a characteristic or two.

For present purposes, *communities* can be defined as groups of people who have some common and continuing organization, values, understanding, history, and practices. As John Dewey pointed out: "There is more than a verbal tie between the words common, community, and communication. [People] live in a community in virtue of the things which they have in common; and communication is the way in which they come to possess things in common" (1916, p. 5).

A community involves people trying to accomplish some things together, with some stability of involvement and attention to the ways they relate to each other. Being a community requires structured communication that is expected to endure for some time, with a degree of commitment and shared though often contested meaning. A community develops cultural practices and traditions that transcend the particular individuals involved, as one generation replaces another.

The relations among the participants in a community are varied and multifaceted. Different participants have different roles and responsibilities, and their relations may be comfortable or conflictual or oppressive. Their relations involve personal connections and procedures for resolving inevitable conflicts in ways that attempt to maintain the relationships and the community. Participants in a community may provide each other with support and are familiar with aspects of each other's lives. They also engage in conflicts, disputes, and intrigues, as seems inevitable when people's lives are connected and the future of the community is a matter of intense interest. Even after leaving, participants in a community often continue to regard their involvement and their continuing relationships as central to their lives, whether this is expressed in affection and loyalty to the community or resentment or efforts to avoid community ways.

A community involves generations that move through it, with customary ways of handling the transitions of generations. To continue to function, a community also adapts with changing times, experimenting with and resisting new ideas in ways that maintain core values while learning from changes that are desired or required.

My use of the term community is not limited to people who are in face-to-face contact or living in geographic proximity. Prototypical communities, in prior times, have involved people who live in the same small village or region for generations. However, people who coordinate with others at a distance, within some form of personal network, relying on some similar assumptions about how things are done and using similar tools within related institutions may also share a community. In such distal communities, people's relationships are still multifaceted; individuals are not just thrown together without some common history, future, traditions, and goals. Communities are composed of people who coordinate with each other over a shared and often contested history.

*Expectable variation within and overlapping
participation among communities*

The questions of variation within a group and of overlapping involvements are not stumbling blocks once we shift to looking at participation in cultural communities rather than thinking of culture as a categorical variable or set of independent factors.

Variations among participants in a community are to be expected. Participants do not have precisely the same points of view, practices, backgrounds, or goals. Rather, they are part of a somewhat coordinated organization. They often are in complementary roles, playing parts that fit together rather than being identical, or in contested relationships with each other, disagreeing about features of their own roles or community direction while requiring some common ground even for the disagreement. It is the *common ways* that participants in a community share (even if they contest them) that I regard as culture.

People often participate in more than one community, and the cultural ways of the various dynamic communities in which they participate may overlap or conflict with each other. To the extent that a nation shares ideas, institutions, and ways of doing things and relating, the traditions and practices of people in that nation can be identified by reference to the national community. At the same time, people participate in cultural traditions and practices that are identified with more local or specific communities. The salience of these overlapping communities is likely to vary for those who participate in them.

For example, many North Americans regard themselves as members of a national community along with communities defined by one or more ethnic heritages (such as Danish, African, Jewish, and Mexican descent), regional traditions (e.g., Appalachian, urban, or Southern Californian), and religions. Academia (or intelligentsia) can also be regarded as a community that often extends across national and ethnic boundaries (Walker, 2001). Likewise, the communities of commune dwellers of the 1960s in the United States included people of quite varied family roots and values (Weisner & Bernheimer, 1998). An individual may regard one or a few of these kinds of community as primary for defining his or her way of life, even while participating in others.

Communities are often in close relationship with one another, frequently in ways that serve to define each other (see Barth, 1994; Nagel, 1994; Wolf, 1997). For example, generational communities such as the "children of the 1960s" defined their values and practices in opposition to those of their parents' generation. Ethnic neighbors or different religious groups may define themselves in terms of historical relationships (of conflict, oppression, assistance, or mutual reliance) across their communities.

Individuals' connections with some cultural communities may take greater prominence and others may become family secrets, depending on the social meaning of involvement in different groups (see Valsiner & Lawrence, 1997). Individuals often identify their cultural heritage differently depending on the situation and audience, reflecting historical relations among communities:

> An individual of Cuban ancestry may be a Latino vis-à-vis non-Spanish-speaking ethnic groups, a Cuban-American vis-à-vis other Spanish-speaking groups, a Marielito vis-à-vis other Cubans, and white vis-à-vis African Americans. The chosen ethnic identity is determined by the individual's perception of its meaning to different audiences, its salience in different social contexts, and its utility in different settings. For instance, intra-Cuban distinctions of class and immigration cohort may not be widely understood outside of the Cuban community since a Marielito is a "Cuban" or "Hispanic" to most Anglo-Americans. To a Cuban, however, immigration cohorts represent important political "vintages," distinguishing those whose lives have been shaped by decades of Cuban revolutionary social changes

from those whose life experiences have been as exiles in the United States. (Nagel, 1994, p. 155, summarizing the work of Pedraza; Padilla; and Gimenez, Lopez & Munoz)

I purposely focus on *participation* rather than *membership* in communities. To be a member of a group usually requires some agreement that the person falls within some established boundaries (like the boxes). However, people often participate in cultural communities without being accorded membership in them. For example, I have participated for several decades in a Mayan community in Guatemala, but people from that community (and I) do not regard me as a member of that community. Nonetheless, my cultural participation in the Tz'utujil Mayan town of San Pedro has been very important to my own development and that of my family, and my involvement has contributed to San Pedro's cultural practices over the years. If we use the more dynamic concept of participation, rather than the categorical concept of membership, I believe that we can more easily focus on the cultural processes involved in both individual development and community histories.

Generalizing about People and Processes

The categorical approach assumes some homogeneity within each category of people, automatically generalizing observations (on average) to all people who share a category designation, such as Japanese, Mexican American, or European American. This approach also wrestles with the issue of "representativeness" of the research participants to the wider population of which they are expected to serve as exemplars (because category members are expected to be relatively homogeneous).

My proposal—that we focus on participation in cultural communities—does not assume that observations are general beyond the people observed. Instead, the question of generality is a matter for investigation, to examine the extent to which observations in one community can be extended to a "neighbor." Far more research needs to be done before we can determine the generality or specificity of the observations to date. Some aspects of membership in broader communities will apply to more specific communities that share a common history and institutions, and other aspects will differ.

The research so far provides little basis for determining the generality of observations. Hence, my approach is to treat findings from particular studies as pertaining to the specific group studied, unless sufficient research in different related communities lends confidence in generalizing.

In summarizing a study, I try to write "*many* European American children *did* such-and-such" rather than "European American children *do* such-

and-such," unless there is evidence that the observations apply more generally across time and place. (It is often difficult to determine cultural information, however. Many published reports provide little information on cultural backgrounds of participants, or refer to broad ethnic categories—using boxes in a "cultural influence" approach—without considering cultural practices.) We need to address how broadly observations generalize by studying patterns of variation, rather than either assuming generality within categories or arguing that cultural communities vary infinitely.

We should also turn our focus to questions of generality of *cultural processes*, not just generality or representativeness of *groups of people,* as in the categorical approach. By suggesting that we search for patterns of regularities of cultural processes, I am arguing for a dynamic approach to examining culture, to replace the static approaches involved in categorizing people in supposedly homogeneous groups.

Research is just beginning to provide clues regarding the dynamic patterns of cultural processes in human development. In this book, I identify some cultural patterns that I see in classic areas of human development, such as social relations, cognitive development, and socialization practices. Although some of the available research employs boxes in the cultural influence approach, it is still useful.

Far more research is needed, however, to help delineate the regularities that may help us make sense of the differences we observe in the ways that people develop in a variety of cultural communities. We have some idea of areas of universality and many examples of cultural variations. But we need more focus on studying the *regularities in the patterns of variation and similarity* in cultural practices across cultural communities.

Because most research on child development has focused on middle-class European American populations, there is more basis for making generalizations about human development in this cultural community than in many others. Unfortunately, little of this research has focused explicitly on cultural aspects of European American middle-class lives, much less on diverse cultural communities that may fit that label. A great deal of research with middle-class European American children assumes that the findings represent children in general (4-year-olds do this, and 6-year-olds do that).

Many participants in this broad cultural community are unfamiliar with considering their practices to be cultural at all. Because cultural aspects of everyday life may be more difficult for people of dominant cultural communities to discern—due to their unique position—I address cultural aspects of middle-class European American communities specifically.

The Case of Middle-Class European American Cultural Communities

The cultural practices, traditions, values, and understandings of middle-class European American communities may be less visible to people of this heritage precisely because people from a dominant majority often take their practices for granted as the norm (Perry, 2001). It has been common for researchers to treat middle-class European American practices and development as "normal" or even "natural" and to refer only to the practices of other communities as "cultural." The dominance of this cultural community in both world affairs and research on human development often makes it more challenging for people who are familiar only with the ways of this community to become aware of their own cultural practices.

Habitual relations between people become expected, *institutionalized* rules and approaches that people come to regard as external to their functioning (Berger & Luckmann, 1966). Such institutions are in effect *cultural habits*, in which previous generations' innovations are used as a matter of routine. They are often regarded as natural; their role in current activities is simply assumed and not noticed or credited (or blamed) for the processes to which they contribute. John Shotter explained how practices become institutionalized and, in the process, become taken for granted:

> For the structure of human exchanges, there are precise foundations to be discovered in the *institutions* we establish between ourselves and others; institutions which implicate us in one another's activity in such a way that, what we have done together in the past, *commits us* to going on in a certain way in the future. . . . The members of an institution need not necessarily have been its originators; they may be second, third, fourth, etc. generation members, having "inherited" the institution from their forebears. And this is a most important point, for although there may be an intentional structure to institutional activities, practitioners of institutional forms need have no awareness at all of the reason for its structure—for them, it is just "the-way-things-are-done." The reasons for the institution having one form rather than another are buried in its *history*. (1978, p. 70)

To understand the cultural basis of human development in all communities—especially any that we are accustomed to—it is crucial to examine other ways of doing things. Cultural research helps to delineate the cultural features of mainstream practices, which otherwise may not be examined due to their dominance and pervasiveness. People who have experienced variation are much more likely to be aware of their own cultural ways, as Dalton Conley discovered in his childhood in New York City:

I am not your typical middle-class white male. I am middle class, despite the fact that my parents had no money; I am white, but I grew up in an inner-city housing project where most everyone was black or Hispanic. I enjoyed a range of privileges that were denied my neighbors but that most Americans take for granted. In fact, my childhood was like a social science experiment: Find out what being middle class really means by raising a kid from a so-called good family in a so-called bad neighborhood. Define whiteness by putting a light-skinned kid in the midst of a community of color. . . .

Ask any African American to list the adjectives that describe them and they will likely put *black* or *African American* at the top of the list. Ask someone of European descent the same question and *white* will be far down the list, if it's there at all. Not so for me. I've studied whiteness the way I would a foreign language. I know its grammar, its parts of speech; I know the subtleties of its idioms, its vernacular words and phrases to which the native speaker has never given a second thought. There's an old saying that you never really know your own language until you study another. It's the same with race and class. (2000, pp. xi–xii)

There is not a commonly agreed-upon way to designate the community or cultural ways of mainstream middle-class European Americans. Some common ways of referring to this general group or their cultural ways include White, American, the dominant majority, mainstream, middle class, Western, and European American.

As a temporary solution, I frequently refer rather loosely to "middle-class European American" practices, traditions, or communities. By this I mean the cultural ways of the group that in recent decades has held a mainstream position in North America. These are people who are primarily of Western European descent, with a social position that is often characterized as middle class on the basis of having participated in high levels of formal schooling and associated occupations. It is interesting, however, that in recent decades, most men and women in the United States have classified themselves as middle class (Kluckhohn, 1949; Shwalb, Shwalb, Sukemune, & Tatsumoto, 1992).

It is perhaps their extensive involvement in the particular cultural institution of formal schooling and the associated occupational roles that most characterize the group, more than their ethnicity or nationality, but these currently often go together. Historically, and still, middle-class European American people are involved in a cultural system that bears some similarities to Western European social practices, economic systems, religions, philosophy, and history of colonialism and expansion (Hollingshead, 1949; Latouche, 1996). Schooling itself is an institution of European and American origins that has spread widely (Meyer, Ramirez, & Soysal, 1992).

However, the middle-class, highly schooled cultural system is not limited to people of Western European ancestry. Indeed, in many large cities all around the world, highly schooled people of very different ancestry increasingly resemble the European American middle class in their occupations, practices, and values.

Important variations from one locale or specific group to another accompany the common cultural approach held by different middle-class European American communities (and middle-class communities in Western Europe and other regions). These differences have seldom been studied. However, the variations reveal the cultural practices related to region, religion, and other distinctions within the "mainstream" of the United States and other nations. Such variation, and awareness of it, is well expressed by a student at a northeastern U.S. university:

> During my first year at [university x], I was acutely aware of not belonging here. I was different from everyone else in so many ways: I was a Southerner, I went to public schools, and I was totally unfamiliar with the urban Northeast and its mixture of cultures and races. My family history was rooted in rural Mississippi and Arkansas, and only in the last couple of generations had anyone in my family gone to college. I felt that my previous education was inferior to most other students. I walked, talked, and even thought more slowly than everyone around me, and often I felt as stupid as many people treated me. . . . I tried very hard during this period to find people and things that reminded me of [hometown x], of "home." I visited Baptist and Episcopal churches around campus, trying to find a church similar to those I attended while growing up. . . . My accent actually became deeper, because I was making such an effort to hold on to my old identity, which was strongly tied up with the part of the country I had come from. (quoted in Diamond, 1999, p. 6)

The variations among middle-class European American neighborhoods from different regions of the country are noticeable enough that it may be difficult to regard them as part of the same community. Likewise, there are important differences among American Indian tribes and among different Pacific Island groups and many other neighboring communities. Nonetheless, there can also be important underlying similarities in values and practices across neighborhoods or tribes that may justify regarding the smaller communities as instances of larger communities for some purposes (Cajete, 1994; Latouche, 1996). For example, Urie Bronfenbrenner speculated on the emphasis on individualism in the United States, broadly speaking. An immigrant to the United States himself, Bronfenbrenner noted

> the special character of those who, since this country's very beginnings, have been emigrating to the United States. As I have summed it up for myself, Americans are mostly descendants of those who could not stand authority, or whom authority could not stand. (1992, p. 288)

A guidebook written to help foreigners understand "American" ways relayed observations based on many conversations with foreign students at the University of Iowa:

> The most important thing to understand about Americans is probably their devotion to "individualism." They have been trained since very early in their lives to consider themselves as separate individuals who are responsible for their own situations in life and their own destinies. . . .
>   You can see it in the way Americans treat their children. Even very young children are given opportunities to make their own choices and express their opinions. A parent will ask a one-year-old child what color balloon she wants, which candy bar she would prefer, or whether she wants to sit next to mommy or daddy. . . .
>   It is this concept of themselves as individual decision-makers that blinds at least some Americans to the fact that they share a culture with each other. They have the idea, as mentioned above, that they have independently made up their own minds about the values and assumptions they hold. The notion that social factors outside themselves have made them "just like everyone else" in important ways offends their sense of dignity. (Althen, 1988, pp. 4–6)

To help foreigners get along in the United States, the guide goes on to describe a number of characteristics ascribed to "Americans" by visitors. Some of the descriptions may strike home and others seem questionable to "Americans":

- A strong desire for privacy
- Discomfort with being treated with obvious deference (such as bowing) but using other cues to indicate status (such as more frequently interrupting others or sitting at the head of a table)
- A belief that they can control the future and that new things are better than old ones
- Treating time as a resource that should be spent well ("One of the more difficult things many foreign businessmen and students must adjust to in the States is the notion that time must be saved whenever possible and used wisely every day"; p. 14)

- Prioritizing efficiency, to accomplish more with fewer resources
- A custom of engaging in "small talk" when meeting another person ("Listening to American small talk leads some foreigners to the erroneous conclusion that Americans are intellectually incapable of carrying on a discussion about anything significant. Some foreigners believe that topics more complex than weather, sports, or social lives are beyond the Americans' ability to comprehend"; p. 23)

As an "American" myself, I recognize some of these characterizations—although I would also argue about their generality. The statements may be helpful to visitors in some general sense, and there is *something* to them. But they would also need to be more qualified when we think about particular circumstances and different immigrant and native communities of "Americans." (The author of the guide recognized this, too.) I include the list here because it is especially useful for middle-class European Americans to consider how they are seen as a group by others, as part of the process of reflecting on their own cultural ways.

Cultural research far from U.S. shores can be an aid in the process of becoming aware of cultural patterns of the U.S. "mainstream," as well as being important for building an understanding of human development that encompasses worldwide regularities and variations. The traditions and practices of middle-class European American communities contribute to the traditions and practices of other communities, along with borrowed ideas, practices, and institutions. Current ways of middle-class European American communities like those of all communities—have transformed from previous ways, derived from genealogical ancestors as well as from other communities. And changes across generations and communities continue.

Conceiving of Communities across Generations

If asked to specify the communities with which they identify, often people find it necessary to give an account of the richly textured historical background of their family, themselves, and even their communities, including whichever features are prominent in their lives: their ancestors' and household members' national origins, historical relations to other groups, recency of immigration, racial features, educational background, gender, generational status or age group, religion, current country and region of residence, involvement in important events (e.g., a great war, holocaust, or enslavement), and so on.

This historical and dynamic nature of community involvement is difficult to address if group membership is treated with a few static categories. To address the changing yet continuing processes by which individuals and communities constitute each other, I find it useful to think of community participation *across generations* (both past and future). Across generations, some continuities from the past are preserved and built on, at the same time that each new generation transforms what is "given."

The patterns of ocean waves is an image that can illustrate the connection between individuals and communities across generations. Imagine the position of a particular, *individual* water molecule as it moves in partial concert with others in the ocean. Its movement is partially all its own (though obviously not as individually determined as the movement of animate individuals such as humans). At the same time, it rises and falls in waves that form predictable patterns. The waves rise and fall in the same places although the individual water molecules differ—just as some community traditions are carried on through the passage of generations. At the same time, as conditions change, the wave form changes. Changes in the position of the moon, geological changes in the ocean bottom, and wind currents—as well as aspects of the water molecules themselves such as their temperature—contribute to changes in the form of the waves.

In like fashion, the traditions of cultural communities change with conditions such as world economic fluctuations, wars, technological inventions, and other contributions of the current generation. Waves themselves are not isolated from other wave patterns: An individual water molecule may participate in the movement emanating from several sources, such as when wave forms overlap and create more complex motion. This is like individuals' participation in the traditions of more than one community: The different traditions may amplify or conflict, just as with wave forms. Of course, individual humans—more than water molecules!—create direction and innovation in their own movement as well as in that of their companions and even in whole "waves."

This wave image helps me to think about the overlapping community traditions in which an individual participates, forming patterns that both endure and change with the passage of generations. The image opens up fascinating questions, ones that require a longer-term view than a few decades. I have begun to see such patterns in my work in a Mayan community during almost three decades, and the patterns fascinate me at high school reunions across an even longer stretch. These give me a viewpoint on individual as well as community and generational continuities and changes that I didn't have when I myself had only a few decades of experience in the world. (But I recognize with some discomfort that one lifetime of experience in a particular historical era in a few locales limits my opportunities to observe longer-span changes across generations firsthand.)

Across millennia, communities have continuously changed their practices (often by force but also by choice or accident), and they have also maintained themes from prior generations. They have borrowed ideas from each other to enhance means of subsistence and artistic expression. They have forced ideas on each other in massive and small-scale crusades of religious practices, formal education, and moral values. They have traded and purchased and stolen ideas and knowledge from each other, such as ceramic techniques, systems of warfare, and writing technologies. And they have combined traditions and heritages as people from different communities intermarry, are captured by enemies, migrate, or engage in common endeavors that require collaboration (see figure 3.5).

An example of individuals borrowing and extending ideas appeared in the newsletter of the Children's Discovery Museum of San Jose, California. The museum director noted the "spontaneous sharing of ideas among people who happen to be in the same place at the same time":

> A couple of weeks ago, a mother and her grown daughter came upon thin strips of mylar in our recycle art space and began to braid the

FIGURE 3.5

Christmas at the Nagano family's home on West 30th Street in Los Angeles in 1930 (Japanese American).

material into marvelously intricate palm-sized pyramids. Turns out the two visitors had learned to make these charming novelties from children in Zaire, who braid a local reed into these shapes in much the same way children in this country fold and weave chewing gum wrappers. In the wonderful way these things happen, our visitors met up with two ideal Museum Discovery Guides . . . who wanted to learn how to do it themselves, and ultimately, pass along the technique to other Museum visitors. An isolated incident? We think not . . .

    Distinctive experience of the world is continuously woven and rewoven, through just such magical moments, into new expressions of culture. (Osberg, 1994, p. 2)

Such borrowing and extending has occurred for thousands of years, as neighboring and distant people encounter each other, peacefully or otherwise, as people have traded, migrated, explored, and waged war and raids on each other. Contacts over great distances are apparent from the ancient historical record, with materials, customs, and products of one continent found among people in another.

Indeed, most readers' family histories would serve to illustrate generational cultural processes of large-scale political, technological, and demographic change, together with creative individual and generational inventions and adaptations of the world as they find it. To help portray generational aspects of communities, I give three accounts that illustrate changes built on enduring traditions across generations and between communities as they borrow, impose, and blend ideas and practices. The three accounts focus on the use of American Indian ways by Europeans, changes and continuities over time in the English language, and an individual's tracking of his family history across several continents and centuries.

Account 1: Use of American Indian inventions by Europeans

For many centuries before the arrival of Europeans, Indian trade routes connected widely dispersed indigenous groups throughout North and South America. The Inca maintained a highway system that stretched for about 3,000 miles, with bridges and gondolas for crossing gorges and rivers, uniting an area larger than Western Europe (Weatherford, 1988). Using this highway system, Inca runners carried government messages throughout the empire at about the same rate of travel as the Pony Express. Ironically, the excellence of the Inca highways and the other routes throughout North and South America facilitated the rapid conquest by Europeans, whose horses and cannons would not have traveled easily through these areas without the paved roads. Thus, areas with the best roads were conquered first, and the Europeans commonly built their roads following the highways and paths of the Indians.

The contact between the "Old World" and the "New World" provides a compelling example of how communities change over generations, how individuals and generations contribute to such change, and how current practices are built on borrowing or imposing ideas across communities. Europeans appropriated many ideas and inventions from Native Americans that transformed cultural, economic, and political systems worldwide.

The whole power structure of Europe changed with the arrival of "the miracle crops" of the Andean potato and maize corn from Mexico (Weatherford, 1988). Before contact with the Americas, the "Old World" primarily subsisted on grains, which frequently suffer from crop failure. Hence political power centered around the Mediterranean, where grains could be more reliably grown. Although the peasants of Europe despised the potato for the first two centuries after its arrival, they eventually accepted it after their rulers forced them to plant it and restricted access to grains in the second half of the 18th century. (The rulers forced the change because a field of potatoes produces more food more reliably, faster, and with less labor than the same field planted with grain.) Once the peasants became accustomed to the potato, their nutrition improved markedly, and the population grew— especially in northern countries. The centers of power in Europe shifted accordingly.

North and South American Indian food products are key ingredients in many foods that are today considered traditional in Europe, such as Italian spaghetti sauces, Hungarian goulash, and french fries. The Indians gave the world three-fifths of the crops now in cultivation (including beans, peanuts, squashes, sunflowers, sweet potatoes, tomatoes, peppers, chocolate, vanilla, maple syrup, avocados, pineapples, cashews, and pecans). They carefully bred such plants through advanced agricultural technology and experimentation to adapt them to human needs using a profound understanding of genetics, varying environmental conditions, and agricultural technologies.

Even more impressive is how forms of government of some American Indian groups contributed to the rise of democracies in other nations. Early European visitors were impressed by social organization without rulers or social classes based on property ownership, the idea of society based on cooperation without coercion, and authority vested in groups rather than in an individual (Weatherford, 1988). The first reports by the visitors gave rise to widespread debate in Europe regarding the possibilities of this form of civilization, as in Sir Thomas More's influential 1516 book *Utopia*. The first French ethnographies on North American Indians, in the late 1600s, focused on issues of freedom and gave rise to adaptations in numerous operas and plays, including one that deeply influenced Jean-Jacques Rousseau, the philosopher whose lifelong concerns with liberty focused on contrasts between these Indian and European ways. In his 1776 call for American independence Thomas Paine used Indian ways as models of how society might be organized.

The Founding Fathers of the United States made use of Indian governance structures in solving the problem of how to make a country out of 13 separate states without each state yielding its own power (Weatherford, 1988). The League of the Iroquois was the original federal system, uniting five major Indian nations in a Council with delegates representing territories that extended from New England to the Mississippi River. It had fascinated the Europeans and American colonists from earliest contact.

Among those individuals inspired by the Indian governance system was Benjamin Franklin, who took the Iroquois system as a model for fashioning a new government (Weatherford, 1988). Franklin had become intimately familiar with Indian political culture and especially with the League of the Iroquois during his first diplomatic assignment. He echoed the 1744 proposal of the Iroquois chief Canassatego that the new American government incorporate features of the Iroquois system of government.

The secretary of the Continental Congress, Charles Thomson, also contributed to bringing these Indian ideas of government to the formation of the Constitution. He spent so much energy studying them that he was adopted as a full member of the Delaware Nation, and his lengthy writings on Indian social and political institutions were included by Thomas Jefferson in his own book. The Constitution followed the model of the Iroquois League in many ways, including separating military and civilian authorities, allowing for the possibility of impeachment, and permitting expansion of the number of states as members rather than as colonies.

Principles of group decision making replaced European authority-based rule among the colonists after many generations of engagement with East Coast North American Indians:

> Another imitation of the Iroquois came in the simple practice of allowing only one person to speak at a time in political meetings. This contrasts with the British tradition of noisy interruptions of one another as the members of Parliament shout out agreement or disagreement with the speaker. Europeans were accustomed to shouting down any speaker who displeased them. . . . The Iroquois permitted no interruptions or shouting. They even imposed a short period of silence at the end of each oration in case the speaker had forgotten some point or wished to elaborate or change something he had said. . . . The purpose of debate in Indian councils was to persuade and

educate, not to confront. (Weatherford, 1988, pp. 140–141, based on Johansen)

These American Indian ideas about the relation between the individual and the state have continued to influence world politics. Henry David Thoreau's writings on civil disobedience in the mid-1800s, which provided his interpretation of Indian personal freedom to refuse cooperation with the state, helped Mahatma Gandhi struggle peacefully for (East) Indian independence from Britain. This in turn inspired peaceful methods for seeking civil rights in the United States, such as the movement led by Martin Luther King Jr. (Weatherford, 1988). Interpretations of American Indian ideas have also been influential in efforts to improve schooling over the years (carried by some of the same individuals, such as Rousseau, Thoreau, and Jefferson).

This account illustrates how, over decades and centuries, individuals and cultural communities carry on and transform traditions. Communities maintain some practices and change others through the contributions of specific individuals and of other communities. While they transform, they also maintain some fidelity to long-standing values. (Another example is the continuity and changes of child-rearing concepts from the early 18th century to the present in Japan, amid major changes in Japanese institutions and everyday lives; see Kojima, 1996.) To understand human development, it is necessary to view it as a dynamic process involving individuals actively, creatively participating in and contributing to powerful and changing cultural traditions.

Account 2: Changes and continuities
in the language of Angle-land

The English language in its current form has developed through a long series of borrowings, conquests, and attempts both to revise the language and to fix it so that it would not continue to evolve, according to the history recounted by Albert Baugh and Thomas Cable (1978). This process illustrates the stabilities as well as continual changes of cultural practices, with contributions by particular individuals and by each successive generation that modifies what it inherits from prior generations. The languages (and other cultural tools) that we currently use are the momentary form of particular overlapping and continually moving currents.

The British Isles have been inhabited by humans for many thousands of years. However, English has been its language for only the past 1,500 years, when tribes from the area of Denmark and the Low Countries— Jutes, Saxons, and Angles—invaded the lands where Celtic and Latin had been spoken, and founded the English nation. The Christianization of

England in 597 brought further contact with Latin, and the Viking invasions of the Danes beginning in the eighth century brought renewed contact with that language tradition. The conquest of England by the Normans (Viking North-men who had earlier invaded France and adopted French ways) in 1066 made French the language of the nobility; English became the language of the lower classes for two centuries. When English again became the language of all classes in England, after 1200, it was greatly changed from prior versions, and it has continued to evolve with the changes in the island people's contacts with other peoples—as is the case with all living languages.

Current English speakers are unable to understand the Old English of a millennium ago. Almost 85% of the old vocabulary has disappeared; many of the words were replaced with others borrowed from Latin and French, which are the basis of more than half of the words now commonly used in English (Baugh & Cable, 1978). However, the Old English words that are still in use are central to English vocabulary. Among them are pronouns, prepositions, conjunctions, and auxiliary verbs as well as words such as *cild* (child), *strang* (strong), *drincan* (drink), *slæpan* (sleep), and *feohtan* (fight).

The printing press, introduced to England in about 1476 from Germany, transformed communication and created forces for the standardization of the language, together with increases in literacy. Toward the end of the 1500s, English was slowly becoming acceptable as a scholarly written language rather than simply a local vernacular, but the idiosyncrasies of written English were an annoyance (Baugh & Cable, 1978). The spelling of English of the Middle Ages had fairly well represented its pronunciation. However, Norman scribes created confusion in their attempts to write English with habits they had learned for writing French. In addition, the spellings gradually became standardized while pronunciations continued to change. Many authors attempted to create rules and systems for standardizing the spelling of English during the 16th and 17th centuries.

With the Renaissance, English people of the 16th and early 17th centuries attempted to improve their language by enlarging the vocabulary. The impulse to learn from classical and other sources prompted borrowing of words from those sources. In technical fields, English had notable shortcomings, which prompted borrowing of foreign terms. A number of authors deliberately and patriotically imported words from more than 50 languages (primarily Latin, French, Greek, Spanish, and Italian), as in the following example from Sir Thomas Elyot in introducing the word *maturity*:

> Wherfore I am constrained to usurpe a latine worde . . . , which
> worde, though it be strange and darke [obscure], yet . . . shall be

facile to understande as other wordes late commen out of Italy and Fraunce. . . . Therefore that worde *maturitie* is translated to the actis of man, . . . reservyng the wordes *ripe* and *redy* to frute and other thinges seperate from affaires, as we have nowe in usage. *And this do I nowe remembre for the necessary augmentation of our langage.* (quoted in Baugh & Cable, 1978, p. 216)

At the same time, the desirability of such borrowing was hotly contested. For example, Sir John Cheke wrote in 1561, "I am of this opinion that our own tung shold be written cleane and pure, unmixt and unmangeled with borowing of other tunges" (p. 216). Thomas Wilson protested that the new terms, if too freely imported, constituted affectations that the English should avoid so as not to forget their mother's language: "Some farre journeyed gentlemen at their returne home, like as they love to goe in forraine apparell, so thei wil pouder their talke with oversea language" (p. 218). Wilson satirized such affectation in a letter he devised, peppered heavily with words that were new in his day, including those italicized in this passage (some of which are common now): "I cannot but *celebrate*, & *extol* your *magnifical dexteritie* above all other. . . . But now I *relinquish* to *fatigate* your intelligence, with any more *frivolous verbositie*" (pp. 218–219).

Many of the words adopted in this period are now so common that it is difficult to imagine that 400 years ago they were strange and controversial—words such as democracy, atmosphere, expectation, halo, agile, expensive, hereditary, insane, malignant, adapt, benefit (first used by Cheke, though he protested such borrowing), disregard (introduced by John Milton), exist, skeleton, system, tactics, enthusiasm. Of course, many other newly introduced terms were rejected, many of the new terms underwent change, and many features of English remained unchanged.

The extent to which the introduction of new words can be traced to a particular individual helps to reveal the mutually constituting processes across generations in the development and use of this cultural tool. For example, Sir Thomas Elyot introduced many words, including analogy, animate, encyclopedia, exhaust, experience, infrequent, irritate, and modesty, and Sir Thomas More brought in anticipate, contradictory, exact, exaggerate, explain, fact, frivolous, paradox, and many others (Baugh & Cable, 1978). And of course, William Shakespeare eagerly accepted new words and, in a number of cases, introduced them himself (including assassination, indistinguishable, obscene, reliance, and submerged).

Such innovators illustrate how individual efforts contribute to cultural practices. At the same time, community and cultural processes, such as historical changes and inventions and controversies, contribute to the direction of individuals' ways of thinking, speaking, and acting. The availability of particular words for expressing ideas—democracy, expectation, hereditary, adapt, system, experience, contradictory, exact, explain, fact—can be seen as contributing to the thoughts and discussions of individuals and generations.

In the 18th century, a desire for systematizing and regulating the language arose from world events. English scholars sought rules by which correctness could be determined and achieved. An ideal of logic reigned, with a "chronocentrism" (if I can coin a word in this context!) that resembles ethnocentrism:

> The eighteenth century, like many other periods in history, was quietly conscious of its own superiority, and not being trammeled by any strong historical sense, any belief in the validity of other ideals than its own, or any great interest in the factors by which the ideals of former ages might be justified, it could easily come to believe in the essential rightness of its judgment and think that its own ideals could be erected into something like a permanent standard. (Baugh & Cable, 1978, p. 254)

Concerns that English had been and continued to be corrupted led to efforts to correct the language and fix it permanently, protected from change. Dictionaries and grammar books arose. Writers expressed fear that their works would be incomprehensible in later centuries. Although earlier scholars had already discerned that language changes are inevitable, scholars of this age (in Italy and France as well as in England) sought permanence.

Of course, historical change makes permanence an impossibility, and with continuing expansion of the British Empire came many other forces of change in English vocabulary, with additions such as moose and raccoon from American Indians; chocolate and tomato from Mexico; barbecue and hurricane from Cuba and the West Indies; calico, cot, jungle, and thug from India. In addition, English grammar has continued to change, with the progressive passive form ("the house is being built") appearing only at the end of the 18th century, resisted as an unwanted innovation but adopted for its usefulness in the following century. Languages are alive and grow, with changes prompted by events and inventions that make new vocabulary and grammatical forms available and needed to express ideas.

The changes of the language of Angle-Land over generations demonstrate the key roles of individuals, social groups, and communities across generations in the continuities and changes of cultural practices. The languages that we use to express our ideas have come to us through the practices of many prior generations and of other lands, and we contribute to their further maintenance and transformations.

*Account 3: Alex Haley's family
heritage across centuries*

Haley's account reflects the roles of individuals across generations, with changing as well as enduring connections with African and American practices:

> I first heard the story of our family, which had been passed down
> for generations, on the front porch of my grandma's house in
> Henning, Tennessee, about 50 miles north of Memphis. I grew up
> there with Grandma Cynthia Murray Palmer, and every summer she
> used to invite various women relatives to stay. After the supper dishes
> were washed and put away, they would sit in the squeaky rocking-
> chairs and talk about the past, as the dusk deepened into night,
> and the lightning bugs flicked on and off above the now shadowy
> honeysuckles.
>
> Whenever they were speaking of our people, Grandma and the
> others spoke—always in tones of awe, I noticed—of a furtherest
> back person whom they called "the African." They would say that
> some ship brought him to some place they would pronounce as
> "Naplis." Somebody called "Mas' John Waller" bought that African
> off that ship, and took him to a plantation in "Spotsylvania County,
> Virginia."
>
> When he had a daughter, Kizzy, he would tell her what things
> were in his native tongue. "*Ko*," he would say, pointing at a banjo, for
> instance. Or, pointing at a river which ran near the plantation, he
> would say "*Kamby Bolongo*." When other slaves would call him
> "Toby" he would angrily tell them that his name was "*Kin-tay*." And
> as he gradually learnt more English he began to tell Kizzy some
> things about himself—how he had been captured, for instance. He
> said that he had been not far away from his village, chopping some
> wood to make himself a drum, when four men had surprised, over-
> whelmed, and kidnapped him.
>
> At 16 Kizzy was sold away, on to a much smaller plantation in
> North Carolina. She had been bought by a "Mas' Tom Lea," and he
> fathered her first child, a boy, whom she named George; later she
> taught him all she could about his African grandfather. In time
> George had seven children; one of his sons, Tom, had seven children
> too; and he, in turn, passed on the family story. There had developed
> almost a ritual in its telling. It would occur mostly during the winter-
> time, after the harvesting was done, and there was more free time of
> an evening. The family would sit around the hearth with the logs
> burning, and sweet potatoes would be roasting in the hot ashes, as

the children listened to and absorbed the stories and the sounds. And the youngest of the seven was Cynthia, who became my maternal grandmother.

When I had heard that story over and again for around 10 years, it had become nearly as fixed in my head as it was in Grandma's, though I never then comprehended that the African they talked about was my own great-great-great-great-grandfather. (1972, p. 28)

More than 30 years later, Haley began to research the story through census records and by asking Africans at the United Nations Headquarters whether they recognized the African words. They were identified eventually as Mandinka words to indicate the Gambia River and the name of a very old clan. Haley followed the information to the Gambia, where he eventually reached a griot, an old man who lived in the back country and held the honored role of remembering centuries of histories of very old clans:

Seeming to gather himself into a physical rigidity [the griot] began speaking the Kinte clan's ancestral oral history. Across the next hours it came rolling from his mouth, the interpreters translating for me . . . the seventeenth- and eighteenth-century Kinte lineage details—predominantly what men took what wives, the children whom they "begot" in the order of their births; those children's mates and children. . . .

The Kinte clan he said, began in Old Mali; the men generally were blacksmiths, and the women were potters and weavers. One large branch of the clan moved to Mauretania, from where one son of the clan, Kairaba Kunta Kinte, a Muslim Marabout holy man, entered the Gambia. He lived first in the village of Pakali N'Ding; he moved next to Jiffarong village; "—and then he came here, into our own village of Juffure." His youngest son was Omoro, who in turn had four sons. Then, said the griot, "About the time the king's soldiers came, the eldest of those four sons, Kunta, when he had about 16 rains [16 years], went away from his village, to chop wood to make a drum, and he was never seen again." (p. 29)

From this information, Haley was able to find the king's soldiers in records in London and to identify the ship that had carried "the African" as cargo along with 139 others, in addition to gold, elephants' teeth, beeswax, and cotton bound for Annapolis. After searching records in Annapolis, he found that 16-year-old Kunta Kinte was listed as one of the "98 Negroes" who had survived the crossing. He found the announcement of the sale of the ship's cargo: "from the River GAMBIA, in AFRICA . . . a cargo of choice, healthy SLAVES . . ."

Haley's remarkable story, which became the television series *Roots*, illustrates the waves of change and continuity that contributed to his family story and traditions. It gives an idea, seldom available to our observational view that spans only a few decades, of how individuals' lives contribute to shaping what follows and are shaped by the practices and traditions of communities that have gone before.

Many other examples from the African diaspora in the Americas could demonstrate communities' creative building on their inheritance, constraints, and opportunities, across generations (Comer, 1988). For example, the histories of jazz and Jamaican reggae music relate to historical circumstances of African-descent groups in the Americas, technological and political changes, and human expression and invention (see Chude-Sokei, 1999). Another example of community traditions maintained and adapted by successive generations is the use of the Gullah language, deriving from West Africa, on islands off the Georgia coast (Smitherman, 1977). Africans and their descendents have contributed mightily to forming mainstream cultural traditions of the Americas (Walker, 2001).

In this chapter, I have developed the proposal to focus on cultural communities changing across generations, to understand the mutually constituting roles of individuals and cultural communities. As individuals and their generational cohorts participate in the everyday lives of their communities, they build on the cultural practices and traditions that they inherit from their predecessors, contributing to both maintenance and invention of cultural ways.

In the chapters that follow, I turn to research on classic topics in the study of human development. These topics include the cast of characters and the opportunities children have to engage in the activities of their communities, transitions in people's roles from infancy through old age, gender roles, interdependence and autonomy, processes of thinking and learning, and the ways in which communities arrange for and assist children's learning. Throughout these chapters, I focus on the ways in which individual participation in sociocultural activities of different communities relate to cultural similarities and variations in development. Although historical research on human development is rare, where possible, I relate the cultural patterns to generational changes of communities. The final chapter of the book returns more explicitly to questions of community change, specifically to the mixing and relations among communities that are increasingly prevalent in daily lives of children and communities around the world.

Child Rearing in Families and Communities

The cast of characters and the scenarios of children's lives are central aspects of human development, as suggested by Beatrice Whiting (1980). The immaturity of human infants requires extensive caregiving for their survival, and children require opportunities to learn mature ways of their community to become capable of sustaining themselves.

Family and community roles in children's development differ quite dramatically worldwide. Some central cultural variations have to do with differences associated with likelihood of infant mortality or survival, availability of siblings and extended family, opportunities for children to engage widely in their community, and cultural prototypes for engaging as groups rather than in pairs.

Around the world, child rearing involves children's families, neighborhoods, and communities in a variety of roles. One community's arrangement of responsibility for child rearing is beautifully illustrated by a childhood experience recounted by Pueblo Indian scholar Joseph Suina:

> My cousins and I were hunting rabbits. Unable to locate the desired game, we began shooting at tin cans and other assorted targets. One of these happened to be a pig. The injured pig drew attention to the situation, causing the two of us to be summoned before the tribal council for corrective measures. During the hearing, a council member disclosed that he had witnessed our reckless shooting. An

older council member inquired what the man had done about the situation. "Nothing," replied the first. He couldn't, he elaborated, because it was about to rain, and then proceeded to remind the other council members of the dire consequences of neglecting a hay crop when a rain threatened. The negligent member was quickly reminded of what happens to the villages' children when they are neglected. For neglecting his duty, the derelict council member was required to pay half the price of the pig; we were required to pay the remainder. (Suina & Smolkin, 1994, p. 117)

Communities' arrangements of responsibilities for child rearing are evident in the observations of Barbara Kingsolver, when she and her 4-year-old daughter from the United States lived for a year in the Canary Islands of Spain:

Widows in black, buttoned-down CEOs, purple-sneakered teenagers, the butcher, the baker, all would stop on the street to have little chats with my daughter. . . . Whenever Camille grew cranky in a restaurant (and really, what do you expect at midnight?) the waiters flirted and brought her little presents, and nearby diners looked on with that sweet, wistful gleam of eye that I'd thought diners reserved for the dessert tray. What I discovered in Spain was a culture that held children to be its meringues and éclairs. My own culture, it seemed to me in retrospect, tended to regard children as a sort of toxic-waste product: a necessary evil, maybe, but if it's not our own we don't want to see it or hear it or, God help us, smell it.

If you don't have children, you think I'm exaggerating. . . . In the U.S. I have been told in restaurants: "We come here to get *away* from kids." (This for no infraction on my daughter's part that I could discern, other than being visible.) On an airplane I heard a man tell a beleaguered woman whose infant was bawling (as I would, to clear my aching ears, if I couldn't manage chewing gum): "If you can't keep that thing quiet, you should keep it at home.". . .

It took a move to another country to make me realize how thoroughly I had accepted my nation's creed of every family for itself. Whenever my daughter crash-landed in the playground, I was startled at first to see a sanguine, Spanish-speaking stranger pick her up and dust her off. And if a shrieking bundle landed at my feet, I'd furtively look around for the next of kin. But I quickly came to see this detachment as perverse when applied to children, and am wondering how it ever caught on in the first place. (1995, pp. 100–101)

Arrangements regarding who cares for children and under what circumstances are intimately related to the support provided by community connections and extended family. As pointed out in the previous chapter, cultural practices surrounding the care of children are both inherited across generations and revised by new generations with novel circumstances and new ideas. Some of the circumstances and new ideas have to do with national and international politics.

Family Composition and Governments

Generational changes as well as continuities in family circumstances can be seen by examining national policies regarding population growth in recent decades. Large family size has alternately been encouraged and discouraged by governments seeking to increase or stabilize the population for political and economic goals. This is especially clear in China's and Mexico's recent population histories, where changes have dramatically altered family composition.

Before 1949, China's population was marked by a high death rate along with a high birthrate, which resulted in slow population growth, according to Lee Lee (1992). In 1949, with government interest in increasing the population, efforts were made to eliminate disease and to encourage conception by restricting the use of birth control and abortion. In 1953, disease had begun to be controlled and the population increased at what seemed to some to be an alarming rate: 50 million people in four years. In 1956, the proposal of a Chinese economist sparked implementation of birth control and population planning, to avoid strains in the standard of living, availability of education, and the national reconstruction goals. However, in 1957, this policy was reversed and everyone worked toward increasing the population until 1964, when the government again noted the critical nature of rapid population growth.

Little was done about the growth until the late 1970s, when China's single-child policy, with strict use of birth control and abortion, was implemented. This has resulted in 90% of 9-year-old children in Chinese cities being only children (Jiao, Ji, & Jing, 1996). The single-child policy results in one child for each two parents and four grandparents. This drastic change from prior Chinese family structure has led to widespread questions about spoiling children, psychological pressure from parents and elders, children's ability to take care of themselves, and peer skills such as sharing and getting along with others (Lee, 1992; Jiao, Ji, & Jing, 1996). Changing nationwide policies regarding child survival and birth relate closely to cultural practices for child caregiving as well as individual development.

Mexico's fluctuations in national policies have also resulted in wide swings in the structure and size of families (Dillon, 1999). Within a generation, the average number of births in a family has dropped from 7 (in 1965) to only 2.5, slightly below worldwide rates. One mother of two, herself the oldest of 14 children, plans to have no more children. She said, "Small families live better," echoing the television jingle that has permeated broadcasts since the government reversed its promotion of growth in 1974.

The Mexican government's earlier policies led to a fivefold increase in the population in a little more than five decades—not including the large numbers who have emigrated to the United States. Early in this period, the Mexican government encouraged rapid growth, in part because of the idea that sparse population allowed the United States to seize Mexican territory (the land from California to Texas) during the previous century.

The about-face of government policy in 1974 came from warnings by Mexican demographers that the rapid growth would entail challenges to national stability. The government set up clinics to help couples control the size of their family, and anticipates that slowing growth will help the national economy, at least while the country benefits from having fewer children to support. However, when the population bulge enters old age, care of older people within the family may be jeopardized by the demographic changes. The changes in the family, related to national policies, are removing the social network of extended family that has provided care to young children and aged parents (Dillon, 1999).

The dynamics of population changes and national policies, as seen in both China and Mexico, have an intimate relationship with the daily lives and upbringing of children as well as the circumstances of their parents. Just consider the divergent concerns of parents if only half the babies survive versus most of them, or the changing relationships occasioned in families of seven children versus one or two. Across generations, child-rearing practices and family relations commonly reflect the patterns and strategies of previous generations, when circumstances may have been different—challenging each generation to build on the cultural approaches they inherit to address their current needs.

This chapter next addresses cultural strategies for dealing with issues of child survival and care, a central issue often overlooked in affluent times. Then it turns to cultural variations in infants' relations with their caregivers and varying role specializations in responsibility for the care of children by families and communities. Finally, the chapter examines children's involvement in the mature activities of their communities and the integration of children in groups or one-on-one engagements.

Cultural Strategies for Child Survival and Care

Issues of child survival are central to child-rearing practices, though often taken for granted in more fortunate families and nations. In communities that experience high infant mortality, parents' priorities for their children may be quite different from communities in which parents can be relatively confident that their infant will grow up (see figure 4.1). In many communities, large numbers of children may be needed to ensure that enough will survive to make needed contributions to the household in childhood and youth, and later to support the aged parents, who lack other forms of "social security."

For many families in the United States, issues of death in childhood or of children becoming orphaned are uncommon compared with prior generations, due to lowered infant mortality and limited likelihood of maternal death in childbirth (Mintz & Kellogg, 1988). During the colonial period in the United States, parents lost many children, and children often were orphaned. For example, Cotton Mather, a New England preacher, was the father of 15 children, but only two of them survived him. In a measles epidemic in 1713, his wife and three of his children died within two weeks. He wrote in his diary:

> November 8, 9, 1713. . . . For these many Months, and ever since I heard of the venemous Measles invading the Countrey sixty Miles to the Southward of us, I have had a strong Distress on my Mind, that it will bring on my poor Family, a Calamity, which is now going to be inflicted. I have often, often express'd my Fear unto my Friends concerning it. And now, *the Thing that I greatly feared is coming upon me!* . . .
>
> To part with so desireable, so agreeable a Companion, a Dove from such a Nest of young ones too! Oh! the sad Cup, which my Father has appointed me! . . .
>
> On Munday [November 9, 1713] between three and four in the Afternoon, my dear, dear, dear Friend expired.
>
> November 17–18, 1713. About Midnight, little *Eleazar* died.
>
> November 20, 1713. Little *Martha* died, about ten a clock, A.M.
>
> November 21, 1713. This Day, I attended the Funeral, of my two: *Eleazar* and *Martha*.
>
> Betwixt 9 h. and 10 h. at Night, my lovely *Jerusha* Expired. She was two years, and about seven Months, old. Just before she died, she asked me to pray with her; which I did, with a distressed, but resigning Soul; and I gave her up unto the Lord. . . .
>
> Lord, I am oppressed! undertake for me! (quoted in Bremner, 1970, pp. 46–48)

FIGURE 4.1A

Nepomoceno Baez in his aunt's arms, at his funeral, ca. 1914 or 1917, in a Latino community of Los Angeles.

Around 1800, U.S. women averaged seven live births, of which a third or a half would not survive to 5 years of age (Ehrenreich & English, 1978). Around 1890, 20% of White children and 40% of Black children died before age 15 (Hernandez, 1993). In the 1900s, child mortality in the United States dropped due to improvements in sanitation and nutrition; by 1973, only 2% of White children and 4% of Black children died by age 15.

However, in many communities around the world as well as some in the United States, issues of children's survival are still of great concern. For example, in economically disadvantaged inner-city ghettos, African American families face many risks in the survival of their children. According to an African American father in a Chicago housing project: "A baby's gotta' cry strong right from birth. A lil' fainty baby might never survive. Gotta' grow up strong in our neighborhood" (quoted in Trawick-Smith, 1997, p. 84). Many youths in such settings do not expect to live past the age of 21 (Burton, Obeidallah, & Allison, 1996). This makes physical survival an important measure of successful adolescent outcome, as explained by a 14-year-old: "I know I'm successful because I know how to survive on the streets. I bet them rich White kids couldn't do what I do" (p. 401).

FIGURE 4.1B

U.S. parents ca. 1850–1860s with their dead child.

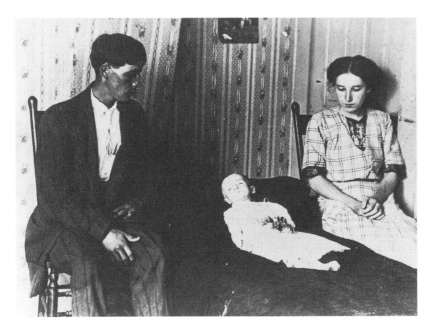

FIGURE 4.1C

Postmortem photograph of a U.S. child with parents, ca. 1930s–1940s.

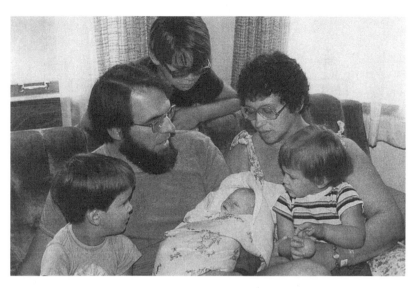

FIGURE 4.1D

U.S. family with their stillborn baby, Adam, 1981.

Robert LeVine (1980) proposed a three-level hierarchy of parental child-rearing goals that varies in different communities. He argued that communities adapt to prevalent circumstances with priorities and practices that reflect such considerations as the danger of death in childhood:

1. In communities with high infant and child mortality, LeVine suggested that parents must first consider a child's *physical survival and health*.
2. Second in LeVine's hierarchy of child-rearing goals are parental priorities involving preparing children to *maintain themselves economically* in maturity.
3. If the first two priorities are met, parents can devote more energy to considering each child's potential to *maximize other cultural values*, such as prestige, religious piety, intellectual achievement, personal satisfaction, and self-realization.

Because the greatest danger of mortality is in infancy, parents in communities with high infant mortality can afford to consider the second and third goals primarily after their child has survived infancy.

An illustration of the connection between issues of infant mortality and child-rearing practices is provided by changing parental goals in Japan in the last half of the 1900s. The infant mortality rate in Japan fell dramatically, from 60 per thousand in 1950 to 10 per thousand in 1975 (Kojima,

1996). In the 1960s, Japanese parents, confident that their children would survive, turned their attention to creating the most successful children. And in the 1970s, Japanese child care books began to include not just routine care and medical care, but advice on the intellectual and personality development of infants.

Parents do not face child-rearing issues on their own. Rather, as LeVine pointed out, each generation of parents relies on cultural practices that have developed historically to meet prior circumstances. They have at hand customary patterns of infant and child care that respond to the most prominent hazards historically experienced by the community. So, in regions of high infant mortality due to disease or danger (such as cooking fires), customs of child care focus on survival and health goals. In regions where making a living is precarious, once a child's survival is assured, child-rearing patterns can focus on enabling the child to make a living in adulthood.

LeVine (1980) illustrated this with child-rearing patterns among agricultural populations of tropical Africa, which are adapted to the prevalence of infant death and the difficulty of assuring subsistence. The child's physical survival and economic future are the most salient goals for parents, and parents' strategy is to have many children. They give each child very attentive physical care during the first two or three years: The infant is breast-fed for 18 to 24 months, sleeps with the mother and is fed on demand, is carried most of the time, and receives a rapid response to crying. This is a kind of "folk pediatrics" to prevent the most common danger, dehydration from diarrhea, by close monitoring and rapid provision of liquid. Once weaned, a child joins the responsible and obedient group of older children, and the mother devotes herself to the next infant and to her agricultural work.

LeVine contrasted these practices with those in middle-class U.S. communities, where infant mortality rate is low, children rarely contribute to family economics, and parents seldom depend on their children for maintenance in old age (but instead rely to a great extent on societal support). Having children entails an economic cost, and the customary strategy is to have only a few children and to focus effort not no much on their survival (though, of course, all parents have some concerns in this regard) but on their eventual attainment of a position in life that is equal to or better than that of the parents. This is a conception of child rearing in which parents make a large investment in each of a small number of children. The nurturance of character traits that are regarded as appropriate to achievement and status (such as independence) are assumed to require extensive parental time and effort from earliest infancy and throughout childhood.

Given the differences in infant mortality and economic circumstances in the two settings, the strategies of middle-class U.S. parents would not be appropriate to the conditions in agricultural communities of tropical

Africa, nor would the strategies of the African parents be appropriate in the conditions of middle-class U.S. life. LeVine argued that local child-rearing strategies are cultural compromise formulas that provide parents with tested solutions that have worked historically for addressing local problems of parenting.

Of course, each generation builds on a moving historical base, maintaining some of the solutions of their parents and grandparents and modifying others with changing circumstances. Imagine the changes in child-rearing practices—along with the efforts to preserve tradition—that are likely to accompany the changing fertility and infant health conditions in China and Mexico and across the centuries of U.S. history.

Infant-Caregiver Attachment

The survival of infants depends on bonds with caregivers who protect and nurture them. The psychological literature commonly presents caregiver-child relationships in terms of an innate bond of attachment and even engrossment between infants and a primary caregiver (usually assumed to be the mother). However, information from other communities and other historical periods has challenged the standards often assumed to be universal in research with current European American infants and children (Fisher, Jackson, & Villaruel, 1998; LeVine & Miller, 1990; Rosenthal, 1999; Serpell, 1993).

The cultural research draws attention to community aspects of infants' and caregivers' attachments to each other, including the health and economic conditions of the community, cultural goals of infant care, and cultural arrangements of family life. Variations in the attachment of mothers with their infants, infants with their mothers, and infants with other family members all make more sense when we consider that these individuals relate to each other as participants in dynamic cultural communities.

Maternal Attachment under Severe Conditions

The idea that current European American middle-class mother-child relations provide a universal standard has been challenged by information on child treatment in other communities. For example, in some settings it has been accepted practice to kill or abandon young children (as in ancient Greece) or to send infants to live with paid wet nurses in the countryside despite high risks of infant mortality (as in the 1700s and 1800s in France). Often, infanticide or child abandonment occurred because of difficulties in supporting the children or when the children were not healthy. In many cases, however, children were abandoned in the hopes that they would be found and raised by other people. In many French cities of the 1700s, about a third of children were abandoned, with higher rates nearing one half in poorer districts (Getis & Vinovskis, 1992).

The most serious challenge to the idea of innateness of middle-class expressions of maternal affection has come from Nancy Scheper-Hughes's observations of mother-infant relations in a shantytown in Brazil. In the desperately poor conditions of recent rural migrants, infant mortality is very high due to disease and chronic undernutrition. The average woman had 3.5 children who had died and 4.5 children who were still alive at the time of Scheper-Hughes's interviews. Most of the child deaths occurred by the end of the child's first year. The mothers reported:

> "they die because we are poor, because we are hungry"; "they die be-
> cause the water we drink is filthy with germs"; "they die because we
> can't keep them in shoes or away from this human garbage dump we
> live in"; "they die because we get worthless medical care . . ."; "they
> die because we have no safe place to leave them when we go off to
> work." . . .
> "They are born already starving in the womb. They are born
> bruised and discolored, their tongues swollen in their mouths. If we
> were to nurse them constantly we would all die of tuberculosis. Weak
> people can't give much milk." (1985, pp. 301, 303)

Under these circumstances, Scheper-Hughes observed maternal detachment and indifference toward infants that mothers judged to be too weak to survive the conditions of their life. The women see life as a struggle in which it is necessary to allow some babies, especially the very sick ones, to die without attention, care, or protection.

These mothers' selective neglect is not motivated by hostility toward the child (as implied in the U.S. concept of child abuse). In this community, severe child battering leading to death is regarded as abhorrent. "Mother love" is celebrated in Brazilian life, and a great deal of physical affection is expressed toward infants, who are frequently held, stroked, tickled, and babbled to by all in the household. Selective neglect of infants along with maternal detachment are seen as appropriate maternal responses to a child who does not show the resilience necessary for survival under the extreme circumstances of the shantytown. The mothers' attitude is one of pity toward these children in the face of inability to change the circumstances.

These mothers preferred babies who evidenced the physical and psychological characteristics of survivors—being active, sharp, playful, precocious, and even a little wild. They spoke of babies whose drive to live was not sufficiently strong or who had an aversion to life. Part of learning how to mother in the shantytown is learning when to "let go." The mothers agreed that it is best if the weak die as infants without a prolonged and wasted struggle: "They die because they have to die. . . . I think that if they were always weak, they wouldn't be able to defend themselves in life. So, it is really better to let the weak ones die" (p. 305). One mother spoke of her two infants as having given her "no trouble" in dying—they just "rolled their eyes to the back of their heads and were still" (p. 304). It is slow, protracted deaths that the mothers fear.

When Scheper-Hughes tried to intervene to save a 1-year-old who was severely malnourished, unable even to sit up, her efforts were laughed at by the local women. The baby himself refused to eat, and the women "said that they had seen many babies like this one and that 'if a baby *wants* to die, it *will* die' and that this one was completely *disanimado*, lifeless, without fight. It was wrong, they cautioned, to fight death" (1985, p. 294). With tremendous effort, Scheper-Hughes forced the child to eat and to live. He was welcomed by his mother when this treatment was successful, and as an adult he reported that his mother was his greatest friend in life.

Other children who survived terrible odds also managed to later win family love and protection. Their mother's earlier detachment and neglect were, by local standards, appropriate to the child's likelihood of survival given the severe limitations of the shantytown. If an infant suffers many crises during its first year but survives, its mother will be proud of the child's triumphs—testimony to the child's inner vitality and will to live.

With an infant death, mothers and others are expected not to shed tears. Sometimes the pain of a loss breaks through the resignation that is the norm, with memories of particular babies in whom a mother's hopes for the future had been invested. Then other women scold the grieving woman, urging her not to go mad with grief but to go on with life.

On the basis of these observations, Scheper-Hughes called into question the assumption that maternal attachment is innate and called for a more contextualized model of the biological and cultural processes involved in mother-child relations. She criticized the hospital practice of encouraging early mother-infant contact to establish an affectional bond without giving attention to ensuring a supportive environment for the mother and child once they left the hospital. She noted the inappropriateness of attributing abuse and neglect solely to failures in early maternal bonding rather than considering societal features surrounding infant care:

> Theories of innate maternal scripts such as "bonding," "maternal thinking," or "maternal instincts" are both culture and history bound, the reflection of a very specific and very recent reproductive strategy: to give birth to few babies and to invest heavily in each one.

This is a reproductive strategy that was a stranger to most of European history through the early modern period, and it does not reflect the "maternal thinking" of a great many women living in the Third World today where an alternative strategy holds: to give birth to many children, invest selectively based on culturally derived favored characteristics, and hope that a few survive infancy and the early years of life. . . .

The classical maternal bonding model . . . grossly underestimates the power and significance of social and cultural factors that influence and shape maternal thinking over time: the cultural meanings of sexuality, fertility, death, and survival; mother's assessment of her economic, social support, and psychological resources; family size and composition; characteristics and evaluation of the infant.
(pp. 310, 314)

Clearly, interpretations of mothers' treatment of infants require consideration of a community's cultural strategies for handling local challenges and an examination of the circumstances of parenting. Mothers' relations with their infants link with mothers' and infants' relations with their community.

Infants' Security of Attachment

Most research on infants' attachment to their caregivers has taken place in the United States and Western Europe. It addresses the question of how securely infants relate to their mothers (and occasionally, to other caregivers). The security of infants' attachment has usually been examined in laboratory situations in a procedure called "the Strange Situation," in which caregivers are asked to leave and reunite with their infants so that the researchers can observe the infants' reactions when slightly stressed.

Infants are judged to have a "secure" attachment if they explore the Strange Situation room and act friendly before the separation from the caregiver, show mild wariness during the separation, and are comforted and do not show anger when reunited with the caregiver. Several alternative patterns are also distinguished. The "anxious/resistant" pattern is characterized by high distress while the caregiver is absent, and when the caregiver attempts to comfort the infant after the separation, the infant is not easily soothed and simultaneously seeks contact and resists proximity. The "anxious/avoidant" pattern involves low distress while the caregiver is away but avoidance of the caregiver upon reunion, turning or looking away.

Most European American infants are classifiable into one of these three categories, with the largest number classified as secure, the category regarded as ideal. However, research in several other communities around the world has noted variations in the prevalence of different patterns (Harwood, Miller, & Irizarry, 1995; Jackson, 1993; LeVine & Miller, 1990; Sagi, 1990; Takahashi, 1990). Although the secure pattern is prevalent in most groups that have been studied, the anxious/avoidant pattern was more common in studies in some Western European countries, and the anxious/resistant pattern was more common in studies in Israel and Japan.

The different patterns of reaction to the Strange Situation seem to reflect cultural values and practices (LeVine & Miller, 1990). For example, the greater frequency of anxious avoidance of the mother in north Germany, upon reunion after stressful separation and approach of a stranger, may reflect cultural emphasis on early independence training (Grossmann, Grossmann, Spangler, Suess, & Unzner, 1985). In contrast, the absence of avoidance among Dogon (West African) infants may stem from their community's infant care practices, which involve responsiveness, constant proximity to mothers, and immediate nursing in response to signs of distress (True, Pisani, & Oumar, 2001).

The greater frequency of anxious resistance to the mother upon reunion in Japan may result from greater stress during the Strange Situation due to infants' unfamiliarity with being left with strangers (Miyake, Chen, & Campos, 1985). In contrast, for African American infants who are used to being tended by several caregivers and who are encouraged to be friendly to the numerous strangers they encounter on frequent excursions, attachment observations in the laboratory may arouse the infants' interest in exploration. The infants in whom a gregarious personality is cultivated are outgoing in the laboratory situation, while still attuned to their caregivers. "There would be no reason for them to be upset by a toy-filled room with a friendly stranger who more or less entertained them while their parent figures were momentarily away" (Jackson, 1993, p. 98).

The importance of community goals for children's early relationships was clear in attachment interviews with Anglo and Puerto Rican mothers (Harwood et al., 1995). Anglo mothers expressed an overriding concern that their children develop an optimal balance between autonomy and relatedness. These concerns mapped well onto the three attachment patterns studied in the Strange Situation, which focus on emotional isolation, insufficient autonomy, and optimally balanced attachment. In contrast, Puerto Rican mothers focused on their children's skill in engaging in appropriate levels of relatedness, encompassed in an idea of "proper demeanor," with courtesy and respectful attentiveness. They distinguished toddlers' behavior in terms of the presence of proper demeanor rather than patterns of autonomy and relatedness.

These studies point to critical issues in assessing the attachment of infants in standardized situations, as well as to cultural variations in the goals promoted and the social relations involved in infant-caregiver interactions. The studies suggest that "infants become attached not only to specific persons but to specific conditions that have given them comfort and that arouse anxiety when they are withdrawn. The meaning of the mother to the baby is partly provided by such conditions" (LeVine & Miller, 1990, p. 76).

Attachment to Whom?

The conditions that give infants comfort often involve other people in addition to the mother. Infants' attachments are intimately related to community arrangements of child care, reflecting historical circumstances and cultural values regarding families' roles in caregiving.

Cultural research questions the assumption that the caregiving role is naturally provided by the mother, or by the parents, or even by a particular adult. Around the world, different people in the family, neighborhood, and community provide different aspects of infant and child care (Fisher, Jackson, & Villarruel, 1998; Mead, 1935; see figure 4.2). Shared responsibility for care of infants does not seem to get in the way of close attachment to mothers (Fox, 1977; Harkness & Super, 1992b; Hewlett, 1991; Jackson, 1993; Morelli & Tronick, 1991; but see also Sagi, van IJzendoorn, Aviezer, Donnell, & Mayseless, 1994).

Care and nursing of infants among the Efe (a gathering and hunting group in the Democratic Republic of Congo) is shared among the women of the community. This practice extends infants' maternal relationships beyond those with the biological mother, but the infants nonetheless distinguish their mothers from their other caregivers (Morelli & Tronick, 1991; Tronick, Morelli, & Winn, 1987). Along with their affiliation with their fathers, Efe toddlers also affiliate with other males of their camp (Morelli & Tronick, 1992). The children's broad relationships with men and boys are important because if parents divorce or parental death occurs (both are frequent), the children remain in their father's group.

The likelihood of parental mortality has been a feature of child-rearing traditions in many cultural communities. In some regions of the colonial United States, stable family life was unusual, with most children having at least one parent die during their childhood (Getis & Vinovskis, 1992). Such situations make relationships with extended family, godparents, and community institutions especially important for the survival of children.

Among Aka foragers of Central Africa, where mothers are primary caregivers and fathers are secondary caregivers, infants are most attached to their mothers and secondarily to their fathers (Hewlett, 1991). At the same

FIGURE 4.2

A man and child among the
!Kung (now Ju'/hoansi), a
hunting and gathering group
in Southern Africa.

time, infants have attachments with many others who care for them. Within
the camp setting, 1- to 4-month-olds are held most of the time, but less
than 40% of the time by their mothers. They are transferred to other caregivers about seven times an hour and have seven different caregivers on an
average day.

The role of fathers with infants varies greatly across communities
(Whiting & Edwards, 1988). The highest involvement of fathers appears to
occur among Aka foragers, where almost half of the father's day (24-hour
period) is spent holding or within arm's reach of his infant; fathers hold infants about 20% of the time they are in camp (Hewlett, 1991); this is still
less than the mothers hold the babies, however. In farming and foraging settings in other parts of the world, fathers have been observed to hold infants
less than 4% of the time, according to Hewlett's summary. However, even
when fathers are seldom in direct interaction with infants, they often play
essential supportive roles (for example, contributing to subsistence and protection). Studies suggest that fetal, infant, and child illness and mortality are
higher for infants without a father (Hewlett, 1991).

In many communities, then, the mother is not the sole caregiver or attachment figure. The other caregivers and their roles vary widely, depending on who else is in the household and their other responsibilities.

Family and Community Role Specializations

In some communities, children's relationships are primarily with parents and secondarily with siblings. In other communities, siblings play a primary role after infancy. In still other settings, the extended family or the neighborhood or even professional caregivers or agencies hold responsibility for children. In Cameroon (West Africa), only unborn babies are regarded as belonging to their parents; from birth on, infants belong to their extended kin group (Nsamenang, 1992). In traditional Japanese households, children were regarded as belonging to the house (Hendry, 1986). If a woman left a house upon divorce or separation, the children usually remained behind and were brought up by the new wife or their father's mother.

Different individuals may specialize in distinct roles with children. For example, some serve caregiving roles, while others are companions and conversational or play partners. In traditional Chewa (Zambian) communities, distribution of child rearing roles changed as children grew up:

> The parents are responsible for bringing forth children. . . . The mother feeds the baby till it is weaned. From then on the responsibility for further rearing and education lies with the grandparents. When the child leaves the [house] of his grandparents [at the approximate age of 7] he passes on to the sleeping quarters of the unmarried and his training becomes more of a community concern than of individual parents. (Bruwer, 1949, p. 197, quoted in Serpell, 1993, p. 59)

Extended Families

Specialization of roles with children have to do with who else is available within the family or neighborhood, as well as with cultural expectations regarding the appropriate roles. Given the mobility and practices of middle-class European American families, children often do not have nearby grandparents, aunts and uncles, or cousins. The census of the year 2000 showed that only about 4% of U.S. households included three generations, with higher levels in regions with many new immigrants (Seligman, 2001). In contrast, the proportion of U.S. households that contain only one person is six times as great (26%).[1]

The nuclear family situation, with one or two parents (and one or two

---

[1]This is a notable change from the 1600s, when the colonies of Massachusetts and Connecticut had laws forbidding single persons from living alone; they were required to arrange to live in a family for the sake of the moral order (Morgan, 1944).

children) living in a separate dwelling perhaps hundreds of miles from kin, is a markedly different child-rearing environment from that experienced by children surrounded by relatives (Chudacoff, 1989; Jackson, 1993; Mistry, Göncü, & Rogoff, 1988; New & Richman, 1996; Seymour, 1999; Tafoya, 1989; Whiting & Edwards, 1988). In Polynesia, for example, even firstborn children usually have older children to play with and care for them, as their parents live with the mother's or father's parents (Martini & Kirkpatrick, 1992). In Kokwet, Kenya, babies are usually in a social group that includes the mother, several siblings, and half-siblings (from their mother's cowives). Babies in Kokwet averaged 6.7 companions, compared with 1.8 in a U.S. community (Harkness & Super, 1985).

The isolated nuclear family in European American communities stems from particular historical circumstances:

> American society was created by people who were consciously trying to leave behind the hierarchies and constraints of Europe and set up a different way of life, where an individual could be himself, the captain of his soul, the master of his fate. Americans therefore think and try to act as if they were individual atoms, much better off if left alone. . . . They believe that individualism plus competition are the foundation of the American way of life, with its promise of material abundance together with the personal freedom to enjoy it. . . . If people are brought up to be individualistic and competitive, they are not likely to leave these traits at the door when they come home. . . .
>
> A lot is demanded of the modern family. Couples expect to share each other's interests, to have fun in each other's company, to enjoy sex together frequently and exclusively, and to find room for personal growth in the sanctuary they have created. We have come a long way from Socrates' Athens, where men never expected to talk to their wives. Yet these high expectations can turn into pressures. . . .
>
> If pressures overwhelm and expectations go unfulfilled, divorce is readily available and frequently chosen. Americans have the highest divorce rates in the world. There is no longer much social pressure to make a marriage work; there may even be a certain encouragement to get out of a marriage where things are not going well. . . . [Americans engage in] serial monogamy, which means that people of both sexes have multiple spouses, but only one at a time. . . .
>
> The "nuclear family" on which Americans pin such high hopes is terribly isolated. Other relatives are usually far away, physically or emotionally, and therefore cannot help. Nor are they really expected to. Meanwhile, the little family haven, which Americans are encour-

aged to think of as a love nest, can sometimes become a place of desperation. [If we were anthropologists from a remote tribal society, we would note] that if a husband batters his wife or parents abuse their children, they are not often restrained by outraged relatives or concerned neighbors. Protected by the privacy that the society values so highly, they are tacitly permitted to continue until somebody is hurt badly enough to bring the family in to court. (Maybury-Lewis, 1992, pp. 112–116)

In contrast, in many African American, American Indian, and U.S. Latino communities of varying economic means, grandparents and other kin are frequently a part of children's daily lives. They often live in the children's immediate household or are otherwise in frequent contact and helping with child care (Harrison, Wilson, Pine, Chan, & Buriel, 1990; Hays & Mindel, 1973; Jackson, 1993; Leyendecker, Lamb, Schölmerich, & Fracasso, 1995; MacPhee, Fritz, & Miller-Heyl, 1996).

Among Hawaiian middle-class Japanese American families, 64% reported that grandparents and parents' siblings provide care for children almost every day. This was reported in only 6% of middle-class Caucasian American families in Hawaii. Even for those with relatives living on the islands, only half saw them on a daily basis (Martini, 1994a). Most of the Caucasian American families saw the children's grandparents or aunts and uncles only once or twice a year for short visits. They relied on day care, preschools, baby-sitters, and school and afterschool programs for daily child care, whereas only 19% of the Japanese American families (with similar parental employment) used such facilities.

Children's involvement with their extended kin also relates to whether they are expected to continue to be a part of their birth family as adults. Often, middle-class U.S. children are expected to "leave home" later in life to form their own, separate families. In some other communities, children are expected to remain involved with and responsible to their family of origin throughout life (Kagitçibasi & Sunar, 1992).

With middle-class children expected to separate from their family of origin, their own parents seldom have a continuing role in their adulthood as members of an extended family with frequent contact and differentiated roles. This contrasts with the differentiated expertise available among extended family members who serve as "funds of knowledge," assisting each other with work, school, language, and other skills and information, as in many Mexican American families (Moll, Tapia, & Whitmore, 1993). The availability of multiple relationships in extended families allows the possibility of differentiation of roles. Different people can provide caregiving, companionship, socialization, and other child-rearing supports.

Differentiation of Caregiving, Companion, and Socializing Roles

Physical care, companionship, and aid in understanding mature roles in the community can each be provided by different people. In some communities, mothers are the main providers of both physical care and social interaction for infants, whereas in others, mothers may meet physical needs while others meet social needs (Edwards & Whiting, 1992; Harkness & Super, 1992b; Leiderman & Leiderman, 1973).

Communities vary in expectations regarding whether parents or other people will serve as playmates in addition to being caregivers of young children. Middle-class Chinese and European American parents and Aka hunter-gatherer parents are often their toddler's playmates (Haight, Parke, & Black, 1997; Haight, Wang, Fung, Williams, & Mintz, 1999; Hewlett, 1992; Rogoff et al., 1993). In contrast, the role of playmate belongs to siblings and other extended family members in other communities, such as East African societies, a working-class town in central Italy, and a Mayan town in Guatemala (Harkness & Super, 1992b; LeVine, Dixon, LeVine, Richman, Leiderman, Keefer, & Brazelton, 1994; New, 1994; Rogoff & Mosier, 1993). When a toddler is playing, Mayan mothers reported, it is time for a mother to get her work done (Rogoff & Mosier, 1993). Although Mayan parents may tickle and jounce their babies affectionately, they seldom play as peers with their toddlers.

African American children in Louisiana watched and listened to adults; they played and talked and tumbled with other children (Ward, 1971). Older children were involved in taking care of younger children and taught social and intellectual skills such as reciting the alphabet, rhymes, and word games and naming colors and numbers. "No child, even the firstborn, is without such tutelage, since cousins, aunts, and uncles of their own age and older are always on hand" (p. 25). Similarly, in a working-class African American community in the Carolinas, girls invented playsongs tailored to language teaching and engaged young children in wordplay, counting, and naming body parts (Heath, 1983). These are topics handled by adults engaging children in nursery rhymes and language routines in middle-class European American communities, but they were not part of adult-child interaction in this working-class African American community.

Even when responsibility for child rearing is assumed by an extended group, mothers usually have primary responsibility for caregiving in the early years. Native Hawaiian preschoolers were involved with an average of 17 people who were active in their caregiving and entertainment (Farran, Mistry, Ai-Chang, & Herman, 1993). Although mothers reported key contributions by others, they described themselves as centrally responsible and involved (Gallimore et al., 1974). Around the world, mothers' roles are usually central, whether they have the sole responsibility for children, delegate responsibility to others, or supervise the shared care of their children (Jackson, 1993; Lamb, Sternberg, Hwang, & Broberg, 1992; Rogoff, Mistry, Göncü, & Mosier, 1991).

Mothers may take care of children as much by ensuring that *others* will consistently provide nurturance and support as by directly doing so themselves. This form of child care thus involves indirect chains of support, managed by mothers or other adults (Weisner, 1997). For example, in home observations when Mayan mothers were asked to help their toddlers operate novel objects, they sometimes recruited one of their older children to play with the toddler. The mothers supervised the sibling and sometimes directed the sibling's interactions with the toddler, but seldom entered into a playmate role themselves with the toddler. In similar executive-style arrangements, Kenyan babies were given three times as much attention as were U.S. babies, although the direct attention from the mothers in both settings was similar (Harkness & Super, 1992b).

Sibling Caregiving and Peer Relations

In many communities in which mothers involve others in the nurturance and support of young children, siblings have a central role, providing care and instruction. The roles of siblings in children's lives are obviously tied to the *existence* of siblings and also to their routine roles in family organization.

The availability of siblings varies widely across cultural communities. In some countries, the average number of births per mother is close to one, yielding no siblings, as in the one-child family mandated in current-day China. In contrast, in traditional societies of Kenya, mothers average more than eight children (Harkness & Super, 1992b).

Over half of all children in colonial America had many siblings; about 36% of all families had nine or more children (Chudacoff, 1989). The number of siblings has decreased across the centuries. In colonial America, women of the 1600s gave birth to an average of 7.4 children; in the U.S. of the early 1800s, the average was 4.9 children; by the 1870s, U.S. women who married averaged only 2.8 children.

In many communities, care of infants and toddlers is traditionally carried out by 5- to 10-year-old children (Edwards & Whiting, 1992; Harkness & Super, 1992b; LeVine et al., 1994; Watson-Gegeo & Gegeo, 1989; Weisner & Gallimore, 1977; Wenger, 1983; Whiting & Edwards, 1988; Whiting & Whiting, 1975). Children may carry a younger sibling or cousin around on their back or hip to be entertained by the sights and sounds of the community and the play of other children. If the young one becomes hungry, the child caregiver returns to the mother to allow the child to nurse. Adults are available to supervise child caregivers, but the entertainment of young children falls to other children.

For example, as they left infancy, Polynesian children became quite independent of parents and active in sibling and child groups (Martini & Kirkpatrick, 1992). Once babies could walk, mothers released them into the care of 3- to 4-year-old siblings, who played nearby, checking periodically on the young ones. Mothers showed siblings how to feed and entertain 4-month-olds, handing them squalling babies to calm. "The young child becomes upset if caregivers do not give him *his* crying baby. The young child takes his job seriously and learns the baby's likes, dislikes, and habits" (p. 211). According to the Polynesian mothers, toddlers are most interested in playing with other children and cry when siblings go off without them, leaving them home with mother. Mothers saw toddlers' interest in wanting to sit and sleep next to siblings as natural, because children's play is interesting to the toddlers and adults' activities are boring to them. Parents oversaw the children rather than being directly involved. Tasks were often assigned to the children as a unit, leaving them to decide who does what; all were held responsible for task completion.

In contrast to the preferred age of 7 to 10 years for child caregivers in many communities, middle-class European American families seldom use baby-sitters younger than 12 years old. This may be because small family size and school attendance limit the experience children have in caring for young children (Harkness & Super, 1992b; Whiting & Edwards, 1988). As a result,

> American toddlers and preschoolers are almost always supervised by adults who set limits, direct activities, schedule eating and resting, comfort children, and resolve children's conflicts. American toddlers play in restricted, baby-proofed settings . . . and are not held responsible for younger siblings. (Martini, 1994b, p. 87)

Unfamiliar with these practices, Kenyan graduate students at Harvard were surprised to see American children seeking interaction with their parents in preference to siblings (Whiting, 1979).

There are other communities in which children seldom tend younger children. Neither girls nor boys are commonly used as child nurses among the foraging !Kung (now Ju'/hoansi) or Aka (Draper, 1975b; Hewlett, 1991). This may result from wide birth spacing, resulting in less need for child care, or to the availability of other adults in the camp who contribute to child care.

In communities in which children have the opportunity to engage extensively with siblings, the role of siblings complements that of parents in an essential way. The organization of children's relations among themselves can be an important ground for young children's development.

Opportunities for young children
to learn from sibling caregivers

Sibling caregiving may provide younger children with special learning opportunities, especially in communities in which such caregiving arrangements are commonplace (LeVine et al., 1994; Maynard, 2002). For example, the playful teasing of slightly older siblings among the Kikuyu (in Kenya) provides children with key guidance on how to act appropriately and how to discriminate what is true from what is not (Edwards & Whiting, 1992). Kwara'ae (Solomon Island) infants benefit from a great diversity of cognitive and social stimulation, both from the sibling caregivers' mobility and from their skill, which is moderate at age 3 and requires no supervision after age 6 to 7 (Watson-Gegeo & Gegeo, 1989).

In observations of working-class Mexican families, toddlers rarely played with their mothers. Instead, they played with mixed-age children, who were much more tolerant and cooperative in supporting the toddlers' play than were working-class U.S. siblings (Farver, 1993). In fact, Mexican sibling-toddler play resembled U.S. mother-child play in its complexity, support for the toddler, and nurturance.

Preschool siblings in the Marquesan Islands (Polynesia) teach 2-year-olds that they can stay with the children's group only if they keep themselves safe and stay out of the way of the group activity (Martini & Kirkpatrick, 1992). The toddlers learn to be self-reliant and nondisruptive. They play on the edge of the group and watch intently until they can keep up with the play. For example, 13 members of a stable play group of 2- to 5-year-olds played several hours a day without supervision while older siblings attended school (Martini, 1994b). The preschool children and their toddler charges organized activities, settled disputes, avoided danger, and dealt with injuries without adult intervention. The play area was potentially dangerous, with broken glass, strong surf breaking on the boat ramp, and steep slippery terrain. The children played on a high bridge and walls and with machetes, axes, and matches that were occasionally left around. In spite of the dangers, accidents were rare and minor.

Children around the world observe other children and may attempt to follow their lead from infancy. Marquesan mothers claim that toddlers develop skills because they want to be with and be like their older siblings. By imitating preschool children, toddlers learn to run, feed and dress themselves, go outside to urinate and defecate, and help with household chores (Martini & Kirkpatrick, 1992).

Children learn collective roles, responsibility, peer mentoring, and how to handle conflicts and compromises as they spend their days in teams of children responsible for child care in West African villages. Children in these teams range from about 20 months to 6 or 7 years of age, under the guidance of one or two older siblings (often girls of 8 to 10 years):

> A multiage, dual-sex team of children move about together under the supervision of older peers. As they play make-believe, group-circle, and other games in the neighborhood, they are expected to fetch water and carry firewood as well as complete any chore they were assigned. When they are hungry, they return to the house to eat the food their mothers left for them; older children feed younger ones. Adults, especially grandparents and sometimes fathers, are usually within shouting or running distance to intervene or help when disasters such as a serious fight, injury, or snake bite arise. (Nsamenang, 1992, p. 153)

Previously, such teams were used as a training ground for leadership roles and, when members became older, as part of the government and law enforcement system.

Children's engagement with related children of different ages provides an organization in which they learn how to relate with others. In some communities, children also—or instead—spend a great deal of time with unrelated same-age peers. Cultural differences in children's involvement with multiage groups versus with same-age peers are important for the social relations that children develop with each other.

Same-age peers: Segregation of children from children of other ages

Children's groups around the world generally include a mix of ages. For example, in the Mayan community where I have worked, children spent less than 10% of their out-of-school time with other children who were just the same age (Rogoff, 1981a). Often, children's companions are siblings and other young relatives of a wide range of ages (Angelillo, Rogoff, & Morelli, 2002).

Grouping children by age is unusual around the world. It requires adequate numbers of children in a small territory to ensure availability of several children of the same age (Konner, 1975). It also seems to be prompted by the growth of bureaucracies and reductions in family size.

Currently, much of North American children's time is spent in age-graded bureaucratic institutions, such as school or camp, where one-year age groups are often formed for adults' convenience. Consistent with this segregation, middle-class North Americans often emphasize children's peer relations over relations with brothers and sisters (Angelillo et al., 2002; Ruffy, 1981; Wolfenstein, 1955). However, outside of bureaucratic settings, contact across age groups may be frequent in some middle-class U.S. communities (Ellis, Rogoff, & Cromer, 1981; Fitchen, 1981; Gump, Schoggen, & Redl, 1963; Hicks, 1976; Young, 1970).

Until relatively recently, when large numbers of children have been required to attend school, children were not divided according to age even in schooling's gradation of the curriculum into steps (Chudacoff, 1989; Serpell, 1993). Gradations in European schools did not begin until the 16th century, and those grades were based on students' progress in learning rather than on chronological age. Gradation based on age began in the early 19th century, but even then, the usual age range dropped only as far as a six-year range within a given class (according to Serpell's 1993 summary based on Ariès's account).

In North America, organized schooling spread in the late 1700s, but there was not a standard age of entry or completion; very young children could be in the same classroom with teenagers (Chudacoff, 1989). The variation in age at school entry and in frequency of attendance made age a poor predictor of extent of children's school knowledge.

In the late 1800s, segregation of U.S. schoolchildren by age became formalized with the advent of compulsory schooling, which required a standard starting age to verify that children were not truant. Age-grading served bureaucratic needs in the face of great increases in the numbers of schoolchildren, due in part to industrialization, urbanization of the population, and huge influxes of immigrants. In the 1870s, 61% of White children ages 5 to 19 attended school, a rapid increase from 35% in 1830 (Chudacoff, 1989). Handling instruction bureaucratically also followed the preference in the late 1800s to codify a "rational" system of uniform classification, curricula, textbooks, and discipline, using age as a metric to categorize pupils (Chudacoff, 1989).

Segregating children in groups of similar ages has a clear impact on the opportunities for sibling care and interaction. For example, now that 5- to 10-year-old Kikuyu (Kenyan) children usually attend school, they are no longer available to serve as child caregivers for their toddler siblings, although they are the preferred age for this job. This means that Kikuyu mothers now need to rely on children under age 5 to help care for and entertain toddlers (Edwards & Whiting, 1992). The age range of interactions among children at home is thereby restricted.

Such age-based restriction reduces schoolchildren's opportunities to learn from engaging with younger (and older) children. Interaction with a broad range of ages provides children the opportunity to practice teaching and nurturance with younger children and to imitate and practice role re-

FIGURE 4.3

In this informal group that includes a range of ages, Guatemalan Mayan children pretend to make a meal using found materials. The younger children observe the oldest girl intently as she pretends to grind corn for tortillas on her makeshift grinding stone.

lations with older children (Whiting & Edwards, 1988; Whiting & Whiting, 1975; see figure 4.3). On the other hand, interaction with agemates seems to promote competitiveness.

The growth in emphasis on age-graded institutions has created a societal structure in which associations with similar-age people has taken precedence in many cases over intergenerational family and community relations. In colonial America, the large families usually did not segment into separate generations, as the oldest children often started families of their own before the parents completed child rearing. The youngest children of the family often had aunts and uncles near their own age and adult siblings living in the same household (Chudacoff, 1989). Family as well as community activities included people spanning different ages and generations.

By the early 1900s, similar-age peer groups were supplanting the integration across generations (Chudacoff, 1989). Many more children attended school and for longer times. Child labor laws separated children from the workforce and restricted exposure to this source of intergenerational socialization. With young people having more spare time, adult concern about wayward pastimes created efforts to control children's leisure activities. These efforts employed age stages postulated by the new theories of development, with play reformers designing the order in which children should engage in particular forms of play and games: "Age-stratified groupings in both school and recreational activities combined to enclose youths in a potent environment that accustomed them to interacting almost exclusively with peers for a significant portion of their daily lives" (p. 78).

In addition, reduction in family size by the early 1900s reduced the spread of ages of siblings, so the children of a family formed more of a peer group. The gap between the children's ages and those of their parents created greater isolation across generations and more connection among those close in age (Chudacoff, 1989). There was also a reduction in the age difference between husband and wife, now that youths had much more contact with each other within age-graded schools and leisure activities.[2] This made the marital relation more of a peer relation as well. The lives of children and adults became increasingly separated into like-age groups.

Now, even very young children in some nations are spending large portions of their day in institutions such as preschools and day care, which are also often age-graded. The age-grading of such institutions contributes to societal debates about the impact on children's development of growing up in such settings. As child care in some nations has become increasingly institutional, the responsibility for child development has become based much more on government policies—a form of community-based caregiving.

The Community as Caregiver

Daily supervision of children may be the responsibility of the whole community, without the need for any particular adult to devote primary attention to the pack of children. In a variety of communities, caregiving and disciplinary duties belong to anyone who is near the child. Babies are usually surrounded by relatives and nonkin neighbors of many ages who take responsibility for them when the mother is away or busy (Gallimore et al., 1974; Munroe & Munroe, 1975a; Rohner & Chaki-Sirkar, 1988; Saraswathi & Dutta, 1988; Ward, 1971).

For example, in Polynesia, children often grow up in an environment where many adults and children have responsibility for their upbringing in enduring social networks (Martini & Kirkpatrick, 1992). Children belong to the community and everyone is expected to comfort, instruct, and correct them. Within the extended family, a new baby belongs to the family,

---

[2] In 1889–90, enrollment in secondary schools in the United States included only 6.7% of the total population age 14 to 17 years; in 1919–20, 32.3% were in school, and by 1929–30, 51.4% were enrolled (Chudacoff, 1989).

and the adults all care for, teach, and discipline the child as it grows. Children have "many laps" to sit in and many models of adult behavior. Often children are adopted and raised by kin other than their biological parents in a system in which children are shared and help to strengthen ties among households.

Likewise, in West Africa, biological parents often delegate the care of their child to foster parents without losing parental rights, as a way of rearing children within the extended social network and cementing kinship and friendship bonds (Nsamenang, 1992). The involvement of the extended kinship network also provides checks and balances in parenting. The presence and involvement of many people, for example, prevents punishment from going beyond culturally permissible boundaries. Parents may be less likely to reach the level of exasperation of parents in communities in which there are not many people around to help buffer such feelings.

Neighbors who are not related to the family by kinship but by long association in a tribal village in India made their opinions known regarding anyone's treatment of a child (Mistry et al., 1988). Nonrelatives were almost always present in toddlers' homes and engaged with them at least as extensively as did relatives. They told the mothers what to do, regulated the children's behavior, and engaged them in playful teasing (Rogoff et al., 1991). These nonrelatives' direct engagement with toddlers contrasted with observations in middle-class U.S., middle-class Turkish, and Mayan homes, where nonrelatives were rarely present, and those who were present usually took a spectator role.

Indeed, many U.S. taxpayers seem to regard the care of children as the sole responsibility of the children's parents (Getis & Vinovskis, 1992; Lamb, Sternberg, & Ketterlinus, 1992). Child care in the United States is seldom treated as an investment of the community in the next generation, which will become responsible for the community and for support of the older generation.

In contrast, some communities assert their roles in rearing children. For example, in a number of cases, Navajo children who have been adopted by Anglo families have been returned to the tribe, which claims the right to raise its children even if parents have agreed to give them up. The kibbutz movement in Israel attempted to encourage children's growth as members of the whole community by raising children (until recently) in a separate house away from their parents. The children were tended by community members specializing in child care (Oppenheim, 1998; Rosenthal, 1992). Church communities have served as powerful forces in the resilience of African American children (Comer, 1988; Haight, 2002).

*Community involvement in the form
of child care specialists*

Specialized paid caregivers, teachers, child-rearing experts, social workers, pediatricians, and child-focused institutions and advice books constitute a form of community responsibility for child rearing in industrialized nations. Most of these roles have arisen following industrialization, little more than a century ago in the United States and many other nations, replacing many of the responsibilities of extended family and neighbors of prior centuries (Chudacoff, 1989; Demos & Demos, 1969; Ehrenreich & English, 1978; Hareven, 1985; Harkness, Super, & Keefer, 1992; Kojima, 1996; Lamb, Sternberg, Hwang, & Broberg, 1992).

Indeed, "experts" stake claims for the right to determine child-rearing practices. This can be seen in laws regulating parental rights and responsibilities and in the policies promoted by social agencies. For example, the *Instructions to Mothers* brochure, given by the Research Hospital of Kansas City to new mothers in 1949, claimed preeminence of medical expertise over the knowledge and advice of family members. Item 24 stated, "Don't listen to careless advice of friends and relatives. Do as your physician advises. He knows more about you and your baby than they do."

The other Instructions to Mothers dealt with such matters as diet, bowel movements (both mother's and baby's), cleanliness, diapering, and how to clean the baby's eyes with boric acid solution. Some items clearly reveal cultural assumptions when considered half a century later:

1. Awaken baby to feed regularly at 6-9-12 A.M.-3-6-10 P.M.-2 A.M. unless otherwise instructed. Regular feeding and careful routine are the first essentials for your baby.

10. Handle infant as little as possible. Do not pick up to show to relatives and friends. Keep quiet and free from commotion and infection.

13. Do not pick baby up every time it cries. Normal infants cry some every day to obtain exercise. Infant is quickly spoiled by handling.

19. Baby should never sleep with you or any other person.[3]

Teachers are perhaps the pre-eminent child care specialists appointed by communities since the late 1800s, when school became pervasive in children's lives in many nations. In colonial America, families were expected to care for children and teach them to read at home. A few primary schools existed for the education of poor children, and grammar schools and colleges educated those few who were preparing to become ministers (Getis & Vinovskis, 1992). Preschool and kindergarten practices were imported to the United States from Europe in the 1800s, impelled by societal efforts to pro-

[3] Thanks to Sally Duensing for showing me this hospital brochure, given to her mother.

vide care and literacy instruction for poor children with mothers working outside the home, to help the children overcome their "disadvantaged" backgrounds (Getis & Vinovskis, 1992). Since then, debates have reflected tensions over the extent to which home and public institutions are the proper place for care and socialization of young children.

Community Support of Children and Families

Children's increased involvements outside of the home and the immediate community have created concerns for the development of youth in many industrialized nations. In U.S. cities, community responsibility for youth seems to have diffused and observers often bemoan lack of adult authority over adolescents. They often blame parents, overlooking the changed role of neighbors and the immediate community. Alice Schlegel and Herbert Barry suggested that adolescent crime results more from community than family breakdown, resulting in delinquency even in adolescents from "good homes": "Parents do not control adolescents unaided by community norms and sanctions; boys in particular [in nonindustrial societies] are likely to behave well when they are much in the presence of men. These men do not necessarily have to be their fathers" (1991, p. 204).

A weakened community support system contributed to family difficulties of Polish immigrants to the United States in the early 1900s. In Polish peasant life in the "old country," parental authority was supported and balanced by the organization of the extended family and whole community, providing parents with a role that was both stronger and more just. The emigrants to America found great friction between parents and children, due to a weaker support system:

> First, there is in America no family in the traditional sense; the married couple and the children are almost completely isolated, and the parental authority has no background. (In a few cases, where many members of the family have settled in the same locality, the control is much stronger.) Again, if there is something equivalent to the community of the old country, i.e., the parish, it is much less closed and concentrated and can hardly have the same influence. Its composition is new, accidental, and changing . . . and has consequently a rather poor stock of common traditions. (quoted in Thomas & Znaniecki, 1984, p. 143)

An example of strong community responsibility for children's healthy development has been found in Japan, where responsibility is shared by the family, school, and workplace (White, 1987). On school fieldtrips, if a mishap occurs, the responsibility is assumed by everyone involved—the child, classmates, the teacher, the principal, the person in charge of the place of the visit, and the parents to an extent—with apologies from everyone. If a high school student is caught driving without a license, the student's schoolteachers, principal, and parents are called to account by the police, along with the student. A young person beginning work for a company can expect superiors in the firm to help in the search for a suitable wife or husband and sometimes to sponsor the wedding ceremony.

Children's freedom and supervision in community caregiving

Children have both freedom of movement and supervised involvement with their broader community in settings in which the community keeps an eye on the children (Comer, 1988; Heath, 1989b). Jane Easton, age 50, recalled New York's Harlem in the 1950s:

> Everybody knew everybody. . . . You could run from one person's house to another and you didn't have to ring the bell 'cause the door would be open. We had fun when we were kids, running around. The neighborhood was safe. Everybody would come downstairs and you'd play, running in the fire hydrant and stuff like that. You could go to the store for your mother and stuff. . . .
>
> You knew everybody. You knew the lady that ran the grocery store. . . . My grandmother's family . . . owned the cleaners. You knew the man that owned the supermarket and the meat market. They knew you personally, you know . . . "Oh, you're Miss ——'s granddaughter." It was a real family thing. (quoted in Newman, 1998, p. 267)

If responsibility for caregiving is widely shared by a community, even very young children may have opportunities to engage in and observe community activities more broadly than if their care is delegated to an adult in an isolated household or an institution specializing in child care. For example, in the Guatemalan Mayan community where I began working almost three decades ago, 3- to 5-year-old children largely took care of themselves, puttering around the neighborhood in small groups rather than having an adult caregiver and being restricted to the home (Mosier & Rogoff, 2002). If help was needed, nearby older children or adults assisted the children.

Under such circumstances, children have the freedom to watch ongoing community activities and to engage in them according to their interest and emerging skills. One Mayan 3-year-old who was more religious than the rest of her family usually went to evening church meetings by herself. She would put on her shawl at about 7:30 P.M. (well after dusk) and walk the four blocks to church, returning about two hours later (Rogoff, 1981a). She was responsible for herself in the presence of many familiar neighbors and took part in community events unrestrictedly. The next section focuses on such participation in—or segregation from—the mature activities of the community.

Children's Participation in or Segregation from Mature Community Activities

One of the most powerful variations in children's lives in different cultural communities is the extent to which they are allowed to participate in and observe adult activities. Segregation of children from mature community activities is taken for granted in middle-class settings, but it is rare in many other communities.

Differences in children's opportunities to learn from ongoing mature activities relate closely to many other differences in cultural patterns of child rearing (Rogoff, 1990; Morelli, Rogoff, & Angelillo, 2002). Children's participation in versus segregation from the range of community activities is central to one of the cultural patterns of regularity that I foregrounded in Chapter 1. Here I focus on describing community differences in children's opportunities to learn through observing and beginning to participate in mature community activities early in life. Later, I relate these differences to other aspects of children's lives, including reliance on formal schooling, the cognitive skills that are valued, children's motivation and interests, communication between caregivers and children, and peer relations.

Access to Mature Community Activities

In some communities, children are included in almost all community and family events, day and night, from infancy (see figure 4.4). Little in the adult world is hidden from small children, who are usually present in adult settings. For example, 2- to 4-year-olds in Kokwet (East Africa) spent much of their time in the company of others, often seated with siblings and half-siblings on a cow hide laid on the ground, watching the goings-on of older family members (Harkness & Super, 1992a). In urban Cairo, "children are totally incorporated into the community and highly visible, no matter what time of day or night" (Singerman, 1995, p. 98). Young Efe children (in the Democratic Republic of Congo) roam wherever they like in their camps, where there are few walls blocking the view of ongoing activities (Morelli & Tronick, 1992). Where toddlers share sleeping quarters with parents, nighttime does not involve segregation from the social life in which they participate by day (Hewlett, 1992; LeVine et al., 1994; Morelli, Rogoff, Oppenheim, & Goldsmith, 1992; New, 1994).

In contrast, middle-class European American infants are in the unusual situation—speaking in worldwide and historical terms—of being segregated from other people throughout the night as well as at times during the day (Morelli et al., 1992; Ward, 1971; Whiting, 1981). Massachusetts middle-class babies were observed to spend their time alternately in intense interaction or in isolation, whereas Italian middle-class babies were much more often in the company of others (New & Richman, 1996). Working-class African American infants were almost never observed being alone; they were held and carried day and night and were usually in the company of more than one other person (Heath, 1983).

In a number of communities around the world, young children have greater opportunity to observe adult work activities than do middle-class

FIGURE 4.4

A small child keeps company, even as she snoozes, with a fisherman as he weaves pieces of reed for the construction of fish pots on the island of St. Lucia (Caribbean).

U.S. children. For example, Aka mothers and fathers (in Central Africa) hunt, butcher, and share game while holding their infants (Hewlett, 1992).

Similarly, toddlers have routinely had the opportunity to observe their families' economic activities in a Mayan town, a tribal community in India, and a hunting-and-gathering community in the Democratic Republic of Congo. They could watch adults weaving, tailoring, and shopkeeping in the home, gathering food and building houses near home, or laboring in fields or in factories (Morelli et al., 2002; Rogoff et al., 1993). In contrast, young middle-class children from Turkey and from several U.S. cities generally stayed with parents or day care providers whose work was limited to household chores, errands, and tending children. The structure of middle-class U.S. adults' days makes it difficult for children to observe and participate in the full range of their community's economic and social activities.

"Pitching in" from Early Childhood

Perhaps related to the early opportunity to observe adult work, children in many communities begin to participate in family work at an early age (see figure 4.5). By age 3 to 5, Marquesan (Polynesian) children learn simple

FIGURE 4.5

A young child in the Ituri Forest of the Democratic Republic of Congo assists an adult in preparing leaves for a building project.

household skills and are expected to gather wood, pick up leaves, sweep, and run to the store on errands. "They watch others work and then perform the task once they know how" (Martini & Kirkpatrick, 1992, p. 211).

Similarly, 4-year-old children from a farming community in East Africa spent 35% of their time doing chores, and 3-year-olds did chores during 25% of their time (Harkness & Super, 1992a). In contrast, middle-class U.S. children of the same ages spent none to 1% of their time doing chores, though they did spend 4% to 5% of their time accompanying others in chores (such as helping the mother peel a carrot or fold laundry).

In West Africa, children often begin to perform errands around the house from the time they begin to walk and have simple duties from age 2 or 3; their roles increase with their competence. They have an important part in the work of their compound and village and see themselves as useful members of their community. The small income their work produces often makes a crucial difference in family survival. Young children participate in the social as well as the economic life of their community, as they are included in all settings. They are part of the adult world, not "in the way." In addition, child work is an essential component of socialization, "the core process by which children learn roles and skills" (Nsamenang, 1992, p. 156; see also Ogunnaike & Houser, 2002).

Aka children (of Central Africa) are almost constantly with their parents, and learn to use knives and digging tools in infancy and to cook on a fire as toddlers. They know most of the skills needed for survival when they are 7 to 12 years old: how to kill and butcher large game, soothe a newborn, identify edible mushrooms, make medicines, trap porcupines, and plant manioc (Hewlett, 1992).

Most 8-year-old girls in a Gusii community (in Kenya) could carry out most household work (LeVine et al., 1994). Two 6-year-olds were observed raising a field of maize from planting to harvest, by themselves.

Nowadays in middle-class communities, children are usually segregated from the work and social world of adults (Beach, 1988; Crouter, 1979; Hentoff, 1976). However, in the colonial period in Western Europe and the United States, workplace and home were typically not separated. Child rearing involved many relatives and nonkin, and learning took place by participating in ongoing activities (Chudacoff, 1989; Hareven, 1989; see figure 4.6). In colonial times, U.S. children as young as 4 years participated skillfully in family economic work (Ehrenreich & English, 1978).

Even now in the United States, if parents work at home, children are often involved (Orellana, 2001). In a study of U.S. children whose parents worked at home, all children who were old enough to talk had concrete knowledge of their parents' work (in occupations such as day care provider, mechanic, chef, translator, cabinet maker, veterinarian, and fine arts dealer;

FIGURE 4.6

"Meal time during field work." Dutch children accompany their family in work (no date given).

Beach, 1988). They were able to label jobs, describe procedures, and name tools. The children were all involved with their parents' work in a developmental progression from playing and watching, to performing simple tasks, to carrying out regular assistance, to engaging in regular paid work.

A 12-year-old girl who chopped vegetables and garnishes for the family restaurant on a regularly paid basis described her gradual introduction to the use of sharp knives through observation: "Sometimes when [Dad's] boning the veal and we have nothing to do cause we don't have TV, so we just set and watch him. . . . [Once] I was watching him and he started to show me how to do stuff [chop vegetables]." The interviewer asked, "The knives must be sharp—how did you learn to use them?" and the girl responded, "We've been using sharp knives since we were little, cause we were always watching my Dad and stuff" (pp. 216–217).

The preschool-age children who were present as their parents worked engaged in playing-watching: playing with scraps of yarn or cloth, needles or tools for a knitting machine, or the paper punch of a secretary. A 7-month-old who was in his mother's beauty shop was given curlers and a shop towel to play with, helped up to the large mirror to play, spun around in the chair, and set under a dryer blowing cool air. The children made an imperceptible transition into helping with simple tasks. An example was provided by a 3-year-old girl who reported how she helps her mother sew sweaters: "I pop it [thread] into the little hole for Mommy and then I put it through the holes in the sewing machine" (p. 217).

Over the 20th century, fewer and fewer mature skills have been employed in U.S. homes that would help prepare children for adulthood (Ehrenreich & English, 1978). Efforts to protect U.S. children from economic exploitation and physical dangers, to extend their schooling, and to remove them from economic competition with adults have reduced the chances of their learning firsthand about adult work and other mature activities.

Excluding Children and Youth from Labor — and from Productive Roles

From the end of the 18th into the beginning of the 20th century in the United States, the expanding industrial economy took shocking advantage of child labor (Chudacoff, 1989; Ehrenreich & English, 1978). When the Industrial Revolution came to America, in the cotton industry in New England, children formed the labor force. In 1801, the first cotton yarn factory's labor force was composed of 100 children, ranging in age from 4 to 10 years (Bremner, 1970). Within a few decades, cotton manufacture grew into a widespread industry; children formed about half of the labor force of the mills in Massachusetts, Rhode Island, and Connecticut. A child under age 10 usually earned about enough in a six-day week (working sunrise to sunset) to pay for six pounds of flour or two pounds of sugar. Advertisers of machinery assured prospective customers that machines could be managed by children from 5 to 10 years old.

Children employed in industry were exploited as cheap labor under extreme and dangerous conditions (Bremner, 1970; Ehrenreich & English, 1978). Four-year-olds worked 16-hour shifts rolling cigars or sorting beads in tenements in New York and 5-year-olds worked night shifts in cotton mills in the South, until they fainted. In 1900, a third of mill laborers in the southern states were children—half of them between 10 and 13 years old, and many younger. (See figure 4.7.)

Child labor in industry was considered ethically as well as economically valuable through most of the 1800s. But between the 1880s and 1930s, prohibitions on child labor arose in response to unhealthy conditions in industry, as well as the labor unions' efforts to protect jobs for adults (Bremner, 1971; Chudacoff, 1989).

The exploitation of children in factories differed in many ways from the participation in work and mature social life that had often characterized U.S. children's "pitching in" in the family's work on small farms or businesses in preceding centuries, and that still occurs in many communities (including some in the Unites States; Orellana, 2001). Children who pitch in as a member of a social and economic family unit work in conjunction with people whose lives they share. Work is not divided from family social life. The children share in the product of their work and generally can see how their role fits in the overall process (as opposed to being limited to a repetitive, small piece in an assembly line).

Of course, children working on the family farm or business are sometimes exploited as well (Nieuwenhuys, 2000). However, the possibilities for learning and satisfaction from contributing to productive work appear greater when children engage with relatives, with whom they have more than an economic relationship. Prior to industrialization, children collaborated with family members in the more varied family work as well as social life that was common before the division of labor of factory life.

Currently, most children and youth in the United States have very few opportunities to contribute to their families and communities or to work with adults to accomplish anything—missing a valuable arrangement that can contribute both to children's learning and to their satisfaction. Al-

FIGURE 4.7

At the turn of the century, "breaker boys" age 8 or 9 years labored "from 7 A.M. to dark picking slate from chutes of dusty, tumbling coal—for wages of $1 to $3 a week. . . . An accident rate three times that of adults" (Boorstin et al., 1975, p. 251). When Lewis W. Hine's photographs, like this one, publicized the situation, states passed laws limiting the work day to 10 hours; not until the 1930s was such child labor made illegal in the United States.

though the kind of pitching in with adults that has been common in child-hood across history is not necessarily limited to work situations, its restriction in the domain of work seems to have limited its use more generally. Commenting on the reduction in circumstances in which adults work side-by-side with youth to accomplish a joint task together, Shirley Brice Heath pointed out the importance of such situations for U.S. child and youth development:

> Currently, aside from agricultural households, relatively few families spend time in cross-age tasks that require planning, practice, and productive work across a period of several weeks or months. Yet these are the very situations in which children are most likely to engage in work on tasks beneficial to them and others and to receive extensive authentic practice [in] planning ahead, linking current actions to future outcomes, and self-assessing and self-correcting their own be-haviors and attitudes. (1998, p. 217)[4]

With a lack of opportunities to observe adult economic activities and social relationships, U.S. children and youth may have little chance to begin to make sense of the mature roles of their community (Panel on Youth of the President's Science Advisory Committee, 1974; Rogoff, 1990). In middle-class communities, instead of an arrangement in which children pitch in with adults in mature activities, childhood often involves adults creating specialized situations to *prepare* children for later entry in mature activities.

Adults "Preparing" Children or Children Joining Adults

An alternative to children's observing and participating in the activities of their communities is for adults to introduce them to mature skills in specialized, child-focused settings that are created to instruct children, outside of mature community activities. A prime site for this is school, which is usually organized to keep children away from adult settings and to "pre-pare" them to enter mature roles by giving them nonproductive, specialized exercises.

Specialized child-focused activities with younger children are common in middle-class families and communities and rare in several communities in which young children more often are in the presence of adult work. These specialized child-focused activities include play with adults as play-

---

[4] Heath's research has identified this as an important feature of a number of voluntary community youth organizations (such as drama, arts, sports, and service clubs) in which young people learn and demonstrate important planning, hypothetical thinking, language, and leadership skills that they often do not show in schools.

mates or as organizers of children's play, lessons given at home in preparation for later engagement in school or work activities, and adults serving as peers in child-focused conversations (Rogoff, 1990; Morelli et al., 2002).

In communities in which children are not segregated from observing and participating in the activities of their elders, the responsibility for learning may fall less on those who "raise" the children than on the children themselves "coming up" (to use the words of the working-class African American community studied by Heath, 1983). Such children can learn about the mature roles of their community as they are embedded in the everyday lives and work of their extended family and community. In these settings, children, with their elders, may be likely to coordinate in groups.

Engaging in Groups or Dyads

In many communities, infants and children are oriented to the group's activities rather than to exclusive, one-to-one (dyadic) interaction with a caregiver. An article questioning the applicability for Nigeria of current Western child development research called attention to the atypicality of interacting in pairs:

> The mother-child dyad may not be any more important than the older sibling-child dyad, the co-wife–child dyad, or the grandmother-child dyad. There may be no one who can be designated as the primary caretaker. Furthermore, the social context of development may rarely include *any* type of dyadic formation: There may typically be more than one person interacting with the child at any given moment. (Wilson-Oyclaran, 1989, p. 56)

Children of different communities have widely differing experience with engaging in groups larger than two. In a study of Marquesan (South Pacific) 3- to 5-year-olds, the children played in groups of three to six children in 75% of the observations and in groups of seven to ten children in another 18% of the observations. They never played alone and they played with just one other child in only 7% of the observations. In comparison, U.S. children played alone in 36% of observations and with just one partner in 35% of observations (Martini, 1994b).

Similarly, book-reading sessions in Tongan, Samoan, and Maori families in New Zealand usually involved more than one other person besides the preschool child. In contrast, book-reading sessions in European-heritage middle-class New Zealand families usually involved only one person reading with the child, even though most of the families contained older children (McNaughton, 1995).

Children's engagement in groups seems to fit in important ways with their community's usual forms of adult engagement and with opportunities to learn from involvement in adult activities. Community differences in children's engagement in groups can be seen in the orientation of caregivers with infants (face-to-face versus oriented to a group). Differences are also apparent in cultural prioritizing of dyadic versus group social relations in homes as well as in instructional settings.

Infant Orientation: Face-to-Face with Caregiver versus Oriented to the Group

It is common for middle-class European American infants to engage primarily with one other person at a time in dyadic, face-to-face interactions. Middle-class European American mothers and infants were observed to engage face-to-face nearly twice as often as middle-class Japanese mothers and infants in home observations (Bornstein, Azuma, Tamis-LeMonda, & Ogino, 1990).

Intimate face-to-face mother-infant interaction may be unusual in communities where infants are participating members of the larger community. In many communities, children are held facing the same direction as the caregiver, oriented to observe the same things as the caregiver and taking part in the same activities (Heath, 1983; Martini & Kirkpatrick, 1981; Sostek et al., 1981; see figure 4.8).

For example, Kaluli mothers in Polynesia encourage even newborns to interact with others, facing their babies outward so that they both see and are seen by others in their social group. Mothers often face infants toward older children and speak for them in a special high-pitched register to which the older children are expected to respond as conversation (Schieffelin, 1991).

Marquesan mothers (in the South Pacific) appeared strained and awkward when asked to interact with their babies in a face-to-face orientation (Martini & Kirkpatrick, 1981). Babies were usually held facing outward and encouraged to interact with others (especially slightly older siblings), not the mother. They were participating members of the community, embedded in a complex social world. Marquesan mothers arranged infants' social interactions with others, encouraging them to engage broadly with community members:

> As soon as infants can sit, caregivers turn them to face outward and encourage them to attend to others: for example, "Wave hello," "Smile at brother." Caregivers interpret slight moves by the baby as attempts to initiate interaction: "Oh, you want to go to sister?"

FIGURE 4.8

An Otavalo Indian infant has the opportunity to look over mother's shoulder to observe the market, reached by walking for miles over trails in the Andean highlands of Ecuador. Mother and infant watch the crowd and linger over each purchase.

> Adult caregivers orchestrate the baby's early interactions. They teach preschoolers how to keep the baby engaged. They discourage babies from becoming self-absorbed, directing them to attend to others. They call their names, jostle them, and tell them to look at so-and-so. If these efforts fail, they assume babies are tired and put them down to sleep. (Martini & Kirkpatrick, 1992, p. 209)

Similarly, West African infants in working-class families living in Paris are encouraged to participate in group relationships (Rabain Jamin, 1994). Mothers oriented 3-month-old babies to interact with third parties by turning the baby to another person and prompting, "Go answer Wendy." Sometimes the third party is not even present, and is evoked in a playful register that brings distant relationships (such as with the grandmother in Africa or brothers and sisters at school) to the present situation through simulation. In comparison with French mothers, whose exchanges with their babies were mostly dyadic and concerned the babies' utterances to a third party in only 9% of their comments, 40% of the African mothers' comments in interaction with the babies involved reference to third parties. The African mothers modeled and simulated communication emphasizing the importance of group relationships in which the children already have prescribed roles, even with distant people. The differences suggest use of distinct cultural prototypes of social relations.

Dyadic versus Group Prototypes for Social Relations

Middle-class European American social interaction seems to follow a dyadic prototype of one-partner-at-a-time. Even when a group is present, individuals often interact dyadically, treating the group as multiple dyads rather than as an integrated multiparty group (Rogoff et al., 1991, 1993).

In contrast, it is common in a Guatemalan Mayan community for the social organization to involve a group of people interacting in a circle, with complex multidirectional shared engagements (Chavajay, 1993; Chavajay & Rogoff, 2002). Toddlers usually appeared to be smoothly integrated into the social fabric, not recipients of exclusive one-person-at-a-time attention (Rogoff et al., 1993). They fit into the flow of ongoing social events, interacting as members of a group, rather than in dyadic interactions or solitary activity. They coordinated their involvement with the different agendas and multiparty interactions of the group.

The interactions of a Mayan 20-month-old illustrate how coordinating with a group involves more than successive dyadic engagements:

> María watched her mother present the jar to explore while María simultaneously handed another toy over to her cousin; she monitored her mother demonstrating the jumping-jack while she extracted a tiny doll from the jar; she noticed everything the interviewers did without breaking her activity with the jar; she monitored her cousin subtly taking various objects while she admired the tiny doll and skillfully put it in the jar; and on and on. (Rogoff et al., 1993, pp. 50–51)

María *could* have interacted with her mother and then with her cousin, in successive interactions with several dyads. Instead, she smoothly coordinated her monitoring and protective efforts toward her encroaching cousin along with her engagement with her mother regarding the novel objects. Her involvements could not have been disentangled into successive one-to-one dyadic engagements but appeared rather to be a complex, multiway intertwining of the various contributions of the participants to the whole event.

Evidence supporting the idea that the dyad is treated as the basic unit of middle-class European American relations is seen in the way that adult conversations are often interrupted by young children. If a mother does not stop what she is doing to attend to the child, the child may grab her chin to turn her head or stand right between the mother and another adult. The children have learned to expect that social engagement is one-to-one and they want their turn.

Middle-class U.S. toddlers more frequently interrupted adult activity than did Mayan toddlers, perhaps because the middle-class mothers were less likely to attend to subtle bids for attention during their other ongoing activity (Rogoff et al., 1993). When engaged with other adults, the U.S. middle-class mothers often ceased interacting with their children. In contrast, the Mayan mothers maintained their supportive and attentive assistance to the children even when interacting with other adults. Thus, when middle-class U.S. mothers were involved in adult activities, toddlers may have had to resort to strong means to get attention, whereas Mayan toddlers received attention as a matter of course even while the mothers were engaged with adult activities.

An example of the middle-class U.S. pattern of dyadic attention and child interruption was provided by 20-month-old Judy, who noticed that her sister had taken the baby doll with which Judy had been playing.

> As her mother chatted with the interviewer, Judy quietly murmured, "Baby, baby, baby." With no response, Judy escalated her tone and shook her head, "*Bay*-be, *bay*-be, *bay*-be . . ." She pulled on her mother's leg, "*Bay*-bee, I *wan* it!" Her mother paid no attention to Judy, and continued talking.
>
> Judy demanded, "*Bay*-bee, I *wan* it!!" over and over, occasionally looking at her sister while her mother continued talking to the adults.
>
> Finally, when her mother finished her story to the interviewer, she looked around, asking with puzzlement, "Well, where did the baby go?" It appeared that the mother really did not know that the sister had taken the doll and that Judy had been trying to get her to help get it back—she encouraged Judy to find it as if it were misplaced. Judy complained, "Mom" in a pitiful tone, and waited for her mother to do something, but her mother asked curiously, "Well, where do you think the baby went?" Judy fiddled with another object and her mother resumed talking with the interviewer.
>
> When her sister moved away with the doll, Judy resumed her requests—"I wanna baby"—softly and persistently several times, then she looked at her mother and said with more force, "I *wan* a baby!"
>
> Not until the sister called across the room—"I *want* it!"—did

the mother attend. She quit the adult conversation and engaged in an extensive child-focused episode to resolve the issue by negotiating with the sister to return the doll to Judy. Then she resumed talking with the interviewer, and Judy gave a sneaky smile to the camera operator. (Rogoff et al., 1993, pp. 96–97)

This incident, full of interruption and dyadic attention by the mother, contrasts with the smooth, unobtrusive multiway group communication without interruptions during an episode involving 18-month-old Nila from the Mayan community in Guatemala. Nila needed help getting cookies from a plastic wrapper during an adult activity:

> During the interview, when Nila held the package up to her mother, her mother asked if she wanted a cookie, and Nila nodded yes. Her mother smiled quietly at Nila and opened the cookie package as she attended to the interviewers.
>
> Nila attended to the interviewers too, so when her mother got the cookie out of the package, she offered it to Nila by moving her own arm, on which Nila's hand rested, so that Nila's hand touched the cookie. Nila took the cookie and ate it, then subtly requested another by gently pushing her mother's hand toward the cookies beside her on the patio. As the mother continued to attend to the interviewers she readily responded to Nila's gesture and picked up the package without looking at Nila or the package. She handed it to Nila, then glanced down at it quietly and took it back [the package was difficult for a toddler to open], and looked back at the interviewers as she took out another cookie. Once the cookie was out of the package, she took Nila's hand and moved it to the cookie that she held in her other hand, still conversing with the interviewers. She only glanced down at the package once during this unobtrusive event. The interaction with Nila did not disrupt the flow of the interview in the least. (p. 97)

Children with experience coordinating in a group may more easily maintain involvement in activities that are not directed to them as audience or dyadic partners. For example, when pairs of 9-year-olds were asked to teach a younger child to play a game, Navajo 9-year-olds were more likely to build on each other's comments to the younger child than were European American 9-year-olds. The European American 9-year-olds more often offered two parallel, unrelated lines of one-to-one instruction to the younger child (Ellis & Gauvain, 1992). The Navajo 9-year-olds remained engaged in the task, observing the other children, even when they were not controlling the game moves. European American 9-year-olds were distracted when their partner and not they were controlling the game, sometimes to the point of leaving the task.

It seems that children who have facility in coordinating with others in a group may have an easier time building on each other's contributions to a shared group endeavor. For example, when first-grade teachers in Oregon started arranging group projects in class, groups of Indian children worked smoothly without designating a leader. They worked quickly and effectively without needing intervention from the teacher and without conflict over who should be doing what (Philips, 1983). In contrast, in Anglo groups, some children tried to control the talk and action of the others, and the groups often disputed how to carry out the tasks. The Anglo groups often needed the teacher's intervention and had trouble completing the task.

Cultural variations in the ways people engage in groups seem also to reflect experience with the dyadic social organization common in Western schooling. Mayan mothers who had little or no experience in Western schooling usually worked in a multidirectional, coordinated way when assembling a puzzle with three related children (Chavajay & Rogoff, 2002). In contrast, Mayan mothers who had extensive schooling experience often divided the task and directed the children to work in pairs or solo, rather than using the more traditional Mayan social organization of fluid collaboration in a multiparty group. Schooling seems to play an important cultural role in the structure of social relations.

Dyadic versus Multiparty Group Relations in Schooling

In traditional U.S. classrooms, where many people are present, interaction is nonetheless usually structured dyadically, as two sides of a conversation. Students are expected to speak only to the teacher and only one at a time or in unison so they can act as one side of a dyad.

The use of cooperative structures in U.S. classrooms has begun only recently. Often, children who are used to a classroom structure that is managed dyadically by the teacher have difficulty learning how to work together effectively in groups (Sharan & Sharan, 1992; Solomon, Watson, Schaps, Battistich, & Solomon, 1990). To incorporate various types of group learning arrangements such as cooperative learning and whole-class discussion, teachers often find that they first have to establish new classroom practices that help children learn group norms of interaction (O'Connor & Michaels, 1996).

Observations of indigenous teachers sometimes illuminate differences between the usual dyadic structure of formal schooling and the multidirectional structure of interaction that seems to be common in indigenous communities. For example, compared with European-descent teachers,

Alaskan Native teachers often employ a more even distribution of speaking turns among students and teachers. In addition, Alaskan Native teachers foster speaking as a group rather than calling on individuals in sequence, as in the following observation in an elementary school classroom with a White teacher and a Yup'ik aide:

> The teacher had arranged the desks of her several students into a large rectangle, and had the students face her and look at her. Her lesson format [was to ask] a question, [wait] for the children to raise their hands to be nominated, and then [call on] a single student to answer. . . . Student responses were brief, in keeping with the focused information requested in the question.
>
> In another corner of the room, a Yup'ik bilingual aide [worked with a group of approximately six students, seated] facing each other, with only half of them facing the bilingual aide. . . . The students spoke to each other and to the bilingual aide in Yup'ik, although the students were not facing the bilingual aide directly. The aide allowed the students to speak "out of turn"—that is, without being nominated by herself and without waiting for a student who already had the floor to finish speaking.
>
> [Then] the classroom teacher walked over to the group. She told the students to face the aide, straighten their chairs, and pay attention. She waited until the students had shifted their positions according to her instructions before returning to her own group of students. . . . After the teacher had left and the aide resumed the story lesson, the students were reticent and spoke very little.
>
> [The next day, the aide said that the teacher assumes] that "everybody face this way" and "all eyes on me" (the teacher) is synonymous with communication in the classroom. [The Yup'ik way of communicating] is a conversation in my class. [The students] speak to each other freely, helping each other out on a subject. [They are] trying to let the other students understand. . . . They build on each other. (Lipka, 1994, pp. 64–65)

U.S. classrooms are commonly structured with the teacher taking a speaking turn between each child turn, in what Philips (1983) refers to as the "switchboard model." Children address only the teacher, seldom taking other children's ideas into account in building their own contributions.

In contrast, Japanese elementary school classrooms often involve conversations in which children build on each other's ideas in exploring a problem (Rogoff & Toma, 1997). Japanese preschool teachers value having a large number of children in a class so that children learn to work together without the teacher as a constant one-on-one intermediary (Tobin, Wu, & Davidson, 1991).

Some innovations in U.S. schooling also prioritize organizing instruction with children building ideas together (Brown & Campione, 1990; Rogoff, Goodman Turkanis, & Bartlett, 2001; Tharp & Gallimore, 1988). A number of scholars have suggested that learning in multiparty groups may be especially appropriate for children of African American, Hawaiian American, Native American, and Latino heritage (Boykin, 1994; Duran, 1994; Haynes & Gebreyesus, 1992; Lee, 2001; Little Soldier, 1989; Losey, 1995; Tharp & Gallimore, 1988).

The cast of characters and scenarios of child rearing, along with cultural prototypes of the structure of relationships, are closely involved in children's development. Attachment between infants and family members is related to issues of survival, cultural values regarding relationships, and community arrangements regarding families. Who else is available relates to how family and community specialize in caregiving, companionship, and instructional roles.

Community arrangements contribute in important ways to children's opportunities to learn the mature ways of their community from observing and joining in with their elders. If young children cannot enter community activities, adults may design specialized child-focused settings for them, such as schooling and the kind of adult-child interactions that often characterize middle-class parenting. Adult-child play, lessons, and child-focused conversations seem to be a specific cultural solution to providing children with preparation for later mature contributions, while segregating them from participation during childhood. Whether interaction in groups is structured in successive one-to-one engagement or in fluid multiparty engagement seems to vary with cultural emphasis on children's broad participation in the community and to connect with the cultural institution of Western schooling.

The next chapter deals with developmental transitions from infancy through adulthood as people develop in phases recognized by their community. Some of the first developmental transitions mark an infant's survival and welcome the new person to the family and community. Many of the later transitions recognize expanding roles in knowing how to coordinate with groups and handle responsibilities of their community's cultural traditions and institutions. Developmental phases marked in the lives of individuals often serve as recognition of their expected roles in their cultural communities, as people transform their participation in sociocultural activities.

5

Developmental Transitions in Individuals' Roles in Their Communities

A central question in developmental psychology has been to identify the nature and timing of people's transitions from one phase of development to the next—from infancy to childhood through adulthood. In ethnographic accounts in many communities, researchers have also documented stages or phases of development identified by the people they study. For example, in the Navajo model of development, the infant's first laugh is recognized as a major transition, as explained by a Navajo mother:

> At two or three months they have the First Laugh ceremony. . . .
> Whoever makes the baby laugh then has to give a big feast for the
> baby. [This person] puts on the feast for the baby, in his place. This
> makes sure that the baby will be generous, and happy, and jokeful,
> and so that he will communicate well. The baby's first laugh is really
> when he becomes a person. (Chisholm, 1996, p. 173)

Developmental transitions are commonly portrayed by researchers as belonging to individuals, as in the stages of cognitive development described by Piaget. However, transitions across childhood can also be considered cultural, community events that occur as individuals change their roles in their community's structure. Often, developmental phases are identified in terms of the person's developing relationships and community roles. For example, development to maturity in the Navajo model is a process of acquiring knowledge to be able to take responsibility for oneself and others. When asked about the goal of development, one Navajo replied:

> Being a leader of the people is the highest form of development, like its goal. The whole thing is responsibility—taking care of things. First you just learn to take care of yourself. Then some things, then some animals, then your family. Then you help all your people and the whole world. Talking real well is when you're ready to help the people, talking real well in front of big crowds of people, then you're ready to start helping. (Chisholm, 1996, p. 171)

Following the pre-stage of infancy, the Navajo model distinguishes the following stages across the life span (according to Chisholm, 1996, building especially on Begishi's scheme):

1. One becomes aware (2–4 years, with the first indicators of self-discipline)
2. One becomes self-aware (4–6 years, with awareness of one's own thought and will)
3. One begins to think (6–9 years, initiating appropriate, respectful contributions)
4. One's thought begins to exist (10–15 years, carrying out responsibilities without needing help or supervision and understanding one's place within the larger scheme)
5. One begins to think for oneself (15–18 years, fully able to manage one's own affairs)
6. One begins thinking for all things (17–22 years, mastery of every aspect of the responsibilities of adult life)
7. One begins to think ahead for oneself (22–30 years, the successes of one's life are manifested in one's children, and one may begin to take responsibility for others' welfare)
8. One begins to think ahead for all things (30+ years)

Many communities mark developmental transitions with ceremonies. Some transition ceremonies mark valued events and achievements, such as the first smile, first communion, graduation, or onset of menstruation. Others recognize age-based passages, such as the *quinceañera* ceremony and celebration for Mexican and Mexican American girls at age 15 (see figures 5.1, 5.2, and 5.3).

In this chapter, I first examine the contrast between distinguishing phases of life in terms of chronological age or events and achievements valued by the community. Then I consider cultural values related to "rate" of development. The chapter then describes transitions from infancy through

FIGURE 5.1

Helen Soto's first communion, 1944 (Mexican American.)

adulthood and considers how communities value and mark changes of developmental status with specialized events, often differentiating roles by gender. These cultural practices often bring individual development explicitly into relation with social and cultural expectations, marking the transitions not only for individuals but for generations.

Age as a Cultural Metric for Development

Time elapsed since birth has become a defining characteristic of individuals and an organizing principle for people's lives in some communities. The centrality of this measure, and its connections with schooling, are apparent in the observations of a very young 20th-century British girl (3 years 10 months) who announced to her preschool teacher:

> CHILD: Do you know, my baby's one now.
> STAFF: Your baby's coming here when she's older.
> CHILD: She'll go to playgroup when she's two, though.
> STAFF: Will she?
> CHILD: Yeah. Because when you're two you go to . . . Whan I was two I went to a playgroup.
> OTHER CHILD: So did I.
> CHILD: That shows you, that people go to playgroup when they're two.
> STAFF: Why do they go to a playgroup?

CHILD: Because they're not old enough to go to school.

STAFF: I see. And how old were you when you came here, then?

CHILD: Three or four.

STAFF: Three or four. Then what happens when you're five?

CHILD: You go . . . When I'm five I'll only . . . I'll go to a . . . I expect
  I won't come to here any more.

STAFF: Where will you be, then?

CHILD: Be? In a different school, of course. (Tizard & Hughes, 1984,
  pp. 99–100)

In contrast with this ordering of life according to years since birth, in many communities age is not tracked (e.g., Harkness & Super, 1987; Mead, 1935; Rogoff, Sellers, Pirrotta, Fox, & White, 1975; Werner, 1979). In the words of Minnie Aodla Freeman, reporting on a twenty-first birthday celebration in her honor in Ottawa:

FIGURE 5.2

Tom Chong holding his grandnephew, Dean Brian Tom, at the traditional celebration of the child's first month of life, 1956. Tom is their family name; as an older Chinese immigrant with a Chinese given name, Tom Chong put his family name first, according to Chinese custom, but the baby's American given name is first and his family name last (Chinese American).

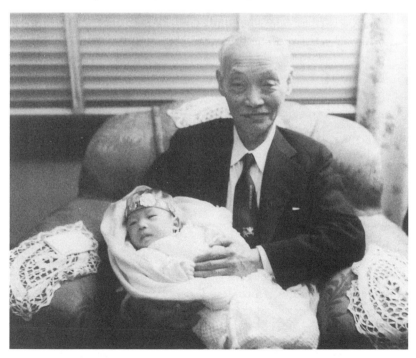

Stella Anaya Ortega and Raul Ortega on Raul's first birthday, July 3, 1948 (Mexican American).

Everybody talked and laughed to each other while I stood in front of the cake, not knowing what to say. I tried to look at each one of them and wondered how many knew that Inuit don't celebrate birthdays, that we don't reckon maturity in terms of years. (1978, pp. 36–37)

In the 1970s in the Mayan community where I worked, mothers' estimates of their children's age usually differed by a year or two from municipal birth records. When I asked the mothers how old they themselves were, they often said, "I don't know, what do you think? 40? Or maybe it's 50." It didn't matter to them.

When I began working in this Mayan town, I was surprised to note that on meeting a child, adults' next question after "What is your name?" was not "How old are you?" but "Who are your mother and father?" Instead of a focus on identity as defined by individuals' progress on a timeline, as is habitual in middle-class European American conversations, the Mayan questions suggest a focus on identity as defined by social relationships and place in the community.

Instead of using time-since-birth as a measure of development, people in small communities like this Mayan town may use relative seniority. People who have known each other all their lives are likely to know who is senior to whom, which may matter for issues of responsibility and privilege. For example, in the local Mayan language, there is one term for older sister and another for younger sister; a female is obliged by the language to distinguish these—there is not a general term for sister that can be used by females. (A similar system applies for males' reference to older/younger brothers.)

Researchers interested in tracking ages can get a pretty good idea of how old people are by investigating who is senior to whom (and whether a person experienced some notable historical event, such as an earthquake or a drought). In addition, people around the world are aware of physical changes across the life span. Sometimes these are used as markers of development, as when the onset of menstruation marks a new phase in female development. Losing baby teeth occurs at a regular enough time in childhood that Western researchers sometimes use this as a substitute for age if they need time-since-birth measurements in communities in which age is not known or recorded. This change is also used as a marker of development in some other communities:

> The Ngoni [of Central Africa] believed that children who had lost their first teeth, and acquired their second, had reached a new stage in their development. The obvious gaps in their mouths were filled, and this might happen between the ages of six-and-a-half and seven-and-a-half, and some of the children might be rather small and slight for their age. Socially, because they had their second teeth, and because it was a sign of physical change recognized for everyone, the Ngoni adult would regard these children as ready for a different kind of life. (Read, 1968, p. 46)

Even in the United States, using time-since-birth as a marker of human development is a rather recent habit. Before the middle of the 1800s, there was little reference to ages in diaries or in expert or popular writing (Chudacoff, 1989). Before the end of the 1800s, people often did not know or have records of their birthdate. It was not until the 20th century that Americans commonly referred to ages and began to celebrate birthdays regularly (see figure 5.4). Cards printed specifically for birthdays did not appear until the 1910s, and not until the 1930s did the birthday ditty "Happy Birthday to You" appear (when it became a hit in a Broadway play). Soon, birthdays became a major industry, and popular culture commonly referred to age norms (for example, popular songs referring to "sweet sixteen" as a time when a person is supposed to first fall in love).[1]

---

[1] The emphasis on age continues in the United States, with age-grading in many institutions, marketing of toys and movies, publications for specific age groups (e.g., *Seventeen* magazine), laws, and advice books.

FIGURE 5.4

Alfreda Masters (on the left)
and sister Shirley, ages 6 and 7,
each with her own birthday
cake, February 6, 1947, in Los
Angeles.

The focus on age as a way to divide the life stream is thus a recent practice, speaking in terms of the history of humanity, now widespread in the industrialized United States and Europe. It fits with other aspects of industrial society's developing priorities and practices, specifically the goal of efficient management of schools and other institutions, modeled on the newly developed factory system, with its division of labor and assembly line:

Awareness of age and the age grading of activities and institutions were part of a larger process of segmentation within American society during the late nineteenth and early twentieth centuries. These periods marked an era in which science, industry, and communications influenced people's lives in revolutionary ways. New emphases on efficiency and productivity stressed numerical measurement as a means of imposing order and predictability on human life and the environment. Scientists, engineers, and corporate managers strove for precision and control through the application of specialization and expertise. These same endeavors were applied to human institutions and activities—schools, medical care, social organizations, and leisure. The impetus for rationality and measurement also included the establishment of orderly categories to facilitate precise understanding and analysis. Age became a prominent criterion in this process of classification. (Chudacoff, 1989, p. 5)

Developmental Transitions Marking Change in Relation to the Community

In some communities, developmental phases are not based on chronological age or physical changes. Instead, they center on socially recognized events, such as naming (see figure 5.5).

FIGURE 5.5

According to Mardell Hogan Plainfeather, this appears to be the end of a picnic feast in honor of the child whom Bear Ground holds in his arms, probably for this Crow child's sacred naming ceremony, at which prayers are offered for the future of the child and clan ties are strengthened. Mary Bear Ground is the little girl on the left, and on the extreme left is Open Eye Old Lady (or With Her Eyes Open), 1910.

The naming of a child marks the beginning of personhood in Cameroon (West Africa). Children serve a spiritual function, connecting with ancestors who have left the world of the living but have not gone far. Pregnancy denotes God's approval of the ancestors' wish to send a representative into the community through this couple (Nsamenang, 1992). The infants are not regarded as belonging to this world until they have been incorporated into the world of the living through naming, usually when the umbilical stump falls off (about the seventh day after birth). Before naming, the newborn is believed to belong more to the spirit world than the material world and could be "taken away" (that is, die) at any time. Children who die before naming are suspected of being "spirit" children, and in some communities are buried without mourning and are not considered as having lived. Naming is thus an occasion for rejoicing in the child's remaining with the world of the living—an initiation into the human community. Because infant mortality is high, a week is a critical period for "assessing God's willingness and final decision regarding the parents' worth for his precious gift" (p. 142). Other local socially marked transitions include the onset of smiling, beginning to talk, social maturity in being trusted to run errands and conduct oneself well, the appearance of secondary sex characteristics, marriage, parenthood, and death.

Around the world, distinctions in stages of development are often defined in terms of the child's beginning to participate in the family or community in a new way. For example, European American middle-class families often distinguish when an infant first makes a social smile or begins to talk—important transitions in infants' relations with their caregivers. Subsequent European American developmental transitions often center on children's participation in a key societal institution—school: preschooler, elementary age, high schooler. Other common U.S. transitions are tightly age-governed, but also mark new types of involvement in community activities, such as ages at which young people are allowed to drive a car, vote, and drink.

Other ways of delineating stages of development also do so with reference to children's relations to other people and the community. Margaret Mead referred to four major age grades:

"Lap children" spend most of their time on someone's lap or in their physical presence.

"Knee children" stay near the knees of a caregiver or move in an area that is closely monitored by caregivers.

"Yard children" roam more widely but stay close to home.

"Community children" go beyond the home and participate in other community institutions, such as school or market.

These phases of development identify children's changing relations with others in their communities (Whiting & Edwards, 1988).

Rates of Passing Developmental "Milestones"

There is a great deal of variation in how soon children reach developmental "milestones," such as beginning to smile, sit, walk, talk, and be responsible for various aspects of family life:

> [Middle-class U.S. children] may be highly precocious verbally, in some cases speaking in full sentences by the age of 2 according to their parents. These children become adept at imaginative play and at competing for the attention and praise of parents and other adults. Typically, however, these children will also frustrate their parents by slow developmental progress in relation to household responsibilities. (Harkness & Super, 1992a, p. 389)

Such variation is partially based on what is valued in children's cultural communities. For example, European American middle-class families stress the early development of verbal articulateness and assertiveness, whereas Italian signs of maturity focus on sensitivity to the needs of others and graciousness in entering and exiting social situations (Edwards, 1994).

Differences in communities' values and expectations underlie varying parental efforts to help children learn skills (Bril & Sabatier, 1986; Super & Harkness, 1997). African infants routinely surpass U.S. infants in their rate of learning to sit and to walk, but not in learning to crawl or to climb stairs (Kilbride, 1980; Super, 1981). This may be because African parents provide experiences for their babies that are intended to teach sitting and walking. Sitting skills are encouraged by propping very young infants in a sitting position supported by rolled blankets in a hole in the ground. Walking skills are encouraged by exercising the newborn's walking reflex and by bouncing babies on their feet. But crawling is discouraged, and stair-climbing skills may be limited by the absence of stairs.

In some communities, walking sooner is valued; in others, it is not desired. In Wogeo, New Guinea, infants were not allowed to crawl and discouraged from walking until nearly 2 years of age so that they know how to take care of themselves and avoid dangers before moving about freely. An infant who showed an interest in moving about would be immediately picked up or put firmly in a corner. Toward the end of the second year, children learned to walk well within two or three days:

So interesting

> No one seems to think that active encouragement of any kind is necessary. When I told the natives how we coax our babies to stand at a

much earlier age, they admitted that such methods might be suitable where there was no fireplace or veranda from which to tumble, but they openly laughed at me for speaking of "teaching" children to walk. A child walks of its own accord, they said, once it has reached the appropriate stage of growth; I would be saying next that trees had to be instructed in how to bear fruit. (Hogbin, 1943, p. 302)

In contrast, learning how to talk in Wogeo was regarded as requiring instruction. Wogeo mothers imitated infants' babbling and repeated words to infants while feeding them. Names of objects were taught by pointing at something and saying its name over and over until the child repeated it:

> As she prepares the meal, for example, [the mother] may say, "This is a pot (*bwara*), pot, pot. I am putting food into a pot, pot, pot. You say it: 'pot, pot, pot.' Now, what is this?—a pot, pot, pot." Other persons present take up the lesson in their turn, remarking, "Yes, a pot, pot, pot. Your mother puts food into the pot, pot, pot." "Pot, pot, pot," replies the child. "Yes, pot, pot, pot," echo the adults. (p. 303)

Guatemalan Mayan mothers reported that their children learned to walk and talk by watching others or with encouragement; few reported teaching the children to help them achieve these milestones. Mothers from a tribal farming community in India often simply shrugged when asked whether and how they taught their toddlers appropriate behavior or etiquette or said simply that children "just learn" (see Seymour, 1999).

In contrast, middle-class mothers in the United States and Turkey reported trying to advance the pace of their children's development, instructing them in walking, talking, or helping around the house (Rogoff et al., 1993). These mothers appeared to be concerned with developmental milestones and to consider themselves responsible for the children's rate of development. One U.S. mother, who had devised an extensive curriculum of games to teach her 17-month-old to read letters and to count, specified her child's progress in terms of Piagetian stages of cognitive development.

Age Timing of Learning

The question of how quickly children can reach developmental "milestones" was referred to as "the American Question" when I studied at Jean Piaget's Swiss institute. In Piaget's developmental theory, the *sequence* of stages in the development of thinking was important, but not the *age* at which new developments occurred. Nonetheless, for years American researchers tried to demonstrate Piagetian stages at earlier ages than the approximate ages that Piaget and his colleagues had identified. Indeed, this was one of the main thrusts of American researchers' response to Piaget's theory.

Concern with being "on time" (or "behind time" or "ahead of time") in daily life appeared in the United States during the 1870s, when standardized measurements became central in the new industrial system (Chudacoff, 1989). Before that, clocks and watches were rare and often not accurate, and people's activities were coordinated by the rhythms of daily life. The regular working hours of factories and the schedules of railroads and streetcars introduced standardized time to regulate people's activities.

By the 1890s, concern with scheduling extended beyond the hours of the day to the years of life, as experts delineated norms for the ideal age timing of life events, prescribing what it meant for an individual's experiences and achievements to be on time (or ahead or behind). Within a few decades, in the early 1900s, the interest in prescribing norms for the age of achievement of particular developmental milestones extended to concerns about characterizing individuals in terms of their degree of "retardation" (or "backwardness") versus "normal" development.[2]

When schooling became compulsory, a standard starting age was required to enforce the schooling laws and catch truants. This allowed schools to move students through the grades in age "batches" given the same instruction. School officials prioritized grouping on age-based "maturity" rather than on progress in learning school subjects (Chudacoff, 1989). In France and the United States, organizing instruction into stages for batch instruction also helped administrators supervise teachers (Anderson-Levitt, 1996).

The growing concern with timing of development stemmed in large part from educational administrators' alarm over the extent to which children were "behind" the grades in school that were designated for them. Such lags challenged the bureaucratic efficiency of age-grading for organizing schoolchildren (Anderson-Levitt, 1996; Chudacoff, 1989).

Mental Testing

Consistent with concerns about children being behind their expected level, mental testing developed about the same time that age-graded classes became common. Efforts to determine "mental age" were based on work in developmental psychology, especially in France and the United States. In France, Alfred Binet and colleagues were the first to develop tests of intel-

---

[2] Likewise during this time, individuals increasingly made reference to their age in describing themselves and others, using age as a guidepost or making comparative statements relative to age norms (e.g., commenting on being "very tall for my age"; Chudacoff, 1989, p. 119).

lectual level, as a practical tool for schools of the early 1900s to sort out children who needed "special" education.

The effort to quantify "intelligence" reflected the era's (and societies') use of age as a systematic way of sorting people for the new compulsory schooling and more "efficiently" processing batches of students through the grades (Anderson-Levitt, 1996; Chudacoff, 1989). Mental age was determined by creating norms using test items that could be distinguished by age across childhood. The Intelligence Quotient was soon invented to compare tested mental age to chronological age (with 100 indicating that the mental and chronological ages are the same, designated as "normal" IQ).[3] "Americans, particularly, became obsessed with defining and measuring mental age, and their efforts to do so riveted age norms and developmental schedules in the public consciousness more tightly than ever before" (Chudacoff, 1989, p. 79).

Ironically, Jean Piaget, whose stage theory of child development has been so influential in developmental psychology, began his career working on intelligence testing in Binet's laboratory (Anderson-Levitt, 1996). He became interested in going beyond the number of items a child got wrong on a test of intelligence to understand the basis of children's differing conceptions of phenomena across stages of mental development.

Development as a Racetrack

The "American Question" is based on a racetrack metaphor for development, assuming that children who pass the milestones of infancy and childhood earlier will be more successful in adulthood:

> Teachers' use of "ahead" and "behind" as the idiom of achievement makes going to school sound like running a race, and the racetrack metaphor fits well. The contestants all begin from the same starting place, that is, at the same age; they all take off at the same point in time, the beginning of the school year; they all move along the same linear path, that is, through the stages or grades of the curriculum. (Anderson-Levitt, 1996, p. 70)

Teachers in the United States and France routinely refer to children's progress along a linear dimension measured now in months, such that children in the same school class are seen as being "ahead" or "behind" expected performance (Anderson-Levitt, 1996). Relevant to such judgments is whether

---

[3] Since the origins of mental testing a century ago, many problems in the assumptions and procedures of such testing have surfaced. Nonetheless, mental testing and chronological age remain common bureaucratic tools for sorting individuals for various educational and career opportunities.

their birthdate falls early or late in the year assigned to a particular grade level. Children who are slower in following predefined stages of learning to read (on the teachers' schedule) are regarded as failing or likely to become failures.

Many parents and politicians in the United States, like many teachers (and developmental psychologists), conceive of development in this unidimensional way, assuming that the timing of passing milestones translates to life success or failure. They impose a single straight path onto the inherently more complex dimensions and directions of human development.

In valued domains, middle-class U.S. parents often emphasize the rate of their children's development in comparison with other children (e.g., "advanced," "way ahead"). Such descriptions of children's comparative rate of development were not found in an East African community (Harkness & Super, 1992a). Anglo-Australian mothers expressed concern that instruction might be left until it was "too late," and most reported teaching their preschoolers the alphabet. Their concern with timing contrasted with Lebanese-Australian mothers, who were less likely to teach preschoolers the alphabet and indicated that if a general willingness to learn is sustained, skills can be learned when needed (Goodnow, Cashmore, Cotton, & Knight, 1984). Now, among some middle-class European American families, hopes for precocity (and fears of delay) push academic training and high expectations for learning into infancy, despite lack of evidence that early achievement of milestones offers any inherent advantage.

In some communities, infants are not expected to rapidly understand the ways of those around them, and adults are comfortable that infants will learn when they are ready if not pushed against their will. Infants' development is not conceived as progressing past a linear sequence of milestones in accord with a timeline. Their efforts are not expected to follow the same rules or linear form of progress as their elders; instead, they are accorded a unique social status.

According Infants a Unique Social Status

In some communities, infants and toddlers are accorded a unique social status in which their acts and responsibilities are regarded as being of a different sort than those of older children and adults. As such, they are not simply "immature" and needing to quickly learn how to behave by the rules of social behavior. They are in a period of moratorium in which they are not expected to follow the same rules and are not hurried to do so.

In such communities, babies and toddlers are expected not to be capable of understanding how to cooperate with the group; they are regarded as incapable of intentionally harming or mistreating others. So there is no sense in hurrying them to follow the rules. They are patiently given their way until they leave infancy and are regarded as capable of intentional acts and of understanding how to cooperate. In the meantime, they are accorded a privileged status in the family (Hewlett, 1992; Martini & Kirkpatrick, 1992; Mosier & Rogoff, 2002).

For example, in the Guatemalan Mayan community of San Pedro, when children under about age 2 want something, other people give it to them. Once when I brought gifts to the children of a Mayan friend, her 4-year-old came back a few minutes later without his toy helicopter, crying, "The baby wanted it." His mother responded, "Good for you, you gave it to him." Because his 1-year-old brother was too young to understand how to share, the right thing for a big brother to do was to support the baby in learning how to be a member of the group by respecting his wishes.

Such treatment of infants and toddlers has been termed "indulgent" by researchers from communities in which children are seen as willful from the start (Blount, 1972; Briggs, 1970; Harkness & Super, 1983; Joseph, Spicer, & Chesky, 1949). In middle-class European American families, 1-year-olds and 5-year-olds may be held to the same rules, with explicit concern for equality. They are often expected to take turns with desirable objects. Although probably given more support and leniency in following the rules than an older child, the toddler's acts are interpreted as willful and needing correction to follow the mature form. Infants' and toddlers' development is supported by holding them to proper behavior so they will understand it.

Contrasting Treatment of Toddlers and Older Siblings

To examine differences in the family status of toddlers, Mosier and Rogoff (2002) visited Mayan and middle-class European American families with a 1-year-old and a 3- to 5-year-old. The middle-class European American children often tussled over desirable objects, and their mothers tried to get them to negotiate dividing the property and to consider each other's equal rights. A mother would say "Why don't you give your brother a turn now and then it will be your turn" or "You've had it for a long time now, give it to your sister." Although mothers were a little more lenient with the 1-year-olds, they tried to get them to follow the same rules as the older children.

In contrast, in the Mayan families, 3- to 5-year-old siblings usually treated 1-year-olds as having a privileged status that allowed them not to follow the usual social rules. The older siblings seldom grabbed things from the toddler, and they usually voluntarily handed over an object if the toddler wanted it. They usually asked the toddler's permission for access to a desirable object, and if the toddler said no, the 3- to 5-year-old would not insist. (Sometimes, the older children cleverly found ways to get the toddlers to allow them to play *together*, so that the older child could also play with the object.) The Mayan mothers did not often need to intervene to get the older siblings to let the toddler have their way, and they did not refer to turn-taking. Occasionally, they reminded the older child to let the toddler have the object because a toddler "does not understand."

The Mayan mothers reported that toddlers are not old enough to do things on purpose; they cannot break things on purpose or understand that hitting or pulling hair hurts. This idea is illustrated by an incident in which a hefty 15-month-old walked around bonking his brothers and sisters, his mother, and his aunt with the stick puppet that I had brought along. The adults and older children just tried to protect themselves and the little children near them, they did not try to stop him. (When the little guy got close to me, I took the puppet out of his hand, and he gave me an indignant look. His mother hurriedly gave him a wink that meant I was just teasing, and he relaxed. What I had done was socially inappropriate—I had forced him to stop what he was doing.) When I asked local people what this toddler had been doing, they commented:

"He was amusing people; he was having a good time."
Was he trying to hurt anybody?
"Oh no. He couldn't have been trying to hurt anybody; he's just a
    baby. He wasn't being aggressive, he's too young; he doesn't understand. Babies don't do things on purpose."

In contrast, most of the middle-class European American mothers reported that their toddler was capable of breaking things on purpose. For example, several mothers said that their toddler destroys other children's toys or rips their artwork on purpose, although they "know better." (Ironically, observations suggested that the Mayan toddlers may have been more aware of and in tune with the actions and meanings of the group than were the middle-class European American toddlers; Rogoff et al., 1993.) The treatment of toddlers in the two communities seems to be based on different assumptions about how children learn to become responsible members of their community.

Continuities and Discontinuities across Early Childhood

In the Mayan approach, allowing toddlers not to follow the rules is based on the idea that their will should be given respect like that of any other person. Between the ages of 2 and 3, the age at which a new sibling is often born into the family, Mayan children are regarded as beginning to understand how to cooperate with the group. Then they change status from ba-

ho have unchallenged access to what they want, to people who un-
.nd how to cooperate and do not insist on access. They can then re-
the wishes of their new little sibling.

This transition involves discontinuity in the specific rules of sharing
from infancy to childhood. It contrasts with the consistency in application
of rules to toddlers and older children found in the European American
middle-class community.

At the same time, the Mayan practices involve continuity in respecting
others' autonomy, even for infants, who do not yet understand community
ways. This is consistent with the deep respect for individual autonomy that
prevails in this community and in some other communities in which infants are accorded a special status. The toddlers are regarded as learning how
to cooperate by having their wishes respected, even though they are not regarded as capable of doing the same for others.

The pattern in Japanese child rearing may be related. Japanese mothers
emphasize letting their small children grow up naturally, allowing their
childish behavior. It is commonly believed that, with development, ob-
streperous conduct will naturally disappear. Through the mother's empathy
toward the child and encouragement of the child's empathy toward her
own and others' feelings, with time, the child brings his or her conduct in
line with cultural norms. "It is implied that social rules cannot be enforced
unless the child is subjectively ready to understand and accept them or to
comply with them voluntarily" (Lebra, 1994, p. 263).

An Inuit infant who is given her way rather than having to follow the
same rules as an older child may seem indulged or spoiled from a middle-
class European American perspective (Briggs, 1970). But Minnie Aodla
Freeman explained the difference from an Inuit perspective:

> [Non-Inuit people] who have gone north and lived in the settle-
> ments, who do not understand Inuit home life or believe in our way
> of child-rearing, think that Inuit children are spoiled.
>
> [When I visited a non-Inuit home in Ottawa], I could not help
> but notice the treatment of the children by the parents. One child
> asked, "Who is that girl?" She was answered with whispers and told
> to leave. Instead of being proud that the child was curious, instead of
> considering the way the child used her words, the parents silenced
> her immediately. To my people, such discipline can prevent a child
> from growing mentally, killing the child's sense of interest. "Is it very
> cold where she comes from? Did she live in an igloo before she came
> here?" Shhhh! the mother was cautioning. "Go outside! Don't do
> that! Move away!" How I wanted to pick up the child and say, "It is
> not very cold where I come from because we wear warm clothes." But

words like "don't," "no," "move" were to me like talking to a dog who was eating from some other dog's dish or who did not obey commands given during sled travel. My culture tells me that the word no leads to disobedient children who become very hard to handle later on. (1978, p. 22)

In middle-class European American communities, the end of infancy is expected to involve a sudden appearance of contrary behavior—the "terrible twos" (Rothbaum, Pott, Azuma, Miyake, & Weisz, 2000; Wenar, 1982). This transition is interpreted as indicating the appearance of autonomy and separateness. It is expected by parents, discussed in magazines, and expounded on by child-rearing experts. For example, a Boston mother and father described their 20-month-old as having entered the "stage" of "terrible twos," which they characterized as being obstinate, negative, and needing independence. They gave this example:

FATHER: When you put her in a car seat, you don't know whether she's gonna straighten out and not allow you to strap her in, or whether . . . She's pretty strong.

MOTHER (GESTURING): Two handed, right before they slide down, because with the polyester snowsuit on, they slide right off. Then you give them a karate chop in the middle . . .

What causes that behavior? Well, you're really sort of chaining them down, and it's exactly what they don't want to have happen, at this age. Because they have no control, they . . . you are forcing them to do something, and there's no way around it, they've gotta do it. And the more you force them into it . . .

FATHER: You can't trick them, because they know that the ultimate is that they get tied into the car seat, or that's my feeling.

MOTHER: And it seems like once she's in there, she is totally resigned to it, and she's fine. But just getting into it, is wicked. Why is control such an issue at this age? Well, I guess it's that whole stage of development, where they have to branch out, and do whatever it is they're going to do on their own, so they're testing everything. The first thing she says all the time is "I'll do it, I'll do it, I'll do it." Because they're not babies any more. (Harkness et al., 1992, p. 168)

In contrast, in many communities, such a transition to negativism and obstinacy around age 2 is not observed or expected (Hewlett, 1992; Rothbaum et al., 2000). For example, Zinacantecan infants in Mexico do not go through this transition; instead, they are watchful and observant, seeking contact with mothers who until then had treated them with a special status now reserved for a new baby (Edwards, 1994). Rather than asserting control and independence from their mother, they change their status from mother's baby to a child of the courtyard children's group—a child who acts as a responsible caregiver to the new baby and helps with household tasks.

Responsible Roles in Childhood

As children leave the toddler years, in many communities they begin to contribute to the work of their family (Harkness & Super, 1992a; Levin, 1990; Martini & Kirkpatrick, 1992; Nsamenang, 1992). In colonial times in the United States, girls of 4 years knitted stockings and mittens and girls of 6 spun wool on a spinning wheel they could reach only by standing on a footstool (Ogburn & Nimkoff, 1955). Mayan children in the Guatemalan town I have worked in began to make a real contribution to household work by age 4 to 6 years—tending infants, delivering messages and running errands around town, and helping with meals and agricultural work. They were valuable and competent assistants by 8 to 10 years—making meals, weaving, supervising the household or family shop in the parents' absence, and tending crops (Rogoff, 1978; see figure 5.6).

FIGURE 5.6

A Mayan 10-year-old boy splitting the family firewood.

Onset of Responsibility at Age 5 to 7?

In many parts of the world, age 5 to 7 years is an important time of transition in children's responsibilities and status in their community. Western, bureaucratic society shifts its treatment of children at this age, and has done so for centuries, viewing these children as becoming able to tell right from wrong, to participate in work, and to begin serious education in institutions outside the family (White, 1976). Developmental research often notes a discontinuity in skills and knowledge at about age 5 to 7 years (White, 1965), which happens to be the age when children begin school in the United States. In Europe, historically, children took on adultlike work status at about this age:

> In the Middle Ages, at the beginning of modern times, and for a long time after that in the lower classes, children were mixed with adults as soon as they were considered capable of doing without their mothers or nannies, not long after a tardy weaning (in other words, at about the age of 7). They immediately went straight into the great community of men, sharing in the work and play of their companions, old and young alike. (Ariès, 1962, p. 411)

Descriptions of age transitions in many communities focus on this age. For example, when they lost their first teeth and began to get their second ones, Ngoni (Central African) children were expected to show independence and were held accountable for discourtesy. They stopped playing childish games and started skill training. The boys left the women's domain and entered dormitories and a system of male life (Read, 1968).

Ethnographies of 50 communities around the world (from the Human Relations Area Files) indicate a widespread change at about age 5 to 7 years in the onset of responsibilities and expectations of children:

> It appears that in the age period centering on 5–7 years, parents relegate (and children assume) responsibility for care of younger children, for tending animals, for carrying out household chores and gathering materials for the upkeep of the family. The children also become responsible for their own social behavior and the method of punishment for transgression changes. Along with new responsibility, there is the expectation that children between 5 and 7 years begin to be teachable. Adults give practical training expecting children to be able to imitate their example; children are taught social manners and inculcated in cultural traditions. Underlying these changes in teachability is the fact that at 5–7 years children are considered to attain common sense or rationality.

At this age also, the child's character is considered to be fixed, and he begins to assume new social and sexual roles. He begins to join with groups of peers, and participate in rule games. The children's groups separate by sex at this time. Concurrently, the children are expected to show modesty and sex differentiation in chores and social relationships is stressed. All of these variables indicate that at 5–7 the child is broadly categorized differently than before this age, as he becomes a more integral part of his social structure. (Rogoff et al., 1975, p. 367)

What seems to happen at about age 5 to 7, as reflected in the ethnographic literature, is that children *begin* to be responsible and teachable. However, at about age 8 to 10, parents often *count on* children to understand and to help, with competence and responsibility (Sellers, 1975).

The expectations for children of age 5 to 7 (or any other age) have some general basis, but it is important not to accord too much specificity to age expectations for particular activities. Although many communities in the survey of 50 ethnographies showed impressive regularities in children's beginning responsibilities at age 5 to 7 years, some had shifts outside that age range (Rogoff et al., 1975). In addition, the apparent regularities may have come partially from the Western ethnographers' expectations; most of them had to estimate ages because in most of the communities, people did not know their age.

It is important not to give too much weight to specific age expectations because the age at which children begin to contribute to specific activities is strongly related to the sort of supports and constraints offered by their community, as described in Chapter 1. Impressive variations occur in the age at which children are expected to carry out complex, culturally valued activities, such as being responsible for infants or handling knives or fire safely, depending on how these activities and children's roles are structured in their communities. The ages of accomplishment are highly related to the opportunities children have to observe and participate in the activities and cultural values regarding development of particular skills.

Maturation and Experience

Sometimes, child development experts in the United States regard adults in other communities as irresponsible if young children handle dangerous materials or tend infants, because they assume that young children can't do such things. However, middle-class U.S. families also expect children to do some things that are seen as inappropriate or even dangerous in other places, such as sleeping by themselves from the first months of life (Morelli et al., 1992) or engaging in school-like discourse or beginning to learn to read in the toddler years (Heath, 1983).

Many activities that a community may treat as having a "natural" point of transition are only natural given the assumptions and the circumstances and organization of that community. Instead of assuming that age transitions are inherent to children's biological maturation, independent of circumstances, it is reasonable to ask how children in a particular community become responsible enough to take care of themselves in the ways expected and supported in that community. The impressive changes that come with biological maturation are accompanied by powerful changes in communitywide expectations and opportunities for children's participation in the activities valued in the community.

For example, in middle-class communities, the role of a particular cultural institution—formal schooling—is so central that its contributions to children's developmental transitions are often overlooked. Researchers commonly interpret children's age as a measure of maturation plus generic experience with the world (Wohlwill, 1970). Differences in development often are considered to be differences in the rate of maturation along a natural developmental time course, perhaps sped up or retarded by generic environmental circumstances. Such an approach overlooks the near complete association of age with the specific experience of schooling in nations where school is compulsory (Laboratory of Comparative Human Cognition, 1979). This is despite the fact that common age labels in the United States specifically refer to children's schooling—preschoolers and school-age children.

Many changes that occur in middle childhood in the United States may be largely a matter of having learned the skills or ways of doing things that are promoted in this institution. Because the ubiquitous role of schooling is usually overlooked, there is little basis for determining how maturation and experience work together to produce many of the transitions in middle childhood that are commonly described in developmental psychology research.

Adolescence as a Special Stage

Some observers have argued that certain phases of development treated in middle-class communities as "natural," such as adolescence, are cultural inventions unique to certain cultural conditions (Hollingshead, 1949; Saraswathi, 2000). Nonetheless, some transition time is usual between childhood and adulthood. A delay between the onset of puberty and adulthood appears to be universal for boys in nonindustrial societies. They are rarely deemed marriageable before their late teens, apparently due to the time needed to show sufficient responsibility to provide for a wife and children (Schlegel & Barry, 1991). Girls may marry as early as 13, but in a majority of nonindustrial societies, at least a short time intervenes between puberty and full assumption of adult roles. Adulthood usually occurs at marriage (although the woman is still often under the supervision of elders of the family or in-laws). A longer delay between puberty and the attainment of adult status is more common in communities in which marriage involves setting up a separate household than in those where the young couple usually lives with the bride's or the groom's parents.

Often, the years surrounding the attainment of physical maturity are treated as a special phase in which responsibilities and independence are greater than those of children but not yet those of adulthood (Schlegel & Barry, 1991). Adolescents may not be allowed to marry, to work, to vote, or to drive, or they may have many responsibilities of adulthood but under the supervision of parents or in-laws. In some settings, teens may have adult responsibilities at home but be treated as children at school, as expressed by this African American 15-year-old living in an inner-city neighborhood:

> Sometimes I just don't believe how this school operates and thinks about us. Here I am a grown man. I take care of my mother and have raised my sisters. Then I come here and this know-nothing teacher treats me like I'm some dumb kid with no responsibilities. I am so frustrated. They are trying to make me something that I am not. Don't they understand I'm a man and I been a man longer than they been a woman? (quoted in Burton et al., 1996, pp. 404–405)

In some communities, adolescence is regarded as a time of rebelliousness, emotional crisis, or self-centeredness. This goes beyond the existence of a transition period between childhood and adulthood, which is common in most communities but does not necessarily involve conflict or crisis.

Various authors have suggested that discord in adolescence is a function of young people's segregation from productive roles in society, which they are otherwise ready to fill. Beginning in the 1800s, adolescence became increasingly separated from childhood and adulthood in some regions of the United States. Lydia Child's 1835 *Mother's Book* expressed concern about the growing separation of young and older people, and other sources reported mood fluctuations in youth (Demos & Demos, 1969).

The first formal expression of the concept of adolescence came with psychologist G. Stanley Hall's influential treatise in 1882 on the storm and stress of this stage of life, cast as a serious crisis. Other scholars, such as anthropologist Margaret Mead in her study of development of children and youth of Samoa, called into question the idea that adolescence was necessarily a separate stage involving crisis. However, Hall's ideas have prevailed in U.S. folk and academic psychology.

The appearance of the concept of adolescence at the end of the 19th century has been attributed to the transformation of the United States from an agricultural into an urban industrial nation (Demos & Demos, 1969). In farm families, which most U.S. families were before the 19th century, children and adults shared work, entertainments, friends, and values. When Americans began to move to cities and work in factories, these relationships changed drastically. City children had less economic function and came into greater contact with others of their age and with diverse backgrounds and values. If they had employment, they also had greater economic freedom from adults (Schlegel & Barry, 1991).

By the end of the 19th century, child-rearing experts discussed the dangers and temptations of urban life that threatened youth. Urban life appeared as a corrupting force, with its varied social and economic life, its commercialism, and its entertainments. By about 1900 the situation had become clearer, with many writers addressing the problems of gangs and juvenile delinquency and the need for vocational guidance (Demos & Demos, 1969).

Late 19th-century authors expressed concern about the growth of peer-group contacts. They were perhaps witnessing the origins of "youth culture," with its own styles, language, and priorities and the societal treatment of adolescence as a distinct and troubled stage of life (Demos & Demos, 1969). Ironically, most features of current U.S. youth culture—such as music, videos, video games, and sports—are commodities produced by adults for teenage markets. These markets are manipulated by adults according to what they believe adolescents will buy (Schlegel & Barry, 1991).

U.S. youth culture contrasts with the adolescent peer activities that were common in some preindustrial societies, in which teenagers would compose their own songs or organize village festivities:

> Given little responsibility to society and little authority over certain, albeit small, domains of social life, modern adolescents seldom act as autonomous groups in constructive, socially meaningful ways. If young people are successful during their adolescent years, it is as talented individuals or in activities organized by adults for adolescents like school sports, not through peer groups who plan their own actions and are rewarded by appreciative adults. Opportunities for adolescents are constrained and their scope of activities determined by adults in all societies, but in many parts of the world, peer groups seemed to play larger social roles before their transitions to modern and modernizing societies than they do today. Ironically, adolescents are losing incentives to plan and act at the same time that they are becoming increasingly emancipated from the control of parents and other adult authorities. (Schlegel & Barry, 1991, p. 202)

Consistent with this concern for the restrictions in the roles of adolescents accompanying industrialization, Shirley Brice Heath (1998) pointed out that it is in the context of planning and working on shared efforts that youth learn to plan, collaborate, think, and speak in skilled, complex ways. She argued for the importance of opportunities for collaborative activities with adults in youth-based organizations such as community youth clubs, art groups, and sport leagues.

In some societies, elaborate initiation rites dramatize the developmental changes of adolescence and may help to ease the transitions (Demos & Demos, 1969). Youth culture may be a substitute for cultural rites to mark this developmental transition.

Initiation to Manhood and Womanhood

In many communities, boys and girls undergo an initiation to bring them to manhood and womanhood. Adolescent initiation rites may involve circumcision for boys and girls; they invariably emphasize gender distinctions (Ottenberg, 1994). A boy at initiation may be physically wrenched from his mother by older men and removed from his home for an extended time, with cultural symbolism of death and rebirth (Grob & Dobkin de Rios, 1994). Initiations may include strenuous tests to move from childhood into adulthood: survival or endurance tests, withstanding circumcision without screaming, being able to keep calm when frightening things happen, tests of strength or verbal skill or silence. A positive reaction to these tests is seen as a sign of growing maturity. However, individuals seem almost always to be initiated no matter how they react (Ottenberg, 1994).

Communities that employ initiation in adolescence seem to differ in systematic ways from those without this rite of passage. Many reasons for initiation have been suggested, including

> status change to adulthood, recognition of sexual maturity, incorporation into the larger society, creating a sense of ethnic identity and/or of social solidarity, a working through of Oedipal or of early childhood experience, preparing for adult gender roles and identifying with the proper gender, channeling assertive aggressive and sexual tendencies of the young into socially acceptable adult roles, maintaining gerontocratic control of the younger generation, inculcating the basic cultural values of the society into the maturing individuals, and teaching new skills and attitudes. (Ottenberg, 1994, p. 353)

The use of initiation rites with circumcision for boys may relate to low male salience in infancy and childhood, according to speculations based on a worldwide sample of communities (Burton & Whiting, 1961; Munroe, Munroe, & Whiting, 1981). Initiation/circumcision rites are more frequent in communities in which households are formed of mothers and children and the father stays somewhere else. This often occurs in polygynous societies, where the child's father usually stays in a men's dormitory or a hut of his own or moves from one wife's house to another's. Researchers have speculated that initiation/circumcision rites provide a symbolic rebirth from childhood to manhood for young boys in polygynous households with few male role models.[4]

Initiation rites are more frequent for girls than for boys. Boys' initiations often focus on issues of responsibility, whereas girls' initiations often focus symbolically on issues of fertility. The difference may reflect the fact that communities are concerned about women bearing children, children not dying, and mothers not dying in childbirth (Ottenberg, 1994).

Among the Navajo, a special rite ushers girls into adult life within the community; no such ceremony occurs for boys. *Kinaalda* is a four-day ceremony to celebrate a Navajo girl's first menstruation. It is designed to impart the moral and intellectual strength the young woman will need as she herself can now create new life and continue Navajo culture (Deyhle & Margonis, 1995). The rite ensures the continuation and expansion of matrilineal networks in the community. The young woman is lectured to and prayed over during the ceremony, formalizing her commitment and obligation to the family and community. (This perspective contrasts with neighboring Anglo society, where adolescence is viewed as establishing the independence of the individual.) One young woman explained the importance of Kinaalda:

> "My mom won't let anybody go out without one. My mom says if you get one you are an okay lady. On my aunt's side, they didn't do any of those. They're just running around out there somewhere." Her sister laughed, "White people try to hide it. We celebrate it. It is womanhood. And everything." (p. 139)

---

[4] In societies where boys have low contact with male role models but without initiation/circumcision rites, two alternatives have been suggested to substitute. One is that young men may gang together, creating their own passage to manhood through gang activities. Another is that males may yearn for female roles, as in the custom called *couvade,* in which men experience symptoms resembling pregnancy when their wife is pregnant (Burton & Whiting, 1961; Munroe & Munroe, 1975b; Vigil, 1988). In couvade, when the mother has morning sickness, the father feels sick too; when the mother is in labor, the father feels pain, sometimes to the point of going into a labor bed when the wife does and sometimes with sympathetic feelings with lesser "symptoms."

Some Navajo elders see a connection between the decreased use of Kinaalda and an increase in the number of Navajo young women who have difficulties staying on an appropriate cultural track.

Initiation rites for young women and men recognize and promote developmental transitions that mark (and instruct) status changes within the structure of the community. The gender roles that are widely used to structure people's community roles and status are examined in greater depth in a later section of this chapter.

Marriage and Parenthood as Markers of Adulthood

In many communities, marriage and parenthood are markers of the transition to adulthood, even though the young couple/parents are often still supervised and supported by elders. Although some countries set age limits for marriageability,[5] a transition to adulthood upon marriage is a developmental transition based on the change in roles rather than on age (Schlegel & Barry, 1991).

For example, in Cameroon (West Africa), young people of 14 or 15 years may become adults by virtue of marriage and parenthood, whereas persons 24 years of age are considered immature if they are unmarried and childless (Nsamenang, 1992; see also LeVine et al., 1994). Full adult status requires that a person be married with children. The birth of the first child is more important for the parents' status than was their marriage. Parental status is further enhanced at the point that the baby is named, as parents become known and addressed as the mother or father of so-and-so, rather than by their personal names.

In the United States, young people seldom regard parenthood as an essential criterion of adult status, but those who have become parents generally regard this transition as the most important marker of adulthood for themselves (Arnett, 2000). In general, U.S. young people experience an extended phase between adolescence and adulthood, in their late teens and twenties. During this time, most reply to the question of whether they feel they have reached adulthood, "In some respects yes, in some respects no." They are often still in school and not yet settled into a career or marriage, but they do not indicate these transitions as markers of adulthood. Rather,

[5] For example, "Principles of English common law, adopted by statute in the United States, set the age at which a minor was deemed capable of marrying at fourteen for males and twelve for females. Marriage at younger ages required parental consent, although common law voided marriage below age seven even with parental consent. By 1886, laws in most American states had raised age limits considerably" (Chudacoff, 1989, pp. 85–86).

FIGURE 5.7

The wedding of John and Helen Cummings in the yard of the groom's family, about 1920, in Watts, Los Angeles (African American).

they regard adulthood as accepting responsibility for oneself and making independent decisions and, often, becoming financially independent—individual character milestones that may strike readers as particularly "American."

Even in the United States, with its emphasis on individuality, the roles of individuals connect with family and community functioning when a couple marries. This is clear in the family involvement common in marriage ceremonies (see figure 5.7). Marriage is often an arrangement by the community or family, not just the two individuals.

Indeed, the choice of spouse is often made by family and community. In fewer than 20% of preindustrial societies have young people chosen their own mate (Schlegel & Barry, 1991). For example, in Ireland in the last half of the 1800s, the couple's fathers arranged the marriage (at which point, the groom's status changed from boy or lad to adult, often at about age 40; Horgan, 1988). Historically, in the majority of the world's communities, marriages have been arranged by family members rather than the bride or groom (Levine, Sato, Hashimoto, & Verma, 1995).

This is illustrated in an account from Oscar Magarian, regarding his older brother's marriage in an Armenian American community in the early 1900s:

> When he began to show more than a casual interest in the other sex, Mother and Dad decided it was time for them to find Martin a wife. Because the old country traditions were still considered the best way to do things, Martin let the folks look all over Massachusetts and Rhode Island for a suitable wife. . . . We younger children were all ears as friends and relatives told of the various girls they knew. I think I learned the genealogy, the physical dimensions and specifications, and the matrimonial qualifications of every available Armenian girl within a hundred miles.
>
> Father and Mother made many trips and visited many homes. The routine seemed to be one of casual interest and almost invariably the girl in question would serve refreshments consisting of Turkish coffee scalding hot in tiny cups, along with some other delicacies reminiscent of the old country. I never learned whether the poor girl ever learned how well she scored on her performance. But we younger brothers wasted no opportunity to eavesdrop and to learn how she walked and whether her frame was suitable for producing healthy grandchildren and still be able to do her share of the work. But the search eventually ended and the selection seemed to register well with my brother. (recollections written in 1958; Oscar himself found a wife on his own, at college)

Before the Industrial Revolution, marriage in the United States was largely a practical arrangement between two families. According to a U.S. writer in 1832, it was common for parents to choose a husband for their daughter, who was consulted only as a formality (Ogburn & Nimkoff, 1955). Families sought mates for their children who were industrious, held similar values, and had respectable personal qualities; love and personal attraction were secondary considerations. In rural villages, where most people lived, people were quite familiar with each other and family background and the character of the young people were widely known. The young people were expected to demonstrate their ability to support a household. For example, it was the expectation several centuries ago in the United States that a young woman would not marry until she had spun linen for herself, her bed, and her table (hence, the legal term "spinster" to designate all unmarried women).

Differences in conceptions of the role of love in selecting a mate are widespread in modern nations (Saraswathi, 2000). In a recent international study, more than 80% of university students from the United States, England, and Australia—but less than 40% from India, Pakistan, and Thailand—reported that they would not marry a person without being in love, even if the person had all the other desired qualities (Levine et al., 1995).

An emphasis on romantic love as a basis for marriage appears to accompany an emphasis on individual gratification. This contrasts with marriages that are supposed to protect, strengthen, and elaborate bonds across families and generations.

Romantic love and intense emotional attachment are sometimes seen as a threat to the extended family structure (Levine et al., 1995; Seymour, 1999). Romantic love can even be regarded as a danger to the integrity of the structure of the community or nation. Such disruption occurred in Spanish New Mexico in the early 1800s, when marriage based on romantic love—prioritizing individual autonomy—replaced the practice of marriages arranged by parents to protect the family and class economic structure (Gutierrez, 1991). Hindu adults explain the problems of using romantic love as a basis of marriage: "A marriage is something that affects so many people, relatives, ancestors, neighbors, and friends, in serious ways. How can you possibly leave it up to one young person, driven by lust and passion, to make a sound decision?" (Shweder, Mahapatra, & Miller, 1990, p. 198).

Midlife in Relation to Maturation of the Next Generation

In some middle-class communities of the 21st century, a middle period of adulthood is distinguished, after the childbearing years and before retirement. Midlife as a distinct stage of life appeared in the United States in the early 1900s, with the increased emphasis on age as a measure of the life course in that era (Chudacoff, 1989):

> Walter Pitkin's bestselling book, *Life Begins at Forty*, published in 1932, ratified the recognition of middle age in American culture. Proclaiming that his title reflected "the supreme reward of the Machine Age," Pitkin, a psychologist and journalist, urged that one's middle and later years could be productive and enjoyable. According to his scheme of adulthood, the years between ages seventeen and twenty-four were a sort of apprenticeship, when "we learn the social life." Between twenty-four and forty, the demanding tasks of getting a job, buying a house, and raising children consumed a person's energies. In previous eras, Pitkin observed, "men wore out at forty." But now, because of new technology, better standards of living, and increased access to leisure time, "life after forty has been much more exciting

and profitable than before forty." To prove his point, Pitkin listed famous people who had "blossomed" after age forty, and he asserted further that "in some fields, the woman past forty is best qualified to think and to lead." (pp. 108–109)

Pitkin's book became the best-selling nonfiction book in 1933. Its title was taken up by the media, appearing in magazines, radio shows, movies, popular music, and everyday conversation. (This contribution to the national conception of the life course is a good illustration of the role played by individuals and generations in creating cultural practices, as well as the role of cultural practices in individual lives, subsequent to the approach introduced by Walter Pitkin and his generation.)

Now, among the middle class of the United States, the boundaries of midlife are sometimes conceived in terms of chronological age, such as the fortieth birthday. This phase of life is also sometimes marked by physiological changes such as menopause. However, it is often also marked by community-based events involving relationships, such as the children leaving home ("empty nest syndrome") or workplace transitions.

In many other communities, midlife is not distinguished as a distinct life stage to be discussed or diagnosed (Shweder, 1998). But even if not recognized as a stage of life, adults often undergo major life transitions with changes in their responsibilities and relationships, such as when their children reach adolescence and marry:

> Midlife actually is marked by its being yoked with the adolescent developmental transition. Many cultures have adolescent initiation ceremonies, or relatively early marriage and associated negotiations and ceremonies soon after puberty, and there are accompanying changes of residence, transfers of property, and realignments of kin and affinal relations as a result. All these kinds of cultural markers are coded ethnographically and thought of as adolescent linked. But who is arranging all those ceremonies? Transferring that property? Rearranging where family members live and sleep? Having grandchildren in their lives? Parents at midlife, of course. Midlife transitions *are* there in the ethnographic record, but are described and *represented* as the adolescent and marital transitions of parents' adolescent children rather than as distinctive life stages of the parents themselves. (Weisner & Bernheimer, 1998, p. 217)

Being a parent connects an individual with later generations and in some communities with immortality. For example, in West Africa, the self moves through three phases: a spiritual phase beginning at conception and ending with naming soon after birth; a social phase from naming until death; and an ancestral phase that follows biological death (Nsamenang, 1992). Having children immortalizes the parent, providing the only remedy against complete death. Therefore, most people would rather die poor and be survived by offspring than die rich and childless: "The confidence level with which old people face death depends on the number of competent offspring who live with their 'blood'" (p. 147). Similarly, among the Gusii of Kenya, a childless man or woman is pitied as "an incomplete person who has not attained the foothold necessary for full adulthood and spiritual continuity" (LeVine et al., 1994, p. 32). Further, to reach the respected adult status of "elder," a woman or man must have married children preparing to continue the lineage.

From infancy through adulthood, people's assumption of roles expected of their developmental phase, and the skills associated with them, reflect community goals, technologies, and practices. The next section focuses specifically on girls' and boys' gender roles as they prepare to take (and may transform) the roles expected of men and women in their communities.

Gender Roles

The widespread gender differences of children around the world relate closely to the adult gender roles of their communities. This is the case for the gender differences that vary across communities as well as those that are similar around the world, especially the widespread expectation that maturity involves parenthood.

In most communities, gender roles until recently have been closely tied to the biological roles of women as mothers and men as fathers, with associated opportunities and constraints.[6] In some cultural communities, such as traditional societies of eastern Africa, all women married and there were no roles for adult women that did not involve bearing and rearing children (Harkness & Super, 1992b). (Marriage was often necessary for survival. In many traditional communities, the division of labor along gender lines makes both men and women indispensable to each other.) It has only been a few decades since the cultural invention of reliable methods of birth control has altered the likelihood that most women will be pregnant and nursing for most of their adult lives.

---

[6]Although the expectation of parenthood and gendered responsibilities for maintaining the family generally involve heterosexual household structure, in most communities that have been studied, homosexual relations are also found. In different societies, treatment has ranged from prohibition and punishment to expectation of homosexuality during certain phases of most men's lives or as an important societal role for some individuals (Bolin & Whelehan, 1999; Potts & Short, 1999; Whitehead, 1981).

Of course, as humans continue to transform their cultural practices, gender roles change at the same time as maintaining long traditions. The next centuries will undoubtedly hold different possibilities for gender roles, resulting from mutually constituting cultural and biological processes (as discussed in Chapter 3).

From a sociocultural perspective, it is no surprise that children, as they observe and participate in the gendered roles of their communities, are quick to take them on. Children's gender role development can be viewed as a process of preparing for the adult roles expected in their community. These adult roles build on the human species' gender specialization in the bearing and rearing of the next generation.

Parental treatment of daughters and sons in daily interaction reveals communication of expected roles, relations, and skills. An example of communication of gender roles occurred as a Nyansongo (Kenyan) mother worked in the garden with her 6-year-old son. Challenging fellow workers to competition is common in Nyansongo adult work groups, and this mother engaged her son in friendly competition that included reference to his future manly role and her own female role:

> Aloyse, hoeing a field beside his mother . . . "You've gotten so close to me here, I must work hard.
> MOTHER: I'm not so close. You're defeating me by digging so quickly.
> ALOYSE (RESTING): Oh, you're almost overtaking me, I must work hard.
> MOTHER: Who dug here so crudely? You, Aloyse?
> ALOYSE: No . . . I'm afraid you are overtaking me.
> MOTHER: No, you are an *omomura* [circumcised boy, or young man—not really true of Aloyse, of course]. I'm just a woman— I can't overtake you.
> ALOYSE: I'm almost reaching the end! You're going to pass me again, and finish before me. It's because I dig properly.
> Mother laughs. (from LeVine and LeVine's 1956 field observations, quoted in Whiting & Edwards, 1988, pp. 95–96)

This section first discusses the centrality of child rearing and household work in gender roles, and then examines historical cultural changes in mothers' and fathers' family roles. Next it summarizes cultural similarities and differences in gender roles pertaining to occupational roles and power. It concludes by examining gender differences in social relationships such as aggression and nurturance, which relate to the roles in which males and females participate in communities around the world.

The Centrality of Child Rearing and Household Work in Gender Role Specializations

Worldwide, child rearing is more often done by women and girls than by men and boys (Weisner, 1997; Whiting & Edwards, 1988). Birth is the province of women, and until the invention of the baby bottle, infant feeding was limited to women. Other aspects of child care are also more frequently carried out by females. Even among Aka foragers of Central Africa, where fathers have an extremely large role with infants (spending 47% of their day holding or within arm's reach of their infants), their involvement with infants is still less than that of mothers (Hewlett, 1991). These fathers' caregiving often occurs while mothers carry heavy loads, collect firewood, or prepare food.

In many communities, women tend to stay closer to home than men, partly because of child care responsibilities (Draper, 1975b; Martini & Kirkpatrick, 1992). In communities where birth control is not prevalent, a woman is generally pregnant or nursing for most of her childbearing years. A woman who is nursing can either take the baby with her or leave the baby home with a caregiver and be close enough to be fetched to nurse. It seems reasonable to account for women's greater proximity to home in terms of such responsibilities.

Gender roles of girls and boys parallel those of women and men in their communities as they begin early to follow the patterns of their elders. However, the roles of both young boys and girls are often more involved with female activities, as young children are more commonly in the company of women than of men (Munroe & Munroe, 1975b; Rogoff, 1981b; Whiting & Edwards, 1988).

After early childhood, however, boys are less commonly near home than girls. Girls' whereabouts are more often known by their parents and they are more often supervised by adults than boys, who are often further from home and adults and in the company of other boys (Draper, 1975a; Munroe & Munroe, 1997; Nerlove, Roberts, Klein, Yarbrough, & Habicht, 1974; Rogoff, 1981b; Whiting & Edwards, 1988; Whiting & Whiting, 1975).

Compared with boys, girls in many communities around the world are more likely to do household work (Edwards, 1993; Munroe et al., 1977; Whiting & Whiting, 1975). Consistently across observations in 16 communities, girls from age 3 onward were observed to spend more of their day in work such as child care, housework, and gardening than were boys, who spent their time more in undirected activity or play (Edwards, 1993). In observations of Mayan 9-year-olds, girls were more frequently working than boys. The girls' work often involved child care and household chores and production, whereas the boys' work more often included tasks carried out at some distance from home, such as agricultural work (Rogoff, 1981b).

In the United States as well, household responsibilities seem usually to be in women's realm. Men pitch in to help to varying degrees in different U.S. cultural communities. In Hawaii, middle-class Japanese American mothers receive more household help from husbands and children than do middle-class Caucasian American mothers (Martini, 1994a). Only a few of the Japanese American mothers did 80% to 100% of the work, whereas almost half of the Caucasian American mothers did this level of household work. In the Japanese American families, most fathers did 20% to 60% of household work; in contrast, in the Caucasian American families, a majority of fathers did less than 20% of the household work.

Although women often bear primary household responsibilities, the "Betty Crocker" ideal—housewives devoted solely to care of house and children—is uncommon worldwide. Women's household responsibilities are often in conjunction with other occupations, and women do not spend their day solely taking care of the house and children. They have contact with other adults throughout the day through their work and extended family. An extended family makes it possible for women to share in the supervision of children, allowing women the freedom to do errands or community work out of the home. Also, in many cases, the home itself requires less care, with fewer possessions, clothes, and "labor-saving" devices than currently in middle-class households. Societal changes in family structure and economic arrangements—over millennia as well as over decades—are closely related to changes in women's and men's responsibilities.

Sociohistorical Changes over Millennia in Mothers' and Fathers' Roles

For 99% of human existence, a foraging way of life characterized how humans lived. From the time of human origins, about 5 million years ago, a nomadic gathering-hunting lifestyle prevailed, until about 10,000 years ago, when some human groups began to settle and to domesticate animals and cultivate plants. Adrienne Zihlman (1989) speculated that the gender division of labor of modern societies developed recently in human evolution, possibly when hunting became effective or still later, when groups of people gave up nomadic life.

Flexible and egalitarian gender roles have been observed in several hunting and gathering groups in which women make a large contribution to the family's available food (Hewlett, 1991, 1992). Until changes in subsistence patterns occurred among !Kung foragers of Botswana (now known as Ju'/hoansi), women's work of gathering wild vegetables provided more than half of all food (Lee, 1980). The women retained control of the distribution of the food, in contrast to many other societies (even ones in which women nominally own the land and household property), where men usually control the production and distribution of resources (Draper, 1975b):

> The gathering work of !Kung women can be done by women alone. They do not need to ask permission to use certain lands; they do not need the assistance of men in order to carry out their work, as in the case of many agricultural societies where men must do the initial heavy work of clearing fields, building fences, and the like, before the less strenuous work of women can begin. (p. 85)

!Kung women's roles were heavily shaped by their child-rearing as well as food production responsibilities. Along with food gathering, !Kung women were primarily responsible for infants. Women carried children under age 4 with them on gathering trips (averaging 2 to 12 miles roundtrip several times a week) and on camp moves (Lee, 1980).

As !Kung (Ju'/hoansi) have turned increasingly from the nomadic foraging way of life to agriculture and a sedentary (settled) life, women's work roles require less walking, and their traditional four-year birth spacing has become substantially shorter, increasing the number of pregnancies in a life span (Lee, 1980). Change to a sedentary life has decreased women's autonomy and influence, apparently related to the changing nature of their subsistence contribution as well as to a number of features of sedentary living:

- Decrease in the mobility of women as contrasted with men
- Increasing rigidity in sex-typing of adult work
- More material goods requiring upkeep
- Tendency for men to have greater access to and control over important resources such as domestic animals, knowledge of language and culture of neighboring settled people, wage work
- Male involvement in politics beyond the village
- More permanent attachment of the individual to a particular place and group of people (making for disputes rather than simply separation when people do not get along)
- Increasing household privacy (from Draper, 1975b, p. 78)

In nonforaging groups in some parts of Africa, women are currently both "prolific" mothers and influential in the labor force (Nsamenang, 1992). However, most men still attempt to control the use of their wives' income in a struggle to maintain control over female labor; wives' financial independence is a source of marital discord.

Changes in U.S. women's and men's roles in recent centuries also have been tied to changes in family organization and economic structure. As in Africa, changes in U.S. gender roles have been accompanied by controversy and discord. Understanding changes across generations in the biological and cultural nature of gender roles may help us to get beyond the limitations of dichotomies and allow us to determine where we are now going.

Sociohistorical Changes in Recent Centuries in U.S. Mothers' and Fathers' Roles

During the 19th century in the United States, many women's roles changed from productive economic activities centered in the farming home to a middle-class ideal concentrated on motherhood and household management (Mintz & Kellogg, 1988). U.S. households in prior centuries usually involved all members in a productive economic unit connected with community life. (This generality is based on national averages; the pattern was quite different for some portions of the U.S. population, such as those who were slaves, whose work and families were not their own.)

Late in the 19th century, groups of women organized into "the mothers' movement," with an interest in rearing children "scientifically," and child-rearing experts appeared on the scene (Ehrenreich & English, 1978). Such "specialist" approaches to child rearing and running the household became the focus of many women's attention. This was a dramatic change from the days when child rearing and household maintenance were simply a "natural" part of the ongoing economic efforts of the whole household.

During much of the 20th century, roles for many women in the United States and in other nations shifted back and forth between work in the home and outside it, as their country needed them to work in wartime factories, or conversely, needed women's jobs for the men returning from war (Lamb, Sternberg, Hwang, & Broberg, 1992). Ideologies of the importance of patriotic work ("Rosie the Riveter") and of the full-time responsibilities of motherhood have accompanied these swings.

Across the generations of the dominant population of the United States over the past century and a half, parental roles of fathers and mothers have changed dramatically. Donald Hernandez (1994) documented these changes closely. First, in the late 1800s and early 1900s, fathers turned from farm to wage work, the number of children per family dropped rapidly, and the extent of participation in schooling increased dramatically. After 1940, two more great changes occurred in family organization: Mothers greatly increased their participation in the labor force and the incidence of mother-child families (with no father present) rose. This section of the chapter examines this series of changes across generations, based on Hernandez's account (see figure 5.8).

Fathers turned from farm to wage work. A century ago, there was a rapid shift from family farming to an arrangement involving father-as-breadwin-

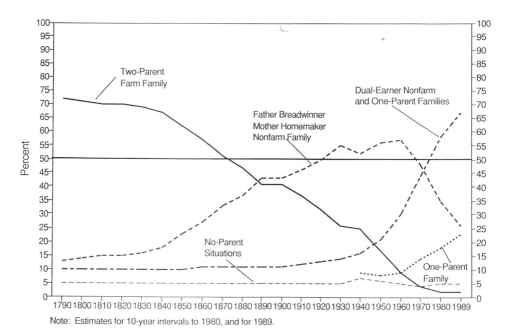

Note: Estimates for 10-year intervals to 1980, and for 1989.

FIGURE 5.8

Children up to age 17 in farm families, father-as-breadwinner families, and dual-earner families, 1790–1989 (Hernandez, 1993).

ner working away from home (to gain higher income in urban jobs) and mother-as-homemaker. For much of the population, two-parent farm families with family members working side-by-side had been the primary family organization for hundreds of years. (In 1800, only 6% of the U.S. population lived in the 33 sites with a population over 2,500, according to Ogburn & Nimkoff, 1955!)

The majority of U.S. children (70%) in 1830 lived in two-parent farm families; a century later, fewer than 30% lived in such families (Hernandez, 1994). During that time, the proportion of children living in nonfarm families with breadwinner father and homemaker mother rose from 15% to 55%.

Family size decreased. There was a great decline in number of children per family during this time. The move from farms meant that the expenses of supporting children had to be managed with cash, making the cost of each child more noticeable. In addition, children's potential for contribution to family economics was reduced by the implementation of child labor laws and compulsory schooling. From 1865 to 1930, smaller families (with only one to four children) grew from 18% to 70%. The median number of siblings in the families of adolescents dropped dramatically from 7.3 to 2.6.

Schooling expanded rapidly. Compulsory schooling was sponsored by movements that also restricted children's work: Labor unions tried to protect jobs for adults, and child welfare workers fought for laws protecting children from dangerous working conditions. (For some portions of the population, the increases in schooling derived from quite different motivations, such as political attempts to "civilize" Native Americans.) In any case, many more children began to spend far less time with their family. From 1870 to 1940, school enrollment increased from 50% for children age 5 to 19 years to 95% for children age 7 to 13 years and to 79% for children age 14 to 17 years. During this time, the number of days spent in school each year also doubled, and higher levels of schooling were required for economic advancement (see figure 5.9; also Chudacoff, 1989).

Mothers turned to wage work. In the middle of the 1900s, an upsurge occurred in mothers working outside the home, paralleling fathers' earlier departure from working in the homestead. From 1940 to 1990, the proportion of children with mother in the labor force increased sixfold, from 10% to nearly 60% (see figure 5.8). (However, in a significant portion of the U.S. population, women have consistently needed to work outside their home throughout the 20th century, as was the case for many African American women.)

Like the turn of fathers to the labor force in previous decades—which increased children's enrollment in formal educational settings—the surge of mothers joining the labor force also increased children's involvements outside the family. By 1940, the increases in formal schooling had released mothers from direct child care responsibilities for about two-thirds of the workday for about two-thirds of the work year, except during early childhood. As mothers, like fathers, began increasingly to work outside the home, children under age 6 spent increasing time in preschool and day care settings.

Having a second wage-earner in the family yielded economic advantages, especially with the insecurities of employment during and since the Great Depression. (At least a fifth of U.S. children since 1940 lived with fathers who experienced part-time work or joblessness during any single year, and this gave a strong incentive for mothers to work for pay.) With a rise in divorce rates, paid work also became important security for women.

Mother-only families increased. From the 1860s to the 1960s, the prevalence of divorce increased steadily to a rate that is eight times as great as a century before. According to Hernandez, in preindustrial farm life, husbands and wives were economically interdependent, requiring them to work together to support the family. But with wage labor, fathers could easily leave the family and take their income with them, as could mothers decades later if they were in the labor force. In addition, the move from

FIGURE 5.9

The student body of a school in Hecla, Montana, a mining camp town, faces the camera with teacher Miss Blanche Lamont, 1893. "In the eventful year of 1864, when Montana became a Territory, vigilantes of the gold-mining towns of Bannack and Virginia City hanged 23 outlaws (including a sheriff and two deputies) for 102 murders—and each town started its first school. Said Territorial Governor Sidney Edgerton: 'A self-ruling people must be an educated people, or prejudice and passion will assume power. . . . Children are in a sense the property of the public and it is one of the highest and most solemn duties of the state to furnish ample provision for their education.' Other Western states and territories shared the sense of public responsibility and, like Montana, established school systems among their first official acts" (Boorstin et al., 1975, p. 126).

small farm communities decreased social controls that previously discouraged divorce, and economic and employment insecurities also contributed to the increase in mother-only families.[7]

These demographic changes in the United States over the past two centuries are clearly tied to current U.S. male and female occupational roles, realms of power, and social relations. In other parts of the world also, the gender roles of each generation relate to such demographic changes.

[7]Economic recessions between 1970 and 1982 are estimated to have accounted for about 50% of the increase in separated or divorced mothers. And the great increase in joblessness among young Black compared with young White men since 1955, when the differences were negligible, may account for increases in never-married Black mother (Hernandez, 1993).

Occupational Roles and Power of Men and Women

There are both similarities and differences across cultural communities in expected occupational roles and power for men and women. Some of the commonalities across communities have to do with physical differences in size (from birth, males are larger) and strength. Men (on average) specialize in the kind of strength used for strenuous bursts of activity, and women (on average) specialize in the kind of strength involved in endurance for the long haul (Parker & Parker, 1979).

If agricultural work involves heavy machinery or large animals, men tend to be involved; otherwise, agriculture is more frequently women's domain. Males' work around the world seems to be characterized by requirements for greater physical strength (especially with bursts of energy) and for travel away from home (Hewlett, 1991; Parker & Parker, 1979). In hunting and gathering communities, hunting of large game is men's work; gathering is done mostly by women but also by men (Hewlett, 1991).

In some communities, the gendered divisions of labor are more flexible than in others, with one gender filling in for the other easily. For example, among !Kung (Ju'/hoansi) gatherer-hunters, some jobs usually belong to men or to women. However, adults of both genders (but men more than women) have been willing to do the work of the other, as illustrated by the following episode:

> I came across Kxau, a rather sober middle-aged man, industriously at work building his own hut. Building huts is predominantly women's work, and I had never seen such a thing. It happened that Kxau's wife was away visiting at another settlement many miles distant, or she would have made the hut. However, Kxau's daughter, an unmarried girl about seventeen years old, was in camp, and even she did not offer to make the hut or help him once he had started. Kxau proceeded to build the structure methodically and without embarrassment. . . . No one commented or joked with him about how his women were lazy. (Draper, 1975b, p. 87)

Gender roles are also egalitarian and rather flexible among several other foraging groups in Africa, making it acceptable for males to care for and entertain infants and young children (Hewlett, 1991; Morelli & Tronick, 1992). In contrast, among neighboring horticultural groups, greater separation of gender roles includes less involvement of males with young children. In some other communities, such as traditional Turkey, male and female roles are very distinct and not flexible (Kagitçibasi & Sunar, 1992).

Differences in the societal value placed on people's roles in the home and in the community accompany differences in the kind of power that women and men have (Kagitçibasi & Sunar, 1992; Ember, 1981; Parker & Parker, 1979; Whitehead, 1981). The power that women have in the household for decisions regarding children and everyday household events may be overlooked or downplayed (as with European American middle-class references to being "just" a housewife).

The current societal value placed on work in the public sphere developed over recent centuries as industrialization separated household activities from income generation through wage labor (Deyhle & Margonis, 1995; Ogburn & Nimkoff, 1955). Now, U.S. households no longer have many of their educational and productive functions. Instead, they have become based on the more tenuous ties of affection and mutual interest, often conflicting with family members' work roles and relationships outside the family (Mintz & Kellogg, 1988).

The power that men often have in community affairs is not so frequently overlooked. Men in many communities (though not all) are more likely to be involved in politics (Best & Williams, 1997). Community decision making, such as dispute settlement and decisions regarding territorial boundaries and warfare, is at least formally done by men in almost all nonindustrial societies (Schlegel & Barry, 1991).

There are communities, however, where women hold powerful community roles equal to or greater than men's roles. Among the Navajo, women are at the foundation of society as the guardians of strong family networks (Deyhle & Margonis, 1995). Women are at the core of Navajo religion and are on an equal basis with men in agriculture, child rearing, religion, and politics. Navajo society traditionally required men to move into their wife's mother's home after marriage and provided inheritance rights to women for homes and livestock. (These practices largely continue, except for individuals who move away to cities.) The family is the place where most decisions are made in the community, rather than in a separate political sphere. Within the family, women have at least as much authority as men do.

In some gathering and hunting societies, where women play a crucial role in producing food as well as in bearing and raising the next generation, their strategically central position contrasts with the situation in agricultural and industrial societies. In agricultural societies, women's work is often heavy but not high in status. In industrial societies, women's role is marginal, as they have often been confined to the home and excluded from the labor force or relegated to menial jobs (Draper, 1975b; Lee, 1980). The occupations and relative power of adult women and men guide the social relations that are expected, encouraged, and practiced in childhood.

Gender and Social Relations

In many communities, boys and girls separate into gender-segregated groups by middle childhood, especially when they are with same-age peers (Edwards, 1993; Harkness & Super, 1985; Kagitçibasi & Sunar, 1992; Rogoff et al., 1975; Whiting & Edwards, 1988). Boys and girls often move into their own circles, with boys doing male activities with boys and girls doing female activities with girls. The proportion of time that children spend in gender-segregated groups is stable across communities that have enough children to segregate by gender (Schlegel & Barry, 1991).

In adolescence in nonindustrial societies, peer groups are more salient (and tend to involve greater numbers) for boys than for girls. Adolescent boys are often excluded from adult activities and thus encouraged to associate with other boys. Boys are less likely to be in the company of or have close relationships with men than are girls to be in the company of and have close relationships with women (Schlegel & Barry, 1991). This may relate to the observation that, from early ages, girls in a number of societies are more obedient and compliant to adults than are boys (Whiting & Edwards, 1988).

Gendered aspects of assertiveness vary across communities (Goodwin, 1990). In some communities, verbal jousting (such as playing the dozens in African American communities; Slaughter & Dombrowski, 1989) seems to be more common among males than females. Youths challenge each other to verbal duels to determine who is more clever with insults or more convincing in arguments. However, African American girls in some communities play very active roles in disputes (Goodwin, 1990).

Some researchers have noted a "crisis of confidence" that appears among middle-class European American girls in the preadolescent years. These girls become less confident and more deferential, concerned with their appearance and with being liked (Gilligan, Lyons, & Hanmer, 1990). In contrast, at this age, many African American girls become more assertive and self-sufficient (Eckert, 1994). This difference may reflect different perspectives on gender roles in the two communities.

Differences between boys and girls in social relations, such as aggression and nurturance, reflect a clear relationship to the roles expected of men and women in many cultural communities. Physical aggression and adolescent antisocial behavior are more common among males than females around the world, although its frequency is quite variable across societies (Draper, 1985; Schlegel & Barry, 1991; Schlegel, 1995; Segall, Ember, & Ember, 1997). Cultural observations systematically find boys being more physically aggressive than girls and girls more often engaged in nurturant and responsible behavior (Edwards, 1993; Edwards & Whiting, 1992; Weisner, 1997;

Whiting & Edwards, 1973). But girls show greater relational aggression, such as malicious use of ostracism, gossip, and manipulation, in some communities (see French, Jansen, & Pidada, 2002).

In groups where women have had a central role in gathering food, such as among the !Kung or Aka foragers, both genders maintain a peaceful demeanor. The common finding of greater physical aggressiveness by males than females and violence against females is not found (Hewlett, 1991):

> In societies where aggressiveness and dominance are valued, these behaviors accrue disproportionately to males, and the females are common targets, resulting in a lowering of their status. !Kung women are not caught by this dimension of sex-role complementarity. They customarily maintain a mild manner, but so do their men. (Draper, 1975b, p. 91)

It is not surprising that gender differences among children are consistent with the adult roles of the current generation of women and men in many communities around the world. After all, from the earliest years, children participate in and prepare to assume the adult roles of their communities. Developmental transitions across the life span often encourage, test, and celebrate individuals' changing community roles.

Developmental transitions in roles across the life span will undoubtedly continue to be closely aligned with cultural communities' traditions and practices. But the nature of those traditions and practices, including those involving gender roles, are likely to change in subtle and not-so-subtle ways with coming generations. At the same time, they are likely to maintain some continuities with roles that humans have developed over millennia, based on biological, ecological, and cultural constraints and supports. The next chapter deals directly with cultural approaches to the relation of individuals with their communities, by addressing the relation of autonomy and interdependence.

6

Interdependence and Autonomy

*Western concepts of autonomy stress the freedom of the person to pursue
individual goals unencumbered by social obligations . . .*

　　　*Marquesans view mature adults not as those who give up personal goals . . .
to conform to the group, but rather those who coordinate their own goals with
those of the group.*
—*Martini, 1994b, pp. 73, 101*

Many authors have characterized European American cultural practices as
stressing individualism and independence (Harrison et al., 1990; Harwood
et al., 1995; Kagitçibasi, 1996; Strauss, 2000). And middle-class European
American parents have identified independence as the most important
long-term goal for their infants (Richman, Miller, & Solomon, 1988).

　　When asked what is important in raising young children, college-educated European American mothers focused on a concept of independence
involving individuality, self-expression, and freedom from others in action
and thought. In contrast, Chinese mothers who had immigrated to the
United States focused on a different sort of independence—becoming self-
reliant and developing the life skills to become successful, contributing
members of the family and society (Chao, 1995).

　　Adolescence in the United States often has the goal of shedding dependence on parental nurturance to start a separate life, with attempts to
"stand on one's own two feet" and be self-made (Lebra, 1994). However,
there are vast cultural differences in whether maturity is considered to lead
to independence from the family of origin or to renewed ties and transformed responsibilities to the family of origin. For example, in Japan great
attention is given to continued reciprocity and primary ties with family.

　　In Hawaii, middle-class Japanese American parents reported that parenting is a long-term process of preparing children for lifetime engagement
with the family. In contrast, middle-class Caucasian American parents treated

parenting as a process of extensive involvement with young children, followed by connecting them with external training institutions, and then monitoring them as they guide their own development to "leave the nest" (Martini, 1994a).

In everyday life, and in cultural research, issues of social relations bring to attention the ways people consider self-interests and collective interests to operate. In some models, individual and community interests are assumed to be in opposition, such that if one is given prominence the other is diminished. In other models, they can work in conjunction. In either case, the topic requires consideration of individual, interpersonal, and cultural-institutional processes.

Some of the most dramatic issues of autonomy and interdependence have to do with social relations across generations, between adults and children. Through participation in these relationships, and those with peers, the next generation learns about its community's models of how individuals and communities relate. In the process, each generation may question and revise the practices of its predecessors, particularly when distinct practices of different communities are juxtaposed in their lives.

Without juxtaposition of alternative ways, cultural traditions often remain implicit, as simply the unquestioned "common sense" of people in their own communities. Even if implicit, or perhaps especially so, cultural traditions and values pervade individuals' and communities' informal interactions as well as the proceedings of their formal institutions.

In examining mutual involvement and autonomy, this chapter first considers variations in sleeping arrangements that are presumed to relate to the development of independence. The chapter then considers how in communities stressing interdependence, in which people's mutual involvements are emphasized, individuals' autonomy in making decisions may also be prioritized. Next, the chapter examines issues of adult authority and control of children, teasing and shaming as indirect means of control, and cultural perspectives on moral relations with others in the community. The chapter concludes with a discussion of cultural variation in children's cooperative and competitive approaches with others and the ways that social relations may be guided by cultural institutions such as schools.

Sleeping "Independently"

U.S. middle-class families often report that it is important for a child's developing independence and self-reliance to sleep apart, with some stating that separation at night makes daytime separations easier and helps reduce the baby's dependence on them (Morelli et al., 1992). A mother who was born in

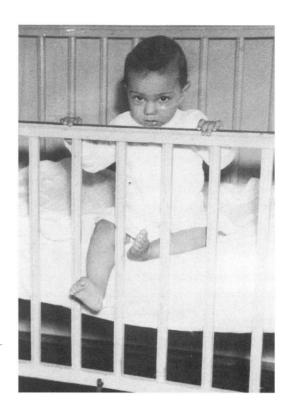

FIGURE 6.1

This 9-month-old middle-class U.S. infant is placed in a crib to sleep by himself.

Greece but had lived in the United States for most of her life said that she had the baby sleep apart from her because "It was time to give him his own room . . . his own territory. That's the American way" (p. 604; see figure 6.1).

However, putting babies to sleep apart from their mother is an unusual practice when viewed from a worldwide and historical perspective (Super, 1981; Trevathan & McKenna, 1994). In a study of 136 societies, infants slept in bed with their mother in two-thirds of the communities, and in the other communities the babies were usually in the same room with their mother (Whiting, 1964). In a survey of 100 societies, American parents were the only ones to maintain separate quarters for their babies (Burton & Whiting, 1961).

In interviews, middle-class European American parents reported that their infant slept separately from them by a few weeks of age, usually in another room (Morelli et al., 1992; Rogoff et al., 1993). Some U.S. parents who occasionally had their infant in bed with them commented that they knew it was counter to the way things are supposed to be done; they recognized that they were violating cultural norms (Hanks & Rebelsky, 1977; Morelli et al., 1992).

Folk wisdom in European American middle-class communities has portrayed nighttime separation of infants from their parents as essential for healthy psychological development, to develop a spirit of independence (Kugelmass, 1959; Trevathan & McKenna, 1994). This belief is reflected in the advice parents have received since the early 1900s from child-rearing experts: "I think it's a sensible rule not to take a child into the parents' bed for any reason" (Dr. Spock, 1945, p. 101).

Middle-class U.S. parents often feel obliged to avoid giving their children comfort during the night (Morelli et al., 1992). One mother reported putting a pillow over her head to drown out the sounds of her crying baby, consistent with the advice of some child-rearing specialists (e.g., Ferber, 1986). Infants and parents in this community frequently engage in conflicts over independent nighttime sleeping, in which parents and infants often act as adversaries in a battle of wills.

Comfort from Bedtime Routines and Objects

Middle-class U.S. infants are encouraged to depend not on people for comfort and company, but on objects—bottles, pacifiers, blankets, and other "lovies." Bedtime routines involve elaborate grooming and storytelling, sometimes taking an hour. Once in bed, however, the children are expected to fall asleep by themselves, often with the help of a favorite object such as a blanket (Morelli et al., 1992).

Middle-class U.S. infants and young children were found to spend about 10% of their time in bedtime activities. In contrast, Kokwet (East African) children of the same ages were not involved in such activities at all (Harkness & Super, 1992a). Toddlers in Turkish families that have recently made a transition from rural roots to the urban middle class usually still slept in the same room as their parents and seldom had bedtime routines or attachment objects (Göncü, 1993).

Similarly, Mayan parents reported that there was no bedtime routine (such as bedtime stories or lullabies) to coax babies to sleep. Toddlers slept in the same room with their parents (and often siblings as well), usually in their mother's bed (Morelli et al., 1992; Rogoff et al., 1993). It was a rare toddler who used security objects to fall asleep, and babies did not rely on thumb sucking or pacifiers. There was generally no need for a bedtime routine to ease a separation because the babies went to sleep with their family, in the same place, whenever they got sleepy.

[handwritten margin notes: toddler in / snack attack / had toy]

Social Relations in Cosleeping

In many communities, the social relations of daytime hours continue through the night. Children sleep with family members when they fall asleep, rather than having a separately designated place and time for sleep.

Communities that practice cosleeping include both highly technological and less technological communities. Japanese urban children have usually slept next to their mother in early childhood and continued to sleep with another family member after that (Ben-Ari, 1996; Caudill & Plath, 1966; Takahashi, 1990). Space considerations appear to play only a minor role.

Berry Brazelton noted that "the Japanese think the U.S. culture rather merciless in pushing small children toward such independence at night" (1990, p. 7). Indeed, Japanese parents have reported that cosleeping facilitates infants' transformation from separate individuals to being able to engage in interdependent relationships (Caudill & Weinstein, 1969). This contrasts with reports that U.S. parents believe that infants are born dependent and need to be socialized to become independent.

A Mayan researcher, Marta Navichoc Cotuc (personal communication, 1986), speculated that if infants are integrated members of the family group, they may have an easier time identifying with their family's values than infants who are forced to spend the night alone. Mayan parents responded with shock, disapproval, and pity on hearing that many middle-class U.S. toddlers are put to sleep in a separate room. One mother asked, "But there's someone else with them there, isn't there?" When told that they are sometimes alone in the room, she gasped. Another responded with shock and disbelief, asked whether the babies do not mind, and said that it would be very painful for her to have to do that. Similarly, "It would be unthinkable in the East African context for a baby to cry itself to sleep; this U.S. custom is considered abusive by East Africans" (Harkness & Super, 1992b, p. 453; see also LeVine et al., 1994). This shock at others' cultural practices parallels the disapproval often shown by European American middle-class adults over the idea of children sleeping with their parents.

A case reported in the *San Jose* (California) *Mercury News* highlights the cultural meaning and social relations involved in sleeping arrangements. In San Jose, Child Protective Services intervened with a family from the Iu Mien tribe of Southeast Asia because their 7-year-old child went to school with some bruises. Adults in the school thought that there was a chance that the child had been abused. Soon the four children were removed from the home, with very little explanation to the parents about what was happening and where the children were being taken. One of the children was a 5-week-old baby, who was placed in a foster home. The baby died there of Sudden Infant Death Syndrome (see also Fadiman, 1997).

Members of the family's community were incensed at what happened for two reasons. First, when families are having trouble (for example, a child is being beaten by his father), neighbors and other familiar people are the ones who are supposed to intervene and help. Second, Iu Mien babies stay with their parents constantly, sleeping in the same bed. (Recall the speculation that sleeping with others may assist some infants in regulating their breathing, and that sleeping apart might contribute to Sudden Infant Death Syndrome.) A spokesman for the Lao Iu Mien Culture Association said:

> Parents believe it's traumatic for families to be separated. A community leader traditionally would intervene with the extended family if there were trouble. . . . "It's wrong, morally wrong, to take away a 1-month-old child from parents without knowing the background and history of the family. Just that action itself hurt both the parents and the child." (Feb. 16, 1994, back page)

Within the United States, families in a number of communities commonly engage in cosleeping. In some African American and Appalachian settings, infants frequently sleep with or near parents (Abbott, 1992; Lozoff, Wolf, & Davis, 1984; Ward, 1971). Rosy Chang, a Ph.D. student in California, describes her immigrant family's interpretation of U.S. sleeping arrangements from the perspective of their Lao and Chinese heritage:

> We had limited sleeping quarters so I would always sleep in the same room as my grandmother since I was the youngest. . . . Another reason I shared a room with my grandmother for most of my childhood was so that I wouldn't become scared. I remember preferring it that way. I would have too many nightmares without her (when she stayed elsewhere). When my friends spent the night, we would sleep in the same room with my grandmother too. I remember thinking my friends probably think it is strange, because when I spent the night at my friend's house, we would sleep in one of the guest rooms. They actually had rooms that were unoccupied! I thought, how could they live in such a big, empty house (compared to the amount of people living there)?
>
> Also, we all liked living together in a tight niche. That's the tradition my family was used to and it's more warm and inviting. I remember it would be so rare to have someone not be home. It was fun living with a big family. We were all close and did activities close to each other in proximity. Rooms would not be unoccupied and scary. They were friendly and occupied.
>
> I'm not sure if these sleeping arrangements influenced me and my siblings to be less independent, but even if it did, that wouldn't be inconsistent with our values. In my culture, parents are supposed to take care of their children for a long time, perhaps even until age 30, until after they finish school and even after they find stable work. After they maintain full independence after acquiring a job,

marriage, and a house, children are expected to take care of their parents. . . .

I'm the exception because I chose higher education away from home, but typically children stay home until ready to make a stable living on their own. They are not thrown out of the house as soon as they finish college. I always thought it was so wrong that my best friend had to begin paying rent as soon as she finished high school. The only exception was if she attended college. Then she was thrown out of the house after college. On the contrary, my brother, who is older than I am, has finished college but is still working and living at home, saving enough money to become independent. Another is still attending school and living at home. My parents would have it no other way. They want my brothers to save enough money to put a down payment on a house or [wait] until they are married to leave the house. It makes no sense to do what my best friend did and leave her parents' home while she is working, because she would not be able to save money, but would waste money on rent. My mom felt pity for my best friend for moving out on her own and thinks that White parents force this on their children because they don't love them as much. (personal communication, 1997)

Independence versus Interdependence with Autonomy

Child-rearing practices in many cultural groups contrast with the training toward separate individuality stressed in the European American middle class. In many communities, children are socialized to interdependence—responsive coordination with the group—rather than separate individualism.

Children in some communities are encouraged to interact in a multi-directional way with groups of people (see Chapter 4). In environments with other people constantly present, infants seldom sit alone and play with objects or engage in one-on-one, face-to-face interaction. Rather, they spend most of their time oriented to the group and ongoing events (Paradise, 1994). Instead of facing the caregiver, an infant may face the same direction as the caregiver ("outward") and learn from the caregiver's activities and interactions with other people (see figure 6.2).

In some communities, this social engagement involves close physical contact, with infants held, sleeping cuddled in arms, and carried on backs or hips. The term for taking care of a baby in Kipsigis (a Kenyan language) literally means holding the baby (Harkness & Super, 1992b; see also LeVine et al., 1994). Skilled working-class African American caregivers know how to hold a baby as though "he's a part of you" (Heath, 1983, p. 75). In con-

FIGURE 6.2

This 11-month-old from the Ituri Forest of the Democratic Republic of Congo faces the same direction as her mother and can observe what her mother does and interact with the people her mother engages with from this vantage point.

trast, middle-class U.S. infants were held for approximately half the time as Kenyan Gusii infants (Richman, Miller, & Solomon, 1988).

However, in some communities where interdependence is stressed, close physical contact is not necessarily a part of being involved with the group. For example, Marquesan (Polynesian) adults either attend to the baby or put the baby down, rather than carrying infants in a "blending" fashion (Martini & Kirkpatrick, 1992).

With or without close physical contact, interdependence involves orienting to the group. However, engagement with the group can simultaneously emphasize individual autonomy. It can be based on voluntary, individual choice, as among the Marquesans:

> Marquesans value group participation but reject the idea of persons submitting to authority. The ideal situation is one in which people have similar or complementary goals and willingly collaborate in a mutually beneficial activity without anyone dominating anyone else. Young children learn that autonomy is valued and then learn when and how to exercise it while still being group members. (Martini & Kirkpatrick, 1992, p. 218)

lual Freedom of Choice in an Interdependent System

ε can both coordinate with others and act autonomously. The usual view in psychology associates freedom of choice with independence and treats coordination among members of a group as lack of autonomy (see Kagitçibasi, 1996). This dichotomy persists in some cultural approaches (e.g., Greenfield & Suzuki, 1998; see Strauss, 2000 for a critique). Contradicting the dichotomous opposition of individual choice and interpersonal coordination, a number of observations suggest that in many communities interdependence also involves respect for the autonomy of individuals.

To be a part of an interdependent group, people in many communities have the responsibility to coordinate with the group but the freedom to do otherwise. For example, individuals' decisions are respected among the Kaluli of Papua New Guinea: "One can never compel another to act. One can appeal and try to move others to act, or assert what one wants" (Schieffelin, 1991, p. 245).

The cultural pattern of interdependence with respect for individuals' autonomy challenges commonly held assumptions in U.S. research regarding the nature of individuality and independence:

> There seems to exist in Western societies an eternal, inescapable tension between autonomy and cooperation—between the individual's right to do as he or she pleases, and the need for the individual to control his or her ego for the common good. For the Navajo, on the other hand, far from being opposed to cooperation, individual freedom of action is seen as the only sure *source* of cooperation. . . . Navajo people place immense value on cooperation . . . while simultaneously holding great respect for individual autonomy. (Chisholm, 1996, p. 178)

"Inviolability of the individual" is a central value widespread among North and Central American Indians (Ellis & Gauvain, 1992; Lamphere, 1977; Paradise, 1987). At any age, people have the right to make their own decisions about their own actions; it is inappropriate to force others to do something against their will (Greenfield, 1996, building on a concept borrowed from Downs).

An example of respect for others' decisions in a Mayan community was provided by Lois Paul (personal communication, 1974). A mother whose 3- or 4-year-old got a bean stuck up her nose asked Lois Paul to remove it. She asked the mother to hold the child still, and the mother said, "I can't; she doesn't want to." Holding the child still would be intruding too much on the child's self-determination and will. The respect for personal autonomy is not breached even for another's well-being.

According respect for others' freedom of choice is a foundation of interdependence in native northern Canadian and Alaskan ways:

> Nonintervention or mutual respect for the individuality of others is an essential element of system stability [of the community]. Without reciprocal nonintervention there would be no larger system. The potential runaway autonomy of individuals is held in check by the mutual respect of others which is held in equally high regard.
>
> We have then the seeming paradox that . . . the autonomy of the individual can only be achieved to the extent that it is granted to one by others. Individual autonomy is, in fact, a social product. One gains autonomy to the extent one grants it. . . . Each person in each situation is constrained only by his own wish to be granted autonomy. Even in this the autonomy of the individual is preserved. One respects others as one's own choice motivated by one's own wish for mutual respect. (Scollon & Scollon, 1981, p. 104)

Learning to Cooperate, with Freedom of Choice

Nonintervention is practiced in some communities even with very young children, who may not be prevented from actions other than those that would cause severe physical harm. Minor harm, such as burns from touching a stove, are usually treated as less serious than interfering with a child's actions, so native northern Canadian/Alaskan children are rarely told not to do something (Scollon & Scollon, 1981). Respect for the autonomy of the individual is also a core value among Aka foragers of Central Africa, where infants' actions are not interfered with except if an infant begins to crawl into a fire or hits another child (Hewlett, 1991).

Individual autonomy is respected with Mayan infants because it is inappropriate to go against other people's self-determination, even if they themselves do not understand how to act in a responsible interdependent way. For example, Mayan mothers were much less likely than middle-class European American mothers to try to overrule toddlers' wishes by insisting on their own way (even though the Mayan toddlers were twice as likely to refuse or insist on their own way; Rogoff et al., 1993). Middle-class European American mothers more often tried to supersede the children's will, trying to force the children to follow the mother's agenda.

By the standards of the Mayan community, forcing amounts to lack of respect for the children's autonomy. Mayan parents often tried to persuade, but stopped short of forcing a child to comply, as when 18-month-old Roberto did not want to have his cloth diaper and trousers put on:

First his mother tried coaxing, then bribing with false promises, "Let's put on your diaper. . . . Let's go to Grandma's. . . . We're going to do an errand." This did not work, and the mother invited Roberto to nurse, as she swiftly slipped the diaper on him with the father's assistance. The father announced, "It's over!" and as a distraction offered Roberto the ball that we had brought.

The mother continued the offer of the toy, with her voice reflecting increasing exasperation that the child was wiggling and not standing to facilitate putting on his pants. Her voice softened as Roberto became interested in the ball, and she increased the stakes: "Do you want another toy?" Roberto listened to both parents say, "Then put on your pants." They continued to try to talk Roberto into cooperating, and handed him various objects, which Roberto enjoyed. But still he stubbornly refused to cooperate with dressing. They left him alone for a while. When his father asked if he was ready, Roberto pouted "Nono!"

After a bit, the mother told Roberto that she was leaving, and waved goodbye. "Are you going with me?" Roberto sat quietly with a worried look. "Then put on your pants, put on your pants to go up the hill." Roberto stared into space, seeming to consider the alternatives. His mother started to walk away, "OK then, I'm going. Goodbye." Roberto started to cry, and his father persuaded, "Put on your pants then!" and his mother asked "Are you going with me?"

Roberto looked down worriedly, one arm outstretched in a half take-me gesture. "Come on, then," his mother offered the pants and Roberto let his father lift him to a stand and cooperated in putting his legs into the pants and in standing to have them fastened. His mother did not intend to leave; instead she suggested that Roberto dance for the audience. Roberto did a baby version of a traditional dance, looking up slightly poutily at the interviewer. (Rogoff et al., 1993, pp. 83–84)

These Mayan parents' persuasive and distracting tactics (including promises and threats that were not carried out) seemed to maintain a boundary of not forcefully intervening against the child's will.

Learning to collaborate with the group, with respect for individual self-determinination, seems to be accomplished by age 3 to 5 years in this Mayan community. Siblings at this age voluntarily respected toddlers' autonomy without being forced, allowing toddlers to have access to objects they themselves wanted (Mosier & Rogoff, 2002). Usually without prompting, they gave desired objects to the toddler, whose self-interest was treated as characteristic of being too young to understand how to be a cooperating member of a group.

The 3- to 5-year-olds cooperated, according to the Mayan view, because by this age they understood how to be a cooperating member of a group. Also, they were used to functioning within a consistent system of respect for individuals' autonomy. They had not been treated adversarially themselves as babies; they had been treated in a way that gave them a chance to observe how other people respected their own and others' autonomy. They were no longer the one given leeway, but all their lives they had participated in the system in which responsibility to other people and respect for each other's autonomy are inherent in human relations.

In Mazahua families (indigenous to Mexico), *respeto* for the person also extends from infancy throughout life, in a general noninterfering approach that adults take toward children and others (Paradise, 1987). With this continuity of a respectful approach, Mazahua babies' privileged status transforms into a responsible child status in a few years:

> It is precisely by taking on the various roles of others, and practicing those roles in interactions with others, that the child learns to organize all of the different and often complementary attitudes he or she encounters. . . . For instance, the basic values that indicate that a baby be appreciated and respected, dealt with gently, and that care be taken that his or her will not be thwarted, are experienced from a baby's perspective, and then from another position that corresponds to a different social status. (pp. 132–133)

Paradise connected the children's early experiential understanding of *respeto* with traditional leadership, in which elders protect and guide rather than giving orders or dominating. Group integration involves each individual following his or her own path without being "organized" by anyone else, in a smoothly functioning coordination that is not preplanned or directed by a boss.

This ethos of respect for individual autonomy contrasts with the treatment of toddlers, common in some middle-class European American families, as willful, independent persons (even adversaries) with whom to negotiate, sometimes in battles of will or tugs-of-war. For example, battles and negotiations are common in parental efforts to get infants and toddlers to sleep by themselves, for fear that if they let the baby "win," they will have lost parental authority.

Adversarial relations may follow historical antecedents in Puritan child-rearing practices of the 1600s. Children were viewed as wicked by nature and needing parental correction—beginning in infancy—to enforce the habit of righteousness to facilitate the children's salvation (Moran & Vinovskis, 1985; Morgan, 1944). Similarly, John Wesley, the founder of Methodism, in the late 1700s exhorted the importance of correcting children: "Break their wills betimes, begin this work before they can run alone, before they can speak plain, perhaps before they can speak at all. Whatever pains it costs, break the will, if you would not damn the child" (in Cleverley, 1971, p. 15, quoting from Southey, 1925).

Middle-class European American mothers frequently intervened as judges and negotiators when their children tussled (Mosier & Rogoff, 2002). They helped the children learn to defend their individual rights and respect the individual rights of others, in accord with their local cultural values. Mothers often established rules for equal, separate turn-taking (never suggested in the Mayan families). The older siblings' negotiation and use of adversarial roles fit a system in which they themselves have participated since infancy. Their roles with younger siblings may assist the toddlers in learning to stand up for their own self-interest in an individualistic model of family relations.

Nonintervention is sometimes misunderstood by people unfamiliar with this cultural system. For example, the practice of allowing American Indian children to cooperate by their own will is often not understood by school personnel. In becoming self-reliant and responsible for others in the community, the children make mature decisions on their own (Chisholm, 1996; Joseph et al., 1949; Lee, 1976). However, European American teachers and administrators in schools on the Navajo reservation often infer that parents have "no control" over their children (Deyhle, 1991). For example, if a school counselor asks a Navajo family about their 14-year-old who has missed school for a week, his parents may say he is probably staying with his uncles somewhere, and the school counselor may tell them to make sure he is in school tomorrow. To Navajo families, especially with a child of 14 but probably also with a younger child, forcing them to do this would intrude on their autonomy.

Training for interdependence with autonomy also appears in accounts of Japanese child rearing, where autonomy and cooperation are compatible qualities that both fall under one term, *sunao,* which may be translated as "receptive":

> A child who is sunao has not yielded his or her personal autonomy
> for the sake of cooperation; cooperation does not suggest giving up
> the self as it may in the West; it implies that working with others is
> the appropriate way of expressing and enhancing the self. . . . How
> one achieves a sunao child . . . seems to be never go against the child.
> (White & LeVine, 1986, pp. 58–59)

In traditional Japanese belief, young children learn autonomously, and use of parental controlling behavior such as anger and impatience leads children after age 10 or 11 to resent and disobey authority rather than to cooperate with others (Kojima, 1986). The next section examines issues of cooperation and control in adult-child relations.

Adult-Child Cooperation and Control

Questions of adult control and discipline relate closely to the ideas of interdependence and autonomy. Underlying many discussions of discipline are questions of control, of who has authority over whom, in adversarial roles. This is clearly at odds with the approach of communities in which respect for others' autonomy is a basic premise, as described in the previous section. However, in U.S. research and middle-class folk beliefs, it is often assumed that if adults don't have control, children do, and vice versa.

When child-rearing books became common in the United Stattes, after 1825, most of the concerns expressed in them had to do with issues of authority (Demos & Demos, 1969). The public was concerned that parental authority was waning, and authors urged parents to establish control early to combat the willfulness and inherent selfish nature of children. Demos and Demos provided a telling quote from Burton's 1863 *Helps to Education*:

> It must be confessed that an irreverent, unruly spirit has come to be a prevalent, an outrageous evil among the young people of our land. . . . Some of the good old people make facetious complaint on this. . . . "There is as much family government now as there used to be in our young days," they say, "only it has changed hands." (pp. 38–39)

During the 20th century, child-rearing advice, educational debate, and psychological research focused on the issue of authority. Often, the debate cast adult and child authority as alternatives such that only one "side" could be in control (Eccles et al., 1991; Giaconia & Hedges, 1982; Greene, 1986; Stipek, 1993; see figure 6.3).

An alternative was promoted by John Dewey (1938), who sought educational changes to support the widespread involvement of all Americans in democratic processes. Dewey claimed that adults have the obligation to guide children but that this does not imply that adults must control them. Adults and children do not necessarily need to be on different sides; rather, they can collaborate, with different roles and responsibilities in the group (Engeström, 1993; Kohn, 1993; Rogoff, 1994). This view is reflected in discussions of collaborative classrooms and family relations in which adults and children engage in shared endeavors, with varying leadership and responsibility (Brown & Campione, 1990; Kobayashi, 1994; Newman, Griffin, & Cole, 1989; Rogoff et al., 2001; Tharp & Gallimore, 1988; Wells,

FIGURE 6.3

A teacher in charge of a public school class in Clayton, New Mexico, 1914.

Chang, & Maher, 1990). Cooperation and control are central to issues surrounding both parental discipline and teachers' classroom discipline.

Parental Discipline

Focusing on parental discipline in the United States, Diana Baumrind (1971) distinguished three styles: an authoritarian style, in which adults control children; a permissive style, in which children have free rein; and an authoritative style, in which parents guide children as well as consult them, setting clear standards while encouraging their independence and individuality, with a verbal give-and-take between parents and children. In European American middle-class populations, parents' authoritative style has been associated with greater social and academic competence among children than parental authoritarian or permissive styles.

Cultural variations have been observed in the prevalence of authoritarian, authoritative, and permissive treatment of children by parents, as well as in the relation of these styles to other aspects of parents' and children's lives (Baumrind, 1972). For example, in Kenya, parents with more schooling were likely to negotiate conflicts with their children and to allow the children to question their authority, which contrasts with traditional parent-child relations (Whiting, 1974).

Chinese parents have been judged as using a more authoritarian parenting style than U.S. counterparts. However, several authors suggest that using the Western concept of authoritarianism with Chinese parents may be misleading. Authoritarian child rearing stems from a history of several centuries of American evangelical religious fervor, which stresses domination and "breaking of the child's will" (Chao, 1994, p. 1113). "In contrast, in Chinese parenting, 'training (*guanjiao*)' takes place in the context of a supportive, involved, and physically close mother-child relationship. It involves caring, devotion, and sacrifice as well as strict discipline and control" (Fung, 1995, p. 7; see Stewart, Bond, Zaman, McBride-Chang, Rao, Ho, & Fielding, 1999, for similar findings in Pakistan). Although prevalence of parental styles in China differed from those in European American populations, similar relationships with children's social and academic competence were found in one study (Chen, Dong, & Zhou, 1997).

Within U.S. populations, differences have been noted in both the prevalence and patterns of relationship of parental discipline styles and their children's social and academic competence. Asian, Black, and Hispanic adolescents from northern California reported their parents as more authoritarian and less authoritative than did White adolescents. Also, the Black adolescents reported less permissiveness than did White adolescents, whereas Hispanics and Asians reported more permissiveness than did White adolescents (Dornbusch, Ritter, Leiderman, Roberts, & Fraleigh, 1987). Within the White and Black groups, authoritarian and permissive styles were associated with low grades, and an authoritative style was associated with higher grades—but the relations were more variable within the Asian and Hispanic groups.

Parental control of decision making seems to have distinct meaning and varying implications for life adjustment in different communities. Among European American youth, those who reported that their parents controlled their decisions—curfews and choice of classes and friends—showed more deviant behavior and poorer academic and psychosocial functioning a year later (Lamborn, Dornbusch, & Steinberg, 1996). In contrast, there was no relation between reports of parents controlling decisions and later adjustment for Asian American and Hispanic American youth. Among African American youth, those who reported that their parents controlled decisions showed *less* involvement in deviant behavior and higher academic performance, regardless of their social class and the affluence of their neighborhood. (In all groups, the adolescents who reported little involvement of parents in their decisions were more likely to show poor adjustment a year later than were those who indicated that decisions were joint with their parents.)

Physical punishment also seems to have different meanings for the children of different communities (Hale-Benson, 1986). European American mothers' use of physical punishment of their kindergarten-age children was associated with the children's development of more aggression toward peers and conflict with teachers. In contrast, no such relationship existed for

African American mothers and children (Deater-Deckard, Dodge, Bates, & Pettit, 1996). Perhaps the use of physical punishment in European American but not in African American families indicates "out-of-control" parents. (Physical abuse, on the other hand, relates to aggressive behavior by children of both ethnic groups.) The greater acceptability of spanking in African American communities may relate to many African American parents' concerns regarding anticipated dangers of the children's neighborhood (such as racist attacks or police violence; Whaley, 2000).

Youth of different communities vary in their interpretations of parental strictness. Many North American adolescents associated strict parental control with parental rejection and hostility and felt that it infringed on their right to be autonomous. However, Korean adolescents viewed parental strictness as an indication of parental warmth and necessary for the youths' success (Rohner & Pettengill, 1985). The researchers attributed the Korean adolescents' perspective to their cultural system, in which individuals are viewed as a part of a more significant whole—the family. Parents' role in protecting the family's welfare is to firmly guide their children and participate in any decision affecting them. The researchers reported that children's role (even in adulthood) is to defer to their parents' wisdom and authority on all matters, including choices of career and spouse.

A follow-up study found that living in a new setting altered judgments regarding parental control (Kim & Choi, 1994). Whereas Korean adolescents associated parental control with high parental warmth, Korean Canadian and Korean American adolescents related parental strictness to hostility, neglect, and rejection. The Korean immigrant youth were in a societal context that stressed individualistic values of independence rather than mutual responsibility in a collective, which may reduce the adaptiveness of the traditional practice in the new setting.

Often, immigrant youth and their families mix and match the approaches of their country of origin and their new country, contributing to changing adaptations across generations. Children and parents who are in the midst of such change negotiate solutions to the new circumstances, sometimes with tension, sometimes with ease. This Asian American college freshman's advice to high school seniors applying to college seems to reflect both his ancestral traditions and his current surroundings. Eric Chun, from San Diego, told an interviewer, "I only applied to two art schools because I didn't think my parents would let me come to art school." The interviewer asked how he convinced his parents to let him go to the school he wanted. Eric explained:

> I wasn't too insistent about going, but I didn't just give up. Something in between. I never said I was going to art school no matter

what. It's not the end of the world if you don't go to the school you want. Loyalty to parents is more important. ("How We Got into College," 1998–99, p. 29)

Teachers' Discipline

In some nations, teachers rap heads or knuckles with rulers; such forms of physical punishment may be seen as an important teaching method (see figure 6.4). In the United States, teachers were prohibited from using corporal punishment several decades ago. (I was in fourth grade when corporal punishment was outlawed in my state, and I recall being relieved, although I had never seen or heard of such punishment in school.) Questions of how to "control" classrooms continue to be central in teachers' training and follow some of the same distinctions seen with parental discipline.

A variety of educational prescriptions urge teachers to depart from their traditional authority roles to engage in dialogue with students (Sutter & Grensjo, 1988; Tharp & Gallimore, 1988). European research indicates that in classrooms in which teachers exert control through commands and questions, children respond tersely. Children are more active and equal participants when teachers instead use noncontrolling talk (such as commentary on their own ideas and demonstration of their own uncertainty) and increase the amount of time allowed for children to respond (Subbotskii, 1987; Wood, 1986).

One approach that is often recommended is for teachers to soften their directives or veil their commands to students in the interest of creating a more egalitarian climate. However, this softening of directives may be confusing to some students. Lisa Delpit pointed out that middle-class veiled commands may be cast as questions (for example, "Isn't it time for your bath?") but are understood as directives. This contrasts with the more direct commands often used by working-class mothers (see also Hale-Benson, 1986; Moreno, 1991). Delpit pointed out that such veiled directives may confuse students who are used to straightforward directives:

> A Black mother, in whose house I was recently a guest, said to her eight-year-old son, "Boy, get your rusty behind in that bathtub." Now I happen to know that this woman loves her son as much as any mother, but she would never have posed the directive to her son to take a bath in the form of a question. Were she to ask, "Would you like to take your bath now?" she would not have been issuing a directive but offering a true alternative. . . . Upon entering school the child from such a family may not understand the indirect statement of the teacher as a direct command. . . .

FIGURE 6.4

This 16th-century school scene comes from a Persian manuscript. "The old, bearded teacher, who holds a stick in his hand to encourage good performance, is instructing one attentive pupil, and others seem to be concentrating on their manuscripts, but theschool-room is not very orderly. Two boys play in the courtyard while another pulls a friend's ear, and pen boxes and inkpots are scattered about" (Burn & Grossman, 1984, p. 84).

But those veiled commands are commands nonetheless, representing true power, and with true consequences for disobedience. If veiled commands are ignored, the child will be labeled a behavior problem and possibly officially classified as behavior disordered. In other words, the attempt by the teacher to reduce an exhibition of power by expressing herself in indirect terms may remove the very explicitness that the child needs to understand the rules of the new classroom culture.

A Black elementary school principal in Fairbanks, Alaska, reported to me that she has a lot of difficulty with Black children who are placed in some White teachers' classrooms. The teachers often send the children to the office for disobeying teacher directives. Their parents are frequently called in for conferences. The parents' response to the teacher is usually the same: "They do what I say; if you just tell them what to do, they'll do it. I tell them at home that they have to listen to what you say." (1988, p. 289)

Observations by a North American preschool teacher compellingly reveal cultural assumptions regarding effective authority. Cindy Ballenger (1992; 1999) was interested in understanding how her Haitian-background colleagues successfully managed classrooms of Haitian preschoolers in Massachusetts, while she herself was having trouble. In a friendly and cheerful fashion, Ballenger's class of 4-year-olds consistently followed their own inclinations rather than her directions. In her colleagues' classrooms, the children did follow directions in an affectionate and cheerful way.

On speaking with Haitian teachers at another center about this problem, Ballenger learned that the teachers were extremely concerned about behavior problems that they saw with Haitian children. They felt that the way teachers are taught to deal with children's behavior was part of the problem. Haitian parents felt that the schools were tolerating disrespectful behavior. Haitians often perceive North American children as being fresh and out of control. In contrast, North Americans often perceive Haitians as too severe, both verbally and in their use of physical punishment.

Ballenger was helped by an account given by a Haitian woman, Clothilde, who was student teaching in a day care center where she felt that the North American teachers were not controlling the children well:

One day, as Clothilde arrived at her school, she watched a teacher telling a little Haitian child that the child needed to go into her classroom, that she could not stay alone in the hall. The child refused and eventually kicked the teacher. Clothilde had had enough. She asked the director to bring her all the Haitian kids right away. The director and Clothilde gathered the children into the large common room. . . .

CLOTHILDE: Does your mother let you bite?

CHILDREN: No.

CLOTHILDE: Does your father let you punch kids?

CHILDREN: No.

CLOTHILDE: Do you kick at home?

CHILDREN: No.

CLOTHILDE: You don't respect anyone, not the teachers who play with
you or the adults who work upstairs. You need to respect
adults—even people you see on the streets. You are taking good
ways you learn at home and not bringing them to school. You're
taking the bad things you learn at school and taking them home.
You're not going to do this anymore. Do you want your parents
to be ashamed of you?

According to Clothilde, the Haitian children have been well-behaved
ever since. Other Haitian teachers . . . confirmed that that was what
the children needed to hear. (1992, p. 202)

Clothilde pointed out to Ballenger that in her speech to the children,
she did not refer to the children's emotions. She noted that North American
teachers frequently refer to children's feelings and interpret them for the
children (e.g., "You must be angry"). North American teachers often talk
about the consequences of misbehavior (e.g., "If you don't listen to me, you
won't know what to do"). Haitian teachers rarely do this; they assume that
the children are already aware that the particular behavior is wrong. Instead,
the Haitian teachers focus on the values and responsibilities of group membership and sometimes talk about affection for the children.

Ballenger began to adopt some of the ways that she learned from the
Haitian teachers and parents, and found that the children paid close attention. Sometimes the other children thanked her earnestly for her intervention with a classmate. On one occasion, she was scolding the children for
not waiting for her while crossing a parking lot:

CINDY [BALLENGER]: Did I tell you to go?

CHILDREN: No.

CINDY: Can you cross this parking lot by yourselves?

CHILDREN: No.

CINDY: That's right. There are cars here. They're dangerous. I don't
want you to go alone. Why do I want you to wait for me, do you
know?

"Yes," says Claudette, "because you like us."
    Although I was following the usual Haitian form, . . . I had been

expecting a final response based on the North American system of cause and effect, something like, "Because the cars are dangerous." Claudette, however, although she understands perfectly well the dangers of cars to small children, does not expect to use that information in this kind of an interaction. What, then, *is* she telling me? One thing that she is saying, which is perhaps what the solemn children also meant, is that, from her point of view, there is intimacy in this kind of talk. This is certainly the feeling I get from these experiences. I feel especially connected to the children in those instances in which I seem to have gotten it right.

. . . I have learned from working with Haitian children and teachers that there are situations in which reprimands can be confirming, can strengthen relationships. (1992, pp. 205, 206)

In another cultural system, adult indirectness is especially valued, but with explicit supports for children in learning how to interact. Visitors to Japan from North America often are surprised by the extent of freedom given to very young children, who sometimes seem undisciplined. However, by the time Japanese children are in first grade, they are more attentive than U.S. children and spend less time behaving inappropriately (Abe & Izard, 1999; Lewis, 1995; Stevenson et al., 1987).

Indeed, Japanese first-graders take on responsibility, with no direct management by an adult, for managing such aspects of school as quieting the class for lessons to begin, breaking into small groups to carry out and discuss science experiments, and running class meetings. When a teacher is absent, the class runs itself, with other teachers or a principal occasionally checking in. Catherine Lewis (1995) has suggested that the impressive behavior of the Japanese children is due to the freedom and supportive empathy of the early years at home and at school. The feeling of belonging that is fostered leads to a feeling of responsibility for the welfare of the group. With muted adult authority, children take strong roles in determining class norms. Teachers encourage children's own problem solving and reflection on the problems that arise, as learning opportunities.

Japanese students' impressive ability to engage together is also supported by explicit prompts indicating classroom formats, such as classroom posters that suggest wording for how to organize a discussion. Lewis gave an example of a 45-minute class meeting run by two 6-year-old class monitors while the teacher sat quietly for most of the time, occasionally raising her hand to be called on. The two students referred to a poster that listed six steps for leading a discussion and announced the first part of the meeting together: "Today's topic for discussion is choosing our next special activity for the class."

Students' hands shot up, and suggestions were plentiful: a talent show, a tug-of-war, a class play, clay projects. The monitors initially called on children in turn, but soon all children were shouting at once. The factions for a talent show and a tug-of-war shouted the most loudly. Ms. Mori did not speak.

After several minutes of shouting, a boy sprang to the front of the class and shouted, "Let's take a vote between talent show and tug-of-war." One of the monitors pulled the teacher's chair over to the blackboard and stood on it to tally votes on the board. The class quieted to vote. One monitor counted the hands and the other recorded the tallies. "The talent show wins," they announced and then led the class in deciding the date for the show, which groups would perform, and which would be audience. . . .

Even when there was a short scuffle between two boys over which groups would perform, the teacher did not intervene. The monitors settled the scuffle by asking the two boys to abide by the results of the hand play "scissors-paper-stone."

Referring again to the poster, the monitors asked, "Do we have anything else to decide?" With no responses, the monitors summarized what had been decided, and one monitor wrote each decision on the board: to have a talent show, its date, which groups would perform and which would be audience, and the dates for practice. (1995, pp. 111–112)

Teachers' comments during such discussions often challenged students to justify what they had said or to reconcile their comments with those of other students. In reflection questions at the end of the school day, teachers asked students to think privately about such questions as "Did today's class discussions involve all classmates or just a few classmates?" and "Did I volunteer my ideas sometime today?" With an emphasis on social and ethical development, these Japanese teachers viewed students' shared participation and personal commitment to rules as important measures of educational success. The teachers' contribution was to guide the children in their collectively developed standards, not to enforce adult-designed rules.

In this setting, as with the others in this section, children's participation in considering the ways of the community or group play a central role in classroom functioning. In such classrooms, the teacher can encourage the children's attention to the practices developed in the class, school, or community, and the children can develop responsibility to the group. Although the particulars of the cultural formats vary, along with distinct preferences for explicitness or indirectness, these classroom examples have in common a respect for autonomy in interdependence.

Teasing and Shaming as Indirect Forms of Social Control

In some communities, teasing by adults or peers is a way to inform people indirectly that their behavior is out of bounds or to indicate the appropriate way to act (Camara, 1975; Edwards & Whiting, 1992; Schieffelin, 1986). This is a form of social control that does not require forcing people to adapt to culturally appropriate ways. Instead, it marks transgressions and motivates people to learn the ways that will not single them out for teasing.

Especially in small interrelated communities, people avoid intrusive or hostile interactions for expressing everyday criticisms or complaints, to avoid jeopardizing long-term relationships (Eisenberg, 1986; Houser, 1996; Schieffelin, 1986). In such settings, teasing provides an indirect means to express criticism, carried in discourse that is softened by humor and that does not call for a serious response:

> Effective Lakota [American Indian] teasing is ambiguous; it conveys affection and humor along with a public message that the individual being teased has done something which the speaker—and the audience—find worthy of amusement and criticism. The victim is expected to take the teasing in good humor. The relationship between teaser and teased may and should continue, but the teaser has had an opportunity to express criticisms of conduct. (Houser, 1996, p. 20)

Paul Tiulanga, a leader of the King Island Eskimo people, explained how King Islanders controlled people making problems for others. The local form of social control was systematized in a combination of teasing by cross-cousins (these are children of a brother and a sister) combined with support from partner's cousins (children of same-sex siblings):

> Cross-cousins were supposed to tease each other, to make fun of each other when somebody did something wrong. Partner's cousins were supposed to help each other throughout life.
> Cross-cousins could make any kind of jokes, try to make each other feel bad. And if a person lost his temper because of something a cross-cousin said, he would be called a bad apple. Whenever someone misbehaved or did something foolish, someone would tell his cross-cousin about it and the cross-cousin would tease, make up jokes or songs to make the person feel funny. This went on throughout life.
> Partner's cousins would stick together, talk to each other and work together. If a person got in trouble, a partner's cousin would feel badly about it. If one partner's cousin thought the other one were causing a problem for someone else, he would not say anything directly. He would not call a partner's cousin a problem to his face. He

would tell a cross-cousin about it and the cross-cousin would do all he or she could to make the problem person feel funny.

People knew, they observed, whether a person were bad or not. A lot of times they gave a person a second chance, a third chance. They tried to make some kind of a relationship with a problem person. They could not just ignore the person because he or she would become more of a problem. (Senungetuk & Tiulana, 1987, pp. 30–31)

Teasing is also used to help children learn culturally appropriate emotional responses to challenging situations. In a community in which teasing is common, such as among the Kikuyu (of Kenya) or the Kaluli (of New Guinea), teasing helps children learn from toddlerhood to discern the difference between what is real or true and what is not, and to deal with symbolic meaning (Edwards & Whiting, 1992; Henze, 1992; Schieffelin, 1986).

Toddlers were encouraged to learn to handle emotional situations and to determine what is true in a Balinese teasing drama in Margaret Mead and Gregory Bateson's film, *Sibling Rivalry in Three Cultures*. In one incident, several Balinese mothers pretended to reject their own 1-year-olds in favor of another infant (borrowed from another mother). The adults supported the infants in how to handle their angry feelings in a safer situation than when a mother actually has a new baby. After all, it is just play, and a 1-year-old's anger is part of the drama. Parents teasing babies by acting out preference (with someone else's child) may help children learn that teasing is pretend, as well as that life will not always favor them.

The lessons learned from teasing exchanges are likely to differ across communities. The kind of teasing practiced in working-class White families in South Baltimore seems to encourage children to assert themselves, to retaliate, and to speak up in anger—highly valued skills in that community (Miller & Hoogstra, 1992). South Baltimore caregivers playfully provoke their children into defending themselves. Mothers threaten, challenge, and insult their daughters, and encourage even physical aggression against themselves in their daughters' retaliations. Their own experiences have convinced them that their girls need such skills to be able to protect themselves in life (Gaskins, Miller, & Corsaro, 1992). By 30 months, the children were skilled in communicating anger and aggression and began to show ability to justify these responses on the basis of another person's instigation.

Learning how to engage skillfully in teasing repartee appears to serve as anticipatory training for self-protection in U.S. Black lower-income communities (Slaughter & Dombrowski, 1989). The teasing repartee called *signifying* is ritualized language play involving the trading of clever insults. This is seen in *playing the dozens* ("Your mama is so stupid, when she heard

90% of all crimes occur around homes, she moved," and the rapid-fire comeback that follows: "*Your* mama . . . ") or *capping* ("I went to your house and wanted to sit down. A roach jumped up and said, 'Sorry, this seat is taken.'" Response: "So, I went in yo house and stepped on a match and yo mama said, 'Who turned off the heat?'" [Lee, 1991, p. 296]).

Among African American adolescents in many social settings, a person who cannot signify is regarded as inept and having neither status nor style (Lee, 1991). The audience that is present during the entertaining exchange admires skilled players for their verbal fluency and quick-wittedness. African American students in my undergraduate class reported that such teasing among friends (it does not take place between strangers) helps people face up to their shortcomings and not be oversensitive about them. They noted that this prepares members of a minority community to shrug off more serious insults that they can be expected to receive outside their community (Wales & Mann et al., personal communication, March 1996).

Teasing among other groups may serve as lessons in stoicism. For example, among Athabascans in northern Canada, young children learn to accept teasing without losing their composure. They learn to remove themselves emotionally from such situations (Scollon & Scollon, 1981). Similarly, among other people of the Arctic area, teasing may help children develop equanimity in the face of provocations, as caregivers encourage children to respond to teasing affronts by ignoring them or laughing (Briggs, 1970). This kind of teasing of young children is regarded as a form of teaching, not cruel or vengeful. It instructs them in appropriate behavior and strengthens them to not lose face in front of others (Crago, 1988).

Likewise, beginning in toddlerhood, Marquesan children in Polynesia learn to control emotional displays through being taunted. Children learn to withstand the frustrations of social life and to deal with social binds through social criticism and teasing by peers (Martini, 1994b). They learn not to give in to the group or withdraw but to respond to attacks by deflecting them with humor. Teasing and social criticism build resilient concepts of self in these preschoolers. Children move to leadership roles in the peer group when they master self-control in response to other children's teasing. At times, children frustrate younger children until they cry, and then show them more appropriate ways to deal with frustration—to stand up and attend to the group and to make light of an attack.

> The everyday social hazing that Marquesan four-year-olds learn to handle with poise and humor would devastate most American preschoolers. . . .
>
> The Marquesan children learn not to take these events personally and not to assume that others' attacks are aimed directly against their

persons. They learn to define their selves as something more stable than their (frustrated) plans of the moment and as something more worthy than how they are portrayed by their tormenters.

In this sense, although Marquesan children attend and respond extensively to the group, they seem less vulnerable to the inevitable disappointments of social life. In the end they may be less affected by shame and group opinion than are their American counterparts. (pp. 100–101)

Marquesan parents use shame to teach children proper action and attentiveness to observers' opinions. Children also use shame to influence each other, lecturing or showing disgust at another's inappropriate actions. They shame others for endangering themselves or others, making mistakes, going beyond the limits of acceptable behavior, and for acting too bossy or self-centered (Martini, 1994b).

In some communities, shame is both a method of helping children learn moral precepts and a virtue to be developed. Shame has been seen as a virtue since the time of Confucius in China (Fung, 1995). In modern China, the parents of 2- to 4-year-olds reported that their favored way of disciplining the children was to situate the lesson in concrete experience rather than to preach. They reported that the immediate concrete experience helped the children understand how the rules work and to remember and to follow the lesson. By preschool age, children already felt shame if they knew they had disappointed their parents. The parents felt that it was necessary to make their children feel shameful when they had transgressed, but only to teach them to know right from wrong. Too much shame might cause the child to avoid interaction, harming self-esteem and leading the child to try to escape responsibilities and lose motivation to improve. So adults and children were expected to maintain well-balanced shaming.

Shaming occurred commonly as part of family life, about five episodes per hour, for two young Chinese children who were observed at home over several years (Fung, 1995). Caregivers often made use of the experience while it was still fresh, to bring the lesson home. Although shaming involved threats of ostracism and abandonment, all participants handled most shaming events in a playful manner. By age 4, the children were able to incorporate a broader variety of roles and to return challenges or shame other people. Shame was used to teach the children how to be a part of society, to include them and protect them from being set apart by being condemned by people outside the family or by society in general.

Teasing and shaming, like discipline by parents and teachers, involve cultural variations in ways of compelling, persuading, or guiding children to behave in accepted ways. Many moral issues, examined in the next section, also have to do with cultural conceptions of autonomy, responsibility to the group, interdependence, and control.

Conceptions of Moral Relations

Notions of fairness and morality are tied to cultural conceptions of how individuals relate to others in their community. In some communities, emphasis may be on negotiating equal treatment and resources for each person; in others, priority is placed on playing a responsible role in relation to the group (in interdependent autonomy).

The importance of the relation of individual rights and group interests is clear in many moral issues. For example: Is infanticide or infant neglect always immoral or can it be moral to allow one individual to die if that person's survival threatens the survival of the group or of many other people? What is the relation between expenditure of material resources and the prolongation of a single life (such as organ transplants for individuals not likely to live long)?

Moral Reasoning

Research on moral development across communities has often involved tests of moral reasoning (see Eckensberger & Zimba, 1997). For example, in Lawrence Kohlberg's work, individuals were presented with moral dilemmas, such as: If a man's wife is dying for lack of a costly new drug, should the man steal it? In this line of research, the respondents' justifications for their views are classified according to the six stages of Kohlberg's (1976) scale of moral reasoning:

- Kohlberg's first two stages focus on a relatively egocentric account of moral decisions, using one's own perspective and assuming that others do the same, and prioritizing the avoidance of harm or punishment.
- At Stage 3, people take a group perspective and operate according to the Golden Rule ("Do unto others as you would have them do unto you"). They use the rules and customs of the group as a guide in moral justifications; this perspective assumes that there is one right set of rules.
- At Stage 4, society is seen as a system involving competing groups with conflicting interests, mediated through institutions such as the courts, which can change the rules. But the rules that are in place are to be upheld.

- Stages 5 and 6 involve a philosophical approach in which people consider "higher-order" obligations or principles of justice that may supersede the rules of society at a particular time.

Responses to moral dilemmas in different communities fall at varying positions on this scale, with "lower" performance in communities other than those in which the scale was developed. In many societies, most adults respond to such moral dilemmas in Kohlberg's Stage 3. They refer to the notion that society is built on mutual reliance, interdependence, and agreements associated with specific role relations, such as parent to child or friend to friend (Shweder et al., 1990). Most judge morality as conformity to the group's preferences and do not report that there are higher-order obligations that take priority over the will of the group (as in the higher stages of Kohlberg's system).

The research often treats people's justifications for their statements as an indicator of their moral approach to life. This is like treating people's ability to *state* grammatical principles as equivalent to their ability to *use* them (Shweder et al., 1990). People's reasons for doing what they do are not always easy for them to explain. People in some communities, especially those with experience in formal schooling, place much higher priority on articulating the reasons for personal judgments, or self-reflection, than do others (Fiske, 1995; Scribner, 1974). Indeed, "higher" stages of moral reasoning are associated with secondary or greater levels of schooling (Edwards, 1981).

Cultural research has suggested that the moral reasoning scale may also reflect the system of values and political structure of the societies of the researchers. The scale may not apply to people functioning in other political systems (Edwards, 1981). The bureaucratic systems perspective (Stage 4) fits a political frame of reference in a large industrialized society, but may be inappropriate for people in small traditional tribal societies:

> The two types of social systems are very different (though of course both are valid working types of systems), and thus everyday social life in them calls forth different modes of moral problem solving whose adequacy must be judged relative to their particular contexts. (p. 274)

Morality as Individual Rights or Harmonious Social Order

Dora Dien (1982) located roots of the Western system of morality—emphasizing individual autonomy and responsibility for one's own actions—in the Judeo-Christian image of man as created with freedom of self-determination and Greek philosophy emphasizing rationality as the key to morality. It is this system, noted Dien, that is reflected in Kohlberg's six-stage scale of moral reasoning.

In China, Dien argued, the doctrine of Confucianism has served as a system of ethics in which people have a sense of justice and moral conduct that does not involve notions of individual rights, as in the West. In the Confucian system, the universe is regarded as moral, designed in a just, good way. Humans have the duty to act according to the absolute morality of the universe, subordinating their own identity to the interest of the group to ensure a harmonious social order. The Confucian ideal is a sage who has developed deep empathy for others and sensitivity to the delicately balanced forces of the universe, able to judge human affairs with consideration of all the aspects of a particular situation. In China, moral maturity involves the ability to make judgments based on "insight into the intricate system of cultural norms of reciprocity, rules of exchange, various available resources, and the complex network of relationships in a given situation" (p. 339). In contrast, Kohlberg's highest stage emphasizes analytical thinking, individual choice, and responsibility.

Dien noted that the mode of resolving conflicts in the West relies on the protection provided by an elaborate set of laws that assume individual choices and responsibilities. This contrasts with the Chinese preference for resolving conflict through reconciliation, to preserve harmonious interdependent social life. The Confucians have argued against control by penal law, claiming that it is difficult for laws to cover all possible circumstances and that law controls through fear of punishment, which may result in people trying to evade the law rather than to change their ways of thinking and acting.

A similar contrast was made by African American Sea Islanders (South Carolina), who settled disputes through mediation (Guthrie, 2001). Plantation members "thrashed out" grievances within the church, with the aim of restoring harmony. People who took their grievances to the court of law were criticized for not working toward a constructive solution, but stirring up trouble. The court's focus on establishing guilt and seeking restitution was seen as exacerbating problems.

The traditional Navajo peacemaking resolution process aims to restore harmony within the community and clan by seeking the root causes of problems, using spiritual resources to apply moral principles of the Navajo way. The peacemaker does not force a wrongdoer to comply with someone else's will, as in the U.S. legal system. Instead, the "one who speaks wisely and well" uses persuasive powers and focuses on relationships and one's responsibility to find solutions that restore harmony (Witmer, 1996). The peacemaking process was reinstated in the Navajo Nation in 1982 to resolve disputes in a nonadversarial way, after an elder mentioned it during a legal proceeding.[1]

---

[1] Navajo Nation Supreme Court Chief Justice Robert Yazzie has been a proponent of the system, and all 14 Navajo tribal justices refer cases to a peacemaker, sometimes in conjunction with the U.S. legal system (Witmer, 1996). The system has aroused interest from the Canadian government and the American Bar Association, among other groups.

Learning the Local Moral Order

An extensive study in Bhubaneswar (India) and Chicago indicated that children as young as 5 years already have a considerable understanding of the moral precepts of their society (Shweder et al., 1990). By age 5 to 7, children of both communities judged moral situations quite differently, and quite similarly to the adults of their community. There were some precepts that were agreed on in both communities, such as the importance of keeping promises, respecting property, allocating resources fairly, protecting the vulnerable, avoiding incest, and avoiding arbitrary assault. However, many other actions were viewed as neutral or virtuous in one community while being seen as vices in the other.

The differences in moral precepts seemed to cluster in ways that suggested distinct worldviews in the two communities. The basic worldview of the middle-class U.S. adults and children seemed to be organized around the idea that what is moral is what independent individuals agree to—contracts, promises, consent. In contrast, the view of the Bhubaneswar adults and children seemed to be based on the idea that customary practices are part of a natural moral order, in which roles and relationships are specified (Shweder et al., 1990).

The rapid learning by children of their community's moral order may be accounted for by the everyday events in which the child is provided with a moral commentary indicating what is good and pure and what is bad and despicable. It is expressed in the reactions of family members to the child's actions or their reactions to each other, in children's games, and in everyday events like the following:

> "*Mara heici. Chhu na! Chhu na!*" is what a menstruating Oriya [Bhubaneswar] mother exclaims when her young child approaches her lap. It means, "I am polluted. Don't touch me! Don't touch me!" If the child continues to approach, the woman will stand up and walk away from her child. Of course, young Oriya children have no concept of menstruation or menstrual blood; the first menstruation arrives as a total surprise to adolescent girls. Mothers typically "explain" their own monthly "pollution" to their children by telling them that they stepped in dog excrement or touched garbage, or they evade the issue. Nevertheless, Oriya children quickly learn that there is something called "*Mara*" . . . and when "*Mara*" is there, as it regularly is, their mother avoids them, sleeps alone on a mat on the floor, is prohibited from entering the kitchen. . . . In interviews, most six-year-olds think it is wrong for a "polluted" ("*mara*") woman to cook food or to sleep in the same bed with her husband; most nine-year-olds think that "*mara*" is an objective force of nature and that all

women in the world have a moral obligation not to touch other people or cook food while they are "*mara*." (Shweder et al., 1990, p. 196)

With increasing age, the Chicago participants in this study more commonly stressed the context dependence of judgments and relied more on the idea of social agreement. In contrast, the Bhubaneswar participants increasingly viewed their practices as universal and unalterable, arguing, for example, "that it is wrong to let young children sleep alone in a separate room and bed because children awaken during the night and are afraid, and that all parents have an obligation to protect their children from fear and distress" (Shweder et al., 1990, p. 170).

However, a few Indian informants expressed context-dependent moral thinking, such as that provided by some Brahmans from Bhubaneswar, who argued that

> it is immoral for a Brahman widow to wear brightly colored clothes and jewelry because (a) she will appear attractive; (b) if she appears attractive she will invite sexual advances; (c) if she gets involved with sex she will disregard her meditative obligations to the soul of her deceased husband and behave disloyally.
>
> But it is acceptable for American widows to wear bright clothes and jewelry because (a) it is the destiny of America, *at this stage in its development as a civilization*, to be a world conqueror and the ingenious inventor of technology; (b) the offspring of illicit sexual unions are more likely to be clever, dominating, and adventurous; (c) widow remarriage and other American practices, adolescent dating, and "love marriage," encourage illicit sexual unions, thereby producing those qualities of character appropriate to the stage level of American civilization.
>
> A more abstract formulation of that context-dependent moral argument goes something as follows. America is a young civilization. India is an ancient civilization. It takes a long time for a civilization to figure out and evolve good or proper practices and institutions, those that are in equilibrium with the requirements of nature. You should not expect the young to possess the wisdom of the old. America is doing what is fitting or normal for its early stage of development. (Shweder et al., 1990, p. 182)

Mandatory and Discretionary Concepts in Moral Codes

There are apparently some mandatory concepts in the moral code of any society. These include the idea that higher-order obligations supersede individual preference or group agreements, the principle of avoiding harm, and the principle of justice whereby like cases are to be treated similarly (Shweder et al., 1990). At the same time, some discretionary features are held in some societies but not others:

- Some societies base their higher-order obligations on a conception of natural *rights* of individuals (such as the right to liberty). In contrast, others focus on natural *duties* of individuals (such as the duty to uphold the obligations of a prescribed role) or *social goals* (such as the goal to preserve national security).
- Societies vary in which is more fundamental: the individuals who play roles or the roles and statuses themselves. In Kohlberg's system, the fundamental entity is the individual. The individual is considered independent of social roles, with an intrinsic and equal value independent of relational or personal characteristics. Society is seen as deriving from the agreements between individuals. An alternative is to assume that social arrangements are fundamental. This approach prioritizes consideration of social roles and accepts inequality of status and personal characteristics. The idea is that social arrangements are natural and more basic than the individuals who come to inhabit them.
- Definitions of who or what counts as a person vary. Do illegal aliens have the same rights as citizens of the country? Should corporations, fetuses, and cows be protected from harm?
- Where the boundaries around the self are placed varies. Is it our bodies and physical possessions that are to be given protection, or should our feelings and honor also be protected?
- Societies vary in emphasis on whether each person's claims are to be treated as equal, with the good or harm to each individual counting equally. One perspective holds that "saving more lives is better than saving fewer lives, regardless of who it is that is saved, the old or the young, the good or the wicked" (p. 150). In another perspective, rules vary according to differences between individuals or roles.
- Whether or not the concept of divine authority is accepted as a feature of the moral order varies from one community to another.

The world community struggles with how to determine what are moral acts as the practices and values of different communities come into increasing contact. In considering various moral stances, it is useful to understand how cultural institutions such as religion and formal schooling play a role in people's moral decisions and in how they explain their decisions. Debates about morality between groups center on issues of autonomy, independence, interdependence, and social control, as do cultural standards for cooperation and competition, examined in the next section.

Cooperation and Competition

Many observers have remarked on cultural differences in the extent to which individuals cooperate or compete with each other. Some communities prioritize cooperation among group members and competition with other groups; in others, competition is prioritized even within a person's closest group (Harrison et al., 1990; Swisher, 1990).

For example, societal differences in the role of cooperation have been noted in dealings between American Indians and the U.S. government. Senator Henry L. Dawes of Massachusetts complained in 1883 about the natives in Indian Territory: "There is no selfishness, which is the bottom of civilization" (quoted in Spring, 1996, p. 179). Dawes went on to say that owning land in common prevents the enterprising motivation to make one's home better than that of one's neighbors. Competition to accumulate property was one of the values that the colonists and the U.S. government tried to instill in the native population, as the settlers sought (and got) access to Indian land. As quoted in an 1888 Congressional Report, "Commissioner of Indian Affairs John Oberly believed that the Indian student should be taught the 'exalting egotism of American civilization, so that he will say "I" instead of "We," and "This is mine" instead of "This is ours"'" (Adams, 1996, p. 35).

Cultural differences in children's cooperation are apparent from a very early age. Middle-class Korean American children responded to Korean American preschool classmates' play initiations in a more cooperative way than middle-class Anglo-American children responded in Anglo-American preschools (Farver, Kim, & Lee, 1995). The Korean American children usually responded by accepting a play initiation, accepting an object, or beginning to play with the initiator. The Anglo-American children did so in less than half of the play initiations, and more frequently ignored or rejected an invitation, left, or turned away—and sometimes responded by hitting or pushing.

Mary Martini suggested that because middle-class European American children are not skilled in cooperation, they may have a rigid sense of self that "may become stressed when a child is frustrated in reaching his or her goals as is often the case in complex social situations. In these cases, American children may retreat to carefully negotiated contacts or to solitary play" (1994b, p. 99). She pointed out that American preschool teachers and adults take the responsibility for monitoring the peer group to ensure that it operates fairly, helping children take turns and negotiate their individual interests in ways that do not impinge on the individual interests of others. This fits with a moral order organized around individual rights and also protects children who may have difficulty collaborating with each other.

Cooperative versus Competitive Behavior in Games

Several studies have employed a game situation in which cooperation among partners could yield a better result for each player. Children on Israeli kibbutzim—communal settlements founded on premises prioritizing cooperation among people—cooperated. In contrast, Israeli city children were more likely to compete with each other, even though that meant that each person achieved less than if the children had cooperated (Shapira & Madsen, 1969). Urban New Zealand children (of both European and Maori descent) had more difficulty cooperating even when their competitive approach gained them fewer rewards, compared with rural Maori and Cook Island children (Thomas, 1975).

Similarly, rural Mexican children were more likely to cooperate than were urban children of three ethnic groups in the United States (Anglo-American, African American, and Mexican American). The U.S. urban groups competed vigorously with each other even though it meant that none of the partners could win (Madsen & Shapira, 1970). There was no sign of competition among any of the rural Mexican children, and there were no instances of group cooperation in the three U.S. urban groups. In fact, for many of the Anglo-American and African American groups, the children engaged in such vigorous competition that the experimenter had to hold the game board down with both hands to keep it from flying through the air. Competition may be so ingrained in these children that they compete even when this strategy works against what they are trying to accomplish.

A related set of studies involved a coin distribution game, in which coins are to be distributed among four to five players. The participants have the choice of distributing things in a generous way, with others getting at least as many as themselves, or a rivalrous way, in which each person tries to get as many as they can for themselves without regard for what others are getting (Graves & Graves, 1983). Traditional Cook Island adults (in Oceania) distributed the goods in a generous fashion, whereas adults who were living in more modernized circumstances in the Cook Islands used rivalrous distribution. The traditional adults had little schooling, were more likely to live in extended families, and used more traditional ways of making a living.

When Cook Island children played the coin distribution game, they were generous at age 5 or 6—near the beginning of schooling. But by grades 4 to 6, there was much more rivalrous distribution of the goods, and with each grade after that, rivalry increased, suggesting that schooling may have something to do with rivalrous distribution (Graves & Graves, 1983). Within these grade levels, the children who acted in a more rivalrous fashion were those who achieved more in school and had a positive attitude toward school (those who dressed and carried themselves in the fashion that the school required). These findings suggest that schooling increases the likelihood of acting competitively.

Schooling and Competition

The findings of more competitive behavior among schooled individuals may relate to schooling's common encouragement of competition among individuals. Schooling often uses grades and comparisons across individuals to regulate access to various opportunities. University students who are not subjected to competition for grades report being more likely to learn from each other in a cooperative manner—treating each other as resources rather than as obstacles.

Grading on a curve ensures that some people fail and all are in competition with each other. This procedure, invented by particular individuals in a particular cultural milieu, now provides a competitive learning environment for many children and young adults worldwide. The idea of grading on a curve was introduced by Max Meyer in 1908 in the prestigious journal *Science.* He proposed that grading should follow the "normal" curve, with the top 3% ranked excellent, the next 22% labeled superior, the middle 50% judged medium, the next 22% inferior, and the bottom 3% failing. Grading on a curve caught on a few years later during the era of "scientific efficiency," in which education experts and administrators applied industrial models for factory production to schools. (Other assessment practices, such as evaluating how well each student reaches a desired level of skill or understanding, do not place students in competition with each other, with one student's achievement ensuring another's loss.)[2]

Many U.S. classrooms are structured competitively, with teachers singling students out to answer questions and praising or correcting individual students publicly (Lipka, 1998). However, a teacher's use of individual competition to structure the classroom may be at odds with some students' community values. For example, in American Indian students' community values, groups may compete with each other, but individuals' roles are to contribute to the success of the group (Swisher, 1990). If the teacher calls on a child, that child may sink down in the seat and do his or her best not

---

[2]A focus on grades seems to be detrimental to student learning (Milton, Pollio, & Eison, 1986). College students who focus on grades (rather than on learning the material) claimed that they got irritated by discussions that went beyond what they need to know for exams, were more distracted during class lectures, and performed worse on exams than students who focus on learning. They had less effective study habits, reported high levels of anxiety, and were twice as likely to report having cheated repeatedly.

to respond, to avoid singling himself or herself out of the group. An example occurred in a novice teacher's classroom serving Pueblo Indian children:

> Ed [the teacher] turns to the class and tells them to introduce themselves to us [visitors]. No one speaks. Ed calls on one of the children to begin. The boy is almost inaudible; we lean forward to hear better. The next child is the same. None of the children makes eye contact with us, although they are glancing at one another. (Suina & Smolkin, 1994, p. 125)

The children were embarrassed because introducing oneself requires rising out of the group, and this was not among the few occasions in which being singled out is appropriate by Pueblo community standards (see figure 6.5).

Navajo high school students may not treat tests and grades as competitive events in the way Anglo students do (Deyhle & Margonis, 1995). A teacher of Indian students explained:

> You put them out on the basketball court and they are competitive as can be. But in the classroom they don't want to compete against each other. I can ask a question and when a student responds incorrectly

FIGURE 6.5

A U.S. Indian School classroom in Santa Fe, New Mexico, 1900.

no other student will correct him. They don't want to look better than each other or to put another student down. The Anglo students are eager to show that they know the correct answer. They want to shine; the Indian students want to blend into the total class. (quoted in Swisher & Deyhle, 1989, p. 7)

Singling out an individual as exceptional may endanger the social structure or the person's relations with others. An Anglo high school counselor reported that Navajo parents complained about their children being singled out when the counselor put up a "high achiever" bulletin board with photos of students with B averages or better (Deyhle & Margonis, 1995). The counselor "compromised" by putting up happy stickers with the students' names on them. A Navajo student, staring at the board, said, "The board embarrasses us, to be stuck out like that" (p. 157). The school's ethic of promoting individual competition was at odds with the community ethic of individuals contributing their strengths to the community.

In contrast, public evaluation of an individual's performance, as in the lavish praise often provided by middle-class European American parents, makes self-sufficient achievement a valued part of their children's identity (LeVine, 1980). It involves drawing attention to individual achievement, sometimes even with supportive roles of other people ignored. A middle-class European American adult may congratulate a child on an achievement, even as the adult carries out most of the activity: "Good girl, you did that all by yourself!" Middle-class U.S. parents regard children's attention seeking and "look at me" behaviors as precursors to valued striving for achievement and reward such behaviors with praise and recognition (Whiting & Edwards, 1988).

Middle-class U.S. children were observed to be far more likely to seek attention than African children, who avoided public attention from their elders because it implies disapproval of misbehavior (Whiting & Whiting, 1975). The early experience of the middle-class U.S. children leads them to expect attention to be intrinsically rewarding, yielding "the peculiar tendency" to misbehave in order to attract attention, even at the risk of being punished (LeVine, 1980). Rather than relying on praise, the African children studied by Robert LeVine learned to take competence in a wide range of skills for granted rather than seeing it as a badge of honor or competitive distinction.

Adults in some communities believe that praise is bad for children because it makes them conceited, painfully embarrassed, and potentially disobedient, and thus disrupts their relations with the group (LeVine, 1980; LeVine et al., 1994; Lipka, 1998; Metge, 1984). Calling attention to good fortune or good personal qualities may be seen as jeopardizing the quality praised or as arousing dangerous envy among others. In Japan, praise is to be deflected to show appropriate humility (Wierzbicka, 1996).

In some communities, satisfaction with a child may be expressed indirectly, to avoid dangers involved in praising:

> When a Bengali mother wants to praise her child . . . she might give the child a peeled and seeded orange. Bengali children understand completely that their mothers have done something special for them, even though mothers may not use words of praise—for to do so would be unseemly, much like praising themselves. (Rohner, 1994, p. 113)

Marquesan and Inuit parents conveyed praise indirectly, by mentioning children's skills to others (Briggs, 1970; Martini, 1994b). Maori children in New Zealand understood the approval given indirectly by a look or a touch and by the giving of tasks and responsibilities to learners who do well (Metge, 1984). Yup'ik (Native Alaskan) teachers seldom directly praised students' performance, but when a student accomplished a difficult task, they might comment approvingly to the child that she or he is now ready to help the family with that skill (Lipka, 1998).

In addition to its use of competitive grading and praise, the contribution of schooling to competitiveness and willingness to stand out individually may also derive from segregating children into age groups. Observations in a variety of cultural communities indicate that children who are mostly with children of their own age tend to be more competitive than are children who spend time with older or younger children (Whiting & Whiting, 1975; Whiting & Edwards, 1988). Thus, being segregated into grades strictly by age may increase the likelihood of competitiveness. Consistent with this idea, Hungarian 6- to 8-year-olds who began school later and spent more time after school at home tending siblings were less competitive than children who spent their time with same-age peers in an educational setting beginning at about age 2 (Hollos, 1980).

Of course, not all schooling is structured in terms of competition. Children who attended a U.S. public school that promoted collaboration among children more often built on each other's ideas in a collaborative way than children who attended a traditional U.S. public school (see figure 6.6; Matusov, Bell, & Rogoff, 2002).

Although cooperation is often contrasted with competition, an intriguing case study makes the point that some forms of competition may fit with a social orientation rather than with individual distinction. In Sally Duensing's (2000) study of the Yapollo science museum in Trinidad, she noticed that competition among museum visitors was a culturally priori-

FIGURE 6.6

This public school in Utah is organized around children's collaboration with each other and with adults (Rogoff, Goodman Turkanis, & Bartlett, 2001). The children in the foreground are working together on a geometry problem; those on the left are planning letters to the U.S. Congress in support of public television; the group in the back is writing and drawing posters; and the child at the cabinet is choosing her next activity.

tized form of social engagement, echoing calypso competitions and other local social forms. Trinidadian museum visitors were energized by competition when museum staff encouraged them to guess how something works, setting up a competition with other visitors or the staff member. However, the fun of the competition was the interaction, not necessarily proving oneself:

> Competition is a common style of interaction in the science education activities at Yapollo and is also part of the fabric of daily life in Trinidad as well, including various popular musical competitions. But it is competition with a social attitude. Rather than an individualistic competition process that I was familiar with, a process that excludes rather than includes, the practice of competition at Yapollo and other non school type competitions had a highly social almost collaborative spin, promoting social interaction, not winners and losers. . . .

> Social competition is a common cultural practice throughout the Caribbean. As Burton (1997) said, "Ritualized conflict becomes a means of binding the community together." (pp. 75, 91)[3]

Such inclusive and performative competition in informal social situations contrasts with the kind of competition that Trinidadians experience in the British-based school system. Museum staff speculated that this might be because in school, rather than enjoying "educated guessing," teachers are seldom open to learning from wrong answers. They are concerned with not making mistakes themselves and with teaching correct answers (in preparation for the frequent exams), rather than exploring ideas. This is fueled by the school system's exclusionary structure, selecting students for the limited places available in secondary schools and university.

In schools and other formal and informal institutions, children learn not only the "curriculum," but also the ways of relating to each other and to adults that the structure of the institution embodies. By participating in the everyday formats and routines of cultural institutions and traditions, children engage in their underlying cultural assumptions. Often, these are taken on unreflectively as simply the way things are done. However, individuals and whole generations may question and transform a community's traditions and institutions, especially if the values conflict with those of another community in which the individuals also participate.

Cultural assumptions regarding individual or community priority, or their mutuality, are carried in the habitual relationships of everyday life. The assumptions can be seen in cultural practices regarding where infants sleep and in young children's reactions to a toddler wanting a coveted object. They are apparent in parental disciplinary styles, the formats and structures of classrooms, and the social influence wielded in teasing. Issues of morality bring questions of individual rights versus harmonious social order to center stage. Individual achievement can be sought and recognized

---

[3] The social nature of such competition in Trinidad resembles that seen in Jewish argumentation, which, as Deborah Schiffrin (1984) argued, is a form of sociability in which speakers disagree and compete with each other in ways that promote and protect their solidarity and intimacy. The importance of sociability in argument is beautifully illustrated by Deborah Meier, in an anecdote about her father: "Friday-night ritual required him to dine, he explained, with his parents. One Friday night, eager for an early release, he found himself agreeing to whatever proposition his father presented during the dinner-table conversation. 'Yes, Poppa, you're right,' he said over and over again, until his father finally exploded. 'Such disrespect from my eldest son I never expected to hear!' Which is to say that I grew up in a family in which arguing was the ultimate sign of respect, and too-ready agreement the ultimate put-down" (1995, pp. 132–133).

in ways that prioritize competition, or can be appreciated as a contribution to community functioning. Throughout these issues in human social relations, autonomy and interdependence are negotiated according to cultural traditions and renegotiated as new generations consider alternative approaches.

7

Thinking with the Tools and Institutions of Culture

Although thinking is often regarded as a private, solo activity, cultural research has brought to light many ways that thinking involves interpersonal and community processes in addition to individual processes. The study of cognitive development now attends to more than the unfolding of children's understanding through childhood. It includes attention to how people come to understand their world through active participation in shared endeavors with other people as they engage in sociocultural activities.

The field's changing perspectives on individual, interpersonal, and community roles in cognition have built on several decades of research in the area of culture and cognition (Rogoff & Chavajay, 1995). The early work involved comparisons of cognitive test performance on tasks that were commonly regarded by European and American researchers as examining "general" cognitive processes—tests of Piagetian reasoning, classification, logic, and memory. Cross-cultural psychology in the 1970s and earlier generally examined what happened when cognitive tasks that had been developed in Europe and the United States were used in other cultural settings.

Results indicated that performance on these tasks was not general, operating irrespective of the circumstances. The generality of the tasks, which at the time was assumed to be broad, was questioned by researchers' observations that people who performed poorly on cognitive tasks in the research room showed impressive thinking in their everyday lives. This contributed to a theoretical transformation, discussed in Chapter 2, to resolve the puzzle that people who seemed not to solve logical problems in a test situation showed skillful logic in other situations.

In addition, the research increasingly implicated people's experience in Western schooling in their performance on many of the tests. Rather than measuring experience-free general abilities, cognitive tests (especially in the areas of logic, classification, and memory) related closely and somewhat narrowly to people's experience with this cultural institution. Until this cross-cultural research, the role of schooling in cognitive test performance had been less visible. After all, virtually all of the research "subjects" in cognitive investigations in the United States and Europe have spent years in school, and the researchers themselves have spent almost their whole lives in this institution. It was easy to take it for granted.

Scholars searched for theoretical guidance that would help them understand how people's thinking relates closely to their cultural experience, to replace the idea that cognition was a general process that could be "influenced" by culture. Many found inspiration in Vygotsky's cultural-historical theory, which posited that individual cognitive skills derived from people's engagement in sociocultural activities. According to this theory, cognitive development occurs as people learn to use cultural tools for thinking (such as literacy and mathematics) with the help of others more experienced with such tools and cultural institutions.

The sociocultural approach also offers an integrated approach to human development. Cognitive, social, perceptual, motivational, physical, emotional, and other processes are regarded as aspects of sociocultural activity rather than as separate, free-standing capabilities or "faculties," as has been traditional in psychology. An integrated approach makes it easier to understand how thinking involves social relations and cultural experience, without an artificial separation into isolated parts.

This perspective has shifted our understanding of cognition from a focus solely on the thoughts of supposedly solitary individuals to a focus on the active processes of individuals, whether momentarily solo or in ensembles, as they engage in shared endeavors in cultural communities. From this perspective, cognitive development is not the acquisition of knowledge or of skills; rather, it takes a more active form. Cognitive development consists of individuals changing their ways of understanding, perceiving, noticing, thinking, remembering, classifying, reflecting, problem setting and solving, planning, and so on—in shared endeavors with other people building on the cultural practices and traditions of communities. Cognitive development is an aspect of the transformation of people's participation in sociocultural activities.

This chapter begins by examining cross-cultural cognitive research that drew attention to the idea that cognition was "situated in" specific contexts rather than being general abilities that are applied without regard for the context of use. I examine the role of familiarity with practices from a specific cultural institution—Western schooling—in cognitive test performance, focusing on research on classification and memory. Next, I discuss distinct cultural values regarding what social and intellectual approaches to problems are intelligent and mature. I examine how people generalize experience from one situation to another and learn to adapt their learning flexibly to circumstances. Then, I consider individual, interpersonal, and community processes in using cultural tools of thinking, especially literacy and mathematics. To conclude the chapter, I discuss how thinking is distributed across cultural tools as well as the people using them.

Specific Contexts Rather than General Ability: Piaget around the World

Jean Piaget proposed that children's thinking transforms in stages as they revise their concepts of physical phenomena and mathematical ideas. He was interested in children's intellectual development as a way of understanding how scientific ideas changed over time. His work was primarily carried out in Geneva, Switzerland, and the responses were assumed to represent universal processes. Cultural variation was not of interest.

However, when scholars began examining Piagetian tasks in other cultural communities, they found that people from different cultural backgrounds performed differently on them. For example, in one of Piaget's tasks that is used as an indication of reaching the "concrete operational stage," European and U.S. children of about age 7 indicate that they know that pouring water from one of two identical beakers into a wider vessel does not change its quantity, unlike younger children, who often respond that the water in the taller (or wider) beaker now has more water. But research on the concrete operational stage around the world yielded variable findings (Dasen, 1977; Rogoff, 1981c). In some studies, there were no differences across populations or advantages for people from non-European/European American communities or for those with less schooling (Goodnow, 1962; Kiminyo, 1977; Nyiti, 1976; Strauss, Ankori, Orpaz, & Stavy, 1977). Often, however, people displayed concrete operational thinking at an age that was much later than in Geneva (Greenfield, 1966; Kelly, 1977; Laurendeau-Bendavid, 1977; Okonji, 1971; Page, 1973; Philp & Kelly, 1974; Stevenson, Parker, Wilkinson, Bonnevaux, & Gonzalez, 1978). Although Piaget was not especially interested in the ages at which stages were achieved, the great variability in ages of passing the tests was striking. (This led some researchers to infer "retardation" in development, based on the questionable assumption that development necessarily follows a linear track along one dimension, Piaget's sequence of stages, with European and European American children setting the norm.)

The variability across communities, and within communities for people with greater experience in school, sparked consideration of contextual aspects of the testing that might create differences in performance. One interpretation of the variable findings in the Piagetian tasks had to do with familiarity of the materials and concepts (Irwin & McLaughlin, 1970; Irwin, Schafer, & Feiden, 1974; Kelly, 1977; Price-Williams, Gordon, & Ramirez, 1969). A number of studies examined Piagetian concepts using local materials such as rice, potting clay, and familiar containers, to see if these adjustments accounted for findings of cultural differences.

Scholars also began to examine familiarity with how objects and concepts are used in a task (Cole, Sharp, & Lave, 1976; Greenfield, 1974; Lave, 1977). They began studying the kinds of activities people did in their own communities and how that related to what the researcher was trying to get them to do. This involved noticing people's "everyday cognition" (to use the phrase coined by Rogoff & Lave, 1984) as they make complicated woven patterns, calculate costs in the market, or skillfully persuade others.

A persuasive study demonstrated differences in children's reproduction of patterns depending on the familiarity of use of particular materials in particular processes (Serpell, 1979). The children performed well when reproducing the pattern in a familiar medium and poorly if the medium was unfamiliar. Zambian children performed well when modeling with strips of wire, a familiar activity in their community (see figure 7.1), but poorly with unfamiliar paper and pencil. In contrast, English children performed well with paper and pencil, a familiar medium for reproducing patterns in their community, but poorly with unfamiliar strips of wire. The two groups performed equally well when reproducing the patterns in clay, a medium that was equally familiar to the two groups.

Another innovative study examined Piagetian reasoning using local concepts and children's familiar system of relationships—their own kinship network (Greenfield & Childs, 1977). Zinacanteco (Mexican Indian) children's performance did not differ whether they were schooled or nonschooled. For both groups, clear developmental trends occurred in understanding the logical relationships used in kinship terms. Younger children thought about their kin relations from their own egocentric perspective, not noting that their sibling necessarily has a sibling. At later ages, they understood kinship terms involving reciprocal relations between two of their siblings, such as noting that their two sisters are each other's sister. Finally, children understood kinship terms "reversibly"—from two points of view, even when they were part of it personally—noting that they themselves are their sibling's sibling.

FIGURE 7.1

A bicycle constructed of wire by a Zambian boy. Boys also construct model cars of wire, with operational wheels and steering (Serpell, 1993).

Researchers noticed that lack of generality was especially apparent in tasks used for Piaget's "formal operational stage," which involves reasoning systematically about physical and mathematical properties even when no concrete objects are present to manipulate. People in many cultural communities did not seem to "reach" Piaget's formal operational stage at all without extensive schooling (Ashton, 1975; Goodnow, 1962; Laurendeau-Bendavid, 1977; Super, 1979).

These observations led Piaget in 1972 to conclude that formal operational thinking was tied to people's experience with the specific kind of scientific thinking of this stage, such as the kind of hypothesis testing used in high school science classes. Thus, when the cultural research drew attention to the problems of assuming that the stages were general, Piaget revised his claim of universal stages to say that this stage was contextually variable, depending on experience in particular domains.

The field moved more generally beyond the assumption of generality in cognitive development with the help of this research, showing that not everyone went through the same stages and that performance shifted greatly with familiarity of materials, concepts, and activities. Scholars began to shift from the idea that thinking involved generic processing of information, independent of the type of information and people's familiar activities (Laboratory of Comparative Human Cognition, 1983).

The move toward specificity rather than generality in thinking took several directions. One was to subdivide processing into domain-specific areas, such as separating thinking about biological and physical processes, or emphasizing different kinds of intelligence. More common among cultural researchers was a move to integrate thinking with contexts of thought (see Laboratory of Comparative Human Cognition, 1983; Rogoff, 1982a). This was the foundation of the sociocultural approach, which turned from examining general abilities of individuals to examining particular cultural activities in which people think. The focus on cultural activities was partly prompted by increasing evidence that a particular type of "background" experience—experience with Western schooling—related to performance on many kinds of tests.

Schooling Practices in Cognitive Tests: Classification and Memory

Cross-cultural studies in nations in which schooling was not obligatory repeatedly found correlations between extent of Western schooling and performance on the kinds of cognitive tasks that were being used.[1,2] The relation of cognitive tests to schooling was difficult for researchers to see prior to the cultural research, because most of the research at the time had been conducted in nations in which schooling is compulsory. Children of the same age were almost always in the same or nearby grades in school, so their life experience was very much tied to this institution. With virtually no opportunity to unlink the relation between age and children's extent of

[1] The role of many other institutions in cognition and development could also be explored fruitfully (e.g., economic systems, religion; see Dorsey-Gaines & Garnett, 1996); however, the institution of schooling repeatedly shows up as centrally related to the kinds of cognitive performance that have been studied.

[2] Although school is not a homogeneous institution, the research that examined the relation between schooling and performance on cognitive tasks seldom considered variations in school practices. The consistency in findings may relate to the fact that in many nations, formal schooling is an institution derived from European and American practices, with some key commonalities across time and place. Later research has begun to pay more attention to variations in what actually happens in schools, including schooling of indigenous origin. My references to schooling in this book are limited to Western (secular) schooling, with recognition that other formal schooling traditions exist, for example, "bush schools" for teaching specialized knowledge in a number of African societies and various religious schooling traditions (Akinnaso, 1992; Haight, 2002; Lancy, 1996).

schooling, researchers explained age differences on cognitive tasks in terms of maturation, overlooking the close tie to children's amount of experience with this cultural institution.

Variation in performance across schooled and nonschooled groups seems to be due largely to differential familiarity with the common formats and activities of Western schooling that are used in the cognitive tests. This explanation is more convincing than the idea that schooling has some sort of general impact on thinking, because research has found only local relationships between school practices and specific cognitive activities (Cole, 1990; Rogoff, 1981c; Wagner & Spratt, 1987).

Individuals with experience in Western schooling show a variety of cognitive skills that resemble the activities of school (Rogoff, 1981c).

- Schooling seems to foster perceptual skills in analysis of two-dimensional patterns and in the use of graphic conventions to represent depth in two dimensions.
- Schooling appears not to relate to rule learning or to logical thought *as long as* the individual has understood the problem in the way the experimenter intended. However, nonschooled people seem to prefer to come to conclusions on the basis of experience rather than by relying on the information in the problem alone (as in story problems and in the research on logical syllogisms presented in Chapter 2).
- Schooling may be necessary for the solution of Piagetian formal operational problems, which involve systematically testing hypotheses, as in high school science.
- Schooling is closely related to performance on tests of classification and memory, which are examined next.

Classification

Adults in Western nations tend to classify test items into *taxonomic categories,* for example, putting animals in one group, food items in another, and implements in another. However, adults in many communities sort items into *functional groups,* such as putting a hoe with a potato because a hoe is used to dig up a potato. Especially if the research participants did not have much schooling, they sorted things according to their function rather than according to their taxonomic categories (Cole et al., 1971; Hall, 1972; Luria, 1976; Scribner, 1974; Sharp & Cole, 1972; Sharp et al., 1979).

People who had not attended much school were also less likely to offer a rationale for their sorting when asked to explain their classification. Schooled people showed greater facility in shifting to alternative dimensions of classification and in explaining the basis of their organization. (Explaining and analyzing one's thinking or other events is not a valued pastime in some communities, as it is among scholars; Fiske, 1995.)

As scholars began to look at the history of schooling (see Cole, 1990), they noticed that one of the functions of early schooling and literacy was to sort things according to taxonomic categories. In an account of the uses and historical development of literacy, Jack Goody argued that writing "is a tool, an amplifier, a facilitating device . . . which encourages reflection upon and the organization of information" (1977, p. 109). Using illustrations from early written records, Goody suggested that making lists is dependent on writing, and that comparison, classification, and hierarchical organization of items are greatly facilitated by spatial arrangement of items in a list. He proposed that classifying information by category and remembering lists of items are skills that derive from literacy.

Memory

Schooled people are skilled in deliberately remembering disconnected bits of information and in organizing the unrelated items to be remembered. In many memory tests, research participants remember lists of unrelated pieces of information, such as lists of isolated words. Lists may be remembered better if a strategy is used to coordinate the items, such as rehearsing, categorizing, or elaborating connections between items. Nonschooled people typically have difficulty with such memory tasks and often do not spontaneously employ strategies to organize such lists (Cole et al., 1971; Cole & Scribner, 1977; Scribner, 1974).

The first conclusions from the observations of poor recall and rare use of strategies focused on inferences about people's general memory ability. But evidence from everyday life suggested that the people who were doing poorly on the recall tasks could remember well in other situations, such as remembering where things were or recalling complicated narratives. For example, nonschooled griots in Africa maintain oral histories spanning centuries of people's moves, marriages, offspring, and important events.

An example of impressive memory appears in Gregory Bateson's study of the Iatmul, in New Guinea. His account also referred to contexts in which this impressive memory skill might be learned:

> Vast and detailed erudition is a quality which is cultivated among the Iatmul. This is most dramatically shown in the [sport of] debating about names and totems, and I have stated that a learned man carries in his head between ten and twenty thousand names. . . .
> In a typical debate a name or series of names is claimed as totemic property by two conflicting clans. The right to the name can

only be demonstrated by knowledge of the esoteric mythology to which the name refers. But if the myth is exposed and becomes publicly known, its value as a means of proving the clan's right to the name will be destroyed. Therefore there ensues a struggle between the two clans, each stating that they themselves know the myth and each trying to find out how much their opponents really know. In this context, the myth is handled by the speakers not as a continuous narrative, but as a series of small details. A speaker will hint at one detail at a time—to prove his own knowledge of the myth—or he will challenge the opposition to produce some one detail.

Footnote: . . . I do not know of any debating in the junior ceremonial house in which the erudition of the older men is copied. There are, however, a number of games in which children test each other's knowledge, e.g. of species of plants in the bush, etc. (1936, pp. 222–227)

The ways in which schooling could produce differences in performance on memory tasks became a focus of study (Rogoff & Mistry, 1985). Remembering lists of items unorganized by meaningful schemas may be an unusual experience except in school, where pupils frequently have to recall material they have not understood. Less-schooled individuals may have less practice organizing isolated bits of information.

In contrast, people from all backgrounds remember information that is embedded in a structured context, and they use meaningful relationships as an aid to recall. For example, waitresses in a short-order restaurant, who serve as many as 10 customers at once, develop complex strategies for keeping track of orders (Stevens, 1990, cited in Cole, 1996). To keep track of who needs what at what time, they use contextual memory aids, such as the order slip/receipt, the sight of the food or drink in front of the customer, and the customer's location.

With contextually organized materials, there seem to be few cultural differences in memory performance. This is in sharp contrast to performance on tests of memory for lists of items that have been stripped of organization by the researcher.

Indeed, in some communities, nonschooled people perform exceptionally well in remembering the layout of the landscape or important historical accounts. In general, cultural differences in memory for spatial arrangements or for organized prose are either minimal or in some cases favor people from communities with emphasis on spatial way-finding or oral history traditions (Briggs, 1970; Cole & Scribner, 1977; Dube, 1982; Kearins, 1981; Kleinfeld, 1973; Klich, 1988; Levinson, 1997; Mandler, Scribner, Cole, & DeForest, 1980; Neisser, 1982; Ross & Millsom, 1970).

In a study examining memory for spatially organized information, Guatemalan Mayan 9-year-olds performed at least as well as middle-class Salt Lake City children (Rogoff & Waddell, 1982). This contrasts with difficulties for Mayan children in recalling lists of isolated items, like the difficulties that are usually found for individuals with limited schooling (Kagan, Klein, Finley, Rogoff, & Nolan, 1979).

In the contextually organized task, each child watched as a local researcher placed 20 familiar miniature objects—such as cars, animals, furniture, people, and household items—into a model of a town with landmarks such as a mountain, a lake, a road, houses, and trees (see figure 7.2). After the 20 objects were removed from the model and reintegrated into the pool of 80 objects from which they had been drawn, the child was asked to reconstruct the scene. The Mayan children performed slightly *better* than the Salt Lake City children, perhaps because of a school strategy—rehearsal —that the Salt Lake City children often tried to use. Rehearsal would work

FIGURE 7.2

A Mayan researcher and a 9-year-old, who is studying the model, with its houses, volcano, lake, and other scenery, along with the objects to be remembered. At the bottom of the photograph is the pool of objects with which the to-be-remembered objects will be mixed.

for lists at school but may get in the way when learning information that is contextually organized.

This study supported the idea that schooling provides people with experience with particular memory strategies that may be helpful for remembering some kinds of information, such as unorganized lists. But the same strategies may get in the way with information that can be remembered with reference to an existing context.

The role of schooling in cognitive test performance is thus apparently tied to particular schooling practices. The role of specific practices is also apparent in the skilled remembering in Bateson's observations in the Iatmul and other skilled memory performances.

The relation between schooling and cognitive skills may be widespread in part because of the historical relationship between schooling and mental testing. It is not an accident that cognitive measures relate to schooling. After all, mental testing (including testing of intelligence) is based on school skills. Its goal is to predict performance in school (Cole et al., 1976; see also Tulviste, 1991).

As researchers noticed the similarity between cognitive tests and schooling, they also became aware of the cultural values involved in definitions of intelligence and situations in which it was observed. Indeed, the social relations built into the testing situation itself became a focus, as scholars noticed the culturally specific and often unfamiliar formats in which cognitive development was being "measured."

Cultural Values of Intelligence and Maturity

For many years, cognitive testing procedures were regarded as context-free, supposedly allowing observation of people's cognitive skills in some sort of pure fashion, unrelated to their life experiences. Along with noticing the importance of familiarity of language, concepts, and materials in test performance, researchers began to consider the familiarity of the values and everyday experience connected with the test format.

Of course, the values embedded in some widely used tests can be part of their role as selection devices for ensuring that certain children get access to opportunities. They can also be political tools to influence public policies:

> In 1912, when racism in America swelled on a rising tide of immigration, the U.S. Public Health Service hired psychologist H. H. Goddard to help screen out the imagined menace of inferior minds that were poised to contaminate the (equally imagined) pellucid American gene pool. Goddard, who invented the term "moron," created his

own test for mental deficiency. Gould's *Mismeasure of Man* gives a remarkable account of how Goddard's test questions were fired at immigrants as they stepped bewildered and exhausted off the boat at
Ellis Island. (Many had never before held a pencil, and had no possible frame of reference for understanding what was being asked of
them.) Goddard arrived at these staggering results: 83 percent of
Jews, 87 percent of Russians, 80 percent of Hungarians, and 79
percent of Italians were diagnosed as morons. . . . Ethnic quotas on
U.S. immigration were in place within the decade. (Kingsolver, 1995,
p. 77)

Even without such motives, value systems are built into the procedures and
interpretation of tests. This section examines how cognitive testing is a kind
of cultural practice involving academic institutions and forms of communication between a tester and the person being tested. Then it turns to how
communities vary in their definitions of intelligence and maturity.

Familiarity with the Interpersonal Relations Used in Tests

Cognitive tests rely on particular conversational forms that are often central
in schools. Schooled people are familiar with an interview or a testing situation in which a high-status adult, who already knows the answer to a
question, requests information from a lower-status person, such as a child
(Mehan, 1979; see figure 7.3).

Even before attending school, children in some communities where
schooling is central begin to participate with their family in the sort of discourse that often occurs in tests and schools. Middle-class European American parents often play language games with their toddlers that involve test
questions in the same format as the known-answer questions used by teachers and testers (such as "Where is your belly button?"). Familiarity with
questions that serve as directives to perform in specific ways can make a difference in whether children respond as expected by the tester, creatively play
with the materials, or warily try to figure out what is going on (Massey,
Hilliard, & Carew, 1982; Moreno, 1991).

In some cultural settings where schooling is not a central practice, culturally appropriate behavior may depart from what a researcher expects.
The situation may call for showing respect to the questioner, or it may call
for attempting to avoid being made a fool of by giving an obvious answer
to what must be a trick question—otherwise why would a knowledgeable
person ask it?

Judith Irvine suggested that Wolof (North African) research participants' interpretation of an experimenter's purpose may have conflicted with

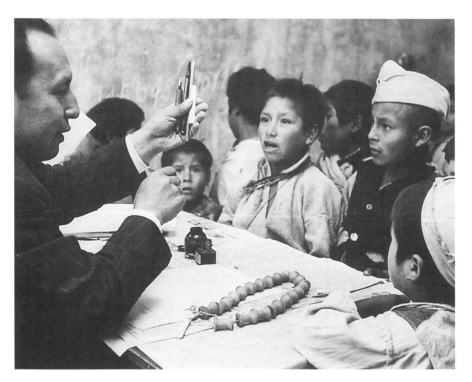

FIGURE 7.3

The principal of the Vicos school in Peru tests Quechua-speaking students' knowledge of the Spanish terms for objects (Collier & Collier, 1986).

giving straightforward answers to Piagetian questions. In a prior study, Wolof adolescents had responded that the quantity of water in a conservation test had changed because the researcher had poured it (Greenfield, 1966). Irvine reported that, except in school interrogation, Wolof people seldom ask questions to which they already know the answers: "Where this kind of questioning does occur it suggests an aggressive challenge, or a riddle with a trick answer" (1978, p. 549). When Irvine presented the task as language-learning questions about the meaning of quantity terms such as *more* and *the same,* using water and beakers for illustration, her informants' responses reflected understanding of conservation.

Values about social relationships influence people's responses to cognitive questions. For example, rather than performing and competing as individuals, children in some communities avoid distinguishing themselves from the group by volunteering an answer (see Chapter 6; Philips, 1972; Whiting & Whiting, 1975). In tests, as in many Western schools, reliance on a companion for help may be considered cheating, whereas in many cultural settings, not to employ a companion's assistance may be regarded as folly or egoism.

Similarly, ideals about relationships between children and others may lead children to place primacy on appropriate social relations rather than to focus on a cognitive puzzle. In many communities, for instance, the role of children may be to observe and carry out directives but not to initiate conversation or talk back to a person of higher status (Blount, 1972; Harkness & Super, 1977; Ward, 1971). In some communities, displaying a skill before it is well learned (as in a test) is considered an important part of the learning process. However, it is regarded as premature and inappropriate in others, where careful, thoughtful problem solving is prioritized (Cazden & John, 1971; S. Ellis, 1997; Swisher & Deyhle, 1989).

Cultural models of social relations, which implicitly or explicitly provide rationales for children's and adults' appropriate behavior and ways of relating (Super & Harkness, 1977), are not held in abeyance in cognitive tests. Indeed, they are centrally involved in each community's definitions of intelligence and maturity.

Varying Definitions of Intelligence and Maturity

Many differences among cultural communities in performance on cognitive tasks may be due to varying interpretations of what problem is to be solved and different values defining "proper" methods of solution (Goodnow, 1976). For example, the appropriateness of treating a cognitive task as a self-contained intellectual puzzle independent of the social context varies across communities. Likewise, speed of problem solving may be regarded either favorably or negatively. Ugandan villagers associated intelligence with adjectives such as *slow, careful,* and *active,* whereas Ugandan teachers and Westernized groups associated intelligence with the word *speed* (Wober, 1972). The reflective pace valued among the Navajo may account for the greater planning and fewer errors by Navajo children, compared with Anglo children, in determining routes in a maze game (Ellis & Siegler, 1997).

Some groups define children's intelligence in terms of both capability in specific situations and social responsibility (Serpell, 1977, 1982). For example, Mexican American ideas of intelligence are reflected in being *educado,* which has a broader meaning than the English term *educated.* It refers to attaining, through orientation by the family, a sense of moral and personal responsibility and respect for the dignity of others that serves as the foundation for all other learning (Munoz, personal communication, February 2000).

Popular conceptions of intelligence held by middle-class European American groups differ from those of some other groups in valuing technical intelligence as distinct from social and emotional skills. The Ifaluk of the western Pacific regard intelligence as not only having knowledge of good social behavior, but also performing it (Lutz & LeVine, 1982). Kipsigis (Kenyan) parents interpret intelligence as including trustworthy, responsible participation in family and social life (Super & Harkness, 1983; see also Ogunnaike & Houser, 2002).

To study what is meant by intelligence in a rural community in Zambia, Robert Serpell asked adults to identify particular children in their village whom they would select for a series of imaginary tasks and asked them to explain why. Some of the imaginary tasks were:

1. (a) If a house catches fire and there are only these children present, which child would you send to call others for help? Why would you choose this child? [Each question was followed with such a request for justification.]
   (b) Which child would you want to stay with you to help you?
2. Suppose you go to a house early in the morning where you are not expected and you find all the adults are absent having gone to work. Then these children come to you shouting "thief," "knife," "he has run away." The things the children are saying are not clear at all. Which child would you ask to explain clearly what happened?
3. (Girls) Suppose you are washing your clothes and you see that the place where you usually spread them out (to dry) is muddy (dirty); which of these girls would you send to search for another good place to spread your clothes?
   (Boys) Suppose you are doing some work on a house, such as repairing the thatch where the roof is damaged or replacing an old door, and you see that a tool such as a hammer is needed. However, you do not have a hammer. Which of these boys would you send to make a substitute tool which you could easily use to finish the job quickly?
4. If you are sitting together in the evening and you tell a riddle, which one of these children would you expect to answer well? (1993, p. 28)

The adults often justified their choice of a particular child with the concept of *nzelu*, which resembles the English *intelligence*. However, whereas the English term has a primarily cognitive meaning, *nzelu* seems to correspond with the areas that in English are called *wisdom*, *cleverness*, and *responsibility*. The concept of *nzelu* does not apply to people who use their intelligence for selfish purposes (such as the mischievous and manipulative cunning of the character Brer Rabbit), only to those who use their intelligence in a socially productive way (Serpell, 1993).

A central meaning of the socially responsible dimension of *nzelu* is the idea of being trusted to carry out something for others, from toddlers who are frequently asked to bring an adult something they cannot reach without standing up, to friends commissioned to make small purchases on a trip. To be sent on such errands is recognition of being both a responsible person and a comrade. It requires understanding of the demands of the task as well as a cooperative attitude.

Serpell summarized similar concepts of intelligence in other African communities, which also include the idea of social responsibility. For example, the concept of *o ti kpa* (from the Baoulé of the Ivory Coast) involves

> the performance of tasks which contribute to the family's welfare . . . with the connotation of responsibility and a touch of initiative as well as know-how. . . . What is important is that the child should help out, pull his weight in domestic and agricultural work. But it is not just a matter of performing these tasks: the child is more *o ti kpa* the more he performs them well, spontaneously, and responsibly. (Dasen, Barthélémy, Kan, Kouamé, Daouda, Adjéi, & Assandé, 1985, pp. 303–304; translated and cited by Serpell, 1993, p. 44)

In the United States, the term *intelligence* also seems to be used more broadly among laypeople than by psychologists. Psychologists from around the United States and the general public in New Haven, Connecticut, differed in how they rated behaviors as characterizing an intelligent person (Sternberg, Conway, Ketron, & Bernstein, 1981). Both psychologists and laypeople included problem-solving ability and verbal ability in their concept of intelligence; laypeople also included social competence, comprised by characteristics such as admitting mistakes, having a social conscience, and thinking before speaking and doing.

Ideas of developmental maturity, precocity, and retardation are tied to judgments regarding what aspects of human intelligence and behavior are valued in the community. Among the Abaluyia (in Kenya),

> mothers use evidence that a child has the ability to give and receive social support, and assist others, as markers of a child's more general developmental level, much as an American parent might use literacy skills such as knowing the alphabet, or verbal facility, to show how grown-up or precocious his or her child is. (Weisner, 1989, p. 86)

An indicator of intelligence and social acuity among Chamulas (Mayan Indians of Mexico) is boys' and young men's virtuosity in highly structured, improvisational verbal dueling (Gossen, 1976). Pairs of youths trade rapid-fire insults that must echo the prior turn with only small changes in the sounds of a phrase, at the same time giving a clever response to the partner's turn. The fellow who can keep the game going longest (sometimes hundreds of turns), returning lewd original puns that follow very exacting rules, is regarded as superior. Boys of 5 or 6 routinely beat small boys of 2 or 3, but truly good players do not emerge until adolescence. By engaging in verbal dueling, boys and young men develop the locally valued form of intelligence—eloquence. Grace and power in the use of language, shown in the arena of verbal dueling, are key in evaluating young men for adult careers:

> Virtuosity [in this form of talk] bodes well for a boy's political and social future. With the reservoir of social rules and thorough knowledge of language which the genre inculcates, a consistent winner in verbal dueling is well equipped to begin the genuine play for rank and prestige which is an important aspect of adulthood. (p. 144)

Value judgments regarding which skills are desirable in young children include considerations of the meaning of the skill to the larger community, not just precocity or virtuosity itself. For example, recent policies in China have caused concern that very young children may be becoming *too* skilled in adapting their behavior to the circumstances:

> The single-child policy has constructed families . . . where the children are often treated as the "center of the universe" at home, while at the day-care center they are but one among many. The rules of conduct are strictly enforced in day care but are often ignored at home. These mixed messages have created toddlers who . . . have a heightened awareness of the appropriate verbiage and conduct for a particular context. They learn at an early age how to deal with events in appropriate ways and know what "face" to put forward at what time. This ability may appear to the Westerners as a great achievement for toddlers of 2 and 3 years of age; in fact, it is an impressive achievement. Nevertheless, it is of concern to many Chinese adults because these children's behaviors are often void of honesty and sincerity. These behaviors are often opportunistic and are used to placate adults, particularly teachers. Thus, to some extent, the goal of educating children to become moral beings is in jeopardy. (Lee, 1992, p. 391)

Each community's goals or endpoints of development, methods of facilitating development, and assessments of progress toward an endpoint involve value judgments (Goodnow, 1980). The designation of certain goals or certain ways of solving problems as more sophisticated or important than others is itself a cultural process worthy of study (S. Ellis, 1997; Wertsch, 1991).

Research on culture and cognition has come to include recognition of the appropriateness of different approaches to tasks, depending on the ways that maturity and intelligence are conceived in different communities. Thus, over a few decades, the conception of cognitive development has changed dramatically from the assumption that thinking ability is a general characteristic of individuals. Cultural research has called attention to the specific nature of thinking as situated in the practices of cultural communities. Not only does it matter how familiar people are with the conservation or classification or memory task they are given, but cultural definitions of intelligent behavior and formats for social interaction come into play in any observation of thinking.

With the realization that cognitive tests examine specific skills, often ones that were practiced in school, the puzzle of how people apply what they have learned across situations is not yet resolved. The problem remains of accounting for how people generalize from their experience in one situation to another.

Generalizing Experience from One Situation to Another

Since it became clear that generality could not be assumed across situations, scholars have continued to struggle with the question of how to handle the specificity of thinking. Is every situation different from every other, resulting in total specificity? Clearly not, or people would never be able to handle anything new or even to use language. There must be some ways in which understanding gained in one situation relates to a new situation.

Researchers sometimes write as though broad generalization of thinking processes is the goal of learning. However, generalization is not necessarily a good thing. Automatically doing the same thing in a new situation may or may not fit the new situation. For example, the Salt Lake City children who rehearsed the names of objects when asked to reconstruct a scene inappropriately generalized a familiar strategy for memorizing lists to a new problem (Rogoff & Waddell, 1982). Rather than needing to apply strategies broadly, they needed to know which strategies are helpful in what circumstances. The goal is *appropriate* generalization.

The likelihood of appropriately using understanding developed in one situation when faced with a new but related situation is based partly on achievement of conceptual understanding (Hatano, 1988). People do not appropriately generalize procedures across relevant circumstances without having some understanding of the procedures. For example, people familiar with mathematical procedures from school or from everyday nonschool experience may not appropriately apply the procedures in relevant new situations unless they understand the principles involved (Schliemann, Carraher, & Ceci, 1997).

However, understanding the principles in a certain situation does not automatically lead to applying them in another one for which they are relevant (Nunes, 1995). This has puzzled scholars who assume that people treat problems with the same structure similarly or are automatically able to apply their knowledge to new problems within the same domain (such as within the domain of biology or of cooking or of addition).

In a sense, these scholars regard the process of generalization as residing within the problem structure or domain of knowledge. Such a stance falls short of considering the need to *discern relevance* to the new situation. This requires relating the goals of the new situation to those of prior situations, not just access to "pieces" of knowledge or the principles underlying them. Once we abandon the idea of generalization being automatic (within similar problems or domains), the question of the extent of generalization is open to investigation rather than assumed to be mechanically driven by characteristics of the "problems."

For a person to discern relevance of prior understanding to a new situation requires considering how the purposes of each are related. The unit of analysis used in sociocultural theory—the whole activity—helps researchers to focus on the goals that people pursue by thinking and to understand how people's participation in one activity relates to their participation in another. The idea is that individuals handle later situations according to how they relate to prior ones in which they have participated (Rogoff, 1998).

This view of cognition moves beyond the idea that development consists of *acquiring* knowledge and skills. Rather, a person develops through *participation in* an activity, *changing* to be involved in the situation at hand in ways that contribute both to the ongoing event and to the person's preparation for involvement in other similar events. The focus is on people's active transformation of understanding and engagement in dynamic activities (Arievitch & van der Veer, 1995; Cobb & Bowers, 1999; Gibson, 1979; Leont'ev, 1981; Pepper, 1942; Rogoff, 1990; Rogoff, Baker-Sennett, & Matusov, 1994).

Seeing connections between the old and the new situations often involves support from other people or institutions pointing out similarities. People may not see the underlying similarities of several problems unless someone suggests that the problems resemble each other (Gick & Holyoak, 1980). For example, Carol Lee (1993, 2001) suggested that the widespread African American practice of *signifying* involves the same facility in analogical reasoning that is needed in classroom interpretation of literature. (Signifying includes but is not limited to trading of insults in playing the dozens and capping, described in Chapter 6.) Students generally do not see this connection automatically; a skilled teacher can help them see the applicability to classroom activities. Thus the students can generalize on the basis of coming to see the relevance of what they already know for the new situation—but generalization does not arise automatically.

For individuals and groups to generalize appropriately across experiences involves what Giyoo Hatano (1982, 1988) has called *adaptive expertise*. Development of adaptive expertise is supported by the extent to which people understand the goals and principles of relevant activities and gain experience with varying means to achieve them. Cultural practices and social interaction support learning which circumstances relate to each other and which approaches fit different circumstances.

Learning to Fit Approaches Flexibly to Circumstances

Learning to fit approaches flexibly to circumstances is itself an important aspect of cognitive development. It is needed for making decisions in the various realms of intelligence that are prioritized in different communities, whether technical or social. Consistent with a sociocultural approach to cognitive development, some of the most relevant research on fitting approaches to circumstances comes from research on social relations, not just in more narrowly cognitive problem-solving situations.

In some communities, learning to distinguish appropriate circumstances is an explicit goal in child development. Takie Lebra (1994) referred to this goal in Japanese child rearing as *boundary training*, in which children learn to conduct themselves according to their various roles: as a schoolchild, as a neighbor, as the child of a doctor, and so on.

The Japanese educational system encourages children to learn the circumstances in which they should act one way or another (Ben-Ari, 1996). For example, in the preschool years, rather than trying to achieve consistency across mother-child and teacher-child relations, children are helped by parents and teachers to distinguish the contexts and the approach that is appropriate to each. In middle childhood, children are immersed in an elementary school system that promotes harmonious learning in the group with little emphasis on competition or individuals standing out; by junior high school age, many of the children also attend private afterschool *juku* lessons that are organized competitively (White, 1987). In this way, Japanese children learn to participate in both harmonious group relations and individual competition in different contexts and to distinguish the contexts in which these approaches apply.

Similarly, working-class African American families emphasize helping children learn flexible ways of acting and speaking, adapted to shifting roles and situations. Shirley Brice Heath (1983) noted that adults in this community often asked questions that encouraged children to seek appropriate relationships between situations based on the children's experience. The adults thus gave importance to flexibility as well as to metaphorical thinking and speaking.

Marquesan toddlers from Polynesia learn to observe contextual cues to determine when to be obedient and when to be demanding and mischievous (Martini & Kirkpatrick, 1992). Caregivers enjoy toddlers' teasing, as in the case of a toddler who responded to a mother's request for a kiss, "No, Mama, you smell." Parents talk proudly about times their toddler stood up to adult authority. Teasing may give toddlers lessons in how to handle inconsistency, helping them learn under what circumstances somebody is treating them in a truthful, straightforward fashion and under what circumstances somebody is pretending in a way that they should not treat as the truth.

In contrast, middle-class European American child-rearing experts' advice to parents often includes suggestions to "be consistent," treating a child in the same fashion at all times. College-educated European American mothers stressed the importance of providing consistency when asked what they think is important for child rearing (Chao, 1995). A U.S. day care center director explained:

> We feel it's crucial that children get the same sort of messages at home as at school. If we teach children here at school to use words instead of hitting to deal with disagreements [but parents use physical punishment], it undoes what we are trying to accomplish. When situations like this arise, we ask parents to come in to talk about our different approaches to discipline. If we can't resolve our differences, we occasionally have to counsel parents to change schools. (Tobin et al., 1991, p. 111)

Differences in acting appropriately at home and at school are faced by children everywhere, but especially by children whose community ways differ from the ways of Western schooling. For example, American Indian children are often expected to be respectfully silent when learning at home, but their non-Indian teachers may regard their silence as disinterest or even resistance (Plank, 1994). Similarly, a collaborative mode at home may be inconsistent with an expectation at school that students compete with each other and try to show off their knowledge.

Showing respect to an adult at school may require looking him or her in the eye; at home it may require averting one's gaze (e.g., for Navajo, Puerto Rican, and African American children; Byers & Byers, 1972; Chisholm, 1996; Hale-Benson, 1986). However, many European American teachers expect eye contact and infer lack of respect or attention without it ("I don't know if you're paying attention if you don't look at me"). This is problematic if the children have been taught that looking an adult in the eye is an affront that challenges adult authority and shows arrogance. Dolores Mena, a Mexican American graduate student, reflected on this conflict:

> I remember growing up and many times feeling conflicted because what my parents told me to do and what other people told me to do was not always consistent. [My parents] would tell us not to look at older people in the eyes because it was disrespectful but, yet, at school we were told by the teachers to look at them when we spoke or were spoken to. And so at school, averting eye contact was misinterpreted as not being attentive in class. I remember one time when I actually stared my father straight in the eyes when he was asking me to do something for him. Just the look in his eyes sent a chill up my spine and I never again stared him straight in the eyes. (personal communication, October 1999)

To avoid communication problems when home and school practices differ, children must learn to distinguish the appropriate approach for the setting. In the home community, children may be expected to answer a question immediately, whereas in school they may be expected to wait to speak until they are called on by the teacher. At home, several people may be expected to talk at once, whereas at school there may be a rule of one person speaking at time. Alternatively, at home, people may provide a respectful pause between turns at speaking, but at school, children from a background requiring a respectful pause may never get a chance to speak. At home, children may be expected to show respect for others by not contradicting them, but in school, they may be expected to argue ideas in ways that seem like contradiction.

Learning to distinguish the appropriate ways to act in different situations is a very important accomplishment in all communities, for children as well as for their elders. Learning which approach to use at school and home, along with determining which strategy to use in cognitive tests and other problem solving situations, amount to learning to generalize appropriately from one situation to another.

Roseanna Bourke offered an insightful metaphor for thinking about the necessity of learning to adapt flexibly to circumstances:

> Chameleons use their ability to change colour to both adapt to changing environments and to communicate states such as anger, fear, calm and distress. A green chameleon is peaceful, calm and serene, whereas a yellow chameleon is surrendering. It takes baby chameleons a year to learn the language of colours and to read the messages portrayed by these colours through interacting with more mature chameleons. Children also learn the language of their culture,

and learn to adapt to changing environments. Like chameleons, children enter a number of different learning settings. . . . Each setting portrays a particular view of learning which coupled with the students' own conceptions of learning creates numerous ways the learner experiences and participates in learning activities. . . . As with the chameleon, the ability to change *colours* is part of the learner's self preservation repertoire to deal with the diversity of environments, settings and community, and in doing so, the learner becomes adept at being a member of multiple learning cultures and communities. (Bourke & Burns, 1998, p. 2)

Sociocultural theories have built on the realization that thinking is closely tied to particular situations. As this section has demonstrated, the connection between thinking and situations is not mechanical. Rather, individuals determine their approaches to particular situations with reference to cultural practices in which they have previously participated. The creative role of individuals in relating one situation to another is supported by social interaction in which social partners suggest connections. In addition, individuals and social groups build on connections made for them by previous generations, often mediated by cultural tools that they inherit. As people use cultural tools such as literacy and number systems to handle cognitive problems, in the process they often extend or modify the use of such tools for themselves and future generations.

Cultural Tools for Thinking

In early cross-cultural research, there were many indications that schooling and literacy relate to performance on cognitive tests. It became clear that the relation was rather specific to particular aspects of performance on cognitive tests and had to do with specific uses of literacy or particular schooling formats. These findings, along with the inspiration provided by Vygotskian theory, contributed to the transformation of cultural cognitive research to a focus on how one learns to use the cognitive tools of one's cultural community. In this section, I examine the use of several cultural tools for thinking that have received considerable research attention: literacy, mathematics, and other conceptual systems.

Literacy

The invention of literacy has been argued to have had profound historical effects on how societies handle cognitive challenges. With the availability of written records, the importance of memory for preserving chronicles in the form of oral narrative diminished. At the same time, the concept of re-membering information word for word (rather than for its gist) may also have arisen with the possibility of checking recall against written records (Cole & Scribner, 1977).

Literacy, it has been argued, fosters the examination of propositions for their internal logic (Goody & Watt, 1968; Olson, 1976). Written statements may more easily be examined for consistency and can be treated *as if* meaning were contained in the text itself, as in solving logical syllogisms or story problems. Of course, as cultural research has demonstrated, the social con-text of the writer and reader are very much a part of treating text in this manner. The reader's familiarity with such genres and prior knowledge of the specific topic play pivotal roles in making sense of written text.

One of the early claims about the importance of literacy assumed it had a broad, general influence on individuals' cognitive abilities. To exam-ine these claims, Sylvia Scribner and Michael Cole (1981) studied the rela-tion between cognitive skills and literacy of various types. They pointed out that most speculations about literacy focus on the use of essayist text (ex-pository writing). In their research, they worked with Vai people from Liberia who employed several different types of literacy:

> *Vai script* is used for the majority of personal and public needs (such as letter writing) in the villages and is transmitted informally by nonprofessional literates who teach friends and relatives over a period of up to two months. Vai script is an independently de-veloped phonetic writing system, consisting of a syllabary of 200 characters with 20 to 40 commonly used characters.
> In addition, some Vai individuals are literate in *Arabic* from their study of religious texts in traditional Qur'anic schools, which emphasize memorizing or reading aloud, often without under-standing the language.
> And some Vai are literate in *English* from their study in Western-style official schools.

The Vai script has many important uses, but it does not involve writing essays to examine ideas. Hence, Scribner and Cole (1981) predicted that Vai literacy would not have the intellectual consequences that have been sug-gested to result from high levels of school-based literacy, such as those re-viewed above. Indeed, they found little difference between individuals lit-erate and not literate in Vai on logic and classification tasks.

However, specific cognitive skills correlated with particular aspects of the different systems of literacy. For example, in communication tasks re-quiring the description of a board game in its absence, Vai literates excelled, compared with nonliterates and with Arabic literates. Scribner and Cole expected this relationship, because Vai literates frequently write letters, a practice requiring communication to be carried largely in the text, with relatively diminished support from other aspects of context. Vai literates were also more skilled in comprehending sentences presented syllable-by-syllable at a slow rate. This resembles the necessity in Vai literacy to integrate syllables into words, as Vai script is written without word division. Arabic literacy was associated with skill in remembering a string of words in order, with one word added to the list on each trial. This test resembles the method for learning the Qur'an by those literate in Arabic.

Scribner and Cole's (1981) results indicate that literacy relates to cognitive skills through specific practices involved in the use of literacy. Different forms of written script (such as alphabetic or phonemic writing, with or without word divisions) and different uses of literacy (such as essayist prose, letters, story problems, lists, chants) promoted distinct cognitive skills. Variations in the purposes and practices of literacy appear to be closely related to the skills that individuals using a technology gain from its use. Such variations are embedded in the societal institutions in which skill with technologies is practiced and developed.

Variation in the societal uses of literacy is clear in shifts in recent U.S. history in the definition of functional literacy (Myers, 1984, 1996; Resnick & Resnick, 1977; Wolf, 1988): In the United States of the 1700s, literacy was defined as being able to sign one's name or an X to legal documents. In the late 1800s, literacy became the ability to read and recite memorized passages, not necessarily with comprehension, as the United States sought order in recovering from a civil war and incorporating influxes of immigrants, and the machinery of industry warmed up. In the early 1900s, being able to read began to require literal understanding of unfamiliar passages. At this time, Army testers sought recruits for World War I who could read instructions for operating equipment,[3] and the efficiency goals of increasingly centralized industry required workers who could extract information

---

[3] The Army test, the first mass literacy test given in the United States (in 1916), was designed in a project of the American Psychological Association (Myers, 1996). Developed two years after the invention of the multiple-choice item, the Army test employed this new "objective" technology to examine the newly expected skill of extracting information from text, using questions like these: "*Cribbage* is played with *rackets mallets dice cards*. The *Holstein* is a kind of *cow horse sheep goat*. The most prominent industry of *Chicago* is *packing brewing automobiles flour*" (p. 86). Within a decade, the College Entrance Examination Board also turned to multiple-choice testing.

Decades later, schools still struggle with the limitations of this form of testing, designed for a different type of literacy. The use of such tests to assess the work of teachers as well as students often channels classroom instruction toward the study of bits of information gleaned from text and constrains instruction in using literacy to make inferences and develop ideas.

from text. By the late 1900s, "higher" levels of literacy (making inferences and developing ideas through written material) were expected on a mass basis for the first time. This latest definition of literacy was prompted in part by widespread use of information technology in the workplace.

Such historical shifts in the use of a cultural technology underscore the relation between individual cognitive practices and the specific institutions, technologies, and goals of society. Literacy as a cultural tool appears to facilitate particular forms of thinking, in the context of how specific forms of literacy are used as cultural practice in different communities (see Dorsey-Gaines & Garnett, 1996; Serpell, 1993; Serpell & Hatano, 1997).

Mathematics

Similar to the findings for literacy, performance on mathematical tests relates to familiarity with particular numerical practices. For example, experience with schooling was related to Liberian tailors' skill in handling arithmetic problems in the format used in school, whereas tailoring experience was related to skill in solving arithmetic problems in the format used in tailoring (Lave, 1977). Neither schooling nor tailoring provided "general" skill in numeric operations. People's familiar arithmetic strategies used in merchant activities and in schooling usually show only specific relations with tested skills (Carraher, Carraher, & Schliemann, 1985; Ginsburg, Posner, & Russell, 1981; Lancy, 1978; Lave, 1988a; Nunes, 1999; Nunes, Schliemann, & Carraher, 1993; Posner, 1982; Saxe, 1988b; see figures 7.4 and 7.5).

Likewise, Japanese abacus experts showed specific consequences of skill in using the abacus. They mentally calculated without an abacus as accurately as with one, and often faster, imagining problems of many digits on an abacus (Hatano, 1982; Stigler, Barclay, & Aiello, 1982). Visualizing problems on an abacus apparently facilitated specific skill in remembering: Abacus experts recalled a series of 15 digits either forward or backward. However, their memory span for the Roman alphabet and for fruit names was not different from the usual 7 plus or minus 2 units found for most adults in memory-span tasks. The processes involved in their impressive mental abacus operations are tailored to the activities in which they were practiced, and are applied specifically to related activities.

Similar to the research on literacy, research on mathematics has indicated the central role of cultural tools of thought. Such tools include the abacus, school forms of calculation, the pricing structure of candy to be sold on the street, the metric system, and the use of body parts or clay tokens to represent numbers (S. Ellis, 1997; Nicolopoulou, 1997; Saxe, 1981, 1991; Ueno & Saito, 1995). People's strategies for handling mathematical

FIGURE 7.4

A math lesson in a village school serving Otavalo Indians in the Andean
highlands of Ecuador (Collier & Buitrón, 1949).

problems relate closely to the purpose of the calculations and the available
and familiar tools.

Mathematical tools and skills are not all-purpose; rather, they are
adapted to the circumstances. The adaptations made by individuals, as well
as institutions, often prioritize simplification of work and reduction of
mental effort, with the use of specialized strategies to deal with routine situations (Cole, 1996; Lave, 1988a; Scribner, 1984).

When mathematics is used for practical purposes—such as by vendors,
carpenters, farmers, and dieters—people seldom came up with nonsense
results in their calculations. However, calculations in the context of schooling regularly produce some absurd errors, with results that are impossible
if the meaning of the problem being solved is considered:

> The rule-bound solutions traditionally taught in schools seem to pro-
> vide [people] with procedures that are not always understood and
> become useless in generating appropriate solutions to problems out
> of school contexts. In contrast, the strategies developed by individu-

als as tools to solve problems out of school are characterized by their flexibility and by constant monitoring of the meaning of the situation, the problem questions, and the quantities involved.

As summarized by Nunes (1993), the two most important differences between the two types of mathematics are that, (1) while outside of schools mathematics is used as a tool to achieve some other goals, in schools mathematics is an aim in itself, and (2) the situations where mathematics is used out of schools give meaning to computations, while mathematics, as it is traditionally taught in schools, becomes mainly a process of manipulation of numbers. (Schliemann et al., 1997, pp. 197–198)

National differences in skill on international mathematics tests have aroused a great deal of public debate regarding the role of schools and cultural practices in fostering mathematical understanding. The differences are striking: The best-performing U.S. fifth-grade classrooms (in Minnesota) scored lower on the mathematics test than the worst-performing Japanese classrooms and all but one Chinese classroom (Stevenson, Lee, & Stigler, 1986; see also Mathematics Achievement, 1996). Only 1 U.S. fifth-grader

FIGURE 7.5

Brazilian children pricing their candy for retail sale on the streets (Saxe, 1988a).

scored in the top 100 (out of 720 children), but 67 of them appeared in the group of 100 children who scored lowest on the test.

Some of the differences may relate to differences in how numbers are represented in different languages, yielding different cognitive tools for thinking. Some languages represent numbers such as 12 in a base-10 system ("ten-two"), whereas others have a nonbase-10 label ("twelve"). Languages with systematic use of base-10 may facilitate learning of the place value of numbers.

This was confirmed in a study in which children represented numbers using blocks in units of ten or units of one. Middle-class first-graders whose language systematically represents numbers in a base-10 system (Japanese, Chinese, and Korean) showed facility in representing place value. In comparison, middle-class first-graders from France, Sweden, and the United States, whose languages do not systematically represent base-10 numbers in the number labels, had much more difficulty (Miura et al., 1994). Similarly, Chinese 4- and 5-year-olds had less difficulty reciting the numbers and counting objects above 10 than did middle-class U.S. preschoolers, but there were not differences below 10 (Miller, Smith, Zhu, & Zhang, 1995).

Efforts to understand the differences in the fifth-graders' mathematical performances have also focused attention on variations in the structure of schooling (Stevenson et al., 1986). U.S. children spent about half as much classroom time devoted to academic activities as children in Japan and China. U.S. teachers spent a much smaller proportion of their time imparting information than did Japanese or Chinese teachers; the U.S. teachers spent more time giving directions than imparting information. These differences are compounded by the fact that the school year is much shorter for the U.S. children (178 days) than for the Japanese and Chinese children (240 days). The U.S. school day is also shorter and U.S. children spent less time on homework than did Japanese or Chinese children.

The impressive achievements of Japanese children in mathematics are accompanied by other differences in values and community organization surrounding academic achievement and group relations (Lewis, 1995; Stevenson et al., 1986; White, 1987). Attitudes toward achievement emphasize that success comes from hard work (not from innate ability). In classes averaging 42 students, Japanese teachers focused on the children's engagement in their work rather than on discipline; classes were noisy but spent more time focused on learning. Japanese teachers also delegated more classroom responsibility to children and supported the development of peer group structures as part of the learning environment. Classmates served as resources in examining mathematical concepts rather than solely as competitors for the teacher's attention. Teachers examined a few problems in depth rather than covering many problems superficially; children's errors were used as learning tools for the group. Catherine Lewis gave an example from a first-grade math lesson:

> Ms. Ogawa read a word problem to the class: "Seven children boarded a train, two got off, and three more boarded the train. How many were finally on the train?"
>
> She asked children to write equations to represent the problem, and she asked several children, who had each written a different equation to represent the problem, to put their equations on the board. Hiro's equations were very puzzling to the class: $3 - 2 = 1$ and $7 + 1 = 8$. Hiro himself could not explain his reasoning, although he tried for several minutes. Ms. Ogawa asked whether anyone in the class could explain his reasoning, but no one volunteered.
>
> When she asked, "Do Hiro's equations represent the problem correctly?" most students answered no. Ms. Ogawa again encouraged Hiro to explain his equations: "Tell us what you were thinking as you wrote these." After another unsuccessful attempt to reconstruct his own thinking, Hiro looked distressed, and Ms. Ogawa said, "Touch my hand in a baton touch and empower me to speak for you. And I will try to speak your thoughts." Hiro reached out his fingertips to touch Ms. Ogawa's, and she explained that the first equation might represent the net difference between people who boarded and left the train. She went on to help the class reason through why Hiro's equations represented the problem correctly. At the end of class, Ms. Ogawa asked Hiro to tell the class "how you felt when everyone in the class said your solution was wrong." "I didn't feel good," Hiro said. "I think he was very courageous to try and give an explanation when everyone thought he was wrong," said Ms. Ogawa, and the class looked to Hiro and burst into applause. (1995, pp. 169–170)

Perhaps surprising in view of Japanese children's impressive test scores, the emphasis in early childhood is on social development, not on instruction in academic subjects (Abe & Izard, 1999; Lewis, 1995; Tobin, Wu, & Davidson, 1989). Very few Japanese parents emphasize academic goals as reasons for children to attend preschool; they emphasize social goals such as developing empathy for others. U.S. parents, on the other hand, usually emphasize academic goals for preschool. Japanese kindergartners spend four times as much time in free play as in the United States, and Japanese elementary schools emphasize children supporting each other in learning together, not test scores. Lewis suggested that the Japanese children's impressive test performance grows from the attention given in preschool and early elementary school to developing a sense of community in the classroom, so that the children feel a part of the group and are responsible to it, allowing a deeper and more focused attention to the subjects taught.

U.S. awareness of national differences in mathematical performance sparked intense interest in the Japanese system of elementary schooling (especially during Japan's economic boom). However, often it was one or two specific techniques that attracted U.S. attention, rather than how the system fits together, integrating mathematics learning, school structure and practices, and family and community practices and values. As Giyoo Hatano and Kayoko Inagaki (1996) pointed out, adoption of specific techniques (such as focusing class attention on individuals' errors) may not help and could be counterproductive without examining how specific procedures fit together in cultural systems of values and practices.

Interestingly, the system of Japanese elementary education has itself incorporated European and American ideas for over a century. In the late 1800s, the Japanese government invited a German scholar of the Herbart educational movement to teach at the University of Tokyo, and Japan adopted aspects of the Herbartian approach (especially standardized teaching methods to centralize control of education; Serpell & Hatano, 1997). The first Japanese kindergartens, in the late 1800s, were inspired by European theories (of Froebel) of early childhood education; they served as a means for the Japanese government to introduce Western ideas (Shwalb et al., 1992). In the early 1900s, the Western ideal of child-centered "free education" was emphasized in early childhood education (Shwalb et al., 1992). In addition, the prominent American educator John Dewey consulted in Japan; his influence on Japanese elementary education has been extensive (Kobayashi, 1964).

Skilled use of cultural tools such as mathematics is intimately connected with many aspects of the practices and values of the communities in which they are used. The use of cultural tools such as mathematical systems relates to properties of the tools themselves (such as whether a number system uses base-10 systematically), community values regarding uses of the tools and how they can be learned, and interpersonal and intercommunity relations in uses of the tools.

Other Conceptual Systems

In addition to literacy and number systems, other conceptual tools provide cultural technologies that support and constrain thinking. The following complex cultural knowledge systems help their users organize information and facilitate decision making:

- Scientific systems such as classification of animals and plants in the folk biology of various cultural communities provide extensive codification of local knowledge (Berlin, 1992).
- The tools available in star maps and spatial metaphors provide navigational systems that guide impressive seafaring expertise in Polynesia (Gladwin, 1971).
- Narrative and schematic maps along with a strategy of continual updating of orientation support extremely accurate wayfinding on land among aboriginal groups in Australia (Chatwin, 1987; Levinson, 1997).
- Linguistic distinctions regarding location and shape along with geographic narratives may support Inuit skill in spatial cognition and wayfinding in the Arctic (Kleinfeld, 1973).
- Folk psychology provides systems of assumptions for organizing beliefs about other people's understanding, desires, and intentionality (Lillard, 1997).

Observations of highly skilled logical systems have also focused on expertise in indigenous games, to go beyond the investigation of logical systems using the literate cultural tool of logical syllogisms (like the one about white bears in Chapter 2). For example, throughout Africa, boys start playing the game *nsolo* in early adolescence (Serpell, 1993; see also Lancy, 1996). This game employs two or four parallel lines of holes in a log or in the ground along which stones are moved according to a complex system of rules, requiring strategic planning and calculation (see figure 7.6).

Linguistic labels for concepts also serve as cultural tools for thinking. The relation between thought and language has long been debated, and from numerous angles. The early hypothesis derived from Benjamin Whorf, that language systems determine thought, appears overly deterministic. At the same time, the idea that language systems simply derive from thought that is unrelated to language is also oversimplified. Recent work suggests that children more easily learn classification systems that are supported by concepts that receive labels in their community's language (Lucy & Gaskins, 1994).

Language systems are tools of thinking that both channel and result from communitywide ways of thinking and acting. Concepts that are easily expressed in the language system of a community provide a tool for thinking. At the same time, important community practices and traditions often find expression in words, to facilitate communication among people. That is, through participation in community practices as well as in communication about them, both thinking and language develop in ways that

FIGURE 7.6

(*Top*) Nsolo game board for moving stones in a game of strategy in Zambia, and (*bottom*) game of nsolo in progress (Serpell, 1993).

support each other (as in the historical changes in the language of Angle-Land, Chapter 3).

Cultural preferences in use of language go beyond the words that are used to express concepts. The narrative structure that is valued in each community gives form to the ways that people express ideas in conversation and writing (Gee, 1989; Michaels & Cazden, 1986; Minami & McCabe, 1996; Mistry, 1993a; Scollon & Scollon, 1981; Wolf & Heath, 1992).

For example, Japanese narrative structure often follows a succinct three-part scheme resembling the Japanese poetry form *haiku*. The narrative omits information that the listener is judged to be able to easily infer if the listener were to take the narrator's perspective, consistent with Japanese valuing of empathy and collaboration (Minami & McCabe, 1995, 1996). To European American teachers, Japanese children's narratives appear unimaginative and sparse. However, Japanese children are encouraged in this cultural form, regarded as elegantly compressed. They are very familiar with hearing haiku-like, succinct storytelling, and their mothers encourage them to narrate everyday events in this format through the kind of conversational accompaniment the mothers provide.

In contrast, European American narrative formats are more descriptive of settings and emotions, elaborating on a single experience, often with a high point resolving a problem (Minami & McCabe, 1995). European American children's narratives were much longer than those of Japanese children. The preferred narrative structure was encouraged by mothers, who often asked the children questions that encouraged them to elaborate on details, even those that a listener might readily infer.

Distinct narrative structures may contribute to habits of thought that relate to such cognitive domains as how one examines evidence to support a claim and how one specifies ideas to oneself and others. For example, the formats for writing scientific articles have a narrative structure that both guides and constrains a scientist's thinking, embodying the structure of thought and communication termed "the scientific method." As is well-known, the scientific method may not be followed in the research process, but eventually the scientist recasts the process in terms that fit with this culturally valued format for others to understand the work.

Individuals' and generations' uses of cognitive tools—such as narrative structure, words, and systems of numbers and writing—make it clear that thinking is a process involving interpersonal and community processes, in addition to the usual focus on individual processes. The next section focuses on the idea that thinking is widely distributed across people and tools, as people use cultural tools for thinking together.

Distributed Cognition in the Use of Cultural Tools for Thinking

The cognitive development of individuals occurs within communities of thinkers in which more than one person is working on a particular topic. Historical and material aspects of other people's efforts are available to each thinker in this extended conversation (Bruffee, 1993; Cole, 1996; John-Steiner, 1985, 1992; Nicolopoulou, 1997; Schrage, 1990):

> As civilized human beings, we are the inheritors, neither of an inquiry about ourselves and the world, nor of an accumulating body of information, but of a conversation, begun in the primeval forests and extended and made more articulate in the course of centuries. It is a conversation which goes on both in public and within each of ourselves. . . . [Each new generation enters] an initiation into the skill and partnership of this conversation. And it is this conversation which, in the end, gives place and character to every human activity and utterance. (Oakeshott, 1962, p. 199)

As Ed Hutchins (1991) pointed out in his studies of how sailors collaborate in the calculations and planning required for navigating large ships, cognition is *distributed* across people as they collaborate with each other and with tools designed to aid in cognitive work. Figuring out how to turn a massive vessel progressing at a certain speed to come to dock in a small harbor is done through the coordination of many people. They work with cognitive devices developed by predecessors to handle some aspects of the necessary data gathering, calculations, and interpersonal problem solving. Similarly:

> An ethnographer studying a group of machine technicians came to a blunt rethinking of what expertise means in the context of the workplace. His analysis was that expert knowledge among technicians is less a matter of what each individual knows than of their joint ability to produce the right information when and where it's needed. . . . In other words, expertise is a social affair. (Schrage, 1990, p. 49)

Another example of how thinking involves interpersonal and cultural tools is the planning that takes place during Girl Scout cookie sales (Rogoff, Baker-Sennett, Lacasa, & Goldsmith, 1995; Rogoff, Topping, Baker-Sennett, & Lacasa, 2002). The Scouts' planning and keeping track of orders and routes occurred in collaboration with other Scouts, kin, customers, and troop leaders and involved cognitive tools provided by the institution (such as memory and calculation aids on the order form). The girls also contributed new tools for handling cognitive problems (such as thinking of using Post-it notes to organize orders).

The impressive invention of a system of writing by Sequoyah for the Cherokee people, in the beginning of the 1800s, was also distributed across people and tools. Sequoyah is reported to have been impressed with the message-sending facility provided by the "talking leaf" used by Whites and devised an alphabet for his people. His alphabet of 85 letters has been used for years for correspondence and newspapers. Sequoyah's feat is notable for his personal genius, the interpersonal basis of his inspiration (in seeing the use of the "talking leaf"), and the adapted cultural technology on which his achievement was based (Carpenter, 1976). This individual's innovation also contributed to others' interpersonal communication and to the cultural tools available to future generations.

Cognition beyond the Skull

The idea that cognition is distributed across individuals, other people, and cultural tools and institutions may be difficult to consider if one assumes that cognition resides wholly inside individual heads. From the perspective that human development is a process of transformation of participation in sociocultural activities, the assumption that thinking occurs completely inside the skull is rejected.

The assumption that there is an arbitrary boundary between the individual and the rest of the world has created unnecessary complications in understanding development and thinking. It has also gotten in the way of understanding the relation among individual, interpersonal, and community processes (discussed in Chapter 2). Gregory Bateson exquisitely illustrated the problems of such boundaries:

> Suppose I am a blind man, and I use a stick. I go tap, tap, tap. Where do *I* start?
>
> Is my mental system bounded at the handle of the stick? Is it bounded by my skin? Does it start halfway up the stick? Does it start at the tip of the stick?
>
> But these are nonsense questions. The stick is a pathway along which transformations of difference are being transmitted. The way to delineate the system is to draw the limiting line in such a way that you do not cut any of these pathways in ways which leave things inexplicable. (1972, p. 459)

For young infants, use of limbs requires the same sort of learning as does Bateson's stick; they learn to use their own limbs as tools in reaching and moving. In learning to use language and literacy, children also learn the use of physical movements and objects as mental tools. Arbitrary sounds, and their relative positions to one another, come to have such meaning that, for skilled speakers, the tools and the process of learning become almost invisible. Likewise, for a skilled reader, the process of moving from ink spots on a page to meaningful ideas is so automatic that the role of the tools of literacy and the author's and other people's contributions to the process of reading may be easily overlooked. For novices, however, the distributed roles of the material tool, other people, and themselves are much more obvious as they learn to use a cognitive tool such as spoken language or literacy. Especially with such mental tools, cognition is distributed not only across individuals and material objects but also across ideas and communication with other people (see figure 7.7).

Collaboration in Thinking across Time and Space

Collaboration in thinking may take place with prior generations, as when Michelangelo studied ancient sculpture and Pablo Casals practiced Bach's music each day. Exceptionally creative writers, painters, and physicists discover their own teachers from the past, engaging with "an intense and personal kinship that results when the work of another evokes a special reso-

FIGURE 7.7

Grandma Smith reads with the Spencer girls, 1923.

nance in them. . . . In this way, they stretch, deepen, and refresh their craft and nourish their intelligence" (John-Steiner, 1985, p. 54).

Shared endeavors also involve engagement with the lives of people who are to follow, even if they are not yet known or even born. For example, a writer must consider ways of expression that will make sense to a future generation (Rogoff, 1998). Consider my efforts at this moment to communicate with you. Part of the cognitive challenge is to attempt to foresee what you may need explained because you are unlikely to share all of my experiences. You probably have a different background than I and may be of a different generation. You may have a different educational tradition, first language, and purpose for engaging with ideas regarding culture and cognition. All these aspects of communication are central to my cognitive efforts in writing at this moment. Thus I am involved in a shared cognitive endeavor with people long gone (such as Vygotsky and Dewey) and not yet born, as well as with technologies and practices that we have inherited (such as literacy and the computer) that we participate in transforming.

The historical and future involvements with other people in solving cognitive problems are apparent in the account of author Patricia MacLachlan, who described how she relied on both an anticipated reader and an absent editor to solve problems in writing:

> I try to anticipate the experience of the reader. I myself, of course, am the first reader, and I try to envision a small, objective, heartless Patty MacLachlan looking over my shoulder saying, "Aw, come on!" when I am clumsy or self-indulgent. But the small Patty MacLachlan somehow turns into a Charlotte Zolotow [MacLachlan's editor]. Her voice has become ingrained in my consciousness; I can hear her.
>
> I've passed this on. My daughter Emily is becoming a wonderful, imaginative writer herself, and we spend a good deal of time discussing her work. "When I write a theme in class," she told me the other day, "I hear your voice in my ear." (1989, pp. 740–741)

Similarly, researchers found that "ideas in the air" (at UC Berkeley's School of Education) led them to synergistic ideas that could not have derived from the work of any one individual working alone or in another local research community (Schoenfeld, 1989). Discussions among research group members as well as apparently extraneous conversations with other colleagues on other topics were important in the development of the ideas of a research project. The conversations at the time did not seem significant to the research problem, but analysis in retrospect revealed their centrality to the endeavor across time and contexts.

Collaboration Hidden in the Design of Cognitive Tools and Procedures

Some cultural tools—such as computers, literacy, workbooks, and diagrams—are particularly designed to foster collaboration and interaction in thinking among people participating in shared activity at a distance (Bruffee, 1993; Crook, 1994; Ochs, Jacoby, & Gonzales, 1994; Pea & Gomez, 1992; Schrage, 1990). The role of such tools in thinking may be easily overlooked.

For example, it would be easy to overlook the role of the problem setup as a tool for learning in the Japanese science education method in which students are presented with a question along with three or four possible answers to discuss. The question and the alternatives guide how students verify their predictions simply in the way the questions are asked and the alternatives worded, providing a range of possibilities that encompass common misconceptions (Kobayashi, 1994). This aids students in discerning both which opinions are plausible and which predictions test out, providing them with clues for restructuring their naïve understanding into scientific concepts. Without considering the collaborative role of those who devise such cognitive tools and the structure of the tools themselves, the students' learning process would be incompletely understood.

The computer plays such an important cultural role as a cognitive tool that it is sometimes regarded as an interactive partner itself (Hawkins, 1987; Schrage, 1990; see figure 7.8). Of course, thinking with the aid of a computer also involves remote collaboration with the people who designed the hardware, the software, and the computer setting that is being used. For example, in classrooms, some forms of guidance can be provided by either a computer or a human partner. Both options involve collaboration with human partners acting either indirectly through a device or directly in face-to-face interaction (Zellermayer, Salomon, Globerson, & Givon, 1991).

Similarly, researchers serve as collaborators in children's test performance (Newman et al., 1984; Scribner, 1976). Young children attempt to make use of the examiner's nonverbal cues, such as direction of gaze and hesitations, to answer standardized questions (Mehan, 1976). Jonathan Tudge suggested that even an experimenter's silence is social information in a situation in which an experimenter provided no feedback on children's solutions to balance beam problems: "Silence on the part of an adult typically implies consent—or surely an incorrect answer would be challenged" (1992, p. 1377).

Even when experimenters and research participants are not directly interacting, they are indirectly engaged together. For example, researchers attempt to tailor the problems on which children work to their age level or abilities (Tudge & Winterhoff, 1993), and the materials, instructions, and experimental script are used to communicate to children what they are to

FIGURE 7.8

At 20 months, David-Charles is using a program called "Jardin d'Èveil," designed for children from age 1 to 2. To play, the child has only to click on the computer mouse or hit any key on the keyboard. In one game, with each keystroke or mouse click a farm animal appears and makes an animal sound for the baby to repeat (e.g., beeee, ouaf ouaf, cocorico; Gagny, France).

do and to support their playing their role in the study. Preschool children have difficulty following the experimenter's plans or focusing on the experimental goals unless their role is carefully supported by the researcher and the procedures.

Roy Pea provided an apt illustration of including other people and cognitive tools in notions of intelligence and its development. He recounted a presentation by Seymour Papert of a computer program for building toy machines at a National Science Foundation meeting:

> Papert described what marvelous machines the students had built, with very little "interference" from teachers. . . . On reflection, I felt this argument missed the key point about the "invisible" human intervention in this example—what the designers of Lego and Logo crafted in creating just the interlockable component parts of Lego machines or just the Logo primitive commands for controlling these machines. For there are only so many ways in which these components can be combined. Considerable intelligence has been *built into* these interpart relations as a means of constraining what actions are possible with the parts in combination. What I realized was that, al-

though Papert could "see" teachers' interventions (a kind of social distribution of intelligence contributing to the child's achievement of activity), the designers' interventions (a kind of artifact-based intelligence contributing to the child's achievement of activity) were not seen. . . . [The child] could be scaffolded in the achievement of activity either explicitly by the intelligence of the teacher, or *implicitly* by that of the designers, now embedded in the constraints of the artifacts with which the child was playing. (1993, pp. 64–65).

Artifacts such as books, orthographies, computers, languages, and hammers are essentially social, historical objects, transforming with the ideas of both their designers and their later users. They form and are formed by the practices of their use and by related practices, in historical and anticipated communities (Brown & Duguid, 1994; Gauvain, 1993; Nicolopoulou, 1997; Rogoff et al., 1994). Artifacts serve to amplify as well as constrain the possibilities of human activity as the artifacts participate in the practices in which they are employed (Cole & Griffin, 1980; Wertsch, 1991). They are representatives of earlier solutions to similar problems by other people, which later generations modify and apply to new problems, extending and transforming their use.

An Example: Sociocultural Development in Writing Technologies and Techniques

An example of the sociocultural development of cognitive tools that many literate people now take for granted is provided in the history of writing technologies and techniques. Now that composing and editing electronically is transforming written communication, we may reflect more easily on the importance of our tools. Older readers are likely to have noticed the difference in composing written ideas with the aid of word processing compared with previously available tools—pencil and paper or typewriter. Younger readers may take for granted the ease in editing when changes can be made and tracked electronically.

Few of us stop to think about paper as a writing technology. However, the easy availability of writing surfaces has been essential to the development of written composition. The invention of paper made key contributions to the development of writing and of widespread literacy.

The search for a good writing surface took inventors from many nations a number of centuries, as chronicled by Jolie Velazquez (1999). Consistent with the premise of this book, the development of this technology was a process involving individual creativity and initiative, societal policies and relations, and ecological opportunities.

The move from writing on walls and clay tablets occurred in Egypt in the third century B.C. with the invention of papyrus made of water reeds that grow along the Nile, which are sliced, pounded, and glued together in sheets. The Pharaoh's subjects were forbidden to export papyrus, and within about a century, the Pharaoh's neighbors developed parchment made out of sheepskin as a writing medium. In A.D. 105, true paper made out of pulp was invented in China by a court official named Ts'ai Lun, who developed a way to make pulp (from tree bark, hemp waste, rags, and fish nets) and then spread the pulp onto a screen to dry in a sheet.

This invention was hailed by the Chinese imperial family and was very important to China's development. China kept this technology secret for five centuries, until papermaking spread to Japan and Korea, China's trade partners. Then in the mid-700s, following victory in a battle, Arabs forced Chinese prisoners to divulge the secret, and by the 10th century, commercial centers throughout the Islamic world prospered in paper-making.

Europe did not begin to import paper until early in the 11th century, and the papermaking trade became established in Europe only in the middle of the 12th century. Some credit a French Crusader, Jean Montgolfier, with bringing the secrets of papermaking to France after being taken prisoner and forced to serve several years in a paper mill in Damascus. It was not until the invention of the printing press in the mid-1400s that paper became an accepted medium in Europe. Before that, the Church and governments refused its use for official documents, due to its fragility and "heathen" origins (from the perspective of Christian Europe).

Eventually, the raw materials for paper—linen cloth from the flax plant used by the Arabs, and then cotton from India and the Americas—could not keep up with the demand for paper. Shortages prevailed even with the recycling of rags and old clothes and an English law requiring that bodies be buried only in wool.

Scientific societies offered medals and prizes to inventors to find new fiber sources for paper. Eventually, in 1719, a French naturalist, inspired by observing wasps making nests with digested wood, suggested wood pulp. An Englishman first successfully created wood paper in 1787. In the mid-1800s, improvements made in Germany prevented the rapid deterioration of wood paper. Then, along with industrial production methods, cheap and strong paper became available, allowing the development of novels for leisure reading (*pulp* fiction!).

What we currently take for granted in literate practices includes not only the availability of paper and particular literate genres such as novels, but also the process of drafting a written composition. In recent years, we have been able to witness the ways that the revision of written text has been transformed by the advent of word processing on computers, which for many authors has replaced drafts on tablets of lined paper.

However, before the Middle Ages in Europe, all elaboration of the ideas and expression of text occurred before the material was set in written form (Alcorta, 1994). The person who composed the text was not the one who wrote it; the text's author merely dictated it to a scribe, who wrote it onto the parchment exactly as dictated. In the Middle Ages, with the innovation of using a wax tablet, it became possible to work with an intermediate draft. Then authors began to fill all three roles: the composer of the text, the writer on the wax tablet, and the transcriber to parchment for the final, neat document. It was not until the 1880s in France, soon after cheap paper became widely available, that schoolchildren were expected to express themselves in writing rather than simply putting others' words on paper.

Literate people may now take for granted the tool for thinking that written composition provides, but this cognitive practice has evolved through the centuries from roots in oral traditions, through the development of material inventions and cultural practices, in a collaboration of many individuals from far-flung societies over great periods of time.

Crediting the Cultural Tools and Practices We Think With

Although cognitive tools, and the social roles that they carry with them across history, are easily overlooked, their contribution to thinking is central. James Wertsch provided a compelling example:

Consider the following multiplication problem:

$$343$$
$$\times\ \underline{822}$$

If asked to solve this problem, you could probably come up with the answer of 281,946. If asked how you arrived at this solution, you might say, "I just multiplied 343 by 822!" and you might show me your calculations, which might look like this:

$$343$$
$$\underline{822}$$
$$686$$
$$686$$
$$\underline{2744\ \ \ }$$
$$281946$$

. . . Was it really you (i.e., the isolated agent) who solved the problem? (After all, you said "I multiplied . . . ") To see the force of this question . . . consider what you would do in response to the request to multiply 343 by 822, but without placing the numbers in the

vertical array used above. Most of us would be stumped at this point.
. . . A seemingly slight change in how the problem is written out
seems to make our ability to multiply disappear. . . .

The spatial organization, or syntax, of the numbers in this case is
an essential part of a cultural tool without which we cannot solve this
problem. In an important sense, then, this syntax is doing some of
the thinking involved. We might be unaware of how or why this
syntax should work, and we might have no idea about how it emerged
in the history of mathematical thought. In this sense, we are unreflec-
tive, if not ignorant, consumers of a cultural tool. The extent to
which our performance relies on it, however, quickly becomes clear
when it is not available. This leads me to suggest that when asked
who carried out such a problem, the more appropriate answer might
be, "I and the cultural tool I employed did." (1998, pp. 24–25)

The importance of cultural tools for mathematical thinking has been
noted in passing for centuries. For example, Shakespeare frequently referred
to the use of "counters" (Swetz, 1987). The clown from *The Winter's Tale*
struggled to calculate the amount of money that the wool of 1,500 sheep
("wethers") would cost, if 11 sheep provide one tod (28 pounds):

> Let me see. Every 'leven wether tods; every tod yields pound and odd
> shilling; fifteen hundred shorn, what comes the wool to? . . .
> I cannot do't without counters. (quoted in Swetz, 1987, p. 181)

The role of "counters" opens up a fascinating story of the development
of mathematical understanding across individuals, generations, and continents (Swetz, 1987). In the Renaissance, the merchants of Venice formed
the first capitalist center of Europe, connecting many trade routes among
Asia, Africa, and Europe. Sons of businessmen from northern Europe con-
gregated in Venice to study the mercantile arts, especially commercial arithmetic. The Venetians early appreciated the importance of arithmetic in
business, and from their trade excursions around the Mediterranean and
Barbary coasts, they had learned of the Hindu-Arabic number system and
arithmetic procedures.

One merchant, among others influential in this history, stands out.
Leonardo of Pisa, who is known as Fibonacci (born in 1180), was raised in
a trading colony in what is now Algeria and studied with an Arab master to
learn the Hindu-Arabic arithmetic. He was convinced that these methods
were much more effective than the Roman numerals that were used in Europe, and in 1202, he published a general introduction to the numerals and
the *algorithms* for their use, including uses in commerce (Swetz, 1987). Italian merchants began to use the Hindu-Arabic numerals rather than the

Roman letters in their accounting, influenced by Fibonacci's treatise as well as by Spanish translations of Arabic works.

The derivation of the label "algorithm" for the calculation scheme provides an apt illustration of the relation of individuals, generations, and communities in thinking processes. The label is derived from translation of the name of the Muslim author, Abu Jafar Muhammed ibn Musa al-Khwarizmi, who lived in about 825 and wrote an arithmetic text on the numerals and how to use them for computations (Swetz, 1987). Al-Khwarizmi's work was translated into Latin in Spain in the 1100s by an Englishman, Robert of Chester, who attributed the work to "Algoritmi." As the new form of numerals and computation spread from the Arab world via Spain to Germany and France, the new system was referred to by the Latinized name of this Arab scholar of several centuries before.[4]

When the easier and more effective pen-and-ink methods of the Hindu-Arabic system came to the attention of Europeans, conflicts arose between those who began to use the new methods and those who fought for the traditional abacus and counters (Swetz, 1987). The abacus method employed counters on a tabletop that was marked with place value columns or rows (this in turn was derived from the ancient system using a slab covered with fine dust in which to carry out and erase computations). The controversy raged for several centuries in Europe between the algorists and the abacists.

A large impediment to the change was that computation was much more accessible to the masses with the new numerals and computation methods (along with the new printing technologies used to print arithmetic texts such as the *Treviso Arithmetic* near Venice in 1478). The select few who specialized in the use of counters to calculate and Roman numerals to record the results resisted the new system, which could be more easily learned and did not require as much in the way of apparatus. Indeed, for some years, laws attempted to prohibit the use of Hindu-Arabic numerals in accounting books (e.g., 1299 in Florence; 1494 in Frankfurt; Swetz, 1987). The Italian merchants made the change by the early 1400s, but abacus arithmetic prevailed as late as 1592 in northern Europe.

Eventually, the successors to Shakespeare's clown made use of the pencil-and-paper cognitive tools referred to by Wertsch, usually without thinking of this as a controversial method or even thinking of it as part of their calculation at all. However, neither the clown nor modern-day solvers of Wertsch's multiplication problem could calculate without relying on the cultural tools (conceptual as well as material) available to them from prior

---

[4]Notice that this was during the time that the papermaking trade also came to Europe from Arab sources.

generations and faraway places. And current generations continue to transform the tools used.

This abbreviated account makes clear how cognitive processes develop together with cultural processes across centuries and continents. The developments involve the contributions and collaborations of individuals of renown and those whose names are not remembered, in inventing, borrowing, and modifying cultural tools of thought. Cultural-historical research has pointed to the importance of including cultural tools in the analysis of cognitive processes and led the way to understanding that thinking is collaborative and distributed among people in shared endeavors.

This line of research has also drawn attention to the importance of understanding thinking as a purposeful effort to accomplish something, often with other people. Cultural tools of thought are generally used for purposes that involve other people engaged in shared endeavors—whether in person or across time and space. Cultural institutions such as schools and factories, families and churches, merchant guilds and trade routes and political systems are closely involved in the traditions that are connected with the use of varying cultural tools for thinking.

The field's growing awareness of the centrality of collaboration in thinking has put the processes of communication and ways of learning to use cultural tools at center stage for understanding human development. What are the processes by which Liberian tailors learn the math involved in cutting cloth, sons of German merchants learned the use of the abacus in Venetian "schools of the abacus," and Mayan girls learn how to plan the patterns of complex weaving designs? How people learn through their involvements with other people, in different cultural settings and institutions, is the subject of the next chapter.

8

Learning through Guided Participation in Cultural Endeavors

When I was about 7 years old, I told my mother that I wanted to learn how to bake bread. She told me that it wasn't too hard. She had done it when she was a young girl working in a bakery. But we did not have an oven to bake. So my first task was to build one with her help. First, I was to find a suitable area for the oven. I learned about the weather, erosion, and how to find the best place to build an oven. As my mother was working around the house, I would come inside and ask for her help or instructions for the next step. I gathered bricks, stones, soil (good soil), and grass to begin the task. The job took me about three days, since I had to let parts of the structure dry before moving to the next step. It was about a week after building it before we began to bake bread.

Out of this experience what strikes me the most is that through this process I learned who my mom was and how her life had been as a child. I also learned about parental expectations. Every step of the way in the process of building the oven, there was a story. Language was the tool my mother used to assist me in the task, as well as the tool to teach me the meaning and the importance of what we were doing together. Her stories were filled with values, beliefs, and meaning that reflected our social reality. But most important, her stories showed me that people have survived with imagination and creative action.
—Recollections of Hector Rivera, as a graduate student, of his childhood in El Salvador (personal communication, October 1995)

When scholars of culture and cognition first started to attend to the collaborative nature of cognitive development, they found inspiration in Vygotsky's concept of interaction in the *zone of proximal development*. This is the idea that children learn through their interactions with more experienced adults and peers, who assist them in engaging in thinking that is beyond the "zone" in which they would be able to perform without assistance. In interactions within the zone of proximal development, children learn to use the intellectual tools of their community, including literacy, number systems, language, and tools for remembering and planning.

Although Vygotsky's idea is very important, it seems to focus especially on the kind of interaction involved in schooling and preparation for use of academic discourse and tools. (This is no accident, because Vygotsky was particularly interested in promoting academic skills in his nation.) The focus on instructional interactions tends to overlook other forms of engagement that are also important to children's learning.

In everyday interactions, parents often are not focused on instructing children, even in communities where schooling is emphasized. Everyday conversations that are not designed as instruction frequently provide children with important access to information and involvement in the skills of their community. For example, a 4-year-old British girl helping her mother prepare a shopping list had the opportunity to learn about using lists as planning tools, counting and calculating to make sure they weren't planning too many items for their available cash, and reading items on the list (Tizard & Hughes, 1984).

In addition to such situations when parents engage with children without intending to teach, parents may try to avoid interacting with their children at times. They may simply carry out a task themselves and avoid sharing it with the children if they are in a hurry or don't want to be bothered (Rheingold, 1982). If they do not think that the children will need to know how to do the task later, they may also be less likely to involve them. For example, U.S. mothers shared more responsibility with their 4-year-olds in planning routes through a model grocery store if they had been told that the children would later carry out the task on their own (Gauvain, 1995).

Whether or not parents focus on helping children learn, children may take initiative in observing and becoming involved in ongoing activities (Rogoff, 1990; Rogoff et al., 2003). Children also often initiate conversations with adults or with other children that help them learn. In a study of British working-class and middle-class 4-year-old girls' conversations, the children initiated slightly more than half of their conversations both at home and at preschool. In this example, a girl became curious about a puppet on TV:

> CHILD: How do they make him talk?
> MOTHER: They just talk . . . the man talks in a funny voice.
> CHILD: Is he inside him?
> MOTHER: No, he puts his hand inside, and then makes the puppet move, and then he talks.
> CHILD: What?
> MOTHER: He talks, and it sounds as though the puppet's talking.
> (Tizard & Hughes, 1998, p. 87)

To broaden our view of the collaborative nature of learning that occurs outside of (as well as within) explicit instructional situations, I proposed the concept of *guided participation* in cultural activities (Rogoff, 1990). Guided participation provides a perspective to help us focus on the *varied ways* that children learn as they participate in and are guided by the values and practices of their cultural communities. It is *not a particular method* of support for learning. For example, one form of guided participation is explanation; another is teasing and shaming, when adults and peers point out children's foibles and missteps by holding their behavior up to social evaluation—sometimes with humor and goodwill, sometimes not.

Guided participation is not limited to learning societally desired skills and practices. The same processes are involved when children engage in interactions that assist them in learning skills and practices that many consider undesirable, such as the use of violence to handle interpersonal problems. Such interactions, like others, channel children's learning of particular values and practices.

In addition, guided participation includes efforts by social partners—and by children themselves—to avoid some kinds of learning. There are many topics that adults protect or divert children from learning (such as sexuality and family income in middle-class U.S. families; Goodnow, 1990; Litowitz, 1993). Adults often constrain children's opportunities to explore, for example, in refusing to let a 1-year-old near a fire or censoring documents from children's access (Serpell, 1993; Valsiner, 1984, 1987; Valsiner & Lawrence, 1997). In observations of U.S. toddlers' everyday home activities, the activities were restricted during 8% of observations (compared with being facilitated during 12% and carried out mutually with another person during 21% of observations; Carew, 1980). Such constraints are a part of the participatory and guided nature of development.

The term "guided" in the concept guided participation is thus meant broadly, to include but go beyond interactions that are intended as instructional. In addition to instructional interactions, guided participation focuses on the side-by-side or distal arrangements in which children participate in the values, skills, and practices of their communities without intentional instruction or even necessarily being together at the same time. It includes varying forms of participation in culturally guided activities through the use of particular tools and involvement with cultural institutions.

The concept of guided participation is central to my proposal that learning is a process of changing participation in community activities. It is a process of taking on new roles and responsibilities. A similar concept has been proposed by Jean Lave and Etienne Wenger (1991), who argued that learning is a matter of people's changing involvement as "legitimate peripheral participants" in communities of practice.

Whether or not what is learned and the means used are desirable, I argue that such learning and interaction involve similar basic processes as well as distinct forms of guided participation around the world. The next section examines widespread basic processes of guided participation. In the remainder of the chapter, I discuss distinct forms of guided participation that vary in their prevalence in different cultural communities.

Basic Processes of Guided Participation

Communication and coordination during participation in shared endeavors are key aspects of how people develop. Participants adjust among themselves (with varying, complementary, or even conflicting roles) to stretch their common understanding to fit new perspectives.

This emphasis on mutual involvement contrasts with the "social influence" perspective, which attributes socialization to adults who organize children's learning. From the perspective that development occurs in *participation* in shared sociocultural activities, it is clear that children play actively central roles, along with their elders and other companions, in learning and extending the ways of their communities.

In this section, I discuss two basic processes of guided participation that appear to be common worldwide. The first involves children and their companions supporting their shared endeavors by attempting to bridge their different perspectives using culturally available tools such as words and gestures and referencing each other's actions and reactions. The second is their structuring of each others' involvement to facilitate engagement in shared endeavors. Mutual structuring occurs in the choice of activities children have access to as well as in interactions between children and their companions in the course of shared endeavors. I conclude this section on basic processes of guided participation with a discussion of mutual involvement in several widespread cultural practices with great importance for learning: narratives, routines, and play.

Mutual Bridging of Meanings

In bridging different perspectives, partners seek a common perspective or language through which to communicate their ideas in order to coordinate their efforts. Mutual understanding occurs *between* people in interaction; it cannot be attributed to one person or another. Modifications in each participant's perspective are necessary to accomplish things together. The modifications are a process of development; as the participants adjust to communicate and coordinate, their new perspectives involve greater understanding (Wertsch, 1984).

Bridging between toddlers' and parents' understandings appeared consistently in the widely different communities studied by Rogoff et al. (1993). Toddlers were almost always closely involved in the same agenda with their mothers. For example, a mother and a child might operate an object together, or a mother might attempt to assist a child trying to operate an object. Toddlers together with their mothers actively interpreted and participated in the definition of situations and in the direction of activities.

Bridging between meanings relies extensively on nonverbal means of communication. For example, in *social referencing*, people seek information about how to interpret ambiguous situations from the expressions of others (Feinman, 1982; Sorce, Emde, Campos, & Klinnert, 1985). An example of bridging meanings through social referencing in an ambiguous situation is provided by a 20-month-old Mayan boy and his mother. The toddler sought information regarding whether Play-Doh was edible while patting out a tortilla using the Play-Doh that the foreign researchers had brought to his house:

> The baby broke off a tiny corner of the little tortilla he had made and held it up expectantly to his mother. She absently nodded to the baby as she conversed with the adults present.
>
> The baby brought the piece of play tortilla to his mouth and, looking at his mother fixedly, he stuck out his tongue and held the piece of tortilla toward it, with a questioning expression. His mother suddenly bolted out her hand and snatched his hand holding the piece of tortilla away from his mouth, blurting out "No! Not that!" The baby looked at her with a little surprise but was not disturbed by this clear message that the dough is not edible; he watched quietly as she laughingly put the little piece of dough back on the rest of the tortilla, put it back into the baby's hand and told him that it is not to eat. He resumed patting the dough contentedly. (Rogoff et al., 1993, pp. 235–236)

Social referencing is a very powerful way to gain and give information. From their first year, infants seek information in social interaction, attempting to obtain information from the direction in which caregivers point and gaze. They also seem to use intonation contours as well as timing and emotional tone to understand the gist of a caregiver's message (Butterworth, 1987; Fernald, 1988; Papousek, Papousek, & Bornstein, 1985; Scaife & Bruner, 1975; Trevarthen & Hubley, 1978). Parents taking children to get an injection easily communicate apprehension to their infants through their expression and tension; without knowing what is about to happen, infants can tell that it is a scary situation. Emotional communication between parents and infants is a widespread way of regulating infant mood; Greek, German, Trobriand Island, Yanomamo, Japanese, and U.S. mothers who display happy expressions "infect" babies with happy moods (Keating, 1994).

Words provide children with meanings and distinctions that are important in their community. Roger Brown pointed out this function of language learning in his notion of the Original Word Game, where children and partners label objects. The child forms hypotheses about the category of objects to which a label refers and a partner helps the child to improve the fit between the child's hypotheses and the cultural designations of categories encoded by labels. "In learning referents and names the player of the Original Word Game prepares himself to receive the science, the rules of thumb, the prejudices, the total expectancies of his society" (1958, p. 228; see also Adams & Bullock, 1986; Bruner, 1983; John-Steiner & Tatter, 1983).

Young children make large contributions to their own socialization, assisted by other people's efforts to support their growing understanding (Rogoff, 1990; Shatz, 1987; Tomasello, 1992, in press; Waxman & Gelman, 1986). Mutuality in early language use is especially evident as some infants build discussions with others through successive turns that layer the infants' one-word comments. For example, the baby might say "Shoe" and the caregiver says "Is that your shoe?" When the baby adds "On," the caregiver fills in "Oh, shall I put on your shoe?" (Greenfield & Smith, 1976; Ochs, Schieffelin, & Platt, 1979; Scollon, 1976; Zukow, Reilly, & Greenfield, 1982).

Mutual involvement in bridging meanings occurs worldwide—although it takes a variety of forms in different communities (examined later in this chapter). Another basic process of guided participation is mutual structuring of partners' participation in shared endeavors.

Mutual Structuring of Participation

Children and caregivers and other companions around the world together structure the situations in which children are involved (Rogoff, 1990; Rogoff et al., 1993). The structuring occurs through choice of which activities children have access to observe and engage in, as well as through in-person shared endeavors, including conversations, recounting of narratives, and engagement in routines and play.

Structuring children's opportunities to observe and participate

Caregivers, community practices and institutions, and children's own choices mutually determine the situations in which children are present and have opportunities to learn. For example, as indicated in Chapter 4, there are striking historical and cultural differences in children's segregation from mature activities of their communities. This form of structuring of children's lives is central to their opportunities to observe and participate.

Structuring of children's participation occurs as they choose to (or choose not to) watch TV, do chores, or eavesdrop on their parents. It occurs as parents extend or limit opportunities by making decisions regarding day care or doing chores when toddlers are asleep, and as communities construct institutions that include or exclude children (Laboratory of Comparative Human Cognition, 1983; Valsiner, 1984; Whiting, 1980). Such choices may be made without the intention of providing a learning experience. But at times, the choices may be designed explicitly around children's learning, as in the design of specialized institutions for learning or availability of specialized training objects, such as baby walkers, baby books, and toy implements (see figures 8.1 and 8.2).

Children's active monitoring of events around them makes clear the importance of the choice of events they are allowed or required to be around. Even when events are not staged for children's benefit or adjusted to their viewing, they gain important information through observing (Bandura, 1986; Lewis & Feiring, 1981; Verba, 1994).

FIGURE 8.1

A structure made of stick rails provided by parents to aid a Guatemalan Mayan infant in learning to walk.

FIGURE 8.2

Miniature implements are one way that parents and communities structure children's learning. This Dani father from the mountains of New Guinea demonstrates the use of a toy bow and arrow to his son.

The propensity to seek proximity to and involvement with their elders assists young children everywhere in learning about the activities of the person who is followed (Hay, 1980). Adult involvement with an object attracted European American toddlers to the object, and they carried out markedly similar actions on it (Eckerman, Whatley, & McGhee, 1979; Hay, Murray, Cecire, & Nash, 1985). European American toddlers spontaneously helped their parents or a stranger in household chores that the adults performed in a laboratory or home setting (Rheingold, 1982). A U.S. mother who spent many hours transcribing tape-recorded conversations for her research noticed her 3-year-old emulating her work in play:

> Each day I sit at the word processor, stopping and starting the tape recorder, tapping in the words and referring to the text. And now Lindsey has incorporated my behavior into her play. This morning I discovered her setting up her own office.
>
> She had pulled her small director's chair up to her bed, which served as a desk. It held her "computer" (really a toy typewriter), as well as her small plastic tape recorder. She would play a section of *Star Wars*, and then stop the recording to bang out a message on the plastic keys of her typewriter. Back and forth she went between the recorder and her "computer," playing and typing, playing a new section and typing again, in a way more than a little reminiscent of my efforts at transcription. (Wolf & Heath, 1992, pp. 11–12)

Less amusing are accounts suggesting that children learn from being in the presence of or being subjected to violence. The form of violence may be repeated if the child becomes perpetrator rather than victim: In the United States, violence committed by people who have been physically abused is likely to be physical whereas violence committed by those who have been sexually abused is most likely to be sexual (Haney, 1995; Schwartz, Dodge, Pettit, & Bates, 1997). Consider the following example, which demonstrates the structuring of young children's learning by the situations in which they are present.

> Tracey [an economically disadvantaged U.S. mother] repeatedly told me that she adored her five children [all under the age of 6]. But every time one of them came up to her, she raised her hand in a swift back-handed motion as if expressing, "I'm going to smack your face." . . . She automatically lifted her hand every time one of the two preschoolers at home came near her. And, her son, who is four, had a belt that looked like it belonged to a child, because it had a cartoon belt buckle, but he took it and wrapped it around his hand in a very practiced way and began to beat his younger sister. . . . She's two years old, I think. And it strikes me that there has been some hitting with belts in this family, because he sure knew how to do that. (Musick, 1994, p. 6)

Structuring during direct interaction

In addition to the arrangement of activities in which children can observe and participate, they and their companions collaborate in structuring activities during in-person interactions. In a study of British families, Rudolph Schaffer described the subtle structuring in which British mothers engaged with their infant:

> Watch a mother with her one-year-old sitting on her knee in front of a collection of toys: a large part of her time is devoted to such quietly facilitative and scene-setting activities as holding a toy that seems to require three hands to manipulate, retrieving things that have been pushed out of range, clearing away those things that are not at present being used in order to provide the child with a sharper focus for this main activity, putting things next to each other that she knows the child will enjoy combining (such as nesting beakers), turning toys so that they become more easily grasped, demonstrating their less obvious properties, and all along moulding her body in such a way as to provide maximal physical support and access to the play material. (1977, p. 73)

Middle-class parents often structure their children's contributions to conversations in picture-book reading. They adjust their prompts and assistance according to the children's development. For example, middle-class U.S. mothers reported that they consciously adjust their input and demands (DeLoache, 1984). Mothers of 15-month-olds asked questions ("What's this?") but without seeming to expect an answer; they answered the questions themselves or asked children simply to confirm the label ("Is that an elephant?"). After children began labeling simple objects, mothers began requesting information that was not visible in the picture ("What do bees make?"). If children did not reply, some mothers gave clues, avoiding answering their own questions but aiding children in getting the right answer, adjusting their structuring of the task to the children's level.

In a parallel fashion, African American elders who did not know how to read could assist their grandchildren in learning to read through their support of oral Scripture reading, using their extensive knowledge of the Bible (Dorsey-Gaines & Garnett, 1996). If a youngster missed a word or a verse, the elder would fill in the missing material for the new reader. In this way elders coached the child in both literacy and spiritual understanding important in the community.

Likewise, Guareño children in Venezuela learn the skills of cultivation, animal husbandry, hunting, and fishing with the assistance of adult structuring of their participation. The children contribute in steps that correspond with their advancing skills as adults demonstrate the whole complex and provide well-placed pointers during their shared endeavors (Ruddle & Chesterfield, 1978).

The "curriculum" of apprenticeship for Vai (Liberian) tailors similarly involves steps for approaching the overall body of tailoring skill and knowledge. Apprentice tailors first learn how to sew and then how to cut each garment. The order of the steps allows them to first note the general structure of the garments, then focus more specifically on the logic by which different pieces are attached, which helps them understand the pattern for cutting the pieces. "Each step offers the unstated opportunity to consider how the previous step contributes to the present one" (Lave, 1988b, p. 4).

Mayan girls learn to make tortillas in stages, with maternal support provided in the context of participation (Rogoff, 1990). Toddlers observe their mothers making tortillas and attempt to follow suit; mothers give them a small piece of dough to use and facilitate their efforts by rolling the dough in a ball and starting the flattening process. As a child becomes more skillful, the mother gives pointers and demonstrates holding the dough in a position that facilitates smooth flattening.

In most interactions in all four of the communities studied by Rogoff et al. (1993), mothers and toddlers structured each other's participation as they shared in operating novel objects. Almost all mothers adjusted the object or its position to facilitate toddlers' efforts, divided or simplified the task, and handled difficult moves. Almost all of the toddlers in all four communities were also involved in one way or another in structuring the activity.

The structuring of children's involvement often takes place within cultural practices that themselves are structured through the contributions of prior generations. For example, in recounting, elaborating, and listening to narratives, children and their companions engage in cultural practices that build on structures provided by predecessors. Similarly, children's engagement in routines and in play involve them mutually with their companions in cultural traditions that precede them and that they contribute to modifying as they play with routines and games.

Recounting, elaborating, and listening to narratives

Science, religion, proper behavior, and community tradition and history are taught and learned through narratives in many communities. For example, in West Africa, many lessons are taught through proverbs and folktales with moral themes and virtuous acts for children to emulate, or strange and fearful myths to deter them from doing wrong (Nsamenang, 1992). Dinnertime conversations of European American families provide extensive opportunities to build and test theories to account for everyday events, as family members narrate and contest the meaning of events (Ochs, Taylor, Rudolph, & Smith, 1992).

Some of these narratives serve only incidentally as instruction, during the telling of family history or recounting of religious stories in worship. Other narratives are intended as instruction, as in the following example from Manitoulin Island (a Canadian Indian community):

> [Our parents] let their children make their own decisions. The closest they ever got to formal teaching was to tell us stories. Let me give you an example.
>
> We had been out picking blueberries one time, and while sitting around this guy told us this story. The idea was that he wanted to get us to wash up—to wash our feet because we had been tramping through this brush all day long. He talked about a warrior who really had a beautiful body. He was very well built, and he used to grease himself and take care of his body. One day this warrior was out, and he ran into a group of other people whom he had never seen before. They started to chase him. He had no problem because he was in

such good shape. He was fooling around and playing with them because he was such a good runner. He ran over hills and over rocks, teasing them. Then he ran into another group. The first group gave up the chase. But now he had to run away from this other group, and he was fooling around doing the same thing with them. All of a sudden he ran into a third group. He ran real hard and all of a sudden he fell. He tried to get up and he couldn't. He spoke to his feet and said, "What's wrong with you? I'm going to get killed if you don't get up and get going." They said, "That's alright. You can comb your hair and grease your body and look after your legs and arms but you never did anything for us. You never washed us or cleaned us or greased us or nothing." He promised to take better care of the feet if they would get up and run, and so they did.

This is one of the stories we were told, and we went up and washed our feet right away. (Pelletier, 1970, pp. 25–26)

Stories are central to instruction and learning in traditional American Indian and Alaska Native education. They are used to foster attention, imagination, metaphoric thinking, and flexibility and fluency of thought in understanding the natural and moral world and the meaning of life (Basso, 1984; Cajete, 1994; Kawagley, 1990; Tafoya, 1989). Joseph Suina, a Pueblo (American Indian) professor, described how a narrative by his third-grade-educated father helped him learn to see his place in the greater scheme of things, to understand the proper contextualization of knowledge:

There was going to be a ceremony performed in our village that had not occurred in 40 years, and I wanted to participate. When I questioned one of the tribal elders, seeking permission to come late because of my teaching responsibilities, he said that would be acceptable, but that I should speak with my father concerning the ceremony itself, so that I could be prepared.

I arose early the following morning to visit my father, wanting to know what I needed to do in the ceremony, but conscious mostly of my need to be elsewhere. My father greeted me, but sensing my hurry, my distraction, told me to relax, to sit down. He wanted, I think, to extract me from the very segmented modern society where I had found my profession, to restore me to a sense of integrated wholeness.

My father began to speak, but not about the ceremony. Instead, he spoke of the time when the ceremony had been performed last— the tribal members who had been present, who was alive, who was in office, how the hunt was that year, how the harvest had been that year—what was happening in the world the last time the ceremony was performed. . . . The time when the ceremony was last performed had been just the beginning of World War II, when so many young men were leaving the village, and perhaps that was what had precipitated its need.

The effect my father's speech had on me was the same sense that I get when I look at mountains and boulders, a sense of eternity, a sense of connection between generations, events. I felt connected with people, with long chains of events, and intensely felt that I was just a small piece in all of this. And I knew that the small piece was not what was important, but rather, what was absolutely crucial was the whole picture.

After about 2 hours of recollections, my father finally wended his way to the purpose of the dance, to some of the symbols that were involved. And after a while longer, he spoke of what I would need for that evening in terms of clothing and other paraphernalia. Finally, my father told me how I was to act, and what words I was to use.

When it was over and done with, I no longer felt anxious; it no longer seemed crucial to me to worry about the details of my teaching on this one day. I could see myself again as just one little piece in a much larger picture. (Suina & Smolkin, 1994, pp. 118–119)

In an African American church, narratives play a central role in socialization as Sunday School teachers help youngsters understand the meaning of the Scriptures so that the children could relate the deep points of the Bible to their everyday lives. To encourage this, they recast biblical stories in contemporary Black English. For example, in telling the story of John 21:3–17, a Sunday School teacher quoted the disciples: "So Peter, he gets this attitude. It's like, 'Look, Jesus ain't comin' back. He ain't gonna show up, you know?'" (Haight, 1998, p. 217; see also Haight, 2002). The teachers also use narrative and role play to relate the Scriptures to everyday issues that face the students to encourage application of the principles to life.

The children help coconstruct the narrative or role play using a form of discourse—call and response—that is different from the interaction formats in traditional schools. The pastor commented that the call-and-response format is an important educational tool, as it helps students speak up immediately when the teacher asks a question or requests a comment. (He contrasted this with the more competitive public school practice of requiring children to raise their hand to be called on individually before responding.)

Among the Xhosa of South Africa, stories originating in previous centuries are told dramatically and dynamically in the evening by elders, often grandmothers, with participation of the children in shaping the stories (van der Riet, 1998). Although the central story images might remain constant over time, the teller develops them in a contemporary context and in collaboration with the audience. The primary motif is exploration of the potential fragmentation of Xhosa society from the forces of change and disorder if individuals act in ways that contradict the norms of society. The stories portray Xhosa worldview and proper social relations that families wish to impart to their children and serve as a means of socialization in the moral order of the community. The interactive, constructive, and dramatic nature of the storytelling strengthens its impact.

Similarly, Athabascan children in northern Canada learn how to participate in the construction of the "high language" of narratives through solving riddles. They learn to guess meanings, read between the lines, anticipate outcomes, and communicate through indirectness (Scollon & Scollon, 1981).

Children learn to use the narrative format preferred in their cultural community to recount events. Caregivers collaborate with children in telling stories, guiding them in the local standard, which varies from community to community (Bruner, 1990; Mistry, 1993a; Scollon & Scollon, 1981; Wolf & Heath, 1992). For example, middle-class European American mothers guide their children in producing lengthy dramatic accounts, embroidered with details or side events, whereas Japanese mothers guide their children in producing concise haiku-like accounts that trust listeners to infer some aspects (Minami & McCabe, 1995, 1996).

Children's participation in narrative storytelling, dramatic portrayals, and riddles (see figure 8.3) extends to enacting culturally valued ways of doing things by practicing and playing with the social routines and roles of their community.

Practicing and playing with routines and roles

Children's engagement in routines and play allows them to become familiar with local traditions and practices. Children also extend and modify traditions through their participation and the involvement of generations of children in routines and play formats (Goodwin, 1990).

An example of participation in social routines comes from 2½-year-old Angu and her primary caregiver, playing school in their middle-class living room in Taiwan:

> CAREGIVER: (*smiling*) Stand up, bow, sit down, teacher is going to deliver a lesson. (*Angu, smiling, moves closer to her caregiver.*)
> CAREGIVER: Teacher is coming to the classroom. What should the class monitor say?
> ANGU: Stand up!

FIGURE 8.3

On an island off the coast of Chile, a Rapa Nui great-grandmother tells ancient tales with her great-granddaughter as they practice *kai kai*, traditional storytelling with string illustrations and chants. A small child observes in the foreground.

CAREGIVER: OK. Stand up. (*Angu stands up and bows.*)

CAREGIVER: Sit down. . . . (*They read the story.*)

CAREGIVER: We have finished the story. (*She claps her hands.*) . . . Before we dismiss the class, the class monitor should say: "Stand up! Bow! Sit down!" Stand up! (*Angu stands up.*)

CAREGIVER: Bow! (*Angu bows*). . . .

CAREGIVER: Class is dismissed. Go play on the slide (*indicates imaginary sliding board in the living room.*) . . . Class is dismissed and you are happy. (translated from Mandarin; Haight, 1999, p. 128)

Young children fill slots in social routines managed by their elders, such as saying hello or naming family members, and in social games such as Peekaboo and All Gone. In the process, the children may learn the structure of such events as well as social moves or phrases to apply in conversation (Snow, 1984). For example, young Inuit (Arctic Quebec) children are encouraged to model the talk of their older siblings in greeting routines that help them learn to use kin terms, refer to others, take turns appropriately, and understand the importance of acknowledgment (Crago & Eriks-Brophy, 1994). The following excerpt was part of a much longer sequence of repetition of greeting routines, while 1-year-old Suusi and her mother were sitting at a table with some cousins, including 4-year-old Natali:

MOTHER: Say "greetings girl cousin"
SUUSI: Huh?
MOTHER: Say "greetings girl cousin"
> That one
> Say to her, "greetings girl cousin"
> Say to her, "greetings girl cousin"
SUUSI: Greetings girl cousin
MOTHER TO NATALI: Reply to her
> Say "aah" [the acknowledgment of a greeting] to her
SUUSI (*sic*): Aah.
MOTHER: Say to her, "greetings pretty girl cousin"
> Go on
SUUSI: Greetings girl cousin
MOTHER: Natalii, reply to her
> Natalii, say, "pretty girl cousin" (slightly adapted from p. 47)

In some communities, learning by reciting important oral language models is especially valued. For example, Maori (New Zealand) children's learning emphasizes reciting songs and genealogies that are central to family and community life (McNaughton, 1995; Metge, 1984). In the course of demonstrating these important routines, elders might also intersperse discussions of their meaning. The youngsters have the opportunity to use the material they have learned in ongoing community events, adapting and innovating as well as preserving the valued oral texts.

Other examples of children's engagement in social routines are playful involvement of young working-class Italian children with adults and other children in debate rituals (*discussione;* New, 1994), dispute and gossip routines among U.S. Black children (Goodwin, 1990), and improvisational verbal dueling practiced by Chamula Mayan boys and men (Gossen, 1976). West African caregivers engage infants in preliminary steps of gifting, sharing, and generosity by offering objects and then luring infants to return the "gifts," leading the children to become part of the sharing and exchange norms that bind together the whole social system (Nsamenang, 1992).

In many communities, a culture of childhood games and routines is passed on by generation after generation of children (see figure 8.4). For example, Robert Serpell (1993; see also Lancy, 1996) described a rich child folklore of games, riddles, and songs among Chewa (Zambian) children. The children played group games like hide-and-seek, guessing games, complex sand drawing games, imaginative games representing local work and family routines, skill games like jacks and a rule game (*nsolo*) requiring considerable strategic planning and numerical calculations, and constructing models of wire or clay.

Vygotsky emphasized the importance of playing with rules and roles,

FIGURE 8.4

An African American youth engages a toddler in a childhood game, as they sit
with others involved in child care and homework.

stating that play "creates its own zone of proximal development of the
child. In play a child is always above his average age, above his daily behaviour; in play it is as though he were a head taller than himself" (1967, p. 552;
see also Nicolopoulou, 1993). Vygotsky suggested that in play, children
enjoy ignoring the ordinary uses of objects and actions in order to subordinate them to imaginary meanings and situations. Children experiment
with the meanings and rules of serious life, but place these meanings and
rules at the center of attention. For example, two sisters focus on the rules
of sisterhood as they "play sisters."

In role play and dramatic play, children free themselves from the situational constraints of everyday time and space and the ordinary meaning of
objects or actions to develop greater control of actions and rules and understanding. They work out the "scripts" of everyday life—adult skills and
roles, values and beliefs—as they play (Göncü, 1987; Hartup, 1977; Hollos,
1980; Lancy, 1980, 1996; Piaget, 1926; Sylva, Bruner, & Genova, 1976; Vygotsky, 1967; see figures 8.5 and 8.6).

When children play, they often emulate adult and other community
roles that they observe. They experiment with and practice social roles in
which they may later participate or that complement their current roles (e.g.,

playing mother and father or playing teacher). In communities in which children participate in the mature life of the community, they often play at adult work and social roles (Haight et al., 1999; Morelli et al., 2002). In communities in which children are segregated from the adult community, their play less commonly reflects mature activities; rather, they emulate what they have the chance to observe, such as television superheroes or adult TV drama.

I have focused so far on basic processes of guided participation that are widespread around the world. These two processes—mutually bridging meanings and mutually structuring children's opportunities to learn—take distinct forms in different communities while retaining their centrality everywhere. For example, children's play builds on what they observe, but what they have the opportunity to observe differs greatly depending on whether they are included in the full range of their community's activities or are segregated from many settings that are restricted to adults.

This difference in children's access to involvement in community activities appears to have great importance for other aspects of children's guided participation. I argue that it relates closely to differences in the extent to which caregivers organize specialized child-focused activities or expect children to learn from intent participation in ongoing shared endeavors. The remainder of this chapter examines these patterns, which reveal regularities in some of the most striking variations in the forms of guided participation employed in different cultural communities.

FIGURE 8.5A

Among the Dani in the mountains of New Guinea warfare is common.
(a) In battle games, "groups of boys imitate their elders, charging back and forth and throwing heavy grass-stem spears at each other. This teaches throwing and dodging skills, as well as battle strategy."

FIGURE 8.5B–D

(b) "Kill-the-seed is one of the mock battle games played by boys too young to fight. The opposing berry armies are moved back and forth in charges and retreats."

(c, d) "In detailed imitation of adult life, a seed warrior is placed in the twig watchtower and then removed when his army retreats," as the adults do on the real watchtower in the photo at the right (Gardner & Heider, 1968, pp. 80, 75).

(b)

(c)

(d)

FIGURE 8.6

Two boys in a Mayan town make-believe they are in a cantina soon after the town fiesta. The boy on the left is the bartender; the one on the right is the customer. Copyright 1975 by Barbara Rogoff.

Distinctive Forms of Guided Participation

Scholars have often assumed that children's learning occurs by their being recipients of explicit instruction that is organized and directed by adults. In middle-class families, adults often structure young children's learning by organizing children's attention, motivation, and involvement. They frequently structure adult-child engagement in child-focused activities, such as child-oriented conversations and play, and attempt to motivate the children's engagement in lessons that they provide, removed from the context of ongoing mature activities (Rogoff et al., 1993). Such interactions resemble the type of interaction for which the children are being prepared to participate in school. In school, middle-class children spend years being prepared for adult economic and social life through exercises out of the context of their communities' mature endeavors.

In contrast, in communities in which children have access to many aspects of adult life, children learn from their opportunities to observe and adults often expect them to learn through watching (Rogoff, 1981a). In such communities, children take a leading role in managing their own attention, motivation, and involvement in learning, through their observation and participation in ongoing mature activities. This may have the support of adults, who provide suggestions and responsive—rather than directive—assistance (Rogoff et al., 1993; Rogoff et al., 2003).

Observations in two U.S. middle-class communities support the idea that young middle-class children are often segregated from the mature life of their community and instead receive lessons and engage in child-focused activities. Middle-class 3-year-old children seldom had the opportunity to observe adult work, and instead often were involved in lessons or engaged with adults as partners in play or in conversations focused on the children's interests and activities (Morelli et al., 2002). In a Guatemalan Mayan town and a foraging group in the Democratic Republic of Congo, 3-year-olds more frequently had the opportunity to observe adult work. They seldom were involved in lessons or engaged with adults in play or child-centered conversations.

These distinct patterns in forms of guided participation are important in the organization of children's learning in different communities. However, the differences in patterns are seldom all-or-none. Often, differences lie in the *prevalence* of different forms of guided participation or the *situations* in which different forms are regarded as appropriate for fostering development. Furthermore, I am sure that there are more patterns than the two I am contrasting.

In the following sections, I address some of the differences that make up these distinct patterns, focusing first on academic lessons within family life and then on learning from observation and increasing participation in mature activities of the community. In examining these contrasting patterns, I also consider cultural preferences in the use of speech or silence, gesture and gaze, which sometimes overlap with differences in the use of lessons or participation in ongoing activities as forms of guided participation.

Academic Lessons in the Family

Middle-class European American parents often involve their children in "literate" forms of discourse, in a way of life in which school forms of interaction are integral to communication, recreation, and livelihood (Cazden, 1979; Gundlach, McLane, Stott, & McNamee, 1985; McNaughton, 1995; Michaels & Cazden, 1986; Scollon & Scollon, 1981; Taylor, 1983). After examining how schooled parents involve their children in literate discourse and academic lessons, I discuss parents' efforts to induce children's involvement in such lessons and parents' engagement with children in play and in conversations on child-focused topics.

Learning to do lessons before starting school

In middle-class European American families, children learn to participate in school-like conversations before they enter school. They learn to "talk like a book" before they learn to read.

In a study of mealtime conversations, Caucasian American families in Hawaii used explicit school-style ways of speaking. These are not more or less effective for communicating or for organizing thought than the styles used by other groups, but they facilitate success in schools that use the same structures (Martini, 1995, 1996). Dinner talk was often organized around the discourse structures of giving school reports. Parents asked children to talk about their day and guided them to discuss novel information, turning them from familiar events (such as "then we had lunch") to unfamiliar information ("Yeah, but what did you see on your field trip?"). They cued the children to fill in background information and helped them organize their "report" by recasting what the children said in conventional forms. They provided phrases segmenting the report ("And then . . .," "After that . . ."), and requested that the children sum up and discuss the "point" of their account. The parents guarded a child's turn on stage, telling others to wait until the child finished. When the adults took a turn, they modeled long, conventionally structured reports and told the children not to interrupt. Children sometimes used school ways to get a turn, such as raising their hand when there were cues that a parent was nearly finished.

Children who had more exposure to middle-class ways of talking and to books did better on preschool tests in families of part-Hawaiian ancestry (Martini & Mistry, 1993). Children who had practice in explaining when, where, how, why, and who and in using conventional middle-class formulas for constructing a story and connecting events performed better on standardized language tests. These tests ordinarily examine skills in using such features.

Those who did better on the tests more frequently engaged in school-related activities at home, such as playing school and pretending to read. Children with experience of books and literate stories develop a sense of how text should sound (such as how short and long sentences should alternate for variety and what sentences with subordinate clauses sound like). They imitate the narrative framework, at first without coherent content. One girl, for example, copied adult intonation and phrasing in pretending to read a book. Her sentences sounded like a story but did not make sense. As she turned pages, she spoke in the cadence of reading used in children's books, with repetition, contrast, counting, and exaggeration—smoothly but without coherence.

Another example of imitating literate forms occurred as a boy provided mock definitions while playing with some cards with two younger children. He imitated adult sentence structures in forming a smooth-sounding definition, inserting whatever words came to mind to fill the slots of how a definition sounds. He held up a card and pretended to read it: "A robot." He showed the card to his companions and explained, "A robot is a captain that's connected to the mouth of both of the bad kings" (Martini & Mistry, 1993, p. 180).

Children in some communities are prepared for analyzing the syllables in words through nursery rhymes and games emphasizing rhymes and repetition of sounds (Serpell & Hatano, 1997). Television shows such as *Sesame Street*, designed to help children segment sounds and learn letters that correspond to them, have become a part of children's daily routine in many nations in recent decades.

The extent of involvement in picture-book reading differs between middle-class and low-income U.S. preschoolers. Picture books made of durable materials are offered to middle-class babies, and bedtime stories are part of their daily routine. Upper- and middle-class Canadian parents reported starting to read storybooks to their children when they were 9 months old, on average; their young children had 61 to 80 children's books in the home (Sénéchal & LeFevre, 2002). Early book reading correlates with later school language and reading performance (Sénéchal & LeFevre, 2002; Whitehurst et al., 1994; see figure 8.7).

FIGURE 8.7

In middle-class families, young children learn literate ways at home as well as at school, supported by older family members reading with them, the presence of reading materials and routines emphasizing reading, and adults reading in children's presence. This photo occurred during "children's reading hour" at the Spencer household, 1921, in Hollywood, California.

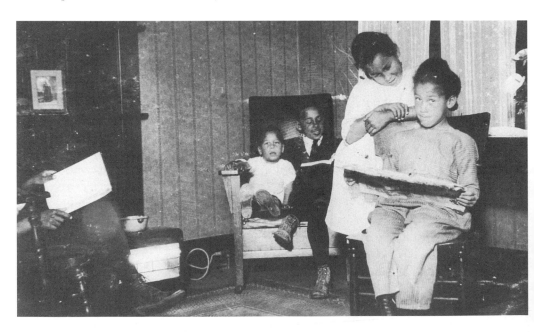

Middle-class African American and European American families were observed to engage in school-oriented practices that prepared their preschool children for literacy (Heath, 1982, 1983). In contrast, early childhood in two other communities did not include reading and writing in the texture of daily life, and the children experienced difficulties with literacy in school. White parents in an Appalachian milltown taught their children respect for the written word but did not involve book characters or information in the children's everyday lives. Their children did well in the first years of learning to read, but had difficulty when required to *use* literate skills to express themselves or interpret text. Working-class African American children in a milltown learned a respect for skillful and creative use of language but were not taught about books or the style of analytic discourse used in school. They had difficulty learning to read, which kept them from making use of their creative skills with language in the school setting.

In many middle-class families, participation in school-like discourse begins by the time children begin to talk. Middle-class 12- to 24-month-olds and their mothers engaged in talk that appears to be lessons in language use, involving utterances that serve no practical function in ongoing activity (Rogoff et al., 1993). Middle-class mothers from the United States and Turkey provided language lessons by labeling objects, requesting labels, giving running commentary on events (for example, saying "Oh, the dolly fell over," although the toddler already saw the event), and playing language games often involving test questions that requested information the mothers already knew (such as "Where are the baby's eyes?"). For example, several forms of language lesson appear in the interaction of a 21-month-old U.S. middle-class boy and his mother as they explored a jar containing a tiny "peewee" doll.

> Sandy's mother held the jar up and chirped excitedly, "What is it? What's inside?" and then pointed to the peewee doll inside, "Is that a little person?" When Sandy pulled down on the jar, she suggested, "Can you take the lid off?"
>
> Sandy inspected the round knob on top and said "Da ball."
>
> "Da ball, yeah," his mother confirmed. "Pull the lid," she encouraged, and demonstrated pulling on the knob, "Can you pull?" Sandy put his hand on hers and they pulled the lid off together triumphantly. "What's inside?" asked his mother, and took the peewee out, "Who is that?"
>
> Sandy reached for the lid, and his mother provided running commentary, "Okay, you put the lid back on." And when Sandy exclaimed "OH!" his mother repeated "OH!" after him. When Sandy lost interest, his mother asked with mock disappointment, "Oh, you don't want to play anymore?" and suggested, "We could make him play peek-a-boo."

When Sandy took the peewee out, she asked, "Where did she go?" and sang, "There, she's all gone" as she covered the peewee with her hands, "Aaall gone." (p. 81)

Another example of language lessons occurred when a middle-class Turkish mother held a pencil box in front of her 23-month-old son and asked excitedly, "Aaaaa, Iskender, what's this?" The boy answered, "It's a toy" (Göncü, 1993, p. 138). The resemblance to school patterns of discourse is clear. These are the kind of known-answer test questions that schoolchildren receive frequently from their teachers, who ask in order to examine the child's knowledge, not to obtain information. This type of specialized conversation was uncommon among Mayan and East Indian mothers and toddlers (Rogoff et al., 1993).

Likewise, among Inuit families, it was rare for mothers of an older generation to ask children questions to which the mothers already knew the answers (Crago, Annahatak, & Ningiuruvik, 1993). On her first trips to northern Quebec, an audiologist who was not Inuit wanted a colleague from the Inuit community to ask children questions such as "Where's your nose?" to test their language comprehension. But the children often just looked at her and did not answer. The colleague said that because she had noticed that children needed to answer such questions in school, she had started teaching her child to reply to test questions such as these. She reported that the younger mothers talk like that to their children more than do the older generation, introducing them to the format of lessons.

Inducing young children to participate in lessons

In school, it is common to offer inducements to children to motivate their cooperation with lessons. The inducements include praise, gold stars, good grades, the avoidance of punishment or bad grades, and materials specially designed to attract children's interest (bright colors in books or bells and whistles in computer programs).

Middle-class toddlers also often receive inducements at home to participate in adult-designed lessons, such as a show of excitement by a parent. Unlike Mayan and tribal Indian mothers, middle-class mothers in the United States and Turkey frequently attempted to motivate children's involvement in operating novel objects by using mock excitement. They pretended to be very interested in the objects, with staged gasps of anticipation and an excited tone of voice and facial expressions (Rogoff et al., 1993). Such mock excitement to attract children into language lessons can be seen in the U.S. and Turkish middle-class interactions described in the previous section.

Another form of inducement in some communities is praising children for the desired behavior; in other communities, praise is seldom seen (Metge, 1984; Whiting, 1996). In middle-class communities in the United States and Turkey, mothers frequently praised their toddlers' accomplishments or performances. Such praise was uncommon in a Mayan community in Guatemala and a tribal community in India, although these mothers were also pleased with their children (Rogoff et al., 1993).

Praise may serve to motivate children to engage in activities in which they otherwise might not choose to participate or in which the value or the success of the efforts is difficult to see. Meyer Fortes, in his classic account of learning among the Tallensi of Ghana, contrasted the form of instruction that often occurs in schools and that which occurs in "real situations." In schools, knowledge is often of unknown utility, but the purpose of the activity is inherent in "real situations" and motivation stems from achieving real results:

> A child repeating the multiplication table is participating in the practical activity appropriate to and defined by the school; but measured by the total social reality it is a factitious activity, a training situation constructed for that purpose. The Tallensi do not make systematic use of training situations. They teach through real situations which children are drawn to participate in because it is expected that they are capable and desirous of mastering the necessary skills. . . . Learning becomes purposive. (1938, pp. 37–38)

Children who enter into the activities of their community from an early age can see that their efforts contribute to the family's sustenance. In the environment of ongoing work, success or failure in the task is obvious and needs no commentary (Jordan, 1989; Whiting & Edwards, 1988). The feedback need not come from a parent or teacher but from the learner's noting the work accomplished. Adults may show approval of children's responsible behavior by assigning more difficult work under less supervision (Whiting & Edwards, 1988).

In a study in which mothers were to help babies learn to do a task, U.S. mothers attempted to arouse the babies' interest in the task and shaped their behavior step by step, providing constant encouragement and refocusing (Dixon, LeVine, Richman, & Brazelton, 1984). In contrast, Gusii (Kenyan) mothers gave their infants responsibility for learning, providing an orientation to the task and often modeling the expected performance in its entirety. They appeared to expect that if the children paid attention, they would be able to carry out the task.

In addition to organizing lessons and inducing children's involvement through providing mock excitement and praise, middle-class parents may enter directly into children's own interests and activities, such as play and child-focused conversation. In this way, adults become peers in children's activities. This may substitute for young children being able to join in adult activities in communities where children are segregated from them.

Adults as peers in play and child-focused conversation

Adults in middle-class communities often engage with children as peers, becoming playmates with children. Many middle-class U.S. parents regard their participation in pretend play as important for preschoolers' cognitive and language development, and some see their involvement as preparing their toddlers for school (Farran, 1982; Farver, 1999; Haight et al., 1997; Harkness & Super, 1992a). Likewise, middle-class mothers in Turkey (who have participated extensively in schooling, like middle-class U.S. mothers) reported that they regarded play as a means of assisting their children's development. As one mother reported, "In school we learned about child development and child language; we learned that playing with children is good for them" (Göncü, 1993, p. 129).

In contrast, in many communities, children's play is not regarded as an activity to be encouraged or entered into by parents. Instead, playing with children is the role of other children or other family members (Gaskins et al., 1992; Mistry, 1993b; Rogoff & Mosier, 1993; Serpell, 1993; Tizard & Hughes, 1984; Watson-Gegeo & Gegeo, 1986b; see also Chapter 4).

In addition to playing with children, middle-class adults often engage with young children as conversational peers, as equals. Middle-class U.S. adults often negotiate meaning with children, cooperate in building propositions, and respond to children's verbal and nonverbal initiations, instead of expecting them to adapt to adult situations, as in Kaluli (New Guinea) and Samoan families (Ochs & Schieffelin, 1984). Out of 12 cultural groups, U.S. middle-class mothers were most likely to interact with children in a friendly, playful, or conversational way as equals. In other communities, mothers maintained an authority role, stressing training or nurturant involvement (Whiting & Edwards, 1988). Children's conversational role may be to speak when spoken to, reply to informational questions, or simply carry out directions (Blount, 1972; Harkness & Super, 1977; Heath, 1983; Schieffelin & Eisenberg, 1984).

Middle-class mothers in the United States and Turkey often placed themselves on toddlers' level by asking their opinions, responding to their vocalizations as conversation, and providing openings for equal dialogic exchanges. The toddlers often offered comments and initiated optional conversation. In contrast, Mayan and tribal Indian toddlers were seldom treated or acted as conversational peers, although they interacted reciprocally with their parents through joint action and communication in the context of exploring objects (Rogoff et al., 1993).

If children are not expected to be conversational partners on child-oriented topics with their parents, their primary conversational partners may be other children (Ward, 1971). In the extended family arrangements of the Inuit of northern Quebec, children have a rich tapestry of relationships and communicative interactions in their home to listen to, participate in, and learn from:

> One mother reported, "If the child has siblings she is taught more to talk by them; when they look after their younger siblings they talk to them. The mother talks less to the baby than the one who is taking care of the baby for her. The mother teaches the child to talk less than the person who is looking after the baby."
>
> INTERVIEWER: Is it the same as the mother, the way the sibling teaches the child to talk?
> MOTHER: The older sibling teaches the younger sibling in different ways. The mother talks about the more important things to the child.
> INTERVIEWER: What are the more important things?
> MOTHER: These different things we have to work on, like obeying, helping others. Obeying what you are told to do is heavier when it is your mother telling you. (Crago & Eriks-Brophy, 1994, pp. 48–49)

In Inuit homes that do not have siblings or grandparents present, a "mother has to be everything all rolled up into one person. She has to be the child's friend, sister, and parent" (Crago, 1988, p. 230). In an Inuit family with a nuclear structure, the parents played with the child in ways that other parents did not. The mother engaged the child in repetition routines that were characteristic of sibling interactions, and the child was a conversational partner with her parents.

Children and caregivers everywhere engage in some forms of conversation. However, families from middle-class communities engage in particular forms of conversation that seem to be specialized for preparing children for schooling. They involve children frequently in academic ways of interacting, such as lessons and literate speech. They offer inducements to participate in such interaction using mock excitement and praise and enter into play and conversation as peers with young children.

These specialized forms of child-focused school preparation form a pattern that contrasts with a pattern in which adults support children's learning from keen observation and participation in mature activities. However, before I discuss learning from intent participation in ongoing community activities, I need to address an associated topic: cultural preferences for extensive use of talk or for taciturn interactions that emphasize use of gaze, gesture, and other forms of communication.

Talk or Taciturnity, Gesture, and Gaze

Everywhere, people use words, silence, gestures, and gaze skillfully to communicate. Yet there also appear to be important differences in how much people talk and in how articulately they communicate nonverbally. Perhaps more important, communities vary in their preferences for circumstances and ways they use speech and nonverbal communication (Cajete, 1999; Deyhle & Swisher, 1997; Field, Sostek, Vietze, & Leiderman, 1981; Jordan, 1977; Leiderman, Tulkin, & Rosenfeld, 1977; Richman, LeVine et al., 1988; Rogoff, 1982b; Scribner & Cole, 1973).

A preference for talkativeness may fit with the academic forms of guided participation that I have been discussing—lessons, efforts to motivate children through mock excitement and praise, and adults entering into children's play and conversational topics. But the differences cannot be as simple as that. For example, taciturnity and attention to nonverbal communication are highly valued in some settings with a long history of schooling, such as Japan. Of course, formal schooling in Japan shows some important differences from formal schooling in "the West."

I open these possibilities without being able to resolve them given the available research. This is a particularly important area for further work. Clearly, the common assumption that school is verbal and learning through observation is nonverbal is an oversimplification. Often, the contrast is treated in an all-or-none fashion, as if some people talk but do not gesture and others gesture but do not talk. This dichotomy is obviously false. People everywhere talk, and those who value taciturnity often also value eloquence. For example, in many communities with great respect for silence, narrative is powerfully used in teaching regarding the moral and natural world. Furthermore, people everywhere employ nonverbal forms of communication to an enormous extent. In addition, individuals can engage in several contrasting formats: Under some circumstances, they may engage in school-like questioning and lesson-format discourse, and under other circumstances, they may engage with taciturnity and keen attention to nonverbal information.

In some settings, there do seem to be some nuanced relations of academic-style learning with talkativeness and intent participation with taciturnity, gesture, and gaze, which I examine below. Some other cultural practices also seem to relate to these. For example, in some communities there may be a connection between taciturnity and cultural views on respect for others' autonomy. In this section, I briefly examine cultural preferences for silence and restraint, conveying indirect messages in stories, and use of articulate nonverbal communication.

Respect for silence and restraint

Socialization for taciturnity has been observed among Inuit of Arctic Quebec, where children are expected to learn from watching and listening. A 7-year-old girl from an Inuit community watched a 3-year-old white middle-class Canadian boy recount a long dream at breakfast one morning and commented to her mother, "Isn't he old enough to learn to control his tongue?" (Crago, 1988, p. 215).

When a non-Inuit researcher observed a young Inuit boy who seemed very bright because his language seemed advanced for his age and he talked frequently, she asked an Inuit teacher for an explanation of his talkativeness. The Inuit teacher responded, "Do you think he might have a learning problem? Some of these children who don't have such high intelligence have trouble stopping themselves. They don't know when to stop talking" (p. 219).

Inuit children's non-Inuit teachers urge them to speak up in class, but this often contrasts with their parents' expectations, as revealed in the following comment from a parent at a report card conference concerning his fifth-grade son:

> NON-INUIT TEACHER: Your son is talking well in class. He is speaking up a lot.
> PARENT: I am sorry. (Crago, 1992, p. 496)

An Inuit author explained, "As [children] grow older, questioning becomes a boring habit; they have gained wisdom and eventually become more intelligent. The more intelligent they become, the quieter they are" (Freeman, 1978, p. 21).

Esther Goody (1978) speculated that U.S. middle-class children are taught to ask questions through the "training questions" asked of them by their caregivers from infancy. In contrast, questions by children to adults are rare in some communities (Briggs, 1991; Goody, 1978; Heath, 1983). For example, knowledge in the Pueblo world cannot be attained by asking questions: It is a gift to be bestowed at the right time in relevant contexts, rather than something to be asked for (Suina & Smolkin, 1994).

In many North American native communities, silence is especially valued, and questions are avoided or purposefully ambiguous (Basso, 1979; Black, 1973; Plank, 1994). Questions can be seen as obliging another person to reply and so constraining their freedom; silence is an appropriate reply when one does not have a response or does not wish to give information. Among other purposes, a taciturn approach signals respect and appropriate nonintervention in others' actions. This has been especially noted in American Indian children's use of silence in the classroom, attempting to employ a respectful form of learning by listening and observing and avoiding asking questions.

Circumspection also characterizes *teaching* in such communities, for the same reasons. For example, Athabascans of northern Canada show a preference for restraint in situations in which speaking may intrude on others, such as when an adult interacts with a child (Scollon & Scollon, 1981). Likewise, among the rural Malinke of French West Africa, speech is carefully used:

> In everything I noticed a kind of dignity which was often lacking in town life; no one ever did anything without first having been ceremoniously invited to do so, even though he had a right to do so. The personal liberty of others was in fact always highly respected. And if their minds seemed to work slower in the country that was because they always spoke only after due reflection, and because speech itself was a most serious matter. (Laye, 1959, p. 53)

In Japanese communication, succinctness is valued and verbosity is frowned upon (Minami & McCabe, 1995, 1996). A collection of observations of "American habits that Japanese grumble about" includes complaints that Americans seem uncomfortable with silence and therefore chatter about unimportant matters (Condon, 1984). Another complaint is that they do not listen well but instead are overly eager to offer their own ideas or ask questions before hearing what others have to say:

> Speaking too much is associated in Japan with immaturity or a kind of empty-headedness. . . . Silence is not simply the absence of sound or speech, a void to be filled, as Americans tend to regard it. Not speaking can sometimes convey respect for the person who has spoken or the ideas expressed. Silence can be a medium that the parties share, a means of unifying, in contrast to words which separate. Silence in conversations is often compared to the white space in brush paintings or calligraphy scrolls. A picture is not richer, more accurate, or more complete if such spaces are filled in. To do so would be to confuse and detract from what is presented.
>
> Japanese and Americans often confuse each other in the way they speak and treat silence. An American asks a Japanese a question and there is a pause before the Japanese responds. If the question is fairly direct, the pause may be even longer as the Japanese considers how to

avoid a direct answer. The American, however, may assume that the pause is because the question was not clearly understood and hence he may rephrase the question. It often happens that the American is himself just uncomfortable with the silence and is trying to fill in with words to reduce his own uneasiness. In any case, the additional verbalization is only likely to make the situation more difficult for the Japanese. Not only has the American asked two or more questions in the space appropriate for one, he has separated himself by not sharing in a thoughtful silence. (pp. 40–41)

Conveying indirect messages in stories

In some communities in which reserve is valued, messages and instruction are conveyed indirectly to people through proverbs and stories. For example, Western Apache people of Arizona find it odd that Anglo–Americans "discourse at length on the patently obvious" (Basso, 1979, p. 87). Yet linguistic play and eloquence are important among the Western Apache, and a specialized story genre is used to indirectly instruct. Historical stories "stalk" people, indicating to a listener that he or she has acted inappropriately and might suffer consequences like the person in the story (Basso, 1984). The place where the story occurred continues to remind the targeted person of the moral message for years.

Keith Basso (1984) gave an example of a story that hit home to a 17-year-old Apache woman. She had attended a serious ceremony in which women wear their hair loose, to respectfully contribute to the effectiveness of the ceremonial. However, she wore pink curlers in her hair, in the fashion of her peers in her out-of-state boarding school. A few weeks later at a large birthday party, her grandmother told the group a historical tale of an Apache policeman who acted too much like a white man and as a result behaved as a fool. Soon after the story's end, the young woman walked off toward her home, without speaking. Basso asked the grandmother why the young woman had left—had she suddenly become sick?—and the grandmother replied, "No, I shot her with an arrow [the story]."

About two years later, Basso ran into the young woman and asked her if she remembered the event. She said that she did, and that she realized that her grandmother was working on her. She said that she didn't like being criticized for acting white, so she stopped acting that way. When they passed the landmark associated with the story of the Apache policeman, Basso pointed at it, and the young woman smiled and said, "I know that place. It stalks me every day."

Nick Thompson, an Apache elder, explained that Apache stories make you think about your life. If you haven't been acting right, someone "goes hunting for you:"

Someone stalks you and tells a story about what happened long ago. It doesn't matter if other people are around—you're going to know he's aiming that story at you. All of a sudden it *hits* you! It's like an arrow, they say. Sometimes it just bounces off—it's too soft and you don't think about anything. But when it's strong it goes in *deep* and starts working on your mind right away. No one says anything to you, only that story is all, but now you know that people have been watching you and talking about you. They don't like how you've been acting. So you have to think about your life.

Then you feel weak, real weak, like you are sick. You don't want to eat or talk to anyone. That story is working on you now. You keep thinking about it. That story is changing you now, making you want to live right. . . . After a while, you don't like to think of what you did wrong. So you try to forget that story. You try to pull that arrow out. You think it won't hurt anymore because now you want to live right.

It's hard to keep on living right. Many things jump up at you and block your way. But you won't forget that story. You're going to see the place where it happened, maybe every day if it's nearby. (Basso, 1984, p. 42)

As discussed earlier in this chapter, narratives seem to have widespread use around the world as a means of instruction. The Western Apache use of stories as indirect personal commentary may be a specialized use in communities that value circumspection in speaking. Eloquence in oratory and virtuosity in verbal dueling may also occur in communities that value reticence in some other interactional settings (e.g., Gossen, 1976). In such communities, there may also be an emphasis on other means of communication besides talk.

Articulate nonverbal communication

Forms of communication other than talk have special importance in many communities where gaze, gesture, posture, and timing of action are used very articulately. People in such communities may be more keen observers of these forms of communication than individuals in communities in which such communicative forms carry less information. For example, Japanese people are reputed to "read" faces and postures to a greater extent and with greater accuracy than do most Americans, preferring nonverbal over verbal messages (Condon, 1984).

Mothers from a Mayan community in Guatemala and a tribal community in India frequently used communicative gaze, touch, posture, and timing cues. In contrast, mothers from two middle-class communities (in the United States and Turkey) less often employed these forms of communication and spoke more to their toddlers. The Mayan and tribal Indian mothers and toddlers appeared to use a more articulated system of nonverbal communication than those from the two middle-class communities, expressing more complex ideas nonverbally (Rogoff et al., 1993).

For example, a father from the Indian community got his 18-month-old's attention to offer him a jar, and then guided him in using the jar by many subtle means, without either father or son saying a single word to each other. At the same time, the father carried on a conversation with the researcher's assistant:

> When the father picked up the jar with the ring inside and shook it (to make the ring rattle) to get Ramu's attention, Ramu moved closer to watch.
>
> As the father answered a question from the researcher's assistant, he drew Ramu's attention to the ring inside the jar and demonstrated the series of actions that could be performed with the jar, by opening the lid, rattling the ring inside briefly, then closing the lid again. He did this as he held the jar out to Ramu, making sure it was in his line of vision and holding it out in an offer.
>
> When Ramu reached for the jar, his father gave it to him and watched as Ramu began to examine the jar while he simultaneously continued his response to questions he was being asked.
>
> Ramu took the lid off the jar, took the ring out and triumphantly showed it to his father, holding it up to his line of vision and smiling happily.
>
> Father nodded, acknowledging what Ramu had accomplished. Then with a quick movement of his eyes together with a sideways nod, he prompted Ramu to put the ring inside the jar again. (Mistry, 1993b, pp. 111–112)

Sensitive nonverbal communication may account for some observations of early toilet training, compared with the two or three years now assumed to be required in the United States. Among the Digo of East Africa, where caregivers and infants use postural and other cues to support the children's control of when and where to urinate and defecate, infants maintain daytime and nighttime dryness by age 4 to 6 months. They crawl into the elimination position with which their caregivers have familiarized them through sensitivity to infant cues of readiness, encouragement to eliminate with the sound "shuus," and pleasurable interaction following the infant's accomplishment (deVries & deVries, 1977).

The separation of middle-class European American infants from other people may necessitate greater use of distal forms of communication in-

FIGURE 8.8

The availability of close contact provides cues to caregivers regarding infants' needs, such as the need to urinate, which may be communicated through postural or other nonverbal cues. Here, a Japanese woman leans out of her mosquito netting to help her sleepy child relieve himself. Woodblock print by Kitagawa Utamaro (1753–1806) in a series depicting the daily customs of women.

volving sound. European American infants have been characterized as "packaged" babies who do not have direct skin contact with their caregivers but spend most of their time encased in clothing and baby pens, cribs, or carriers (Whiting, 1981).

In contrast, children who are constantly close to their caregivers may more easily employ nonverbal cues such as gaze, gestures, facial expression, and postural changes. Japanese mothers hold their babies or have other bodily contact with them more often than American mothers, who talk to their infants more often; Takie Lebra (1994) suggested that more of one leads to less of the other (see figure 8.8).

In communities in which infants are in constant contact with caregivers, tactile and postural forms of communication are readily available. Many anthropologists have commented on the rarity of infant crying in such circumstances, as mothers can respond to infant needs before they break into actual crying (Harkness & Super, 1992b; Whiting & Edwards, 1988). For example, among the Inuit of Arctic Quebec, infants are in almost constant physical contact in a pouch inside their mother's parka.

Infants wiggle and their mothers know they have awakened. They squirm and their mothers sense their hunger or discomfort. In some homes I found that babies hardly needed to cry to have their needs known and responded to. I remember being with one family and finding that a whole day had gone by and I had never heard the one-month-old peep. Her mother would be carrying her in [her parka] and for no reason that was perceptible to me the infant would be taken out and fed. . . . One [non-Inuit] teacher, who had worked in northern Quebec for a number of years, once told me:

> I think the thing I will remember most is how rarely I heard a baby cry. . . . The strength of this initial physical closeness, where infants' bodies are pressed up against their caregivers' bodies for long hours of the day and night, establishes an early pattern of communicative interaction that is not based on the children's vocalizations. (Crago, 1988, pp. 204–205)

Among the reasons middle-class European Americans talk so much, speculated Mary Martini (1995), is that their cultural practices emphasize individual separateness and the construction and explanation to each other of their separate "selves" and mental worlds. Martini pointed out that these children are trained to spend much of their day away from the family, so family members have many unshared experiences to explain to each other, and highly explicit talk is their means for doing this. With individuals seen as inherently separate and having personal mental worlds, social contact is based on talk to communicate an understanding of their distinct selves and to coordinate their separate actions.

This contrasts with arrangements in which children are embedded in family and community life, able to observe the full range of activities and participate in them when ready. In learning through participation in mature community activities, talk is often employed in conjunction with ongoing action. It is more closely coordinated with the activity being learned than in school-style learning, where talk is the primary carrier of information and is often a substitute for actual involvement in the target activity.

Intent Participation in Community Activities

In some communities, children's learning involves "intent participation" in almost the full range of activities of their communities, with keen observation, initiative, and responsive assistance (Rogoff et al., 2003). Children are able to observe and listen in on the ongoing processes of life and death, work and play that are important in their community. They attend to events that often are not designed for their instruction, in which they may not be addressed directly. Rather, they are present and expected to be alert and to pitch in when ready. Children are legitimate peripheral participants (Lave & Wenger, 1991) in the mature activities of their community, watching what is going on and becoming involved.

As infants, they are often carried wherever their mother or older siblings go. For example:

> In subsaharan Africa, Taira [Japan], and Juxtlahuaca [Mexico], lap children [infants] are strapped to the backs of their caretakers for the major part of the day. These societies do not have cribs, baby carriages, playpens, or other means of confining lap children. . . . From their mothers' or siblings' backs they can vicariously participate in the caretakers' activities. . . .
>
> In contrast, in societies such as the North Indian and North American communities, where lap children spend much time in a carriage, playpen, cot, or crib, interaction with others requires that an adult or older child stoop over to come into eye contact. These lap children, as a result, view a world full of legs; they are less able to witness the interaction of their caretakers or to hear their conversation with other individuals and thus vicariously participate in social interaction. (Whiting & Edwards, 1988, p. 168)

Young children may roam the community, free to watch whatever is happening. For example, in the Xavante tribe of the Brazilian rain forest, as soon as babies are confident enough to toddle away from home, they join a flock of children that come and go in the village, observing events:

> Xavante children, like village children the world over, are the eyes and ears of the community. There is very little one can do that escapes their notice, and their curiosity is insatiable. As soon as they see anyone going anywhere, they call out "Where to?" and we very soon learned to give them precise answers or they would follow us to see what we were doing. This could be embarrassing if we were going into the forest to relieve ourselves. (Maybury-Lewis, 1992, pp. 122–123)

Encouragement of keen observation

In many cases, keen observation is encouraged and taught to children by parents and other instructors, as, for example, in learning through watching in Suzuki and school instruction in Japan (Peak, 1986). Likewise, Jomo Kenyatta (1953) described the importance of learning to be a keen observer in his own Gikuyu upbringing prior to the introduction of European rule. He noted that Gikuyu parents took care to teach children to be good observers. In a Mayan community in Mexico, children served as extra eyes and ears for their mothers who stayed at home and extracted information regarding village events from the children. Mothers' questions about events guided the children regarding which aspects of events were significant (Gaskins & Lucy, 1987).

Rotuman (Polynesian) children are subtly encouraged to observe. If a child experiences difficulty, an adult may adjust the child's position to correct an error or refine a movement, but seldom offers verbal instruction. If children ask for explanation, "they are likely to be told to watch a skillful adult in action" (Howard, 1970, p. 116).

Thus, in some communities, children's observation and beginning participation receive extensive support from family and community practices. Most important may be arrangements that allow children to be in places where they can observe and begin to help. Family and community expectations that children should be keenly observing and participating in ongoing activities are another important form of support for this kind of learning. In addition, caregivers and child companions may provide responsive assistance, facilitating children's observation or helping them in ongoing activities.

Responsive assistance

There are striking differences among communities in caregivers' readiness to assist children. In a Mayan town and a tribal community in India, mothers were very responsive to toddlers' efforts to operate novel objects; they were usually poised in readiness to assist the toddlers. This occurred much more rarely in middle-class families in the United States and Turkey (Rogoff et al., 1993). Being poised to help is a responsive way to assist the children that leaves the pace and direction of children's efforts up to them. It involves helping according to the child's need, rather than organizing instruction according to adult plans. An example of responsive attentiveness and readiness to assist is apparent in the interactions of a 20-month-old Mayan boy and his parents, who assisted him in handling a clear jar with a tiny peewee doll inside:

> Juan turned toward his mother and shook the jar—[exclaiming at the peewee doll] "Baby!"—and put the jar into his mother's hand. Although she was involved in an adult conversation, she received the jar and shook it for Juan.
>
> But Juan pointed at the lid, tapping it with his index finger, to request his mother to remove the lid, as she bounced the jar in her hands. When she noticed what Juan was doing (as she continued conversing), she took the lid off and held the jar open long enough

for him to take out the peewee, then closed the jar and held it available in front of him. The interaction continued, with Juan working the jar with his mother ready to assist, as she also attended to the ongoing conversation.

[Later,] Juan smiled and turned to examine the peewee, then touched the peewee to the jar that his mother held, with a quiet request vocalization. She glanced down and understood what Juan wanted. Juan proceeded to work the jar, lid, and peewee with his mother's assistance, smoothly contributed as she attended simultaneously to adult conversation. (p. 82)

Initiative in observation and pitching in

In communities in which observation of community events is possible and children are encouraged to be keen observers, people may be especially active and skilled in observation. Skilled observation requires active management of attention, as reflected in this account of a white middle-class Canadian child's experience in an Inuit community in northern Quebec:

One day when my eight-year-old daughter was watching some girls her age play a game in the house where we were staying, she turned to the mother who spoke English and said:

ANNA: How do I play this game? Tell me what to do. What are the rules?

INUK MOTHER: (gently) Watch them and you'll see how it goes.

ANNA: I don't know how to learn by watching, can't you tell me?

INUK MOTHER: You'll be able to know by watching. (Crago, 1988, p. 211)

Inuit children are expected to take the initiative in learning by observing closely, reasoning, and finding solutions independently, with self-motivation as the impetus (Briggs, 1991). Rural Senegalese children age 2 to 6 years were found to be observing other people more than twice as often as middle-class European American children (Bloch, 1989). The Tallensi (of Ghana) explain rapid learning in terms of keen observation: "He has eyes remarkably" (Fortes, 1938).

Keen observation may promote skilled participation by young children in mature activities. Young children's skills may be remarkable to middle-class observers. For example, Fore (New Guinea) infants have access to all aspects of the environment for observation and involvement and develop a realistic self-reliance, to the point that they handle knives and fire safely by the time they are able to walk (Sorenson, 1979).

Children from many communities begin to pitch in to family work from age 3 or 4, when they begin to see what to do. For example, Kaluli (New Guinea) mothers encourage toddlers to attend to ongoing events and provide a model of how a task is to be done, telling children "Do like that" as they demarcate components of a task, without providing explanation (Schieffelin, 1991). Young daughters spend a great deal of time observing their mothers and are asked to do specific jobs to facilitate a task, such as bringing fire tongs or turning bananas over on the fire. Mothers encourage this assistance and gradually add new jobs as the child gets older; daughters fill responsible roles at an early age, usually by 3 years. Kaluli 3- to 5-year-old girls get together and collect firewood, make a small cooking fire, and cook themselves a bit of food, and Kaluli boys of this age have their own small pocket knives.

Children often assume responsibilities for child, animal, and house care by age 5 or 7, and manage these activities reliably at age 8 to 10 years (see Chapter 5; Rogoff, 1981b; Rogoff et al., 1975; Ward, 1971; Whiting & Edwards, 1988). For example, Black Elk described his own learning as a Sioux child: "The boys of my people began very young to learn the ways of men, and no one taught us; we just learned by doing what we saw, and we were warriors at a time when boys now are like girls. It was the summer when I was nine years old" (Niehardt, 1932, p. 17).

Observing with time-sharing of attention

To learn from ongoing events may require monitoring several events at a time, in a type of time-sharing of attention. A narrow focus of attention would make it difficult to notice nearby events that may be of great interest. If children are responsible for learning by observing, without a parent or teacher telling them what to attend to, alertness to ongoing events is crucial.

An example of time-sharing of attention was provided by a 12-month-old Mayan child who attended skillfully to three events at once: He closed things in a jar with his older sister; he whistled on his toy whistle that his mother had mischievously slipped into his mouth; and at the same time he intently watched a truck passing on the street (Rogoff et al., 1993)! In this way of attending, awareness of several sources is skillfully maintained.

Mayan toddlers often attended to several events at once, with each line of attention maintained as smoothly as if there were no other focus (Rogoff et al., 1993). In contrast, middle-class U.S. toddlers generally alternated attention between the two events or focused just on one. They were also more likely to appear unaware of interesting ongoing events than were Mayan toddlers. The mothers' attentional patterns resembled the patterns of the toddlers. It is striking that the Mayan *toddlers*, age 12 to 24 months, more frequently skillfully attended to several events at once than did the middle-class U.S. *mothers*, who usually alternated their attention between ongoing events.

Examples of alternating attention by a middle-class U.S. mother and child were seen when 21-month-old Sandy tried to reinvolve his mother with the jar and peewee doll after she had resumed conversation with adults:

> As his mother and the interviewer talked, Sandy tried to reach the jar (with a round knob on the lid). He pointed and said "want ball," reached and said "Ball," then grunted, saying "Ball, ball" and finally stretched and barely reached it. His mother eventually saw what he was doing and stopped talking with the interviewer.
>
> She proceeded to interact with Sandy exclusively, picking up the jar, "What is that? You want that back?" . . . with conversational peer questions, vocabulary lessons, and her full attention: "What's in there? . . . The baby?" When Sandy put the peewee in the jar and closed the lid, she prompted, "Say bye-bye."
>
> Sandy became distracted as the camera operator moved the camera, and he too exhibited a focus on one event at a time, as he turned around and watched the camera operator.
>
> At this, the adult conversation resumed . . . . Sandy alternated his attention between the camera operator and his play. (Rogoff et al., 1993, p. 98)

In communities in which children participate in complex social events, sensitivity to information from many sources that call for simultaneous awareness may be heightened. This in turn may facilitate learning to anticipate the plans and direction of a group (Briggs, 1991; Henry, 1955). Consistent with this idea, Samoan transcribers of audiotapes were able to follow simultaneous speech in which three or four people were talking in different areas of a living space. Elinor Ochs (1988) attributed their impressive attentional skills to their socialization as children who were expected to watch and listen to what happened around them. Samoan children early in life monitor others' conversations while carrying on their own.

Community differences in simultaneous attention may reflect cultural *preferences* for use of attention. Middle-class U.S. parents often urge their children to focus on one thing at a time; they may scold their children for attending broadly: "Pay attention to what you're doing!" Likewise, it is improper etiquette for middle-class Turkish mothers and children to interact with one another while the mother is talking to other adults (Göncü, 1993). In contrast, as Pablo Chavajay pointed out, Mayan parents expect their children to attend broadly and scold them if they do not observe:

In the native Mayan culture, caregivers expect children to begin to learn through observation from birth. Indeed, they always tell the children to observe when they are demonstrating any activity. While parents are working, they also attend to their children, and urge the children to pay attention. The children's observation is intensified by the fact that adults do not always give explanations and, if they do, it is always requesting that the child first devote attention through the use of observation. . . .

[Mayan] caregivers always emphasize to the children to be observant in everyday activities. For example, if a child does not do a good job of work in the field, his father would usually scold him, "Haven't you seen how I showed you?" (1993, pp. 163–165)

Intent participation in apprenticeships

Children's learning through observation of ongoing activities in everyday life resembles the structure of learning and assisting of mastery in apprenticeship. Learning "by osmosis," picking up values, skills, and mannerisms in an incidental fashion through close involvement with a socializing agent, is reportedly common in Japanese mother-child interactions, based on a cultural model of learning:

This osmosis model also prevailed in the training of traditional arts and crafts in Japan. The master would not teach. Instead, the live-in disciples, called *uchideshis*, would "steal" the art, together with the professional living style and work ethic, while helping the master with his work and doing household chores. (Azuma, 1994, p. 280)

This *uchideshi* system was also common in academic schooling in Japan until the late 1800s, when teaching became closely patterned after European American schools.

In many communities, people learn their trade through involvement in an apprenticeship. The novices learn largely through their engagement with other apprentices and the master in real production, observing their peers and the master and learning through their own involvement (Coy, 1989a; Lave & Wenger, 1991). Often, work to aid the master's trade is prioritized, with only a small amount of time and attention devoted to instruction per se. The apprentice participates as a peripheral but legitimate contributor to the production: "An apprentice watches masters and advanced apprentices until he thinks he understands how to sew (or cut out) a garment, [waiting] until the shop is closed and the masters have gone home to try making it" (Lave, 1988b, p. 4).

Similar processes may occur in less formal apprenticeships, as when a girl learns from a skilled midwife simply by observing and helping (Jordan, 1989) or daughters learn to weave through daily involvement in their mother's weaving. "Navajos do not teach their children, but they incorporate them in every life task, so that children learn themselves, by keen observation. Mothers do not teach their daughters to weave, but one day a girl may say, 'I am ready. Let me weave'" (Collier, 1988, p. 262).

In some apprenticeships, the master provides pointers (like the Kaluli mothers described in the previous section, who tell their children "Do like that" as they demarcate components of a task):

> Occasionally, Magalgal [a Kenyan master blacksmith] would call my attention to what he was doing to make certain that I was paying attention to something that he felt was important. He would say, "now this is the difficult part," and that was my cue to attend to what he was doing. (Coy, 1989b, p. 120)

Rather than relying on explanations to organize their learning, apprentices may be skilled in picking up information through watching, sometimes even without actually carrying out the central features of the task. Manning Nash (1967) reported that the method of learning to use the footloom in a weaving factory in Guatemala is for the novice (an adult) to sit beside a skilled weaver for weeks, simply observing, asking no questions and receiving no explanations. The novice may fetch a spool of thread for the weaver from time to time, but does not begin to weave until, after weeks of observation, the novice feels competent to begin. At that point, the apprentice has become a skilled weaver by watching, attending to whatever demonstrations the experienced weaver has provided and participating in peripheral aspects of the task.

In intent participation, apprentices and other learners attend to informative ongoing events that are not necessarily designed for their instruction. The purpose of the events is often carrying out the important business of the community and family life—although the presence and keen observation of learners may well be expected or encouraged.

Learning through listening in

Listening in, like observing, is an important form of learning in communities in which children have access to others' conversations. It is important, for example, in Kaluli language learning:

> Although there is relatively little speech directed to preverbal children, the verbal environment of these children is rich and varied, and from the beginning, infants are surrounded by adults and older children who spend a great deal of time talking to each other. . . . [Tod-

dlers'] actions are referred to, described, and commented upon by members of the household, especially older children, speaking to one another. . . . This talk about the activities and interests of toddlers is available for the toddlers to hear, though it is not addressed to or formulated for them. (Schieffelin, 1991, p. 73)

Learning through "eavesdropping" was emphasized by Martha Ward in her description of an African American community in Louisiana: "The silent absorption in community life, the participation in the daily commercial rituals, and the hours spent apparently overhearing adults' conversations should not be underestimated in their impact on a child's language growth" (1971, p. 37). Small children in that community are not conversational partners with adults, people with whom to "engage in dialogue." Questions between children and adults involve straightforward requests for information; questions are not asked for the sake of conversation or to drill children on topics on which the parents already know the answers. If children have something important to say, mothers listen, and children had better listen if mothers speak to them. But for conversation, mothers talk to adults or to a child above about age 8. The children are not encouraged to learn skills in initiating and monopolizing conversation with adults on topics of their own choosing; they hold their parents' attention longer if they say nothing. Toddlers learn to sit very still and listen to adults talk—for as long as three hours.

Shirley Heath similarly reported that working-class African American adults did not treat young children as conversational partners. Rather, the toddlers, who were always in the company of others, moved through phases of echoing and experimenting with variations on the speech around them. At first they were ignored, but gradually they began participating in ongoing conversation. Children were not seen as information givers and were not asked questions for which adults already had an answer. One woman discussed how she expected her toddler grandson, Teegie, to learn:

> White folks uh hear dey kids say sump'n, dey say it back to 'em, dey aks 'em 'gain 'n 'gain 'bout things, like they 'posed to be born knowin'. You think I kin tell Teegie all he gotta know to get along? He just gotta be kéen, keep his eyes open, don't he be sorry. Gotta watch hisself by watchin' other folks. Ain't no use me tellin' 'im: "Learn dis, learn dat. What's dis? What's dat?" He just gotta léarn, gotta know; he see one thing one place one time, he know how it go, see sump'n like it again, maybe it be de same, maybe it won't. He hafta try it out. If he don't he be in trouble; he get lef' out. Gotta keep yo' eyes open. (1983, p. 84)

Inuit men of the Arctic reported that they had learned to hunt as boys from watching the men and that they learned many things by listening. The children's opportunities to learn by overhearing were enhanced if they remained unobtrusive: "When they talked among themselves we weren't supposed to listen. We did in the tents. You couldn't help it. They tell lots of stories in the tents. You learn hard words out on the land. That is where I still learn words" (Crago, 1992, p. 498).

Learning about adult activities as an onlooker or by listening in, rather than as an interacting partner, is a preferred way to learn in some communities. In an Athabascan (native northern Canadian) community:

> The ideal learning situation for a child or young person is to be able to hear the stories of elders. The ideal situation described is that of elders speaking to each other as narrator and audience with the child in a third, observational role. . . . Because the child is not directly required to respond to the narratives, his own autonomy is respected at a time in his life when it is likely to be highly vulnerable. While this three-party narrative situation may not always obtain, those who are able to learn in this way are regarded as very fortunate. (Scollon & Scollon, 1981, pp. 120–121)

The specialized forms of discourse used in preparation for schooling (such as known-answer questions, inducements to participate in lessons, and acting as peers with adults in play and conversation) may seldom be used in communities in which children are encouraged to learn through intent participation in mature activities. Instead, verbal explanations are given in the context of involvement in the process that is being learned (Cazden & John, 1971; John-Steiner, 1984; Kojima, 1986), and children learn through their opportunities to listen and watch important activities of their community.

Of course, with increasing contact around the world, children's chances to observe as well as their likelihood of being involved in Western schooling are changing. The forms of guided participation prevalent in their communities may change as well. The routines of children's lives are increasingly connected with more than one community's practices. This topic is the focus of the next, final chapter.

9

Cultural Change and
Relations among Communities

To understand human development, it is essential to understand the development of the cultural institutions and practices in which people participate. This requires a more long-term view of cultural changes than most people attain through personal experience, as we are all limited to direct observation of only the cultural practices of our lifetime. It is difficult to imagine the lives and cultural communities of our grandparents, much less the generations and world changes that preceded them. Such historical cultural changes contribute to the ways of thinking and living in which current generations live.

Culture change is quite noticeable in today's world; perhaps it always has been (Weisner, Bradley, & Kilbride, 1997; Wolf, 1997). This editorial expresses it well:

> The world is too big for us. Too much going on, too many crimes, too much violence and excitement. Try as you will you get behind in the race, in spite of yourself. It's an incessant strain, to keep pace . . . and still, you lose ground. Science empties its discoveries on you so fast that you stagger beneath them in hopeless bewilderment. The political world is news seen so rapidly you're out of breath trying to keep pace with who's in and who's out. Everything is high pressure. Human nature can't endure much more. (quoted in Disney, 1998, p. 5)

The editorial was published in *The Atlantic Journal* in 1833.

Whether or not the pace of change is faster than before, recent changes have certainly stepped up the pace at which different parts of the world are in contact with each other. The advent of telephones, television, e-mail, fax, and the Internet have contributed to fast communication and contact among small hamlets and large cities all over the earth.

The spread of television has been extremely rapid. It increased from 9% of American homes in 1950 to 65% five years later and 93% by 1965 (Bushman & Anderson, 2001, citing figures from Nielsen Media Research; see figure 9.1).

Television's spread to many other parts of the world means that events almost anywhere can be seen almost everywhere, and programs produced in New York or Hollywood are seen worldwide. In 1974, the year I first arrived in the Mayan town of San Pedro, electricity was installed and the first televisions appeared. I was amazed to watch the Miss Universe contest on TV, with all the values associated beamed into Mayan homes—where very different standards prevailed. Twenty-five years later, most San Pedro homes had televisions, often with cable access to Miami channels.

It is well established that the world portrayed on television provides

FIGURE 9.1

In 1950, the Creason children got right out of the bathtub, eager to look at the new invention their Irish American family just obtained: a television. The family dog, Pretzel, in the chair, is not as interested.

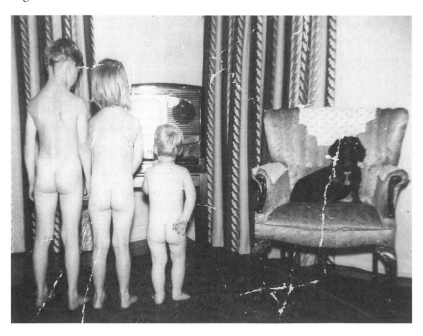

models emulated by viewers. In U.S. studies, for example, it is clear that media violence begets viewer aggression (Bushman & Anderson, 2001; Huston & Wright, 1998). The worldwide cultural and developmental consequences of disseminating programs, whether nonfiction or fiction, from one country to others must be immense.

In addition to changes based on electronic forms of communication, unprecedented numbers of people now live in countries other than those in which they and their parents were born. Global migration is occurring on an enormous scale, and has been for years. The population of the United States, for example, has primarily been composed of immigrants. In the first decade of the 1900s, more than 6 million immigrants arrived, most of them from Southern, Central, and Eastern Europe (Hall, 1990). In recent years (from 1991 through 1998), more than 7 million immigrants joined them and other recent arrivals, with the largest influxes from the former Soviet Union, China, India, the Philippines, Mexico, the Caribbean, and Central America (U.S. Census Bureau, 2000).

The current transformations make cultural change processes readily apparent to observers. They also make culture change and contact among communities an important aspect of most children's development.

In this concluding chapter, I focus on processes of cultural change and relations among individuals and among communities that engage in different cultural systems. First I briefly examine some of the commonly observed issues for individuals and groups as they manage relations across cultural systems. Then I turn to the idea of cultural change as the reality for human existence across millennia and centuries. I focus next on Western schooling, because this institution is one of the most pervasive recent tools of cultural change, and experience with it is so central to issues of human development. I then consider the persistence of traditional ways within changing cultural communities. I argue that rather than trying to substitute one cultural approach for another, communities can build on ideas across different cultural approaches, encouraging people to become fluent in more than one way. In conclusion, I return to the orienting concepts with which I began this book and some of the key patterns that seem to make sense of the variations and similarities across cultural communities.

Living the Traditions of Multiple Communities

With immigration, intermarriage, and other demographic changes, often people today live with more than one cultural approach. Individuals frequently grow up playing roles in several communities. Many have parents of different backgrounds so their own homes and lives function within several cultural traditions (Phinney & Alipuria, 1996). Many live as refugees or immigrants or "minority" group members whose lives span several cultural traditions (Azmitia, Cooper, Garcia, & Dunbar, 1996; Fisher, Jackson, & Villarruel, 1998; Miller, 1995; Mindel, Habenstein, & Wright, 1988; Orellana, 2001). Even those whose cultural heritage matches the dominant one of their nation increasingly participate in neighborhoods, schools, and work composed of a variety of cultural communities.

Immigrant families often rely on young children to serve as translators and culture brokers in dealing with their new country's bureaucracy. This role can be extremely important for the children's development and for the functioning of their families and communities (Valdés, 2002). Indeed, children who serve in this role are central, not peripheral, participants in the life of their communities (Orellana, 2001).

However, the turnabout of expertise can also be disruptive of family roles. As far back as the English arrival in colonial America, the young adapted more easily than their parents to the strangeness and hardships of the "wilderness." They were less bound by remembering the old ways from England and more adaptable to the necessities and structure of their new life. In becoming guides in a new world, the young attained an authority in the family that disrupted the traditional form of family life from the old country (Bailyn, 1960). Similarly, at the beginning of the 1900s, children in immigrant working-class families who had attended a U.S. school knew English and understood U.S. ways while their parents remained uprooted Central and Southern European peasants, with attitudes and language of the old country (Ehrenreich & English, 1978).

Often, differences among cultural systems present difficult challenges, especially when the ways of one community conflict with those of another and are experienced as troubling fragmentation. When a violent rupture separates people from their homes and languages and the familiarity of their cultural ways, the differences of a new system are stark. At other times, differences are experienced as a source of creative combinations (Apfelbaum, 2000; Boykin, 1994; Camara, 1975; Camilleri & Malewska-Peyre, 1997; Fisher et al., 1998; Harrison et al., 1990; McBride, 1996; Mindel et al., 1988; Reed, 1997; Suina & Smolkin, 1994; Vivero & Jenkins, 1999). Some of the creativity as well as uncertainty of the process of living "between" communities is conveyed by Dolores Mena, a Ph.D. student and new mother:

> Even today, I have to decide whether to do something the "Mexican way" (as influenced by my family) or whether I should do it the "American way" (as influenced by my "American" friends and by U.S. formal educational training). An example deals with child-rearing issues, such as whether our son should sleep in the same bed with us

or in his own room. I compromised by having him sleep in the same room with us but in his bassinet from birth to 5 months and now he sleeps in his own room in a crib. . . . My mom is totally against [having the baby sleep apart from us] and, like the Mayan parents, feels that it is inappropriate and neglectful. She tells me that the baby needs physical warmth from the parents to develop "normally" and that all 10 of her children slept in the bed with her and my father (not all at once, of course) until about 2 or 3 years of age. . . . I tell my mom that I am doing things the "Mexican American way." I am not exactly sure what the "Mexican American way" is, I just do what works for me. (personal communication, October 1999)

There are benefits to understanding the various cultural traditions in which one participates. Children who are encouraged to understand the dynamics among communities, to value their own background, and to know how to function in two or more cultural systems are more successful and confident (García Coll et al., 1996; Phinney & Rotheram, 1987). For example, parents of successful African American children raised their children with an emphasis on ethnic pride, self-development, awareness of racial barriers, and egalitarianism (Bowman & Howard, 1985).

Experience with several cultural communities also may provide cognitive and social flexibility and the potential for new syntheses of cultural ways (Harrison et al., 1990). For example, compared with children who speak only one language, children who are fluent in more than one language have greater flexibility in language use and an awareness of language itself, with an understanding of the conventionality of words and an ability to analyze the properties of language (Diaz, 1983). Likewise, the discontinuities among home, neighborhood, and school for African American children can facilitate development of situational problem-solving skills—to recognize, adapt to, circumvent, or change a predicament (Holliday, 1985).

Conflict among Cultural Groups

Although contact among cultural communities can be a source of creativity, it can also be a source of conflict. Indeed, boundaries between groups often maintain hostilities across generations. A large literature documents the roles of interpersonal and institutional prejudice in the lives of children of many communities whose cultural traditions differ from those of the dominant communities (e.g., García Coll et al., 1996; Timm & Borman, 1997; Valentine, 1971).

It is common for children of different groups to segregate in schools and other settings—as do their parents and other members of their home communities (R. Ellis, 1997). For example, a study in Britain found that children whose parents came from the Indian subcontinent to England and White British middle-school students played primarily with those from the same group (Boulton, 1995). Frequently, children were refused entry to games involving children of the other group. However, bullying usually involved perpetrators of the same group. Thus, the majority of both positive *and* negative interactions took place within these segregated groups; however, more of the Asian than the White children reported being teased about their color or race by other-race students.

Treatment of outsiders is often differentiated from the ways that people treat those from their own community, as expressed by a respected Kenyan elder of the Kipsigis group:

> In the past, [Kipsigis] people used to raid cattle from Kisii people, Luo people or Masai people. . . . That act was blessed and the cows multiplied considerably. . . . But it is a sinful thing if you steal from someone you eat with, someone with whom you have shared food. Even if he is your enemy, if he is of your tribe, it is bad to steal from him because you have eaten with him. (Harkness, Edwards, & Super, 1977, p. 18)

Kipsigis elders noted that a stranger, by becoming familiar or "close," would become a member of the group of people to whom one owes care.

The process of forming groups, developing rivalries, and easing hostilities was examined in a clever series of naturalistic studies done with 11- to 12-year-old European American Protestant boys attending a summer camp (Sherif & Sherif, 1969; Sherif, Harvey, White, Hood, & Sherif, 1961; see also Pettigrew, 1998). The researchers experimented with the conditions that would bring the boys (who were strangers) into groups, develop rivalries with other groups that would resemble conflicts between social groups in society at large, and ease those rivalries so that members of the groups could cooperate and respect each other.

They found that boys brought together by chance quickly developed preferences for in-group members and devised shared customs when placed in groups that engaged in a series of interdependent activities, such as cookouts and preparing for athletic activities. When the groups were later placed in repeated competition, intense hostility and aggression developed between groups, with negative stereotypes of individuals in the other group. The competitions began with good sportsmanship, but gradually the groups began to call each other names, hoard resources, engage in physical fights, and attack and destroy each other's property (see figure 9.2). The extent of hostility, and the rapidity of its development, surprised the camp staff.

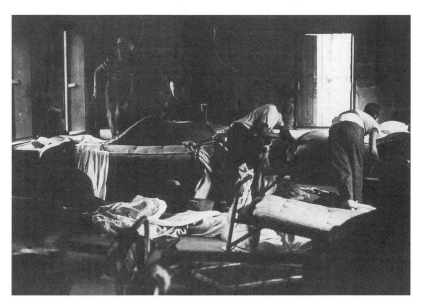

FIGURE 9.2

At camp, after one group was frustrated by the other (by the researchers' design), actual outbreaks occurred in which raids on each other's cabins became the thing to do (not by the researchers' design; Sherif & Sherif, 1969).

It was difficult for the staff to calm the hostilities; many methods that are commonly employed in trying to ease conflict between cultural groups did not work. The staff tried appealing to moral values, but although the boys were enthusiastic about the staff's presentation, they immediately turned to their plans to defeat or avoid the enemy group. The staff provided opportunities for greater contact in activities pleasant to both groups, such as going to the movies, eating in the same dining room, and shooting off fireworks together; however, these situations did not reduce conflict, but instead provided occasions for the groups to attack and insult each other.

What was effective for resolving the hostilities was a need for the two groups to work together to reach superordinate goals in which they needed each other's involvement, such as fixing the breakdown of the camp's water supply and helping get a stalled food truck started. Gradually, such joint efforts led to decreases in the hostilities. Friendships developed across group lines, name-calling ceased, and eventually the groups sought opportunities to intermingle and even to share resources with each other. For example, on the way home from camp, two groups decided to go in the same bus rather than accept the offer of separate buses, and one group bought refreshments for both groups during a stop.

These boys came from homogeneous and very comfortable backgrounds. The likelihood of misunderstandings and hostilities are much greater with groups that have a long history of competition for resources or poor treatment of one by another.

However, social arrangements promoting the need to cooperate to reach a common goal (as in the camp experiment) seem to help. In schools in several nations, children from ethnic groups that often experience friction have been helped to respect and relate to each other by arranging for cooperative learning in which all students have something to offer that the others need (Aronson, Blaney, Stephan, Sikes, & Snapp, 1978; Shachar & Sharan, 1994). Such methods may help promote the respect needed as, increasingly, people deal with others of different backgrounds.

Transformations through Cultural Contact across Human History

Although recent demographic changes seem unprecedented, cultural change and contact among communities have been occurring since the beginning of time. Continual change appears to be a property of living systems, including communities. The changes arise from influences of other communities (whether forced or invited), unforeseen events (desirable or not), and efforts within communities both to maintain traditions and to change in desired directions.

The changes of recent decades have been preceded by other widespread transformations of cultural practices across human history and prehistory. One sweeping economic revolution was the development of farming and herding. This innovation began around 10,000 years ago in the Near East, jumped from Turkey to Greece about 8,500 years ago, and then extended throughout Europe. It permitted great increases in the amount of population beyond that which could be sustained by hunting and gathering (Diamond, 1992).

Another impressive change was the extension of the practices of nomadic herdsmen from the steppes near the Black Sea across thousands of miles, to most of Europe and to Asia, about 5,000 years ago. The domestication of the horse seems to have given the steppe herdsmen such an advantage in warfare and travel that their language and customs came to dominate continents (Diamond, 1992):

> Soon after [horses'] domestication, they may have enabled herdsmen speaking the first Indo-European languages to begin the expansion that would eventually stamp their languages on much of the world. A few millennia later, hitched to battle chariots, horses became the un-

stoppable Sherman tanks of ancient war. After the invention of
saddles and stirrups, they enabled Attila the Hun to devastate the
Roman Empire, Genghis Khan to conquer an empire from Russia to
China, and military kingdoms to arise in West Africa. A few dozen
horses helped Cortés and Pizarro, leading only a few hundred
Spaniards each, to overthrow the two most populous and advanced
New World states, the Aztec and Inca empires. (p. 240)

According to Diamond, the sweeping changes that arose with the herdsmen's conquests resulted in the takeover of many local languages throughout Europe and Asia by the herdsmen's languages. The herdsmen's languages are the ancestors of the native tongues of nearly half of the world's
current population. (This is despite the fact that of the modern world's
5,000 languages, only 140 belong to this Indo-European language family.)

Over the subsequent millennia, the domesticated horse and the languages of their domesticators have dominated much of the world, together
with inventions (such as metallurgy and the plow) of the societies that the
herdsmen overtook. Later waves in this process included the expansion of
European populations into North and South America in the past 500 years.

An Individual's Experience of Uprooting Culture Contact

The process of European expansion in North America, and its role in individual lives, is well illustrated in an account by Ignatia Broker, an Ojibway
elder and storyteller, of the life of her great-great-grandmother. It reveals
some of the enormous changes experienced in prior centuries by Indians
and other indigenous people worldwide, and the effects on a young child:

> There was much excitement in the Ojibway village and the chil-
> dren felt it. It made them fearful. A do-daim, or clansman, from the
> east was visiting and the people held a feast in his honor. After the
> feast, in the evening, the people met in council to hear the news of
> the do-daim. He told of a strange people whose skins were as pale as
> the winter white and whose eyes were blue or green or gray. . . .
> "These strangers," said the do-daim, "are again asking the Ojib-
> way to mark a paper. . . . The Ojibway to the east have made the
> mark, and now they are on the big water where they must stay for-
> ever. The strangers promised never to enter their forests but they
> came anyway to trade for the coats of the Animal Brothers. I have a
> muk-kuk they gave me, and I will leave it to you. It sits right on the
> fire and does not crack. It is called iron kettle, and the strangers have
> promised many of these when the papers are marked."

"Have you studied these strangers well? Are they good people, or are they those who will be enemies?" asked A-bo-wi-ghi-shi-g.

"Some are kind. Others speak good. Others smile when they think they are deceiving," replied the do-daim. "Many of the Ojibway have stayed with these people, but soon our people had great coughs and there were bumps on their skins, and they were given water that made them forget.". . .

"Now," said the do-daim, "these strangers are many. They intend to stay, for they are building lodges and planting food." [He recounts how the strangers have fought for the land of the Mohegan and Cherokee, and how closer kinsmen have been affected and are now only a handful in number.]

"Down by the Chi-si-bi [Mississippi] at the place where the small gulls fly, the forests have become smaller. Strangers are there in great number. All day long they cut the trees and send them down the river. Although these strangers have said they will stay to the rising sun, already they are looking this way, for soon there will be no forest where they are now." [Some of the families decide to hide in deep forests, and others to do as the strangers demanded and go to them at the Lake of Nettles.] The people met and talked for three days on the hill outside the village. They spoke of the many good things that had always been. Of grandfathers and grandmothers who were the dust of the forests. Of those who would be left in the journeying places. The women listened and there was a wailing sound to their voices when they talked together. . . .

[Several days later, little Oona woke to the busy stirrings of the village, listened to discern that something was different, and saw her grandparents making bundles of food and clothing.] Oona was only five years old but she was already trained in many of the ways of a good Ojibway. She knew almost all that she could not do and all that she must learn to do. She went to her grandparents and stood before them with eyes cast down, knowing she could not speak the many questions she wished to ask, for they who are wise must speak first. . . .

"Oona, my child," said Grandfather, "I hope you have slept well. I know by the roundness of your eyes that you are wondering what is doing today." Grandfather paused, sat down, and stretched out his hand to Oona. "Take my hand, and I will tell you what your eyes ask.

"Remember this day, my child," Grandfather continued. "For all of your small life, this village, this place, has been your home, but now we must move toward the setting sun. We have been happy here and we have lived here a long, long time. A very long time even before you were born. At the council it was decided that we shall seek a new place. We move because there is another people who are fast coming into the forest lands. Their ways are different and we wish to be free of them for as long as we can.

"Take the things you wish to take—your corn doll and rubbing rock toy. Put them in a bundle. There is room." Grandfather smiled and Oona felt comforted. [She went to her mother, who told her,] "You must remember the beauty that was here. Go, my daughter, and say the words of friendship to those who were your playmates."

Oona made up her little bundle. Then she went to find her cousin, E-quay (Lady). They joined hands and circled the camp, smiling the smile of friendship to those they would not see again. They then went to the river to wait for the men and the canoes. (Broker, 1983, pp. 18–24)

Community Changes through Recent Cultural Contacts

In an account of cultural changes in West Africa, Bame Nsamenang (1992) pointed out that changes are sparked by contact with the "outside world" but also are deeply shaped by the community's existing practices. He reported that major changes are thought to have begun many centuries ago, with trade exchanges across long distances reaching different continents. The changes intensified when monotheistic religions were established and practices such as enslavement, European cash, taxation, formal education, colonization, and public administration and welfare services appeared on the scene.

Among the most drastic changes are those involving work, especially for women. Traditionally, West African custom was for women to marry and become full-time farmers, homemakers, and mothers. However, when taxes, school fees, and cash crops appeared, family relationships changed. For one thing, the total amount of labor increased for everyone. For example, in the precolonial period, Beti women of Cameroon had to work 46 hours per week; by 1934 they had to work more than 70 hours per week. Men's work hours doubled (although the base still was much lower than that of women) to 25 hours for household heads and 55 hours for dependent males. The change had to do with export crops being in the sphere of men's responsibility. As men's opportunities increasingly lay outside the ancestral land, women had to intensify their farming to balance the loss of men's labor. The establishment of schools, plantations, and industries led to male migration, placing a heavy burden on other family members to produce food and cultivate the absent men's cash crops. At the same time, there was a decrease in women's influence in traditional political life, which was considerable in precolonial times.

Changes in family and community structure were accompanied by changes in parent-child relations (Nsamenang, 1992). The difficulties of work and formal education sometimes separated spouses from each other and from children and kin for extended periods. This necessitated shifts in caregiving arrangements from community and kin-based systems to baby-sitters. For children, increasing involvement in formal education limited their involvement in the home as caregivers (and in other contributions to the family). Busy parents sometimes encouraged toddlers to "sneak" into school to be under the watchful eyes of the peer group and the teacher.

As traditional law changed from considering the rights and obligations of lineages to those of individuals, parental frustration and a sense of powerlessness emerged:

> Parents seem bitter that they are becoming merely "other" members of the family instead of the once undoubted mentors. The erosion of parental authority is further facilitated by the fact that nowadays children know more about contemporary life than do their parents. Consequently, most parents are finding it difficult to guide their children in how to behave in a world in which they are the more ignorant citizens. This approximates role reversal: Children, not parents, are the ones who explain how the world functions. (Nsamenang, 1992, p. 137)

Nsamenang reported that the rapid changes and the clash between traditionalism and modernity produced incompatible role demands and dilemmas that resulted in parental confusion and increases in children's psychological disturbances.

Western schooling has played a key role in this process. Although people in many nations look to schooling as a way of improving their situation, the better jobs that schooling is expected to provide may not be forthcoming. In Africa, the drive for schooling leads sometimes to success but also to loss (Clark, 1988; Serpell, 1993). Not only do young schooled people often lose their mother tongue and ways of life, but they also often end up with no job. As more people seek more schooling, the number of people competing for the available positions has increased, leading to a mass of alienated, unemployed, schooled young people in the major cities of Africa. Some aim for higher degrees in the hopes that this will lead to a job. Many avoid their home out of shame and disgrace at having failed to fulfill the promise offered by schooling.

The idea of schooling leading to a better life is also treated with suspicion by the children of some communities in the United States and elsewhere who have seen the lack of resulting opportunity for their elders (Clark, 1988). John Ogbu (1990) connected attitudes and performance in school with differences in how various groups have come to be part of U.S. society, and their reactions to their subsequent treatment by White Americans.

According to Ogbu, immigrants who moved to the United States voluntarily, in the belief that they would attain improved economic well-being or political or religious freedom, in large part do well in school. They compare their current situation, though difficult, as more favorable than the conditions they left in the "old country" or that are faced by people who are still there. They tend to see discrimination, language differences, and other hardships as temporary barriers to overcome by learning the language and culture of their new land, with the help of the schools, without thinking they are giving up their own cultural ways (see Gibson, 1988).

Ogbu contrasted immigrant minorities with "involuntary minorities" who were initially incorporated into U.S. society through slavery, conquest, or colonization. (In this category, he included American Indians, Black Americans, Mexican Americans in the Southwest, and Native Hawaiians, and pointed out that similar processes operate for some groups in other nations, such as the Maori in New Zealand and Japan's Koreans.) Involuntary minorities do not have the possibility of a favorable comparison with a former homeland situation and often see their hardships as permanent and institutionalized. Ogbu claimed that involuntary minorities are disillusioned about the potential of personal perseverance in institutions such as schools and instead regard collective effort as necessary for getting ahead. They distrust White Americans and their institutions on the basis of extensive experience of discrimination.

Many of the cultural differences between involuntary minorities and the middle class have arisen as involuntary minorities developed coping mechanisms to handle the conditions of subordination. These ways are viewed not just as different from the majority but as in opposition—as boundary-maintaining mechanisms that symbolize cultural identity and preserve a sense of self-worth. Adopting the ways of the majority would challenge cultural identity in ways that changes for immigrants would not. Ogbu claimed that this complicates the learning of middle-class ways and engaging in school for involuntary minorities, but not for immigrant groups. Nonetheless, in both cases, Western schooling has served as a powerful source of cultural change.

Western Schooling as a Locus of Culture Change

Whether sought after or forced, one of the most influential means of culture change for children and families in the past century and a half has been the spread of formal "Western" schooling around the globe. Many communities have long had indigenous forms of formal education, such as religious schooling, apprenticeship, and initiation lessons (Akinnaso, 1992). Widespread involvement with Western formal schooling has been promulgated around the world from European and U.S. origins, accompanying colonization.

However, even within European nations and North America, the role of schooling was quite reduced a century ago compared with now. The practice of requiring all children to attend school for many years is a quite recent phenomenon. For example, in the United States, compulsory schooling began only in the late 1800s.

The first generation of English settlers in America used forms of education that they brought from the old country, where the most important agency of children's learning was not a formal institution devoted to instruction, but the extended family embedded in community and church life. However:

> As the family contracted towards a nuclear core, as settlement and resettlement, especially on the frontier, destroyed what remained of stable community relations, and constant mobility and instability kept new ties from strengthening rapidly, the once elaborate interpenetration of family and community dissolved. The border line between them grew sharper; and the passage of the child from family to society lost its ease, its naturalness, and became abrupt, deliberate, and decisive: open to question, concern, and decision. (Bailyn, 1960, p. 25)

With the reduced role of the family and community, the English colonies in America passed laws in the 1600s attempting to replace the old social order, to control and educate the young. In the Massachusetts statute of 1642, parents and masters of apprentices were exhorted to maintain the old order, condemning "the great neglect of many parents and masters in training up their children in learning and labor" (according to Bailyn, 1960, p. 26). These measures did not restore the old order, and by the end of the 1600s, the surviving elders of the first generation of colonists bemoaned the future, expecting chaos.

Instead, however, a new order developed. Laws in Massachusetts and Connecticut required all towns to maintain teaching institutions, with an urgency stemming from fear of the loss of cultural standards and civilization itself (Bailyn, 1960). The Puritans deliberately transferred the waning educational functions of the family and community to schools. In Virginia, parental efforts to provide for their children's education "suggest a veritable frenzy of parental concern lest they and their children succumb to the savage environment" (p. 28).

By the end of the colonial period, education had been dislodged from its integrated place in family and community life, with the decreasing seamlessness of family and community life. Education became a matter of deliberate attention, shifted to formal institutions—primarily schools—whose purpose was the "transfer of culture" to the young.

Caroline Pratt, a leader in innovative schooling who was born in the mid-1800s, reflected at age 80 on the changes in the role of schooling that continued into the 1900s:

> How utterly the life of a child in this country has changed during my lifetime I would scarcely believe if I had not seen it happen. Three-quarters of a century have spanned the change: my father was a Civil War veteran; I remember the day we all went down to the store to see my mother make our first call on a telephone; I remember watching the explosive progress of the first automobile down our village street.
>
> Put it this way, as the statistics put it: before 1867, the year I was born, only one out of every six people lived in cities of more than 8,000 inhabitants, and there were only 141 such cities; by 1900, one out of three people lived in such a city, and the number of those cities was 547. . . . Nearly half a century has passed since 1900, and the transition from rural and village life to a big-city industrial civilization is a half-century farther along.
>
> I have seen the world of the child grow smaller and smaller. From the wide wonderful place of my childhood, it has become a narrow cell, walled about with the mysteries of complex machinery and the hazards of a motor-driven urban setting.
>
> When I grew up in Fayetteville, New York, school was not very important to children who could roam the real world freely for their learning. We did not merely stand by while the work of our simpler world was done; I drove the wagon in haying time, sitting on top of the swaying load, all the way to the barn. At ten, my great-aunt used to say, I could turn a team of horses and a wagon in less space than a grown man needed to do it.
>
> No one had to tell us where milk came from, or how butter was made. We helped to harvest wheat, saw it ground into flour in the mill on our own stream; I baked bread for the family at thirteen. There was a paper mill, too, on our stream; we could learn the secrets

of half a dozen other industries merely by walking through the open door of a neighbor's shop.

No wonder school was a relatively unimportant place—a place where we learned only the mechanical tools, the three R's, and a smattering about things far away and long ago. Our really important learning, the learning how to live in the world into which we were born and how to participate in its work, was right at hand, outside the schoolhouse walls. (pp. xi–xii)

Pratt became a teacher in a one-room school near her town at the age of 16 (as did my mother and many other young U.S. women for decades). For her, schooling was perhaps not the most important learning experience, but it was not foreign. For many others around the world, schooling is a foreign institution, often accompanying missions to "civilize" other people.

Schooling as a Foreign Mission

The form of schooling that is now widespread in many former colonies of European nations is one of the legacies of colonization. Minnie Aodla Freeman, an Inuit from the Canadian North, wrote about entering a missionary school at about age 7, in the 1940s:

> The missionaries had already come around once to our tent. After that I would hear grandmother and grandfather discuss school and me. Grandmother was very much against it but grandfather said that I had to go. It was just like him. He always believed that refusing people in authority would lead to a bad mark on the refuser. I would hear grandfather explaining over and over that I would be home every Sunday in the afternoons and every summer. Grandmother would question him, "What is her reason for needing to learn the *qallunaat* language [English]?" I never found out how they came to agree, but they both crossed the river from Moosonee to Moose Factory and delivered me to St. Thomas Anglican School.
>
> The three of us were taken upstairs to a little room; sitting there was a great big man who made my grandfather sign papers. I still wonder today what the papers said. Grandmother was crying, the first time I had seen tears in her eyes since I had been in her care. I did not cry. I was too busy looking around. Without any farewell, I was taken to another room by a strange lady. She fascinated me. With her hair and red lips, she did not look at all human.
>
> She brought me into a room with a tub of water, put me in, and washed me all over; her hands were so pale against my little brown body. All my clothing was changed and then I was led to a huge

room. . . . I understood nothing in the *qallunaat* language, least of all reading, writing or arithmetic. Art work, I loved. I soon adapted to the strange routines of the school.

I went home on Sunday as promised, though I saw my family only once. The next Sunday, when the principal and his crew brought me across from Moose Factory to Moosonee, my trained eyes could see that the tents were gone. I wanted to tell the crew that my relatives had left, but I could not. They all looked so huge that I did not dare say anything. We approached the dock area and landed. Finally, one of the men noticed that the tents were not there. We did not bother to climb up the bank of the shore. We turned right around and went back to the empty school. . . . My little mind told me that my grandparents had not come to say goodbye to make it easier on me. They had warned me in the past that their tents would be gone sometime soon [to winter camp], but it did not hit me until it happened. . . .

[By springtime] all the children began to talk about going home for the summer holidays and they gave each other their names and addresses. The dates were set for each child's departure. Mine was not. It did not bother me, because I did not really understand what was going on. Nobody tried to tell me anything. I could not even remember what home was like. . . . I thought I had been kidnapped, but they were pretty kind kidnappers.

[During the next school year] the winter came with the same routine and rules. I began to understand a little more about numbers, reading and the meaning of a *qallunaat* education. . . . [One day] I saw two men approaching. They came closer, and when they entered the gate my little heart jumped and a lump came to my throat. There they were, my grandfather and father. They had come to see me, all the way from Cape Hope Island. I am sure they had come to get me out of school and take me home as they had brought all my Inuit travel clothing. All three of us were brought to the little room where my grandfather and grandmother had left me a year and a half earlier. Then I was sent back to the girls' room and did not see them again until the following evening. I do not know what was said in that little room, but they did not come back the next day, nor the next, nor the next, until finally I put the memory of them out of my mind. I am sure they had come to take me home, but I guess they had no ransom. (1978, pp. 103–107)

The attempts by Western nations to spread this institution to other peoples distinguish it from many local forms of learning. In many other forms of learning, the learners often must convince the teacher to assist them in learning, rather than the teachers attempting to give away their knowledge. As Margaret Mead (1942) pointed out, traditionally knowledge was given as a favor or "stolen" from neighboring groups. In schools and in the exportation of this institution to other lands, knowledge is proselytized.

Indeed, the first Western schools in many colonies were introduced as part of the missionizing process (Spring, 1996). Furthermore, teaching of skills such as literacy was accompanied by insistence on the cultural practices and values of the missionaries. In a sermon, a Methodist minister critiqued

> the failure of our early missionaries to separate the Christian religion from the American way of life. Too often the missionary was identified with a foreign governing power. We often felt that to make Christians out of people, it was necessary to direct the styles of their clothing, the building of their homes, and their table manners as well. (Magarian, recorded in 1963)

Schooling as a Colonial Tool

Proselytizing efforts to teach the ways of the colonizers or reformers were sometimes earnest attempts to help others. However, they often also involved economic and military gains for the nations sponsoring the missionaries and teachers. Colonial education was central to empire building. This can be seen in advice to the British Parliament in 1847 from a well-known educator who claimed that the aim of colonial education was to instill Christianity, habits of self-control, and moral discipline "as the most important agent of civilization for the colored population of the Colonies" (J.P.K. Shuttleworth, quoted in Willinsky, 1998, p. 100). Another example of how schooling was used as a colonial tool is provided by the following account of a school early in the 1900s:

> The American flag hoisted above the one-room school house hung limp in the heavy morning air. Inside, where the stone walls had been papered over with pages torn from back issues of *Harper's Weekly*, the first year students in Alice Magoon's Girls Industrial Work class prepared for the day. The day's lessons included the care and cleaning of homes and laundry work followed by a discussion of the importance of clean ears, teeth and nails for good citizenship. Across the yard, in yet another schoolhouse, the third grade boys' civics club had convened. Readings for the day included an essay on *Habeas Corpus*, and some selections from Benjamin Franklin's *Poor Richard's Almanac*.

The day closed with the recitation of a poem entitled "Luck and Laziness."

This unabashedly American school day could have transpired in Cincinnati, St. Louis, or Seattle. But this school day transpired in the Philippines, a mere four years after the American occupation of the islands. Magoon, and nearly 1,000 more American men and women like herself, had been dispatched to the Philippines beginning in 1901, as a "second wave of troops," following a war of nearly unparalleled violence in the history of American foreign policy. But Magoon, like her fellow passengers who had arrived on U.S. Army transport ships, were not military personnel. They were American school teachers. And yet, despite their civilian status they understood their mission in similarly martial terms. In a journal entry made just after boarding the army transport that would take *her* to Manila, Mary Fee, an American school teacher, described herself as just "one of an *army* of enthusiasts enlisted to instruct our little brown brother, and to pass the torch of occidental knowledge several degrees east of the international date line." (Cleaves, 1994, p. 1)

The colonial strategy was to change Philippine practices of adults through the children, a strategy also used by Spanish priests, backed by soldiers, to drive a wedge between generations of Pueblo Indians in New Mexico in the late 1500s and 1600s (Gutierrez, 1991; see also Spring, 1996).

The Philippine population was to be prepared for self-government through civics training for male students, to instill new attitudes toward wealth and work, and through domestic training courses for female students, to target the Filipino home as "the primary site of moral and social elevation of the population" (Cleaves, 1994, p. 2). An American teacher stated, "Filipino youth [would find] order and neatness the salient features [of the schoolhouse] in contrast to the slovenliness and unkempt conditions of their homes" (p. 5). In daily movements between home and school, children would experience the contrast that would encourage them to rebel against the practices of home and act as a catalyst for change.

The students were told that it was their responsibility to work for change in places that did not live up to the ideal, helping "less fortunate" people who had not had the opportunity to attend school. In their turn, parents took "great pleasure in studying the attractive pictures of American homes found in the primers which the Filipino boys and girls carry home with them daily" (Cleaves, 1994, p. 5). The desire for new things, it was thought, would motivate Filipinos to new standards. A domestic science teacher stated, "It is true we are teaching them to want things they have never had or cared to have before; but the incentive to have more will promote the ambition to work" (p. 7). Clearly, schooling was conceived as a tool for deep changes in the structure and values of the colonized nation.

Schooling as a Tool of U.S. Western Expansion

Schooling has been used similarly as a tool to change practices in Indian communities in the United States, as part of the government's expansion into Indian lands. During the late 1800s and early 1900s, politicians and policymakers viewed schooling as the primary tool for "civilizing" Indians. This led to boarding schools that isolated children from their families and communities for years (Spring, 1996; Yamauchi & Tharp, 1994).

Indian schools set up by the U.S. government were designed to produce obedient, punctual, hardworking Christian students who would become citizens assimilated to the dominant White society (Lomawaima, 1994; Spring, 1996). A major goal of schooling was to create interest in settled agriculture and private property. This would "free up" the forests that the Indians had needed for hunting so that they could be acquired by European Americans (Adams, 1996).[1] The campaign to place Indian children in boarding schools accompanied government moves to get access to Indian lands as pioneers moved westward. In 1887, the "Indian Emancipation Act" aimed to force Indians to accept individual land ownership as a key force in "civilizing" them. (This Act also resulted in an enormous loss of Indian landholdings, reduced from 138 million to 52 million acres between 1887 and 1934; Lomawaima, 1994.)

Boarding schools were purposely established far from students' homes to wrest the children from the influence of their families and communities. General Pratt, a leading figure in the establishment of off-reservation Indian boarding schools, argued in 1881 for the separation of Indian children from their homes:

> I suppose the end to be gained, however far away it may be, is the complete civilization of the Indian and his absorption into our national life, with all the rights and privileges guaranteed to every other individual, the Indian to lose his identity as such, to give up his tribal relations and to be made to feel that he is an American citizen. If I am correct in this supposition, then the sooner all tribal relations are broken up; the sooner the Indian loses all his Indian ways, even

---

[1] Thomas Jefferson wrote, "When [Indians] shall cultivate small spots of earth, and see how useless their extensive forests are, they will sell from time to time, to help out their personal labor in stocking their farms, and procuring clothes and comforts from our trading houses." Elsewhere, he commented, "While they are learning to do better on less land, our increasing numbers will be calling for more land, and thus a coincidence of interests" (quoted in Adams, 1996, p. 49).

his language, the better it will be for him and for the government and the greater will be the economy to both.

Now, I do not believe that amongst his people an Indian can be made to feel all the advantages of a civilized life, nor the manhood of supporting himself and of standing out alone and battling for life as an American citizen. To accomplish that, his removal and personal isolation is necessary. (Pratt's letter to Senator Dawes; in Utley, 1964, p. 266)

By 1900, nearly 85% of Indian schoolchildren were attending boarding schools (Adams, 1996). Children's lives were under strict military discipline and they were not allowed to speak their native language or practice native religion (see figure 9.3). Instead of returning home in the summer, students were placed with White farm families. An Indian woman reminisced about her arrival at an off-reservation school in 1924:

> You were just brought in and dropped there, and they didn't allow you any time with your parents or anything. You're in school and that's it. . . . My main trouble was sleeping . . . that's when I get the loneliest, you know. The lights would go out, and quiet, you had to be real quiet. And then you would think and you would just get so homesick, oh! dear! Homesick is really sick. You can get really sick from it. (Lomawaima, 1994, pp. 42–43)

The Persistence of Traditional Ways in Changing Cultural Systems

Colonial and government efforts to "civilize" native people were characterized by an attitude that there is One Best Way—which, of course, is the way of the dominant group. In scholarly debates and in many intervention projects aiming to improve other people's lives, the assumption that there is One Best Way continues.

The basis of faith in the One Best Way is often merely consensus among an in-group based on their own assumptions and values (along with self-interest in obtaining land and dominating others). Differences in values among communities help to illuminate the cultural systems that otherwise are often taken for granted by people trying to change other people.

Jamake Highwater noted that well-meaning people, wanting to eliminate intolerance, sometimes insist that all peoples are fundamentally the same because all need and want the same things. However, such insistence on a lack of differences means the destruction of the realities of commu-

FIGURE 9.3A

Chiricahua Apaches as they arrived at Carlisle Indian School, Pennsylvania, from Fort Marion, Florida, November 4, 1886. Back row: Hugh Chee, Bishop Eatennah, Ernest Hogee. Middle row: Humphrey Escharzy, Samson Noran, Basil Ekarden. Front row: Clement Seanilzay, Beatrice Kiahtel, Janette Pahgostatun, Margaret Y. Nadasthilah, Fred'k Eskelsejah.

nities other than their own. This would make it difficult to understand why a Navajo family might rip the toilet out of their newly built government house; traditional Navajos believe that it is disgusting to have a toilet under the roof of their living space rather than at a distance. Without understanding cultural differences in values and practices, visitors confuse tradition for squalor, feeling sorry for the lack of indoor plumbing—a feature of housing that they but not the traditional Navajo families desire:

> There is no question that all people feel sorrow and happiness, but the things that evoke these responses and the manner in which such

FIGURE 9.3B

Chiricahua Apaches four months after arriving at Carlisle Indian School. Back row: Samson Noran, Fred'k Eskelsejah, Clement Seanilzay, Hugh Chee. Front row: Ernest Hogee, Humphrey Escharzy, Margaret Y. Nadasthilah (standing), Beatrice Kiahtel, Janette Pahgostatun, Bishop Eatennah, Basil Ekarden.

feelings may be expressed socially and privately can be highly dissimilar from culture to culture. The Mexican poet and scholar Octavio Paz (1967) has stated: "The ideal of a single civilization for everyone, implicit in the cult of progress and technique, impoverishes and mutilates us.". . .

In the process of trying to unify the world we must be exceedingly careful not to destroy the diversity of the many cultures of humankind that give our lives meaning, focus, vision, and vitality. (Highwater, 1995, pp. 209, 210)

Contrasting Ideas of Life Success

The U.S. government, policymakers, and scholars continue efforts to change the lives of Native Americans. And still, differences in cultural practices and values continue to distinguish the perspectives of different players. For example, "mainstream" ideas of school achievement are at odds with Navajo values for life success. In school, individuals are often supposed to get ahead of others by standing out in competition. In contrast, in the Navajo community, individuals may achieve great success in education not for their individual gain but as a contribution to the community's welfare:

> The very individualism that is second nature to much of the middle class is unethical from a Navajo perspective. Whereas the middle class expects individuals to earn their rewards through hard work and often feels no obligation to people who have not earned their own subsistence, many Navajos would think poorly of someone who focused upon their own economic advancement and did not take care of others. (Deyhle & Margonis, 1995, p. 152)

Among Navajo people, priority is generally placed on family and community relations over "getting ahead" materially (Deyhle & Margonis, 1995). It is preferable to live in connection with the community than to sacrifice that for material gain. A Navajo woman who had lived in the city and returned to the reservation contrasted supportive family networks among the Navajo with the situation of nuclear families and individual economic striving that characterizes city life: "The way whites live seems to be lonely. To live alone is kind of like poverty" (p. 152). Another woman stated, "In the traditional way and now, the family is the most important thing you can do. Life is too short to worry about jobs" (p. 156). One father explained:

> "We don't have electricity. And we don't have electric bills. We haul water, and we don't have water bills. And out here we don't have to pay for a [trailer] space." Nightly television watching, lights and the vacuum cleaner only require an adapter and a car battery. His sister added,
>> A medicine man warned us about what happens when you leave. He said, "They educate us to be pawns. We are educated to do a thing, and then we become pawns. Must work for money to pay for the water bills, the electricity. We become pawns." So you see, we have our water, even though we haul it from 16 miles away, we have our warm house, and our meat and food from the land. In town we have to pay for these things and then we become dependent. (p. 151)

From the perspective of national policymakers, Navajo young women are especially at risk because they often do not complete high school and many become pregnant during their teen years. However, within the Navajo community, finishing high school often does not lead to improved employment possibilities because of employment ceilings due to discrimination, and having a child before completing school does not have the negative consequences that would occur in a community without such extended family support (Deyhle & Margonis, 1995).

From another angle, feminist researchers may regard Navajo young women as leading restricted lives. But this also takes their choices out of context. Donna Deyhle and Frank Margonis (1995) pointed out that

> feminist researchers often implicitly invoke the values of the upwardly mobile middle-class individual both in their analysis of women's circumstances and in visions of change. This implicit individualism finds little support in Navajo women's circumstances and attitudes; rather than seeking individual mobility, they strive to make economic mobility consistent with matrilineal networks on the reservation. (p. 158)

Developing a career, with an achievement ethic prioritizing economic gain and individual recognition, does not fit the Navajo priority placed on cooperation in the family and community. The ethic of romance is also foreign, as women's central place in the family derives from their power in the matrilineal community organization, not from a tie between sexuality and finding a romantic partner (Deyhle & Margonis, 1995).

According to Deyhle and Margonis, young Navajo women generally participate in schooling but do not allow it to transform their commitment to the community. For some, success in advanced education can occur together with continuing involvement in their community. For many, there is little appeal in the lonely isolation and the drop in respect that would accompany a shift to the Anglo worldview (given the occupational ceiling and discrimination that pervades the Anglo world with regard to Navajos and women). Hence, most young women accept schooling, but as secondary to Navajo community life and women's roles, including early childbearing.

Thus evaluations of whether change is desirable in Navajo women's lives differ greatly depending on one's point of view. Policymakers prioritize middle-class indicators of success, such as school completion and delay of parenting. Feminists press for public rather than family roles. Navajo women themselves prioritize their respected role as family leaders in communities based on interdependence rather than isolated individual achievement.

These discrepant perspectives fit each group's participation in different cultural traditions as well as ongoing cultural change. Their stances on success in life are based on distinct values regarding such issues as competition, economic independence, material gain, the priority of family and community relations, and judgments of accessibility and desirability of employment. Resistance to interventions that conflict with local values makes sense in the light of differing definitions of life success and the varying cultural organization of community life.

Intervention in Cultural Organization of Community Life

Interventions such as introduction of Western schooling and other change efforts may not actually replace the more traditional ways of a community. But interventions do contribute to subtle and not so subtle changes. In addition to interventions that involve decisions on a political and institutional scale, people's everyday decisions are often a form of intervention in others' cultural ways when individuals come into contact (directly or indirectly) with people of another cultural background. For example, researchers, teachers, social workers, and ministers make many small decisions throughout the day that are based on cultural aspects of others' and their own backgrounds. They often need to judge what is good for others or the directions in which to encourage development.

In making decisions that affect others, it is necessary to consider the potential consequences of one change on other community practices (Seagrim, 1977). Cultural practices work in organic ways, interrelating as living phenomena, not as mechanical objects that can be considered separate entities.

Efforts to improve the lives of people in other communities often have unforeseen consequences when policymakers (and researchers) overlook the cultural organization of particular practices. Gavin Seagrim pointed to the moral dilemmas connected with Western schooling, and its associated values, for aboriginal people in Australia:

> There is undoubtedly a perfectly rational and objective understanding among aboriginal leaders that the white culture is here to stay and that they must learn how to master it if they are to maintain their integrity—their existence as a separate culture. To do this they must master our skills. The problem is, what skills and how to master them? And what will the mastering do to rather than for them? . . .
>
> As one aboriginal said to a school-teacher in the Northern Territory: "We want our children to learn English. Not the kind of En-

glish you teach them at school. But your secret English. *We* don't
understand it but we want our children to do so.". . .

He was making a penetrating and insightful remark: We do have
a secret English, secret in the sense that to understand the thought
that lies behind apparently straightforward verbal utterances you
need to think like an English-speaking person. And you learn to do
that at your mother's knee, in the bosom of the family, where you
learn to interpret and to adopt the value system to which the verbal
utterances give expression.

What he may not realize—and I do not see how he could if he
does not understand the secret English—is what he is letting himself
in for, because, of course, you cannot "have" that English without
also having the attitudes that go with it: the Western materialism, the
"property" mentality, the restricted-extent territoriality, the estima-
tion of monetary as opposed to spiritual wealth. These are incompatible with the maintenance of the aboriginality which he may also like
to preserve. (1977, p. 373)

Intervention efforts often focus on one or a few features of a community, overlooking that feature's relationship to other aspects of community
functioning. Especially likely to be overlooked in intervention efforts is the
way that communities themselves make decisions and coordinate their activities. Organizational assumptions of those intervening may conflict with
the community's own ways of organizing for action.

For example, many communities use a hierarchical (or "vertical") structure, with someone "in charge." This form of organization is common in
bureaucracies (including institutions that are often involved in interventions). This type of organization also fits with cultural practices in families
whose disciplinary practices emphasize control of children by adults.

In other communities, rather than using such hierarchical organization, a "community consciousness" is the prevailing form of organization.
(This fits with earlier discussions of coordinating in a group rather than in
dyads or solo action.) A community can function and solve problems fluently, "like a school of fish. All of a sudden you see them move; they shift
altogether. That is exactly the way most Indian communities function" (Pelletier, 1970, p. 28).

While it didn't have a vertical structure, our community [Mani-
toulin Island, in Canada] was very highly structured. So highly structured that there wasn't anything that could happen that somebody
couldn't almost immediately, in some way, solve. . . . If somebody
died in that community, nobody ever said: We should dig a grave.

The grave was dug, the box was made, everything was set up. . . . The one who baked pies baked pies. Everyone did something in that community, and if you tried to find out who organized it, you couldn't.

. . . In 1964, Prime Minister Pearson came up to the reserve. He had a cocktail party in the hall, and at the same time there was a big buffet organized for him. This was organized by a woman from Toronto. She went up there and set this whole thing up. He had been coming there every year. . . . Every year they turned out a beautiful meal for him, and he never knew who to thank because it was just all of a sudden there; it was done. The people just got together. There was no foreman or boss. There was no vertical structure, and it just happened.

You should have been there in '64. It was chaotic. There were no knives, no desserts, nobody had cut up the heads of lettuce that were all over, because this woman came there and gave orders, and the people wouldn't do anything until she told them what to do. She got so busy that she couldn't tell everybody what to do, and she had four or five turkeys all over the town in different people's ovens, and that's where they sat. They had to go and tell the women to bring the turkeys down because they wouldn't do it on their own. There was someone in charge. Had there not been anyone in charge it would have gone off fine. It was a real mess.

. . . And yet we have the Department of Indian Affairs coming and telling us we have no organization. . . . Every time somebody comes into the community they disrupt the pattern. Every time you remove a resource person from the community you disrupt the pattern. You break it up, and they have to reorganize. But in a lot of communities this is very hard to do, and some of them have been too hurt to make it. Indian resource people begin to drop out of sight and white organizers take over, making it even more difficult for Indian people to function. (pp. 26–27, 28–29)

Cultural practices of different communities are not necessarily mutually exclusive. In thinking about change, we do not have to limit ourselves to considering switching from one cultural system to another in an either/or fashion. Rather than assuming that other communities' ways are simply either noble or barbaric, it is to everyone's benefit to learn from each other's ways. Connections among different cultural patterns can serve as impetus for creative development of new cultural ways. We can consider both how practices already fit together organically and how they can adapt, as a living system, to new circumstances and ideas.

Dynamic Cultural Processes:
Building on More Than One Way

Cultural processes involve continual change, both from choices made by individuals and communities themselves, as well as by the force of circumstances and other people. The continual process of change is recognized by the traditional Inuit image of the ideal genuine and mature person as involved in a lifelong process of growth in their community and environment: "Non-Inuit people often do not understand this value, but hold Inuit and other traditional people to static cultural models. . . . Kinship networks of sharing, for instance, must be modified to deal with money as well as meat from the hunt" (Stairs, 1996, pp. 224–225).

Recognizing that there is more than one way (indeed, more than two ways) for humans to arrange their customs and lives needs to be accompanied by an understanding that cultural practices, although they persist, also change over time. As distinct cultural ways come into contact, communities may develop new ways that build on previous alternatives in a process of cultural development over generations (see Clifford, 1997; Lipka, 1998; Serpell, 1993; Walker, 2001).

Jamake Highwater, who grew up in Montana speaking an Indian language, reflected on the utility of Western tools for Indian people. His statement also highlights the importance of avoiding both deficit models and romanticized images as we think about cultural change:

> Like many young, nearly assimilated primal people all over the world, I became . . . conscious of the "intelligence" at work in my own culture. I ceased being ashamed of it and I ceased trying to justify it. I became aware of the potential of vivifying my heritage rather than sacrificing it.
>
> Of course, there were many isolated and brave Indian spokespersons in the past, but mine was the first generation for whom the use of the Western type of intelligence became a pervasive tool rather than a vehicle of assimilation and ethnic suicide. During the early decades of this century, private and parochial organizations and the federal government sponsored massive Indian educational efforts, often involving boarding schools. As the Oglala Sioux writer Michael Taylor has pointed out: "Disruptive of ordinary tribal life and sometimes brutal and insensitive to human needs, the schools notably failed in their initial purpose of eradicating native languages, religions, and customs. What the schools did accomplish, accidentally, was to provide Indian people from divergent backgrounds [and dif-

ferent languages] with a means of communication—the English language." (1995, p. 211)

Participants in different communities may be able to expand their possibilities by cross-fertilization of ideas, by learning about and mastering forms of communication and learning that are not indigenous to their own community. This can be a mutual enhancement, with some communities learning from others how to engage in the discourse of schooling, for example, and others learning how to engage in skilled observation and coordinated participation in ongoing activities. Rather than looking for One Best Way and regarding cultural patterns as mutually exclusive, each can offer enrichment to others. For example, Pablo Chavajay, a scholar who grew up in a Mayan community in Guatemala, pointed out the benefits of learning to use multiple ways of instruction:

> The different methods of instruction in [Mayan and middle-class European American] cultures are both valid, and result from a long social and historical process. What is emphasized in one culture occurs infrequently in another. This means that both cultures do not take advantage of certain methods of instruction; if the different methods of instruction were used in an adequate and balanced way, it would be to the advantage of all. (1993, p. 165)

The diversity of backgrounds within communities provides children with opportunities to develop a flexible facility with—or at least appreciation of—different patterns of communication that allow them to interact with each other and to provide leadership for their communities. For example, the value of skill in discourse occurring out of the context of productive activities, as well as of skilled observation and coordination in groups, is clear when we consider the challenges of both social harmony and technology that face everyone.

Learning New Ways and *Keeping Cultural Traditions in Communities Where Schooling Has Not Been Prevalent*

The idea that all communities can learn from each other without giving up what they value has implications for participation in the institution of schooling in communities in which schooling has not been prevalent. As traditional communities and minority communities in Western nations seek greater access to Western economic institutions, their children's involvement in schooling appears to be practically inevitable.

Understanding local patterns of communication both in and out of school may facilitate school involvement by people whose communities have not traditionally been involved in this institution. Many observers have referred to the difficulties faced by non-middle-class children in Western schools as a problem of disjunction between the communication styles of home and school (Barnhardt, 1982; Cazden & John, 1971; Dumont & Wax, 1969; Duranti & Ochs, 1986; Erickson & Mohatt, 1982; Foster, 1995; García, 1987; Gay, 2000; Levin, 1990; Lipka, 1998; Tharp, 1989; Valentine, 1971; Vogt, Jordan, & Tharp, 1987).

For people from backgrounds other than middle-class European or European American, learning the discourse practices of school sometimes occurs through instruction in such ways of talking. For example, a successful program for coaching economically impoverished mothers in reading with their preschool children relied on direct instruction in discourse patterns of school. It involved treating the children as conversational peers, asking known-answer (test) questions and praising children's responses, labeling, providing running commentary, and expanding on children's vocalizations (Edwards, 1989).

In addition, learning school discourse practices may be facilitated by extending familiar ways of talking to academic formats (Gay, 2000). African American urban high school students learned to engage in critical analysis of literature by extending their knowledge of the African American discourse practice of *signifying* to the analysis of texts in class (Lee, 1991, 1995). The students' metaphoric and ironic use of language in signifying has important parallels with the kind of critical thinking promoted in schools. (Reasoning metaphorically requires building parallel associations in the unstated relationship between the topic and the words actually used, and ironic reasoning requires rejection of the surface meaning of the words and construction of levels of meaning that contrast or contradict the literal meaning.)

With changes in the prevalence and importance of schooling, family practices change in some communities (e.g., Reese, 2002; Seymour, 1999). For example, during the past 50 years in the Guatemalan Mayan community of San Pedro, schooling has changed from enrolling only a few children for only a few years, to enrolling almost all children, with some achieving Ph.D.s, M.D.s, and law degrees. With greater experience of school, Mayan mothers were more likely to talk with their children in ways that were similar to those of middle-class European American mothers, compared with Mayan mothers with little or no experience in school. The highly schooled mothers gave their toddlers language lessons, acted as peers in conversation and play, and used mock excitement and praise to motivate involvement in their own agenda; with older children, highly schooled mothers took a more managerial role and divided a task rather than approaching it as a collaborative group (Chavajay & Rogoff, 2002; Rogoff et al., 1993). However, some

Mayan practices, such as use of simultaneous attention to ongoing events, do not differ with the extent of mothers' schooling.

In the debates surrounding how to assist schoolchildren from communities that have not traditionally been involved in school practices, many scholars have argued that adaptation of both home and school practices is ideal. Stuart McNaughton (1995) refers to this process as one of developing *dexterity*, in a collaborative approach optimizing both community and school practices. I would add that developing dexterity involves flexible use of several approaches—or combining to produce novel approaches—such that new ways do not necessarily substitute for prior ones, but complement them according to circumstances.

Immigrant Families Borrowing New Practices to Build on Cultural Traditions

People can borrow from the practices of others while building on what is important to them in their own cultural system, as shown in a study by Concha Delgado-Gaitan of how immigrant families modified their child-rearing practices. Mexican immigrant families in the United States often encounter a collision between the kind of thinking valued in schools, in which children are encouraged to question and argue, and their traditional value of respect. In showing respect, children are expected to listen well and participate in conversation with adults only when solicited. Raising questions would be seen as rebellious. Here is an example of a mother requiring respect from her preschool daughter, Rosa:

> Rosa ate her snack and then lingered at the table nibbling on her tortilla, becoming interested in her mother's conversation with her grandmother on the topic of her older brother. Mrs. Baca began to recount that her son's belligerence had been a real problem during the week and that on one day, he missed the school bus. Rosa decided to enter the conversation, "*Y se tuvo que quedar en la casa leyendo*" [And he had to stay home reading]. Mrs. Baca looked at Rosa sternly and said, "*Usted acaba de comer y vaya a jugar afuera. Estas son pláticas de adultos no para niñas. Es falta de respeto estar metiendo su cuchara*" [You finish eating and go outside to play. This is an adult conversation not for children. It's lack of respect for you to be putting in your two cents]. (1994; p. 65)

After several years participating in a parent-community organization that guided parents to carry out academic activities (such as reading stories and writing numbers) with their young children, the new immigrants encouraged their children to raise questions when involved in school-related activities. At the same time, they encouraged them to act with respect, not raising questions, during family routines.

In families that had been in the United States for a generation and had more schooling, respect remained a top priority in child rearing (more so than maintaining the Spanish language). However, negotiation between parents and children had also entered family discourse, indicating a narrowing of the range of application of the value of respect, as in the following example:

> It was after dinner, most of the family was watching TV. Four-year-old Paul called from his bedroom, "I don't want put on my pajamas yet Mom and Steve [older brother] says that I have to." "Well, you don't have to go to bed yet, dear, but I want you to start getting ready. Maybe I'll read you a story," responded his mother. Mr. Mendez then called to him also, "*Mi hijo* [my son], do as your mother says, come on be a good boy." "But how come Steve doesn't have to put on his pajamas right now? You pick on me cause I'm just a kid." "Paul, just put on your pajamas and stop whining." "I'm not whining or whatever you said I'm doing. That's not fair. Okay, if I put my pajamas right now can I come out there and watch TV?" "Okay, *mi hijo*, just for a few minutes," agreed his mother. (Delgado-Gaitan, 1994, p. 68)

Another change for families who had been in the United States for a generation was that family activities now had a conversational character, inviting more of their children's opinions and thoughts than in the new immigrant families. Indeed, those parents who were teachers often spoke to their children in a teacher-student style of discourse. In the Alva family, where both parents were born in the United States and both had attended university, little Philip's conversations with his parents show the kind of school discourse his parents have experienced and promote for their son:

> After school, Philip, who was three years old, his favorite book on zoo animals tucked under his arm, sat on the floor to "read." "Look Mom, look at the puppy." Mrs. Alva, washing dishes in the kitchen, stopped to look at the picture of the puppy in the book, "Yes, that's a coyote, look at his tail. Is that a short or long tail?"
>
> "Yeah, a tail; look Mom; look at the alligator. Oh look, what color is it? Green," he answered himself.
>
> "Look, Lipe [Philip], where does the alligator live?" asked his mother.
>
> Philip: "Water; look, look, look at the water. What color is it? Blue." His answer followed his question. Philip stayed on the kitchen

floor and continued leafing through the book, talking to himself when his mother walked out of the room, "A bear, oh a bear. Look, there's a seal, and more seals. How many? One, two, three, four, eleven." . . .

[At another time, while running errands:] Mr. Alva pointed to a plane and said, "Look, Lipe, there's a plane."
"Look at the plane. Look at the plane, daddy."
"Yeah, there it goes," responded the father. "Oh, look at the long truck, Lipe."
Philip calls out, "Daddy, daddy, the truck, oh look at the truck. What color? It's white," says Philip. (Delgado-Gaitan, 1994, p. 78)

Through the participation of these immigrant families in a parent-community organization in which they decided on their agendas for change, families reflected on their cultural values. They wanted their children to become respectful and cooperative people as they learned to *extend* their language patterns to *include* those learned in school. Parents could choose to help their children become skilled in two discourse patterns, rather than having to reject their language and culture to learn the ways of their new land. "The tacit expectation on the part of the parents is that both can and should co-exist and do not necessarily detract from one another" (Delgado-Gaitan, 1994, p. 82; see also Reese, 2002).

Learning New Ways and *Keeping Cultural Traditions in Communities Where Schooling Has Been Central*

Cross-fertilization of ideas has value for possible changes in schools and middle-class families as well. For example, keen observation of ongoing activity, responsibility for managing one's own learning, and smooth participation in groups may be fostered in middle-class communities in which these are not yet central practices:

The potentially positive interactive and adaptive verbal and interpretive habits learned by Black American children (as well as other non-mainstream groups) . . . represent skills that would benefit all youngsters: keen listening and observational skills, quick recognition and nuanced roles, rapid-fire dialogue, hard-driving argumentation, succinct recapitulating of an event, striking metaphors, and comparative analyses based on unexpected analogies. (Heath, 1989b, p. 370)

Converging efforts to change the conception of teaching and learning in schools build on aspects of learning in communities where informal learning, apprenticeship, and other forms of education prevail. Such restructuring of schools is partially motivated by changes in the organization of work, emphasizing the need to know how to work in groups (Cascio, 1995; Heath, 1989a). The changes do not simply import isolated features of informal or apprenticeship learning into the classroom for part of the day. Instead, the efforts build on coherent ideas from other cultural institutions of learning, creating a new approach.

In the new organization of classrooms as "communities of learners," teachers—along with students—engage in integrated projects of intrinsic interest to class members, often working together (Kasten, 1992; Lipka, 1998; Moll & Greenberg, 1990; Newman, Griffin, & Cole, 1989; Paradise, 1991; Pewewardy & Bushey, 1992; Rogoff et al., 2001; Tharp & Gallimore, 1988; Wells et al., 1990). These communities of learners focus on deliberate instruction; they differ from informal learning settings or apprenticeships in which some other function (such as getting work done) has priority over the instruction of the young.

The communities-of-learners approaches resemble informal learning and apprenticeship processes in several ways. Instead of inculcating skills out of the context in which they are actually used to solve problems, these new approaches focus on learning in the context of communicating and accomplishing goals. With such changes, classrooms move away from dyadic relationships between teachers responsible for filling students with knowledge and students expected to be willing receptacles (given some mock excitement, praise, and other motivators). Instead, the new approach involves complex group relationships among students who learn to take responsibility for contributing to their own learning and to the group's projects (Rogoff, 1994; Rogoff & Toma, 1997).

Cultural Variety as an Opportunity for Learning— for Individuals and Communities

Community change is sometimes treated as adding together several ways of doing things. This is a step beyond the idea that communities have to choose one way, deciding between traditional and outsiders' ways. But inspiration and borrowing of practices across communities may involve the emergence of new ideas, not simply the addition of one alternative to another (see Gutiérrez, Baquedano-López, & Tejeda, 1999; Walker, 2001).

The words of Hopi engineer and artist Al Qöyawayma convey this idea well—and they are applicable to changing practices in middle-class and other communities as well as to processes of change for Indians:

> Indian people today have a foot in two worlds, but we live one life.
> Our footing is often uncertain because each world is in continuous

state of change. The Indian people need to evaluate the best that is in our own culture and hang onto it; for it will always be foremost in our life. But we also need to take the best from other cultures to blend with what we already have. (1991; quoted in Deyhle & Swisher, 1997, p. 166)

Communities develop as generations of individuals make choices and invent solutions to changing circumstances. Borrowing and building on the practices of several communities can lead to cultural practices that creatively solve current problems of child rearing and community adaptation. Such adaptations go beyond the solutions of past generations who adapted to prior circumstances (as described in the accounts of historical change across generations in Chapter 3).

Awareness of a variety of approaches provides us with the chance to reflect on our own customary ways of thinking and doing things, and the chance to consider revisions if another way provides an intriguing idea (see also Camara, 1975). Such revisions constitute ordinary processes of continual development of communities. They do not require wholesale acceptance or rejection of another community's practices, as if a set of cultural practices could be treated as a static, unchanging recipe for life.

The diversity of ways that different communities handle life provide humanity with a reservoir of ideas and resources for the uncertainties of the future. As Piaget and other scholars of human development have observed, the challenge of considering different perspectives on a problem is often what impels advances in thinking. The goal is to learn creatively from each other, to be able to address new issues as well as those with which humans have struggled for generations.

The Creative Process of Learning from Cultural Variation

The creative and open process of learning across different communities' practices was well expressed by Don Miguel Angel Bixcul García, the retired elementary school principal of San Pedro, an indigenous Guatemalan Mayan. Don Miguel was very helpful in the early years of my research in San Pedro, over 25 years ago, helping me get oriented and facilitating my work with the children.

During a visit to San Pedro in 1999, I sat with Don Miguel in the modern living room of his daughter the doctor and reminisced about the striking changes in San Pedro. The town has retained a strong Mayan identity, maintaining Mayan language and ways while adopting many foreign technologies and practices (including cash cropping, facility in Spanish, literacy and schooling, television, fax, and e-mail). These are changes that many other Mayan communities have been slower to embrace.

I asked Don Miguel what he attributed San Pedro's unique character to. He reminded me that, even when I first arrived in San Pedro, families generally welcomed me into their homes. They were interested in conversing and comfortable in responding to my questions. He contrasted this with his own experience interviewing people in several nearby Mayan towns, where "outsiders" (like him) are given the cold shoulder.

Don Miguel explained his theory that San Pedro's openness to new ways—without giving up old ones—is a long-standing characteristic that can be seen across centuries. San Pedro, he explained, is a town that has always mixed cultural approaches, with the predominant Tz'utujil Maya at the base. It has integrated individuals from several other Maya groups (who speak distant as well as similar Mayan languages) and individuals of Spanish origin. Don Miguel pointed out the mixture of Tz'utujil, other Mayan, and Spanish surnames in San Pedro, including his own Tz'utujil and Spanish surnames (Bixcul from his father and García from his mother).

Don Miguel indicated that people in San Pedro have always been interested in new ideas and welcomed people from elsewhere to join the community. These did not challenge the Tz'utujil identity and heritage but enriched it, according to him. His ideas provide a powerful statement of the creative potential of communities that respect both their traditional ways and ideas they may adapt from others.

Another colleague from San Pedro, Don Agapito Cortez Peneleu, described (in 1998–1999) how he managed to maintain Mayan cultural practices and identity while selectively adapting aspects of foreign practices. Don Agapito was one of the town's first teachers who was of Mayan descent. For many decades, he taught the youngest students Spanish as a second language to prepare them for the primary grades, which were taught in Spanish, the national language, rather than the local Mayan language (see figure 9.4). Many of Don Agapito's students have since gone on to professional careers in fields such as teaching, medicine, accounting, and psychology. Don Agapito himself attended only a few grades of school. Years ago when he began to teach, there was a great need for teachers in rural areas and he was given the job without teacher training, as a person with more schooling than most in the region.

Don Agapito developed his teaching methods himself, on the job. They are remarkable for how they bridged the children's Mayan background with the new language and school skills they were learning. Don Agapito's classes contained upwards of 40 students, ranging from 6 to 11 years of age. To help the children learn Spanish, he divided them into teams

FIGURE 9.4

Don Agapito in 1975 teaching his Mayan students Spanish as a second language to prepare them to enter first grade.

of 10 and sent them out around town to observe and report back to the class what they saw. He told them to come back in 20 minutes, which gave them a need to learn numbers and to tell time. When they returned, the teams told their classmates in Spanish what they had seen. When they didn't know how to explain something in this new language, Don Agapito helped them with the Spanish vocabulary or expressions, also using the Mayan language to ensure understanding. The children clamored to tell the others what they had seen and were eager to learn the new vocabulary so they could do so. Don Agapito integrated other aspects of the curriculum into the children's accounts, asking questions such as "What color was the horse you saw?" to bring color terms into the discussion, and "How many legs did the horse have?" to begin a mathematical discussion.

Many other teachers at that time used rote memorization methods, but Don Agapito developed an integrated and motivating curriculum that made use of familiar Mayan ways of learning, such as observing and collaborating in groups. His teaching methods have features that some U.S. schools are beginning to prioritize, such as using the children's interests and contributions to extend their understanding of new concepts and motivating their learning through reporting information to interested classmates.

After Don Agapito had taught for many successful years, in 1970 the Guatemalan Ministry of Education issued an edict that all teachers must wear a tie and shined shoes. This was not a possibility that Don Agapito was willing to consider, as it would require him to give up a mark of his Mayan identity that was very important to him. His colorful traditional Mayan clothes, in the style that has been handwoven locally for generations, are recognizable to all as indicating that a man is Mayan from the town of San Pedro. The edict to wear a tie would require him to give this up. He told the school principal that he could not do so—he did not want to "lose his identity"—and asked the principal to release him from his teaching contract if wearing Mayan clothes was harming his ability to teach the children.

Of course, the principal, the other teachers, and the local families did not want Don Agapito to stop teaching. His colleagues, most of whom were not Mayan, tried to convince him that it was not a big deal to change his way of dressing. They told him that the few Mayan teachers in other towns were giving up their traditional clothing to comply with the government's edict. Don Agapito said, "That is their loss. I want to keep my identity. I am prepared to give up my job."

When his colleagues continued to try to persuade him to change to wearing Western business clothes, he finally said, "All right. I will do as you say. On one condition—I will switch to your kind of clothes, but you must switch to mine." His colleagues replied, aghast, "Oh, no, we couldn't do that!" Whereupon Don Agapito said, "You see? You can't switch to my kind of clothes, and I can't switch to yours. I am not you."

Eventually, the Guatemalan Ministry of Education made an exception in the edict after the state school superintendent presented a petition with a photo of Don Agapito. When Don Agapito retired, he was given a national award recognizing his teaching excellence, which he received proudly wearing Mayan clothes in front of an enormous applauding audience, who were dressed mostly in Western business clothes.

Now, most of the teachers in San Pedro are Mayan—a great many of them having begun their schooling in Don Agapito's class. Although some wear the traditional Mayan attire and others wear Western business clothing, they share pride in their Mayan heritage, continuing to speak Mayan as they fluently help others learn Spanish, and now English as well.

I myself have learned a tremendous amount from the privilege of being included in the lives of people in San Pedro, who have taught me about learning in and outside of school. From engaging with them, I have become aware of the role of participation in community activities as a basis of human development. I am grateful for the opportunity they have given me to step outside of many of my prior assumptions to become aware of regularities in sociocultural processes of human development across communities.

A Few Regularities

In the first pages of this book, I noted that research on human development has devoted a great deal of attention to trying to determine when one should expect children to be capable of certain skills. In discussing the age at which children develop responsibility for others or sufficient skill and judgment to handle dangerous implements, I gave some examples of striking variations across communities. As I then pointed out, it is important to go beyond being able to say "It depends" in response to questions about human development. Clearly, culture matters. The question is, how?

I have tried, in this book, to suggest some ways in which culture matters. In concluding, I would like to mention a few of the regularities that are most striking to me in making sense of the variations and similarities that can be seen in cultural communities around the world. They are regularities that have been discussed throughout this book.

The regularities that I mention are meant to characterize patterns of cultural *processes*—the cultural ways in which people can organize their way of life. I do not assume that the regularities characterize whole communities in an all-or-none fashion. Communities often vary in their use of the cultural patterns, showing different preferences and prevalence under different circumstances, not simply presence or absence of the patterns.

One of the most striking regularities of cultural processes involves the ways that children's learning opportunities are structured. In some cultural systems, children have the opportunity to learn by observing and pitching in to mature activities of the community. Children watch ongoing events keenly and listen closely to narratives and nearby conversations and contribute as they are ready. Their caregivers and companions offer access and often provide support and pointers in the context of shared community activities.

This cultural pattern contrasts with a model in which children are separated from the mature activities of their community and instead do exercises at home and at school to prepare them for their later entry into the adult world. Adults thus organize children's learning, using lessons out of the context of use of the skills and information taught. To encourage children's involvement, the adults try to motivate the children through such means as praise. They often ask known-answer questions to engage the children and test their understanding of the lessons. Instead of children joining adult activities, adults engage with children by entering into child-focused activities such as play and conversations on child-oriented topics.

This contrast seems to relate to broad historical patterns, including industrialization and the organization of people in bureaucratic institutions. For example, the school system organizes children in batches by age and tests their progress (and restricts access to resources) by reference to age and speed of reaching milestones. This places individuals in competition with each other for passing developmental milestones rapidly. The patterns may also relate to other historical changes, such as family size and structure and whether one or both parents work outside the home.

There seem also to be other contrasting patterns of organizing children's learning beyond the two I have focused on here. Another set of regularities centers around whether human relations are organized hierarchically, with one person attempting to control what others do, or horizontally, with mutual responsibility accompanied by respect for individual autonomy in decision making. This contrast relates to disciplinary practices within the family and institutions such as schools, as well as to community leadership and organization. Hierarchical or horizontal relations also seem to relate to whether prototypical relationships are between dyads or among multiparty groups. They seem to connect with the approach of privileging toddlers' desires and decisions until they are expected to understand how to cooperate voluntarily with the group, in contrast to treating infants according to the same rules as older children. Expectations of adversarial, competitive relations or cooperation appear related as well.

Another likely set of regularities involves strategies for child survival and care, connected with family size, infant mortality rates, and specialization of roles for attachment, caregiving, and play in extended families and sibling groups. Cultural patterns having to do with preferences for talk or taciturn engagement that prioritizes silence, gesture, and gaze may connect with some of the other patterns I have mentioned, but they probably also have their own story, yet to be told.

The shape of these and other possible patterns appeared throughout the book as I discussed cultural aspects of classic topics in the study of development, such as transitions across the life span, gender roles, interpersonal relations, cognitive development, and socialization. The regularities seem to relate to each other but not in simple dichotomies between populations. Rather, the processes involved seem to relate in constellations whose form has yet to be made explicit. Clearly, there is a great need for more research in these areas to help determine the patterns of variation and similarity in cultural practices that contribute to human development. My suggestions here are just a beginning.

Concluding with a Return to the Orienting Concepts

I conclude by restating the overarching orienting concept with which we began this exploration:

> *Humans develop through their changing participation in the sociocultural activities of their communities, which also change.*

This overarching orienting concept provides the basis of the other orienting concepts for understanding the role of cultural processes in human development. I hope that each of them is clearer and deeper now, after the intervening chapters. It seems fitting to conclude with them:

> *Culture isn't just what **other** people do.* Broad cultural experience gives us the opportunity to see the extent of cultural processes in our own everyday activities and development, which relate to the technologies we use and our institutional and community values and traditions.

> *Understanding one's own cultural heritage, as well as other cultural communities, requires taking the perspective of people of contrasting backgrounds.* The most difficult cultural processes to examine are the ones that are based on confident and unquestioned assumptions stemming from one's own community's practices. Cultural processes surround all of us and often involve subtle, tacit, taken-for-granted events and ways of doing things that require open eyes, ears, and minds to notice and understand. Children are very alert to learning from these taken-for-granted ways of doing things.

> *Cultural practices fit together and are connected.* They involve multifaceted relations among many aspects of community functioning. Cultural processes have a coherence beyond "elements" such as economic resources, family size, modernization, and urbanization. What is done one way in one community may be done another way in another community, with the same effect, and a practice done the same way in both communities may serve different ends. An understanding of how cultural practices fit together forming patterns of variation and similarity is essential.

> *Cultural communities continue to change, as do individuals.* A community's history and relations with other communities are part of cultural processes, occurring along with individuals' histories and relations with others. Variation across and within communities is a resource for humanity, allowing us to be prepared for varied and unknowable futures.

> *There is not likely to be One Best Way.* Understanding different cultural practices does not require determining which *one* way is "right" (which does not mean that *all* ways are fine). We can be open to possibilities that do not necessarily exclude each other. Learning from other communities does not require giving up one's own

ways, but it does require suspending one's assumptions temporarily to consider others and carefully separating efforts to understand cultural phenomena from efforts to judge their value. It is essential to make some guesses as to what the patterns are, while continually testing and open-mindedly revising one's guesses.

*There is **always** more to learn . . .*

REFERENCES

Abbott, S. (1992). Holding on and pushing away: Comparative perspectives on an Eastern Kentucky child-rearing practice. *Ethos, 20,* 33–65.

Abe, J. A., & Izard, C. E. (1999). Compliance, noncompliance strategies, and the correlates of compliance in 5-year-old Japanese and American children. *Social Development, 8,* 1–20.

Adams, A. K., & Bullock, D. (1986). Apprenticeship in word use: Social convergence processes in learning categorically related nouns. In S. A. Kuczaj & M. D. Barrett (Eds.), *The development of word meaning: Progress in cognitive development research* (pp. 155–197). New York: Springer-Verlag.

Adams, D., & Carwardine, M. (1990). *Last chance to see.* New York: Harmony Books.

Adams, D. A. (1996). Fundamental considerations: The deep meaning of Native American schooling, 1880–1900. In E. R. Hollins (Ed.), *Transforming curriculum for a culturally diverse society.* (pp. 27–57). Hillsdale, NJ: Erlbaum.

Ainsworth, M. D. S. (1977). Infant development and mother-infant interaction among Ganda and American families. In P. H. Leiderman, S. R. Tulkin, & A. Rosenfeld (Eds.), *Culture and infancy.* New York: Academic Press.

Akinnaso, F. N. (1992). Schooling, language, and knowledge in literate and nonliterate societies. *Comparative Studies in Society and History, 34,* 68–109.

Alcorta, M. (1994). Text writing from a Vygotskyan perspective: A sign-mediated operation. *European Journal of Psychology of Education, 9,* 331–341.

Althen, G. (1988). *American ways — A guide for foreigners in the United States.* Yarmouth, ME: Intercultural Press.

Anderson-Levitt, K. M. (1996). Behind schedule: Batch-produced children in French and U.S. classrooms. In B. A. Levinson, D. E. Foley, & D. C. Holland (Eds.), *The cultural production of the educated person: Critical ethnographies of schooling and local practice* (pp. 57–78). Albany: State University of New York Press.

Angelillo, C., Rogoff, B., & Morelli, G. (2002). *Age and kinship of young children's child partners in four communities.* Unpublished manuscript.

Apfelbaum, E. R. (2000). And now what, after such tribulations? *American Psychologist, 55,* 1008–1013.

Ariès, P. (1962). *Centuries of childhood.* New York: Knopf.

Arievitch, I., & van der Veer, R. (1995). Furthering the internalization debate: Gal'perin's contribution. *Human Development, 38,* 113–126.

Arnett, J. J. (2000). Emerging adulthood: A theory of development from the late teens though the twenties. *American Psychologist, 55,* 469–480.

Aronson, E., Blaney, N., Stephan, C., Sikes, J., & Snapp, M. (1978). *The jigsaw classroom.* Beverly Hills: Sage.

Ashton, P.T. (1975). Cross-cultural Piagetian research: An experimental perspective. *Harvard Educational Review, 45,* 475–506.

Azmitia, M., Cooper, C. R., Garcia, E. E., & Dunbar, N. (1996). The ecology of family guidance in low income Mexican-American and European-American families. *Social Development, 5,* 1–23.

Azuma, H. (1994). Two modes of cognitive socialization in Japan and the United States. In P. M. Greenfield & R. R. Cocking (Eds.), *Cross-cultural roots of minority child development* (pp. 275–284). Hillsdale, NJ: Erlbaum.

Bailyn, B. (1960). *Education in the forming of American society.* Chapel Hill: University of North Carolina Press.

Bakhurst, D. (1995). On the social constitution of mind: Bruner, Ilyenkov, and the defence of cultural psychology. *Mind, Culture, and Activity, 2,* 158–171.

Ballenger, C. (1992). Because you like us: The language of control. *Harvard Educational Review, 62,* 199–208.

Ballenger, C. (1999). *Teaching other people's children: Literacy and learning in a bilingual classroom.* New York: Teachers College Press.

Bandura, A. (1986). *Social foundations of thought and action: A social cognitive theory.* Englewood Cliffs, NJ: Prentice-Hall.

Barnhardt, C. (1982, December). *Tuning-in: Athabascan teachers and Athabascan students.* Paper presented at the meeting of the American Anthropological Association, Washington, DC.

Barth, F. (1994). Enduring and emerging issues in the analysis of ethnicity. In H. Vermeulen & C. Govers (Eds.), *The anthropology of ethnicity: Beyond "Ethnic groups and boundaries"* (pp. 11–32). Amsterdam: Het Spinhuis.

Basso, K. H. (1979). *Portraits of "The Whiteman": Linguistic play and cultural symbols among the Western Apache.* Cambridge, MA: Cambridge University Press.

Basso, K. H. (1984). Stalking with stories: Names, places, and moral narratives among the Western Apache. In E. M. Bruner & S. Plattner (Eds.), *Text, play and story: The construction of self and society* (pp. 19–55). Washington, DC: American Ethnological Society.

Bateson, G. (1936). *Naven.* Stanford, CA: Stanford University Press.

Bateson, G. (1972). *Steps to an ecology of mind.* New York: Ballantine Books.

Baugh, A. C., & Cable, T. (1978). *A history of the English language.* Englewood Cliffs, NJ: Prentice-Hall.

Baumrind, D. (1971). Current patterns of parental authority. *Developmental Psychology Monograph, 4,* 1–103.

Baumrind, D. (1972). An exploratory study of socialization effects on Black children: Some Black-White comparisons. *Child Development, 43,* 261–267.

Beach, B.A. (1988). Children at work: The home workplace. *Early Childhood Research Quarterly, 3*, 209–221.

Ben-Ari, E. (1996). From mothering to othering: Organization, culture, and nap time in a Japanese day-care center. *Ethos, 24*, 136–164.

Benedict, R. (1955). Continuities and discontinuities in cultural conditioning. In M. Mead & M. Wolfenstein (Eds.), *Childhood in contemporary cultures*. Chicago: University of Chicago Press.

Berger, P. L., & Luckmann, T. (1966). *The social construction of reality*. New York: Doubleday.

Berlin, B. (1992). *Ethnobiological classification: Principles of categorization of plants and animals in traditional societies*. Princeton: Princeton University Press.

Berry, J. W. (1969). On cross-cultural comparability. *International Journal of Psychology, 4*, 119–128.

Berry, J. W. (1999). Emics and etics: A symbiotic conception. *Culture & Psychology, 5*, 165–171.

Best, D. L., & Williams, J. E. (1997). Sex, gender, and culture. In J. W. Berry, M. H. Segall, & Ç. Kagitçibasi (Eds.), *Handbook of cross-cultural psychology: Vol. 3. Social behavior and applications*. (2nd ed., pp. 163–212). Needham Heights, MA: Allyn & Bacon.

Black, M. B. (1973). Ojibwa questioning etiquette and use of ambiguity. *Studies in Linguistics, 23*, 13–29.

Bloch, M.N. (1989). Young boys' and girls' play at home and in the community: A cultural-ecological framework. In M.N. Bloch & A.D. Pellegrini (Eds.), *The ecological context of children's play*. Norwood, NJ: Ablex.

Blount, B. G. (1972). Parental speech and language acquisition: Some Luo and Samoan examples. *Anthropological Linguistics, 14*, 119–130.

Bolin, A., & Whelehan, P. (1999). *Perspectives on human sexuality*. Albany: State University of New York Press.

Boorstin, D. J., et al. (1975). *We Americans*. Washington, DC: National Geographic Society.

Bornstein, M.H., Azuma, H., Tamis-LeMonda, C., & Ogino, M. (1990). Mother and infant activity and interaction in Japan and in the United States: I. A comparative macroanalysis of naturalistic exchanges. *International Journal of Behavioral Development, 13*, 267–287.

Boulton, M. J. (1995). Patterns of bully/victim problems in mixed race groups of children. *Social Development, 3*, 277–293.

Bourke, R., & Burns, J. (1998, June). *The chameleonic learner: The effect of multiple contexts on students' conceptions and experiences of learning*. Paper presented at the meetings of the International Society for Cultural Research and Activity Theory, Aarhus, Denmark.

Bowerman, M. (1981). Language development. In H. C. Triandis & A. Heron (Eds.), *Handbook of cross-cultural psychology* (Vol. 4). Boston: Allyn & Bacon.

Bowman, P. J., & Howard, C. (1985). Race-related socialization, motivation, and academic achievement: A study of Black youths in three-generation families. *Journal of the American Academy of Child Psychiatry, 24*, 134–141.

Boykin, A. W. (1994). Harvesting talent and culture: African-American children and educational reform. In R. J. Rossi (Ed.), *Schools and students at risk: Context and framework for positive change* (pp. 116–138). New York: Teachers College Press.

Brazelton, T. B. (1977). Implications of infant development among the Mayan Indians of Mexico. In P. H. Leiderman, S. R. Tulkin, & A. Rosenfeld (Eds.), *Culture and infancy*. New York: Academic Press.

Brazelton, T. B. (1990). Parent-infant cosleeping revisited. *Ab Initio, 2*, 1, 7.

Bremner, R. H. (Ed.). (1970). *Children and youth in America. A documentary history: Vols. I–II. 1600–1932*. Cambridge, MA: Harvard University Press.

Briggs, J. L. (1970). *Never in anger: Portrait of an Eskimo family*. Cambridge, MA: Harvard University Press.

Briggs, J. L. (1991). Expecting the unexpected: Canadian Inuit training for an experimental lifestyle. *Ethos, 19*, 259–287.

Bril, B., & Sabatier, C. (1986). The cultural context of motor development: Postural manipulations in the daily life of Bambara babies (Mali). *International Journal of Behavioral Development, 9*, 439–453.

Broker, I. (1983). *Night flying woman: An Ojibway Narrative*. (pp 18–24). St. Paul: Minnesota Historical Society Press.

Bronfenbrenner, U. (1979). *The ecology of human development*. Cambridge, MA: Harvard University Press.

Bronfenbrenner, U. (1992). Child care in the Anglo-Saxon mode. In M. E. Lamb, K. J. Sternberg, C.-P. Hwang, & A. G. Broberg (Eds.), *Child care in context* (pp. 281–291). Hillsdale, NJ: Erlbaum.

Brown, A. L., & Campione, J. C. (1990). Communities of learning and thinking, or a context by any other name. In D. Kuhn (Ed.), *Developmental perspectives on teaching and learning thinking skills: Vol. 21. Contributions in Human Development* (pp. 108–126). Basel: Karger.

Brown, J. S., & Duguid, P. (1994). Borderline issues: Social and material aspects of design. *Human-Computer Interaction, 9*, 3–36.

Brown, R. (1958). *Words and things*. New York: Free Press.

Bruffee, K. A. (1993). *Collaborative learning. Higher education, interdependence, and the authority of knowledge*. Baltimore: Johns Hopkins University Press.

Bruner, J. S. (1983). *Child's talk: Learning to use language*. New York: Norton.

Bruner, J. (1990). *Acts of meaning*. Cambridge, MA: Harvard University Press.

Burn, B., & Grossman, A. (1984). *Metropolitan children*. New York: Metropolitan Museum of Art.

Burton, L.M., Obeidallah, D.A., & Allison, K. (1996). Ethnographic insights on social context and adolescent development among inner-city African-American teens. In R. Jessor, A. Colby, & R. A. Shweder (Eds.), *Ethnography and human development* (pp. 395–418). Chicago: University of Chicago Press.

Burton, R., & Whiting, J. (1961). The absent father and cross-sex identity. *Merrill-Palmer Quarterly, 7*, 85–95.

Bushman, B. J., & Anderson, C. A. (2001). Media violence and the American public. *American Psychologist, 56*, 477–489.

Butterworth, G. (1987). Some benefits of egocentrism. In J. Bruner & H. Haste (Eds.), *Making sense: The child's construction of the world* (pp. 62–80). London: Methuen.

Byers, P., & Byers, H. (1972). Nonverbal communication and the education of children. In C. B. Cazden, V. P. John, & D. Hymes (Eds.), *Functions of language in the classroom*. New York: Academic.

Cajete, G. (1994). *Look to the mountain: An ecology of indigenous education*. Durango, CO: Kivaki Press.

Cajete, G. A. (1999). The Native American learner and bicultural science education. In K. G. Swisher & J. W. Tippeconnic III (Eds.), *Next steps: Research and practice to advance Indian education* (pp. 135–160). Charleston, WV: ERIC Clearinghouse on Rural Education and Small Schools.

Camara, S. (1975). The concept of heterogeneity and change among the Mandenka. *Technological Forecasting and Social Change, 7*, 273–284.

Camilleri, C., & Malewska-Peyre, H. (1997). Socialization and identity strategies. In J. W. Berry, P. R. Dasen, & T. S. Saraswathi (Eds.), *Handbook of cross-cultural psychology: Vol. 2. Basic processes and human development* (2nd ed., pp. 41–67). Needham Heights, NJ: Allyn and Bacon.

Campbell, D. T., & LeVine, R. A. (1961). A proposal for cooperative cross-cultural research on ethnocentrism. *Journal of Conflict Resolution, 5*, 82–108.

Carew, J. V. (1980). Experience and the development of intelligence in young children at home and in day care. *Monographs of the Society for Research in Child Development, 45* (6–7, Serial No. 187).

Carpenter, I. (1976). The tallest Indian. *American Education, 12*, 23–25.

Carraher, T. N., Carraher, D. W., & Schliemann, A. D. (1985). Mathematics in the streets and in schools. *British Journal of Developmental Psychology, 3*, 21–29.

Cascio, W. F. (1995). Whither industrial and organizational psychology in a changing world of work? *American Psychologist, 50*, 928–939.

Cauce, A. M., & Gonzales, N. (1993). Slouching towards culturally competent research: Adolescents and families of color in context. *Focus* (Publication of Division 45 of the American Psychological Association), *7*, 8–9.

Caudill, W., & Plath, D. W. (1966). Who sleeps by whom? Parent-child involvement in urban Japanese families. *Psychiatry, 29,* 344–366.

Caudill, W., & Weinstein, H. (1969). Maternal care and infant behavior in Japan and America. *Psychiatry, 32*, 12–43.

Cazden, C. B. (1979). *Classroom discourse.* Portsmouth, NH: Heinemann Educational.

Cazden, C. B., & John, V. P. (1971). Learning in American Indian children. In M. L. Wax, S. Diamond, & F. O. Gearing (Eds.), *Anthropological perspectives on education* (pp. 252–272). New York: Basic Books.

Chao, R. K. (1994). Beyond parental control and authoritarian parenting style: Understanding Chinese parenting through the cultural notion of training. *Child Development, 65*, 1111–1119.

Chao, R. K. (1995). Chinese and European American cultural models of the self reflected in mothers' childrearing beliefs. *Ethos, 23*, 328–354.

Chatwin, B. (1987). *The songlines.* New York: Penguin Books.

Chavajay, P. (1993). Independent analyses of cultural variations and similarities in San Pedro and Salt Lake. *Monographs of the Society for Research in Child Development, 58* (7, Serial No. 236).

Chavajay, P., & Rogoff, B. (2002). Schooling and traditional collaborative social organization of problem solving by Mayan mothers and children. *Developmental Psychology, 38*, 55–66.

Chen, X., Dong, Q., & Zhou, H. (1997). Authoritative and authoritarian parenting practices and social and school adjustment in Chinese children. *International Journal of Behavioural Development, 20*, 855–873.

Chisholm, J. S. (1996). Learning "respect for everything": Navajo images of development. In C. P. Hwang, M. E. Lamb, & I. E. Sigel (Eds.), *Images of childhood* (pp. 167–183). Mahwah, NJ: Erlbaum.

Chudacoff, H. P. (1989). *How old are you? Age consciousness in American culture.* Princeton: Princeton University Press.

Chude-Sokei, L. (1999). "Dr. Satan's Echo Chamber": Reggae, technology, and the diaspora process. *Emergences, 9*, 47–59.

Clark, C. M. (1988). Mothering in Sub-Saharan Africa and Black America. *Das Argument, 30*, 839–846.

Cleaves, C. (1994, November). *Domesticated Democrats: Domestic science training in American colonial education in the Philippines, 1900–1910.* Paper presented at the meetings of the American Anthropological Association, Atlanta, GA.

Cleverley, J. F. (1971). *The first generation: School and society in early Australia.* Sydney: Sydney University Press.

Clifford, J. (1988). *The predicament of culture.* Cambridge, MA: Harvard University Press.

Clifford, J. (1997). *Routes: Travel and translation in the late twentieth century.* Cambridge, MA: Harvard University Press.

Cobb, P., & Bowers, J. (1999). Cognitive and situated learning perspectives in theory and practice. *Educational Researcher, 28*, 4–15.

Cole, M. (1990). Cognitive development and formal schooling: The evidence from cross-cultural research. In L.C. Moll (Ed.), *Vygotsky and education.* Cambridge, England: Cambridge University Press.

Cole, M. (1995). The supra-individual envelope of development: Activity and practice, situation and context. In J. J. Goodnow, P. J. Miller, & F. Kessel (Eds.), *Cultural practices as contexts for development* (pp. 105–118). San Francisco: Jossey-Bass.

Cole, M. (1996). *Cultural psychology: A once and future discipline.* Cambridge, MA: Harvard University Press.

Cole, M., & Bruner, J. S. (1971). Cultural differences and inferences about psychological processes. *American Psychologist, 26*, 867–876.

Cole, M., & Cole, S. R. (1996). *The development of children* (3rd ed.). New York: W. H. Freeman.

Cole, M., Gay, J., Glick, J. A., & Sharp, D. W. (1971). *The cultural context of learning and thinking.* New York: Basic Books.

Cole, M., & Griffin, P. (1980). Cultural amplifiers reconsidered. In D. R. Olson (Ed.), *The social foundations of language and thought* (pp. 343–364). New York: Norton.

Cole, M., & Means, B. (1981). *Comparative studies of how people think.* Cambridge, MA: Harvard University Press.

Cole, M., & Scribner, S. (1977). Cross-cultural studies of memory and cognition. In R. V. Kail Jr., & J. W. Hagen (Eds.), *Perspectives on the development of memory and cognition.* Hillsdale, NJ: Erlbaum.

Cole, M., Sharp, D. W., & Lave, C. (1976). The cognitive consequences of education. *Urban Review, 9*, 218–233.

Collier, J., Jr. (1988). Survival at Rough Rock: A historical overview of Rough Rock Demonstration School. *Anthropology and Education Quarterly, 19*, 253–269.

Collier, J., Jr., & Buitrón, A. (1949). *The awakening valley.* Chicago: University of Chicago Press.

Collier, J., Jr., & Collier, M. (1986). *Visual anthropology: Photography as a research method* (rev. ed.) Albuquerque: University of New Mexico Press.

Comer, J. P. (1988). *Maggie's American dream: The life and times of a Black family.* New York: Plume/Penguin.

Condon, J. (1984). *With respect to the Japanese: A guide for Americans.* Yarmouth, ME: Intercultural Press.

Conley, D. (2000). *Honky.* Berkeley: University of California Press.

Cook-Gumperz, J., Corsaro, W. A., & Streeck, J., Eds. (1986). *Children's worlds and children's language.* Berlin: Mouton de Gruyter.

Cooper, R. P., & Aslin, R. N. (1989). The language environment of the young infant: Implications for early perceptual development. *Canadian Journal of Psychology, 43,* 247–265.

Coy, M. W. (Ed.). (1989a). *Apprenticeship: From theory to method and back again.* Albany: State University of New York Press.

Coy, M. W. (1989b). Being what we pretend to be: The usefulness of apprenticeship as a field method. In M. W. Coy (Ed.), *Apprenticeship: From theory to method and back again.* Albany: State University of New York Press.

Crago, M. B. (1988). *Cultural context in the communicative interaction of young Inuit children.* Unpublished doctoral dissertation, McGill University.

Crago, M. B. (1992). Communicative interaction and second language acquisition: An Inuit example. *TESOL Quarterly, 26,* 487–505.

Crago, M. B., Annahatak, B., Ningiuruvik, L. (1993). Changing patterns of language socialization in Inuit homes. *Anthropology and Education Quarterly, 24,* 205–223.

Crago, M. B., & Eriks-Brophy, A. (1994). Culture, conversation, and interaction. In J. Felson Duehan, L. Hewitt, & R. Sonnenmeier (Eds.), *Pragmatics from theory to practice* (pp. 43–58). Englewood Cliffs, NJ: Prentice-Hall.

Crook, C. (1994). *Computers and the collaborative experience of learning.* London: Routledge.

Crouter, N. (1979). *The segregation of youth from adults: A review of the literature with recommendations for future research.* Paper prepared for the National Institute of Education, Cornell University.

Dasen, P. R. (1977). *Piagetian psychology: Cross-cultural contributions.* New York: Gardner.

Dasen, P. R., & Heron, A. (1981). Cross-cultural tests of Piaget's theory. In H. C. Triandis & A. Heron (Eds.), *Handbook of cross-cultural psychology* (Vol. 4). Boston: Allyn & Bacon.

Deater-Deckard, K., Dodge, K.A., Bates, J.E., & Pettit, G.S. (1996). Physical discipline among African American and European American mothers: Links to children's externalizing behaviors. *Developmental Psychology, 32,* 1065–1072.

DeCasper, A.J., & Fifer, W.P. (1980). Of human bonding: Newborns prefer their mothers' voices. *Science, 208,* 1174–1176.

DeCasper, A.J., & Spence, M. (1986). Prenatal maternal speech influences newborns' perception of speech sounds. *Infant Behavior and Development, 9,* 133–150.

Delgado-Gaitan, C. (1994). Socializing young children in Mexican-American families: An intergenerational perspective. In P. M. Greenfield & R. R. Cocking (Eds.), *Cross-cultural roots of minority child development* (pp. 55–86). Hillsdale, NJ: Erlbaum.

DeLoache, J. S. (1984). What's this? Maternal questions in joint picturebook reading with toddlers. *Quarterly Newsletter of the Laboratory for Comparative Human Cognition, 6,* 87–95.

Delpit, L. D. (1988). The silenced dialogue: Power and pedagogy in educating other people's children. *Harvard Educational Review, 58,* 280–298.

Demos, J., & Demos, V. (1969). Adolescence in historical perspective. *Journal of Marriage and the Family, 31,* 632–638.

deVries, M. W., & deVries, M. R. (1977). Cultural relativity of toilet training readiness: A perspective from East Africa. *Pediatrics, 60,* 170–177.

Dewey, J. (1916). *Democracy and education.* New York: Macmillan.

Dewey, J. (1938). *Experience and education.* New York: Macmillan.

Deyhle, D. (1991). Empowerment and cultural conflict: Navajo parents and the schooling of their children. *Qualitative Studies in Education, 4,* 277–297.

Deyhle, D., & Margonis, F. (1995). Navajo mothers and daughters: Schools, jobs and the family. *Anthropology & Education Quarterly, 26,* 135–167.

Deyhle, D., & Swisher, K. (1997). Research in American Indian and Alaska Native education: From assimilation to self-determination. In M. W. Apple (Ed.), *Review of Research in Education, 22,* 113–194.

Diamond, A. (1999, Winter). Developmental psychology in its social and cultural context. *SRCD Newsletter, 42,* 5–8.

Diamond, J. (1992). *The third chimpanzee.* New York: HarperCollins.

Diaz, R. (1983). Thought and two languages: The impact of bilingualism on cognitive development. In E. Gordon (Ed.), *Review of research in education* (Vol. 10). Washington, DC: American Educational Research Association.

Dien, D. S-F. (1982). A Chinese perspective on Kohlberg's theory of moral development. *Developmental Review, 2,* 331–341.

Dillon, S. (1999, June 8). Smaller families to bring big change in Mexico. *New York Times,* pp. A1, A15.

Disney, R. (1998, June). Roy Disney '51 claims failure may be key to success. *Pomona College Magazine,* p. 5.

Dixon, S. D., LeVine, R. A., Richman, A., & Brazelton, T. B. (1984). Mother-child interaction around a teaching task: An African-American comparison. *Child Development, 55,* 1252–1264.

Dornbusch, S. M., Ritter, P. L., Leiderman, P. H., Roberts, D. F., & Fraleigh, M. J. (1987). The relation of parenting style to adolescent school performance. *Child Development, 58,* 1244–1257.

Dorsey-Gaines, C., & Garnett, C. M. (1996). The role of the Black Church in growing up literate: Implications for literacy research. In D. Hicks (Ed.), *Discourse, learning, and schooling* (pp. 247–266). New York: Cambridge University Press.

Drake, S. G. (1834). *Biography and history of the Indians of North America.* Boston: O.L. Perkins & Hilliard, Gray & Co.

Draper, P. (1975a). Cultural pressure on sex differences. *American Ethnologist, 4,* 602–616.

Draper, P. (1975b). !Kung women: Contrasts in sexual egalitarianism in foraging and sedentary contexts. In R. R. Reiter (Ed.), *Toward an anthropology of women* (pp. 77–109). New York: Monthly Review Press.

Draper, P. (1985). Two views of sex differences in socialization. In R. L. Hall, with P. Draper, M. E. Hamilton, D. Mc Guinness, C. M. Otten, and E. A. Roth (Eds.), *Male-female differences: A biocultural perspective.* New York: Praeger.

Dube, E. F. (1982). Literacy, cultural familiarity, and "intelligence" as determinants of story recall. In U. Neisser (Ed.), *Memory observed: Remembering in natural contexts* (pp. 274–292). San Francisco: Freeman.

Duensing, S. (2000). *Cultural influences on science museum practices: A case study.* Unpublished doctoral dissertation, California Institute of Integral Studies. (UMI Microform 9949651).

Dumont, R., & Wax, M. (1969). Cherokee School Society and the intercultural classroom. *Human Organization, 28,* 219–225.

Duran, R. P. (1994). Cooperative learning for language minority students. In R. A. DeVillar, C. J. Faltis, & J. Cummins (Eds.), *Cultural diversity in schools: From rhetoric to practice* (pp. 145–159). Buffalo: State University of New York Press.

Duranti, A., & Ochs, E. (1986). Literacy instruction in a Samoan village. In B. B. Schieffelin & P. Gilmore (Eds.), *The acquisition of literacy: Ethnographic perspectives*. Norwood, NJ: Ablex.

Eagly, A. H., & Wood, W. (1999). The origins of sex differences in human behavior. *American Psychologist, 54*, 408–423.

Eccles, J. S., Buchanan, C. M., Flanagan, C., Fuligni, A., Midgley, C., & Yee, D. (1991). Control versus autonomy during early adolescence. *Journal of Social Issues, 47*, 53–68.

Eckensberger, L. H., & Zimba, R. F. (1997). The development of moral judgment. In J. W. Berry, P. R. Dasen, & T. S. Saraswathi (Eds.), *Handbook of cross-cultural psychology: Vol. 2. Basic processes and human development* (pp. 299–338). Boston: Allyn and Bacon.

Eckerman, C. O., Whatley, J. L., & McGhee, L. J. (1979). Approaching and contacting the object another manipulates: A social skill of the one-year-old. *Developmental Psychology, 15*, 585–593.

Eckert, P. (1994). *Entering the heterosexual marketplace: Identities of subordination as a developmental imperative*. Institute for Research on Learning, Working papers on learning and identity, No. 2.

Edwards, C. P. (1981). The comparative study of the development of moral judgment and reasoning. In R. H. Munroe, R. L. Munroe, & B. B. Whiting (Eds.), *Handbook of cross-cultural human development* (pp. 501–528). New York: Academic.

Edwards, C. P. (1993). Behavioral sex differences in children of diverse cultures: The case of nurturance to infants. In M. E. Pereira & L. A. Fairbanks (Eds.), *Juvenile primates: Life history, development, and behavior*. New York: Oxford University Press.

Edwards, C. P. (1994, April). *Cultural relativity meets best practice, OR anthropology and early education, a promising friendship*. Paper presented at the meetings of the American Educational Research Association, New Orleans.

Edwards, C. P., & Whiting, B. B. (1992). "Mother, older sibling and me": The overlapping roles of caregivers and companions in the social world of two- to three-year-olds in Ngeca, Kenya. In K. MacDonald (Ed.), *Parent-child play: Descriptions and implications*. Albany: State University of New York Press.

Edwards, P. A. (1989). Supporting lower SES mothers' attempts to provide scaffolding for book reading. In J. Allen & J. M. Mason (Eds.), *Risk makers, risk takers, risk breakers*. Portsmouth, NH: Heinemann Educational.

Ehrenreich, B., & English, D. (1978). *For her own good: 150 years of the expert's advice to women*. Garden City, New York: Anchor Press/Doubleday.

Eisenberg, A. R. (1986). Teasing: Verbal play in two Mexicano homes. In B. B. Schieffelin & E. Ochs (Eds.), *Language socialization across cultures* (pp. 182–198). Cambridge, England: Cambridge University Press.

Ellis, R. (1997). Color at Cal. In I. Reed (Ed.), *MultiAmerica: Essays on cultural wars and cultural peace* (pp. 395–399) New York: Viking.

Ellis, S. (1997). Strategy choice in sociocultural context. *Developmental Review, 17*, 490–524.

Ellis, S., & Gauvain, M. (1992). Social and cultural influences on children's collaborative interactions. In L. T. Winegar & J. Valsiner (Eds.), *Children's development within social context*. Hillsdale, NJ: Erlbaum.

Ellis, S., Rogoff, B., & Cromer, C. C. (1981). Age segregation in children's social interactions. *Developmental Psychology, 17*, 399–407.

Ellis, S., & Siegler, R. S. (1997). Planning as a strategy choice, or why don't children plan when they should? In S. L. Friedman & E. K. Scholnick (Eds.), *The developmental psychology of planning: Why, how, and when do we plan?* (pp. 183–208). Mahwah, NJ: Erlbaum.

Ember, C. R. (1973). Feminine task assignment and the social behavior of boys. *Ethos, 1,* 424–439.

Ember, C. R. (1981). A cross-cultural perspective on sex differences. In Munroe, R. H., Munroe, R. L., & Whiting, B. B. (Eds.), *Handbook of cross-cultural human development* (pp. 531–580) New York: Garland.

Engeström, Y. (1990) *Learning, working and imagining.* Helsinki: Orienta-Konsultit Oy.

Engeström, Y. (1993). Developmental studies of work as a testbench of activity theory: The case of primary care medical practice. In S. Chaiklin & J. Lave (Eds.), *Understanding practice: Perspectives on activity and context* (pp. 64–103). Cambridge, England: Cambridge University Press.

Erickson, F., & Mohatt, G. (1982). The cultural organization of participation structures in two classrooms of Indian students. In G. Spindler (Ed.), *Doing the ethnography of schooling* (pp. 132–174) New York: Holt, Rinehart, & Winston.

Fadiman, A. (1997). *The spirit catches you and you fall down: A Hmong child, her American doctors, and the collision of two cultures.* New York: Farrar, Straus and Giroux.

Farran, D. (1982). Mother-child interaction, language development, and the school performance of poverty children. In L. Feagans & D. C. Farran (Eds.), *The language of children reared in poverty.* New York: Academic Press.

Farran, D., Mistry, J., Ai-Chang, M., & Herman, H. (1993). Kin and calabash: The social networks of preschool part-Hawaiian children. In R. Roberts (Ed.), *Coming home to preschool: The sociocultural context of early education.* Norwood, NJ: Ablex.

Farver, J. M. (1993). Cultural differences in scaffolding pretend play: A comparison of American and Mexican mother-child and sibling-child pairs. In K. MacDonald (Ed.), *Parent-child play: Descriptions and implications* (pp. 349–366). Albany: State University of New York Press.

Farver, J. M. (1999). Activity setting analysis: A model for examining the role of culture in development. In A. Göncü (Ed.), *Children's engagement in the world: Sociocultural perspectives.* Cambridge, England: Cambridge University Press.

Farver, J. M., Kim, Y. K., & Lee, Y. (1995). Cultural differences in Korean- and Anglo-American preschoolers' social interaction and play behaviors. *Child Development, 66,* 1088–1099.

Feinman, S. (1982). Social referencing in infancy. *Merrill-Palmer Quarterly, 28,* 445–470.

Ferber, R. (1986). *Solve your child's sleep problems.* New York: Simon & Schuster.

Ferdman, B. M. (2000). "Why am I who I am?" Constructing the cultural self in multicultural perspective. *Human Development, 43,* 19–23.

Fernald, A. (1988, November). *The universal language: Infants' responsiveness to emotion in the voice.* Paper presented at the Developmental Psychology Program, Stanford University.

Field, T. M., Sostek, A. M., Vietze, P., & Leiderman, P. H. (Eds.). (1981). *Culture and early interactions.* Hillsdale, NJ: Erlbaum.

Fisher, C. B., Jackson, J. F., & Villarruel, F. A. (1998). The study of African-American and Latin American children and youth. In R. M. Lerner (Ed.), *Vol. 1: Theoretical models of human development* (pp. 1145–1207) of W. Damon (Ed.-in-chief), *Handbook of child psychology* (5th edition). New York: Wiley.

Fiske, A. P. (1995). *Learning a culture the way informants do: Observing, imitating, and participating.* Unpublished manuscript, Bryn Mawr University.

Fitchen, J. M. (1981). *Poverty in rural America: A case study.* Boulder, CO: Westview Press.

Fobih, D. K. (1979). *The influence of different educational experiences on classificatory and verbal reasoning behavior of children in Ghana.* Unpublished doctoral dissertation, University of Alberta.

Fortes, M. (1970). Social and psychological aspects of education in Taleland. In J. Middleton (Ed.), *From child to adult.* New York: National History Press. (Original work published Fortes 1938)

Foster, M. (1995). African American teachers and culturally relevant pedagogy. In J. A. Banks & C. M. Banks (Eds.), *Handbook of research on multicultural education* (pp. 570–581). New York: Macmillan.

Fox, N. A. (1977). Attachment of Kibbutz infants to mother and metapelet. *Child Development, 48,* 1228–1239.

Freed, R. S., & Freed, S. A. (1981). *Enculturation and education in Shanti Nagar* (Anthropological Papers of the American Museum of Natural History, Vol. 57, Pt. 2). New York: American Museum of Natural History.

Freeman, M.A. (1978). *Life among the Qallunaat.* Edmonton, Canada: Hurtig Publishers.

French, D. C., Jansen, E. A., & Pidada, S. (2002). United States and Indonesian children's and adolescents' reports of relational aggression by disliked peers. *Child Development, 73,* 1143–1150.

Frijda, N., & Jahoda, G. (1966). On the scope and methods of cross-cultural research. *International Journal of Psychology, 1,* 109–127.

Fung, H. H. T. (1995, March). *Becoming a moral child: The role of shame in the socialization of young Chinese children.* Paper presented at the Society for Research in Child Development, Indianapolis.

Gallimore, R., Boggs, S., & Jordan, C. (1974). *Culture, behavior, and education: A study of Hawaiian-Americans.* Beverly Hills, CA: Sage.

García, E. (1987). Interactional style of teachers and parents during bilingual instruction. *Ethnolinguistic Issues in Education, 21,* 39–51.

García Coll, C., Lamberty, G., Jenkins, R., McAdoo, H. P., Crnic, K., Wasik, B. H., & García, H. V. (1996). An integrative model for the study of developmental competencies in minority children. *Child Development, 67,* 1891–1914.

Gardner, R., & Heider, K.G. (1968). *Gardens of war.* New York: Random House.

Gaskins, S., & Lucy J. A. (1987, May). *The role of children in the production of adult culture: A Yucatec case.* Paper presented at the meeting of the American Ethnological Society, San Antonio, TX.

Gaskins, S., Miller, P. J., & Corsaro, W. A. (1992). Theoretical and methodological perpsectives in the interpretive study of children. In W. A. Corsaro & P. J. Miller (Eds.), *Interpretive approaches to children's socialization.* San Francisco: Jossey-Bass.

Gauvain, M. (1993). Spatial thinking and its development in sociocultural context. *Annals of Child Development, 9,* 67–102.

Gauvain, M. (1995). Influence of the purpose of an interaction on adult-child planning. *Infancia y Aprendizaje, 69–70,* 141–155.

Gay, G. (2000). *Culturally responsive teaching: Theory, research, and practice.* New York: Teachers College Press.

Gee, J. P. (1989). The narrativization of experience in the oral style. *Journal of Education, 171,* 75–96.

Getis, V. L., & Vinovskis, M. A. (1992). History of child care in the United States before 1950. In M. E. Lamb, K. J. Sternberg, C.-P. Hwang, & A. G. Broberg (Eds.), *Child care in context* (pp. 185–206). Hillsdale, NJ: Erlbaum.

Gewirtz, J. L. (1965). The course of infant smiling in four child-rearing environments in Israel. In B. M. Foss (Ed.), *Determinants of infant behavior* (Vol. 3). London: Methuen.

Giaconia, R. M., & Hedges, L. V. (1982). Identifying features of effective open education. *Review of Educational Research, 52,* 579–602.

Gibson, J. J. (1979). *The ecological approach to visual perception.* Boston: Houghton Mifflin.

Gibson, M. A. (1988). *Accommodation without assimilation: Sikh immigrants in an American high school.* Ithaca, NY: Cornell University Press.

Gick, M. L., & Holyoak, K. J. (1980). Analogical problem solving. *Cognitive Psychology, 12,* 306–355.

Gilligan, C., Lyons, N. P., & Hanmer, T. J. (Eds.). (1990). *Making connections: The relational worlds of adolescent girls at Emma Willard School.* Cambridge, MA: Harvard University Press.

Ginsburg, H. P., Posner, J. K., & Russell, R. L. (1981). The development of mental addition as a function of schooling and culture. *Journal of Cross-Cultural Psychology, 12,* 163–178.

Gjerde, P. F., & Onishi, M. (2000). In search of theory: The study of "ethnic groups" in developmental psychology. *Journal of Research on Adolescence, 10,* 291–299.

Gladwin, T. (1971). *East is a big bird.* Cambridge, MA: Harvard University Press.

Goldberg, S. (1972). Infant care and growth in urban Zambia. *Human Development, 15,* 77–89.

Goldberg, S. (1977). Infant development and mother-infant interaction in urban Zambia. In P. H. Leiderman, S. R. Tulkin, & A. Rosenfeld (Eds.), *Culture and infancy.* New York: Academic Press.

Göncü, A. (1987). Toward an interactional model of developmental changes in social pretend play. In L. G. Katz & K. Steiner (Eds.), *Current topics in early childhood education* (Vol. 7, pp. 126–149). Norwood, NJ: Ablex.

Göncü, A. (1993). Guided participation in Keçioren. In B. Rogoff, J. Mistry, A. Göncü, & C. Mosier, *Guided participation in cultural activity by toddlers and caregivers. Monographs of the Society for Research in Child Development, 58* (7, Serial No. 236, pp. 126–147).

Goodnow, J. J. (1962). A test of milieu effects with some of Piaget's tasks. *Psychological Monographs, 76* (36, Whole No. 555).

Goodnow, J. J. (1976). The nature of intelligent behavior: Questions raised by cross-cultural studies. In L. B. Resnick (Ed.), *The nature of intelligence.* Hillsdale, NJ: Erlbaum.

Goodnow, J. J. (1980). Everyday concepts of intelligence and its development. In N. Warren (Ed.), *Studies in cross-cultural psychology* (Vol. 2, pp. 191–219). London: Academic Press.

Goodnow, J. J. (1990). The socialization of cognition: What's involved? In J.W. Stigler, R.A. Shweder, & G. Herdt (Eds.), *Cultural psychology* (pp. 259–286). Cambridge, England: Cambridge University Press.

Goodnow, J. J. (1993). Direction of post-Vygotskian research. In E. A. Forman, N. Minick, & C. A. Stone (Eds.), *Contexts for learning: Sociocultural dynamics in children's development* (pp. 369–381). New York: Oxford University Press.

Goodnow, J. J., Cashmore, J., Cotton, S., & Knight, R. (1984). Mothers' developmental timetables in two cultural groups. *International Journal of Psychology, 19,* 193–205.

Goodwin, M. H. (1990). *He-said-she-said: Talk as social organization among Black children.* Bloomington: Indiana University Press.

Goody, E. N. (1978). Towards a theory of questions. In E. N. Goody (Ed.), *Questions and politeness* (pp. 17–43). Cambridge, England: Cambridge University Press.

Goody, J. (1977). *The domestication of the savage mind.* Cambridge, England: Cambridge University Press.

Goody, J., & Watt, I. (1968). The consequences of literacy. In J. R. Goody (Ed.), *Literacy in traditional societies.* Cambridge, England: Cambridge University Press.

Gossen, G. H. (1976). Verbal dueling in Chamula. In B. Kirshenblatt-Gimblett (Ed.), *Speech play* (pp. 121–146). Philadelphia: University of Pennsylvania Press.

Graves, N. B., & Graves, T. D. (1983). The cultural context of prosocial development: An ecological model. In D. L. Bridgeman (Ed.), *The nature of prosocial development* (pp. 243–264). New York: Academic.

Graves, Z. R., & Glick, J. (1978). The effect of context on mother-child interaction. *Quarterly Newsletter of the Institute for Comparative Human Development, 2,* 41–46.

Greene, M. (1986). Philosophy and teaching. In M. C. Wittrock (Ed.), *Handbook of research on teaching* (3rd ed., pp. 479–501). New York: Macmillan.

Greenfield, P. J. (1996). Self, family, and community in White Mountain Apache society. *Ethos, 24,* 491–509.

Greenfield, P. M. (1966). On culture and conservation. In J. S. Bruner, R. R. Olver, & P. M. Greenfield (Eds.), *Studies in cognitive growth.* New York: Wiley.

Greenfield, P. M. (1974). Comparing dimensional categorization in natural and artificial contexts: A developmental study among the Zinacantecos of Mexico. *Journal of Social Psychology, 93,* 157–171.

Greenfield, P. M. (1984). A theory of the teacher in the learning activities of everyday life. In B. Rogoff & J. Lave (Eds.), *Everyday cogniton: Its development in social context.* Cambridge, MA: Harvard University Press.

Greenfield, P. M., & Childs, C. P. (1977). Understanding sibling concepts: A developmental study of kin terms in Zinacantan. In P. R. Dasen (Ed.), *Piagetian psychology: Cross-cultural contributions.* New York: Gardner.

Greenfield, P. M., & Lave, J. (1982). Cognitive aspects of informal education. In D. Wagner & H. Stevenson (Eds.), *Cultural perspectives on child development.* San Francisco: Freeman.

Greenfield, P. M., & Smith, J. (1976). *The structure of communication in early language development.* New York: Academic.

Greenfield, P. M., & Suzuki, L. K. (1998). Culture and human development: Implications for parenting, education, pediatrics, and mental health. In W. Damon (General Ed.) & I. E. Sigel & K. A. Renninger (Vol. Eds.), *Handbook of child psychology: Vol. 4. Child psychology in practice* (5th ed.). New York: Wiley.

Griego, M.C., Bucks, B. L., Gilbert, S. S., & Kimball, L.H. (1981). *Tortillitas para Mamá and other nursery rhymes.* New York: Holt.

Grob, C. S., & Dobkin de Rios, M. (1994). Hallucinogens, managed states of consciousness, and adolescents: Cross-cultural perspectives. In P. K. Bock (Ed.),

Handbook of psychological anthropology (pp. 315–329). Westport, CT: Greenwood Press.

Grossmann, K., Grossmann, K. E., Spangler, G., Suess, G., & Unzner, L. (1985). Maternal sensitivity and newborns' orientation responses as related to quality of attachment in northern Germany. In I. Bretherton & E. Waters (Eds.), *Growing points of attachment theory and research. Monographs of the Society for Research in Child Development, 50* (1–2, Serial no. 209, pp. 233–256).

Gump, P., Schoggen, P., & Redl, F. (1963). The behavior of the same child in different milieus. In R. C. Barker (Ed.), *The stream of behavior.* New York: Appleton-Century-Crofts.

Gundlach, R., McLane, J. B., Stott, F. M., & McNamee, G. D. (1985). The social foundations of children's early writing development. In M. Farr (Ed.), *Advances in writing research* (Vol. 1). Norwood, NJ: Ablex.

Guthrie, P. (2001). "Catching sense" and the meaning of belonging on a South Carolina Sea Island. In S. S. Walker (Ed.), *African roots/American cultures: Africa in the creation of the Americas* (pp. 275–283). Lanham, MD: Rowman & Littlefield.

Gutiérrez, K. D., Baquedano-López, P., & Tejada, C. (1999). Rethinking diversity: Hybridity and hybrid language practices in the third space. *Mind, Culture, and Activity, 6,* 286–303.

Gutierrez, R. A. (1991). *When Jesus came, the Corn Mothers went away.* Stanford, CA: Stanford University Press.

Haight, W. L. (1998). "Gathering the spirit" at First Baptist Church: Spirituality as a protective factor in the lives of African American children. *Social Work, 43,* 213–221.

Haight, W. L. (1999). The pragmatics of caregiver-child pretending at home: Understanding culturally specific socialization practices. In A. Göncü (Ed.), *Children's engagement in the world: Sociocultural perspectives.* Cambridge, England: Cambridge University Press.

Haight, W. L. (2002). *African-American children at church: A sociocultural perspective.* Cambridge, UK: Cambridge University Press.

Haight, W. L., Parke, R. D., & Black, J. E. (1997). Mothers' and fathers' beliefs about and spontaneous participation in their toddlers' pretend play. *Merrill-Palmer Quarterly, 43,* 271–290.

Haight, W. L., Wang, X., Fung, H. H., Williams, K., & Mintz, J. (1999). Universal, developmental, and variable aspects of young children's play: A cross-cultural comparison of pretending at home. *Child Development, 70,* 1477–1488.

Hale-Benson, J. E. (1986). *Black children: Their roots, culture, and learning styles.* Baltimore, MD: Johns Hopkins University Press.

Haley, A. (1972). *My furthest-back person — The African.* New York, Paul R. Reynolds. [Quotations from excerpted version in Weitzman, D. (1976). *Underfoot: An everyday guide to exploring the American past.* New York: Scribner.]

Hall, A. J. (1990). Immigration today. *National Geographic, 178,* 103–105.

Hall, J. W. (1972). Verbal behavior as a function of amount of schooling. *American Journal of Psychology, 85,* 277–289.

Haney, C. (1995). The social context of capital murder: Social histories and the logic of mitigation. *Santa Clara Law Review, 35,* 547–609.

Hanks, C., & Rebelsky, F. (1977). Mommy and the midnight visitor: A study of occasional co-sleeping. *Psychiatry, 40,* 277–280.

Hareven, T. (1985). Historical changes in the family and the life course: Implications for child development. In A. B. Smuts & J. W. Hagen (Eds.), *History and research*

*in child development. Monographs of the Society for Research in Child Development,
50* (4–5, Serial no. 211, pp. 8–23).

Hareven, T. K. (1989). Historical changes in children's networks in the family and
community. In D. Belle (Ed.), *Children's social networks and social supports* (pp.
15–36). New York: Wiley.

Harkness, S., Edwards, C. P., & Super, C. M. (1977). *Kohlberg in the bush: A study of
moral reasoning among the elders of a rural Kipsigis community.* Paper presented at
the meeting of the Society for Cross-Cultural Research, East Lansing, MI.

Harkness, S., & Super, C. M. (1977). Why African children are so hard to test. In
L. L. Adler (Ed.), *Issues in cross-cultural research. Annals of the New York Academy
of Sciences, 285,* 326–331.

Harkness, S., & Super, C. M. (1983). The cultural construction of child development:
A framework for the socialization of affect. *Ethos, 11,* 221–231.

Harkness, S., & Super, C. M. (1985). The cultural context of gender segregation in
children's peer groups. *Child Development, 56,* 219–224.

Harkness, S., & Super, C. M. (1987). Fertility change, child survival, and child development: Observations on a rural Kenyan community. In N. Scheper-Hughes
(Ed.), *Child survival* (pp. 59–70). Boston: D. Reidel.

Harkness, S., & Super, C. M. (1992a). Parental ethnotheories in action. In I. E. Sigel,
A. V. McGillicuddy-DeLisi, & J. J. Goodnow (Eds.), *Parental belief systems* (pp.
373–391). Hillsdale, NJ: Erlbaum.

Harkness, S., & Super, C. M. (1992b). Shared child care in East Africa: Sociocultural
origins and developmental consequences. In M. E. Lamb, K. J. Sternberg, C.-P.
Hwang, & A. G. Broberg (Eds.), *Child care in context* (pp. 441–459). Hillsdale,
NJ: Erlbaum.

Harkness, S., Super, C. M., & Keefer, C. H. (1992). Learning to be an American
parent: How cultural models gain directive force. In R. G. D'Andrade & C.
Strauss (Eds.), *Human motivation and cultural models* (pp. 163–178). Cambridge,
England: Cambridge University Press.

Harrison, A. O., Wilson, M. N., Pine, C. J., Chan, S. Q., & Buriel, R. (1990). Family
ecologies of ethnic minority children. *Child Development, 61,* 347–362.

Hartup, W. W. (1977, Fall). Peers, play, and pathology: A new look at the social behavior of children. *Newsletter of the Society for Research in Child Development.*

Harwood, R. L., Miller, J. G., & Irizarry, N. L. (1995). *Culture and attachment: Percep-
tions of the child in context.* New York: Guilford.

Hatano, G. (1982). Cognitive consequences of practice in culture specific procedural skills.
Quarterly Newsletter of the Laboratory of Comparative Human Cognition, 4, 15–17.

Hatano, G. (1988). Social and motivational bases for mathematical understanding. In
G. B. Saxe & M. Gearhart (Eds.), *Children's mathematics* (pp. 55–70). San Francisco: Jossey-Bass.

Hatano, G., & Inagaki, K. (1996, May). *Cultural contexts of schooling revisited.* Paper
presented at the conference "Global prospects for education: Development, culture, and schooling," Ann Arbor, MI.

Hatano, G., & Inagaki, K. (2000). Domain-specific constraints of conceptual development. *International Journal of Behavioral Development, 24,* 267–275.

Hawkins, J. (1987, April). *Collaboration and dissent.* Paper presented at the meetings of
the Society for Research in Child Development, Baltimore, MD.

Hay, D. F. (1980). Multiple functions of proximity seeking in infancy. *Child Development, 51,* 636–645.

Hay, D. F., Murray, P., Cecire, S., & Nash, A. (1985). Social learning of social behavior in early life. *Child Development, 56*, 43–57.

Haynes, N. M., & Gebreyesus, S. (1992). Cooperative learning: A case for African American students. *School Psychology Review, 21*, 577–585.

Hays, W. C., & Mindel, C. H. (1973). Extended kinship relations in Black and White families. *Journal of Marriage and the Family, 35*, 51–57.

Heath, S. B. (1982). What no bedtime story means: Narrative skills at home and school. *Language in Society, 11*, 49–76.

Heath, S. B. (1983). *Ways with words: Language, life, and work in communities and classrooms*. Cambridge, England: Cambridge University Press.

Heath, S. B. (1989a). The learner as cultural member. In M. L. Rice & R. L. Schiefelbusch (Eds.), *The teachability of language*. Baltimore: Paul H. Brookes.

Heath, S. B. (1989b). Oral and literate traditions among Black Americans living in poverty. *American Psychologist, 44*, 367–373.

Heath, S. B. (1991). "It's about winning!" The language of knowledge in baseball. In L. B. Resnick, J. M. Levine, & S. D. Teasley (Eds.), *Perspectives on socially shared cognition*. Washington, DC: American Psychological Association.

Heath, S. B. (1998). Working through language. In S.M. Hoyle & C. Temple Adger (Eds.), *Kids talk: Strategic language use in later childhood* (pp. 217–240). Oxford: Oxford University Press.

Hendry, J. (1986). *Becoming Japanese: The world of the preschool child*. Honolulu: University of Hawaii Press.

Henry, J. (1955). Culture, education, and communications theory. In G. D. Spindler (Ed.), *Education and anthropology*. Stanford, CA: Stanford University Press.

Hentoff, N. (1976). How does one learn to be an adult? In S. White (Ed.), *Human development in today's world*. Boston: Little, Brown.

Henze, R. C. (1992). *Informal teaching and learning: A study of everyday cognition in a Greek community*. Hillsdale NJ: Erlbaum.

Hernandez, D. J. (1993). *America's children: Resources from family, government, and the economy*. New York: Russell Sage Foundation.

Hernandez, D. J. (1994, Spring). Children's changing access to resources: A historical perspective. *Society for Research in Child Development Social Policy Report, 8* (1), 1–23.

Hewlett, B. S. (1991). *Intimate fathers: The nature and context of Aka Pygmy paternal infant care*. Ann Arbor: University of Michigan Press.

Hewlett, B. S. (1992). The parent-infant relationship and social-emotional development among Aka Pygmies. In J. L. Roopmarine & D. B. Carter (Eds.), *Parent-child socialization in diverse cultures* (pp. 223–243). Norwood, NJ: Ablex.

Hicks, G. (1976). *Appalachian valley*. New York: Holt, Rinehart & Winston.

Highwater, J. (1995). The intellectual savage. In N. R. Goldberger & J. B. Veroff (Eds.), *The culture and psychology reader*. New York: New York University Press.

Hilliard, A. G., III, & Vaughn-Scott, M. (1982). The quest for the "minority" child. In S. G. Moore & C. R. Cooper (Eds.), *The young child: Reviews of research* (Vol. 3, pp. 175–189). Washington, DC: National Association for the Education of Young Children.

Hoffman, D. M. (1997, November). *Interrogating identity: New visions of self and other in the study of education*. Paper presented at the meeting of the American Anthropological Association, Washington, DC.

Hogbin, H. I. (1943). A New Guinea infancy: From conception to weaning in Wogeo. *Oceania, 13*, 285–309.

Holliday, B.G. (1985). Developmental imperatives of social ecologies: Lessons learned from Black children. In H. P. McAdoo & J. L. McAdoo (Eds.), *Black children* (pp. 53–71). Beverly Hills, CA: Sage.

Hollingshead, A. B. (1949). *Elmtown's youth: The impact of social class on adolescents.* New York: Wiley.

Hollos, M. (1980). Collective education in Hungary: The development of competitive, cooperative and role-taking behaviors. *Ethos, 8,* 3–23.

Horgan, E. S. (1988). The American Catholic Irish family. In C. H. Mindel, R. W. Habenstein, & R. Wright, Jr. (Eds.), *Ethnic families in America* (3rd ed., pp. 45–75). New York: Elsevier.

Houser, S. (1996). Accountability: What tribal colleges can teach —and learn. *Tribal College Journal, 8,* 18–21.

How we got into college: Six freshmen tell their tales. (1998–1999). *College Times,* pp. 28–29.

Howard, A. (1970). *Learning to be Rotuman.* New York: Teachers College Press.

Howard, A., & Scott, R. A. (1981). The study of minority groups in complex societies. In R. H. Munroe, R. L. Munroe, & B. B. Whiting (Eds.), *Handbook of cross-cultural human development* (pp. 113–152). New York: Garland.

Huston, A. C., & Wright, J. C. (1998). Mass media and children's development. In W. Damon (General Ed.), I. E. Sigel & K. A. Renninger (Vol. Eds.), *Handbook of child psychology: Vol. 4. Child psychology in practice* (5th ed.) pp. 999–1058. New York: Wiley.

Hutchins, E. (1991). The social organization of distributed cognition. In L. B. Resnick, J. M. Levine, & S. D. Teasley (Eds.), *Perspectives on socially shared cognition.* Washington, DC: American Psychological Association.

Institute for the Study of Social Change. (1991, November). Final report of *The Diversity Project,* University of California, Berkeley.

Irvine, J. T. (1978). Wolof "magical thinking"; Culture and conservation revisited. *Journal of Cross-Cultural Psychology, 9,* 300–310.

Irwin, M. H., & McLaughlin, D. H. (1970). Ability and preference in category sorting by Mano schoolchildren and adults. *Journal of Social Psychology, 82,* 15–24.

Irwin, M. H., Schafer, G. N., & Feiden, C. P. (1974). Emic and unfamiliar category sorting of Mano farmers and U.S. undergraduates. *Journal of Cross-Cultural Psychology, 5,* 407–423.

Jackson, J. F. (1993). Multiple caregiving among African-Americans and infant attachment: The need for an emic approach. *Human Development, 36,* 87–102.

Jahoda, G. (2000). On the prehistory of cross-cultural development research. In A. L. Comunian & U. Gielen (Eds.), *International perspectives on human development* (pp. 5–17). Lengerich, Germany: Pabst Science Publishers.

Jahoda, G., & Krewer, B. (1997). History of cross-cultural and cultural psychology. In. J. W. Berry, Y. H. Poortinga, & J. Pandey (Eds.), *Handbook of cross-cultural psychology: Vol. 1. Theory and method* (pp. 1–42) Boston: Allyn and Bacon.

Jiao, S., Ji, G., & Jing, Q. (1996). Cognitive development of Chinese urban only children and children with siblings. *Child Development, 67,* 387–395.

John-Steiner, V. (1984). Learning styles among Pueblo children. *Quarterly Newsletter of the Laboratory of Comparative Human Cognition, 6,* 57–62.

John-Steiner, V. (1985). *Notebooks of the mind: Explorations of thinking.* Albuquerque: University of New Mexico Press.

John-Steiner, V. (1992). Creative lives, creative tensions. *Creativity Research Journal, 5,* 99–108.

John-Steiner, V., & Tatter, P. (1983). An interactionist model of language development. In B. Bain (Ed.), *The sociogenesis of language and human conduct* (pp. 79–97). New York: Plenum.

Jordan, B. (1989). Cosmopolitical obstetrics: Some insights from the training of traditional midwives. *Social Science Medicine, 28,* 925–944.

Jordan, C. (1977, February). *Maternal teaching, peer teaching, and school adaptation in an urban Hawaiian population.* Paper presented at the meetings of the Society for Cross-Cultural Research, East Lansing, MI.

Joseph, A., Spicer, R. B., & Chesky, J. (1949). *The desert people: A study of the Papago Indians.* Chicago: University of Chicago Press.

Jusczyk, P. W. (1997). *The discovery of spoken language.* Cambridge, MA: MIT Press.

Kagan, J., Klein, R. E., Finley, G. E., Rogoff, B., & Nolan, E. (1979). A cross-cultural study of cognitive development. *Monographs of the Society for Research in Child Development, 44* (5, Serial No. 180).

Kagitçibasi, C., (1996). The autonomous-relational self: A new synthesis. *European Psychologist, 1,* 180–186.

Kagitçibasi, C., & Sunar, D. (1992). Family and socialization in Turkey. In J. L. Roopnarine & D. B. Carter (Eds.), *Parent-child socialization in diverse cultures.* Norwood, NJ: Ablex.

Kasten, W. C. (1992). Bridging the horizon: American Indian beliefs and whole language learning. *Anthropology and Educational Quarterly, 23,* 57–62.

Kawagley, O. (1990). Yup'ik ways of knowing. *Canadian Journal of Native Education, 17,* 5–17.

Kearins, J. M. (1981). Visual spatial memory in Australian aboriginal children of desert regions. *Cognitive Psychology, 13,* 434–460.

Keating, C. F. (1994). World without words: Messages from face and body. In W.J. Lonner & R. Malpass (Eds.), *Psychology and culture* (pp. 175–182). Boston: Allyn and Bacon.

Kelly, M. (1977). Papua New Guinea and Piaget—An eight-year study. In P. R. Dasen (Ed.), *Piagetian psychology: Cross-cultural contributions.* New York: Gardner Press.

Kenyatta, J. (1953). *Facing Mount Kenya: The tribal life of the Gikuyu.* London: Secker & Warburg.

Kilbride, P. L. (1980). Sensorimotor behavior of Baganda and Samia infants. *Journal of Cross-Cultural Psychology, 11,* 131–152.

Kim, U., & Choi, S.-H. (1994). Individualism, collectivism, and child development: A Korean perspective. In P. M. Greenfield & R. R. Cocking (Eds.), *Cross-cultural roots of minority child development* (pp. 227–257). Hillsdale, NJ: Erlbaum.

Kiminyo, D. M. (1977). A cross-cultural study of the development of conservation of mass, weight, and volume among Kamba children. In P. R. Dasen (Ed.), *Piagetian psychology: Cross-cultural contributions.* New York: Gardner Press.

Kingsolver, B. (1995). *High tide in Tucson.* New York: Harper-Collins.

Kleinfeld, J. S. (1973). Intellectual strengths in culturally different groups: An Eskimo illustration. *Review of Educational Research, 43,* 341–359.

Klich, L. Z. (1988). Aboriginal cognition and psychological science. In S. H. Irvine & J. W. Berry (Eds.), *Human abilities in cultural context* (pp 427–452). New York: Cambridge University Press.

Kluckhohn, C. (1949). *Mirror for man.* New York: McGraw-Hill.

Kobayashi, V. (1964). *John Dewey in Japanese educational thought.* Ann Arbor: University of Michigan School of Education.

Kobayashi, Y. (1994). Conceptual acquisition and change through social interaction. *Human Development, 37*, 233–241.

Kohlberg, L. (1976). Moral stages and moralization. In T. Lickona (Ed.), *Moral development and behavior*. New York: Holt, Rinehart, & Winston.

Kohn, A. (1993, September). Choices for children: Why and how to let students decide. *Phi Delta Kappan*, 8–20.

Kojima, H. (1986). Child rearing concepts as a belief-value system of the society and the individual. In H. Stevenson, H. Azuma, & K. Hakuta (Eds.), *Child development and education in Japan* (pp. 39–54). New York: Freeman.

Kojima, H. (1996). Japanese childrearing advice in its cultural, social, and economic contexts. *International Journal of Behavioral Development, 19*, 373–391.

Konner, M. (1972). Aspects of the developmental ethology of a foraging people. In N. Blurton-Jones (Ed.), *Ethological studies of child behavior*. Cambridge, England: Cambridge University Press.

Konner, M. (1975). Relations among infants and juveniles in comparative perspective. In M. Lewis & L. A. Rosenblum (Eds.), *Friendship and peer relations*. New York: Wiley.

Kozulin, A. (1990). *Vygotsky's psychology*. Cambridge, MA: Harvard University Press.

Kugelmass, N. (1959). *Complete child care*. New York: Holt, Rinehart, & Winston.

Laboratory of Comparative Human Cognition. (1979). Cross-cultural psychology's challenges to our ideas of children and development. *American Psychologist, 34*, 827–833.

Laboratory of Comparative Human Cognition. (1983). Culture and cognitive development. In P. H. Mussen (Series Ed.), W. Kessen (Vol. Ed.), *Handbook of child psychology: Vol. 1. History, theory, and methods* (pp. 294–356). New York: Wiley.

Lamb, M. E., Sternberg, K. J., Hwang, C.-P., & Broberg, A. G. (1992). *Child care in context*. Hillsdale, NJ: Erlbaum.

Lamb, M. E., Sternberg, K. J., & Ketterlinus, R. D. (1992). Child care in the United States: The modern era. In M. E. Lamb, K. J. Sternberg, C.-P. Hwang, & A. G. Broberg (Eds.), *Child care in context* (pp. 207–222). Hillsdale, NJ: Erlbaum.

Lamborn, S. D., Dornbusch, S. M., & Steinberg, L. (1996). Ethnicity and community context as moderators of the relations between family decision making and adolescent adjustment. *Child Development, 67*, 283–301.

Lamphere, L. (1977). *To run after them: Cultural and social bases of cooperation in a Navajo community*. Tucson: University of Arizona Press.

Lancy, D. F. (1996). *Playing on the mother-ground*. New York: Guilford.

Lancy, D. F. (Ed.). (1978). The indigenous mathematics project. [Special issue]. *Journal of Education, 14*.

Lancy, D. F. (1980). Play in species adaptation. *Annual Review of Anthropology, 9*, 471–495.

Latouche, S. (1996). *The Westernization of the world*. London: Polity Press.

Laurendeau-Bendavid, M. (1977). Culture, schooling, and cognitive development: A comparative study of children in French Canada and Rwanda. In P. R. Dasen (Ed.), *Piagetian psychology: Cross-cultural contributions*. New York: Gardner.

Lave, J. (1977). Tailor-made experiments and evaluating the intellectual consequences of apprenticeship training. *Quarterly Newsletter of the Institute for Comparative Human Development, 1*, 1–3.

Lave, J. (1988a). *Cognition in practice: Mind, mathematics and culture in everyday life*. Cambridge, England: Cambridge University Press.

Lave, J. (1988b). *The culture of acquisition and the practice of understanding*. Institute for Research on Learning, Report No. IRL88–0007.

Lave, J., & Wenger, E. (1991). *Situated learning: Legitimate peripheral participation.* Cambridge, England: Cambridge University Press.

Laye, C. (1959). *The African child: Memories of a West African childhood.* London: Fontana Books.

Lebra, T. S. (1994). Mother and child in Japanese socialization: A Japan-U.S. comparison. In P. M. Greenfield & R. R. Cocking (Eds.), *Cross-cultural roots of minority child development* (pp. 259–274). Hillsdale, NJ: Erlbaum.

Lee, C. D. (1991). Big picture talkers/Words walking without masters: The instructional implications of ethnic voices for an expanded literacy. *Journal of Negro Education, 60,* 291–304.

Lee, C. D. (1993). *Signifying as a scaffold for literary interpretation.* Urbana, IL: National Council of Teachers of English.

Lee, C. D. (1995). Signifying as a scaffold for literary interpretation. *Journal of Black Psychology, 21,* 357–381.

Lee, C. D. (2001). Is October Brown Chinese? A cultural modeling activity system for underachieving students. *American Educational Research Journal, 38,* 97–141.

Lee, D. D. (1976). *Valuing the self: What we can learn from other cultures.* Englewood Cliffs, NJ: Prentice-Hall.

Lee, L. C. (1992). Day care in the People's Republic of China. In M. E. Lamb, K. J. Sternberg, C.-P. Hwang, & A. G. Broberg (Eds.), *Child care in context* (pp. 355–392). Hillsdale, NJ: Erlbaum.

Lee, R. B. (1980). Lactation, ovulation, infanticide, and women's work: A study of hunter-gatherer population regulation. In M. N. Cohen, R. S. Malpass, & H. G. Klein (Eds.), *Biosocial mechanisms of population regulation* (pp. 321–348). New Haven, CT: Yale University Press.

Leiderman, P. H., & Leiderman, G. F. (1973). *Polymatric infant care in the East African highlands: Some affective and cognitive consequences.* Paper presented at the Minnesota Symposium on Child Development, Minneapolis.

Leiderman, P. H., & Leiderman, G. F. (1974). Affective and cognitive consequences of polymatric infant care in the East African highlands. In A. D. Pick (Ed.), *Minnesota symposia on child psychology* (Vol. 8). Minneapolis: University of Minnesota Press.

Leiderman, P. H., Tulkin, S. R., & Rosenfeld, A. (Eds.). (1977). *Culture and infancy: Variations in the human experience.* Orlando, FL: Academic Press.

Lempers, J. D. (1979). Young children's production and comprehension of nonverbal deictic behaviors. *Journal of Genetic Psychology, 135,* 93–102.

Leont'ev, A. N. (1981). The problem of activity in psychology. In J. V. Wertsch (Ed.), *The concept of activity in Soviet psychology* (pp. 37–71). Armonk, New York: Sharpe.

Levin, P. F. (1990) Culturally contextualized apprenticeship: Teaching and learning through helping in Hawaiian families. *Quarterly Newsletter of the Laboratory for Comparative Human Cognition, 12,* 80–86.

Levine, R., Sato, S., Hashimoto, T., Verma, J. (1995). Love and marriage in eleven cultures. *Journal of Cross-Cultural Psychology, 26,* 554–571.

LeVine, R. A. (1966). Outsiders' judgments: An ethnographic approach to group differences in personality. *Southwestern Journal of Anthropology, 22,* 101–116.

LeVine, R. A. (1977). Child rearing as cultural adaptation. In P. H. Leiderman, S. R. Tulkin, & A. Rosenfeld (Eds.), *Culture and infancy: Variations in the human experience* (pp. 15–27). New York: Academic.

LeVine, R. A. (1980). A cross-cultural perspective on parenting. In M.D. Fantini & R. Cardenas (Eds.), *Parenting in a multicultural society*. New York: Longman.

LeVine, R. A., Dixon, S., LeVine, S., Richman, A., Leiderman, P. H., Keefer, C. H., & Brazelton, T. B. (1994). *Childcare and culture: Lessons from Africa*. New York: Cambridge University Press.

LeVine, R. A., & Miller, P. M. (1990). Commentary. *Human Development, 33,* 73–80.

Levinson, S. C. (1997). Language and cognition: The cognitive consequences of spatial description in Guugu Yimithirr. *Journal of Linguistic Anthropology, 7,* 98–131.

Lewis, C. C. (1995). *Educating hearts and minds: Reflections on Japanese preschool and elementary education*. Cambridge, England: Cambridge University Press.

Lewis, M., & Feiring, C. (1981). Direct and indirect interactions in social relationships. In L. P. Lipsett (Ed.), *Advances in infancy research* (Vol. 1, pp. 129–161). Norwood, NJ: Ablex.

Leyendecker, B., Lamb, M. E., Schölmerich, A., & Fracasso, M. P. (1995). The social worlds of 8- and 12-month-old infants: Early experiences in two subcultural contexts. *Social Development, 4,* 194–208.

Lillard, A. S. (1997). Other folks' theories of mind and behavior. *Psychological Science, 8,* 268–274.

Lipka, J. (1994). Schools failing minority teachers. *Educational Foundations, 8,* 57–80.

Lipka, J., with Mohatt, G. V., & the Ciulistet Group (1998). *Transforming the culture of schools: Yup'ik Eskimo examples*. Mahwah, NJ: Erlbaum.

Litowitz, B. E. (1993). Deconstruction in the zone of proximal development. In E. A. Forman, N. Minick, & C.A. Stone (Eds.), *Contexts for learning* (pp. 184–196) New York: Oxford University Press.

Little Soldier, L. (1989). Cooperative learning and the Native American student. *Phi Delta Kappan, 71,* 161–163.

Lomawaima, K. T. (1994). *They called it Prairie Light: The story of Chilocco Indian School*. Lincoln: University of Nebraska Press.

Losey, K. M. (1995). Mexican students and classroom interaction: An overview and critique. *Review of Educational Research, 65,* 283–318.

Lozoff, B., Wolf, A., & Davis, N. (1984). Cosleeping in urban families with young children in the United States. *Pediatrics, 74,* 171–182.

Lucy, J. A., & Gaskins, S. (1994, December). *The role of language in shaping the child's transition from perceptual to conceptual classification*. Paper presented at the meetings of the American Anthropological Association, Atlanta, GA.

Luria, A. R. (1976). *Cognitive development: Its cultural and social foundations*. Cambridge, MA: Harvard University Press.

Lutz, C., & LeVine, R. A. (1982). Culture and intelligence in infancy: An ethnopsychological view. In M. Lewis (Ed.), *Origins of intelligence: Infancy and early childhood* (pp. 1–28). New York: Plenum.

MacLachlan, P. (1989). Dialogue between Charlotte Zolotow and Patricia MacLachlan. *Horn Book, 65,* 740–741.

MacPhee, D., Fritz, J., & Miller-Heyl, J. (1996). Ethnic variations in personal social networks and parenting. *Child Development, 67,* 3278–3295.

Madsen, M. C., & Shapira, A. (1970). Cooperative and competitive behavior of urban Afro-American, Anglo-American, Mexican-American, and Mexican village children. *Developmental Psychology, 3,* 16–20.

Magarian, O. K. (1963, October). Light of the world. Tape recorded sermon [transcribed by E. Magarian]. Opa-Locka Methodist Church, Opa-Locka, FL.

Malinowski, B. (1927). *The father in primitive psychology.* New York: Norton.

Mandler, J. M., Scribner, S., Cole, M., & DeForest, M. (1980). Cross-cultural invariance in story recall. *Child Development, 51,* 19–26.

Martini, M. (1994a). Balancing work and family in Hawaii: Strategies of parents in two cultural groups. *Family Perspective, 28,* 103–127.

Martini, M. (1994b). Peer interactions in Polynesia: A view from the Marquesas. In J. L. Roopnarine, J. E. Johnson, & F. H. Hooper (Eds.), *Children's play in diverse cultures.* Albany: State University of New York Press.

Martini, M. (1995). Features of home environments associated with children's school success. *Early Child Development and Care, 111,* 49–68.

Martini, M. (1996). "What's new?" at the dinner table: Family dynamics during mealtimes in two cultural groups in Hawaii. *Early Development and Parenting, 5,* 23–34.

Martini, M., & Kirkpatrick, J. (1981). Early interactions in the Marquesas Islands. In T. M. Fields, A. M. Sostek, P. Vietze, & P. H. Leiderman (Eds.), *Culture and early interactions.* Hillsdale, NJ: Erlbaum.

Martini, M., & Kirkpatrick, J. (1992). Parenting in Polynesia: A view from the Marquesas. In J. L. Roopnarine & D. B. Carter (Eds.), *Parent-child socialization in diverse cultures: Vol. 5. Annual advances in applied developmental psychology* (pp. 199–222). Norwood, NJ: Ablex.

Martini, M., & Mistry, J. (1993). The relationship between talking at home and test taking at school: A study of Hawaiian preschool children. In R. N. Roberts (Ed.), *Coming home to preschool: The sociocultural context of early education: Vol. 7. Advances in applied developmental psychology.* Norwood, NJ: Ablex.

Massey, G.C., Hilliard, A. G., & Carew, J. (1982). Test-taking behaviors of Black toddlers: An interactive analysis. In L. Feagans & D.C. Farran (Eds.), *The language of children reared in poverty* (pp. 163–179). New York: Academic.

Mather, C. (1709–1724). Diary, in Collections of the Massachusetts Historical Society. Reprinted in Bremner, R. H. (Ed.) & J. Barnard, T. K. Hareven, & R. M. Mennel (Associate Eds.). (1970) *Children and youth in America: A documentary history: Vol. 1. 1600–1865.* Cambridge, MA: Harvard University Press.

Mathematics Achievement. (1996). *Mathematics achievement in the middle school years: IEA's Third International Mathematics and Science report.* Chestnut Hill, MA: TIMSS International Study Center, CSTEEP, Campion Hall 323, Boston College.

Matusov, E., Bell, N., & Rogoff, B. (2002). Schooling as cultural process: Working together and guidance by children from schools differing in collaborative practices. In R. V. Kail & H.W. Reese (Eds.), *Advances in child development and behavior* (Vol. 29, pp. 129–160). San Diego, CA: Academic Press.

Maybury-Lewis, D. (1992). *Millennium: Tribal wisdom and the modern world.* New York: Viking.

Maynard, A. E. (2002). Cultural teaching: The development of teaching skills in Maya sibling interactions. *Child Development, 73,* 969–982.

McBride, J. (1996). *The color of water: A Black man's tribute to his White mother.* New York: Riverhead Books.

McKenna, J. (1986). An anthropological perspective on the Sudden Infant Death Syndrome (SIDS): The role of parental breathing cues and speech breathing adaptations. *Medical Anthropology, 10,* 9–92.

McKenna, J. J., & Mosko, S. (1993). Evoulation and infant sleep: An experimental study of infant-parent co-sleeping and its implications for SIDS. *Acta Paediatrica Supplement, 389,* 31–36.

McLoyd, V. C., & Randolph, S. M. (1985). Secular trends in the study of Afro-American children: A review of *Child Development*, 1936–1980. In A. B. Smuts & J. W. Hagen (Eds.), *History and research in child development. Monographs of the Society for Research in Child Development.* (Serial No. 211, Vol. 50, pp. 78–92).

McNaughton, S. (1995). *Patterns of emergent literacy.* Melbourne: Oxford University Press.

McShane, D., & Berry, J. W. (1986). Native North Americans: Indian and Inuit abilities. In J. H. Irvine & J. W. Berry (Eds.), *Human abilities in cultural context* (pp. 385–426). Cambridge, England: Cambridge University Press.

Mead, M. (1935). *Sex and temperament.* New York: William Morrow.

Mead, M. (1942). Our educational emphases in primitive perspective. *American Journal of Sociology, 48,* 633–639.

Mehan, H. (1976). Assessing children's school performance. In J. Beck, C. Jenks, N. Keddie, & M. F. D. Young (Eds.), *Worlds apart* (pp. 161–180). London: Collier Macmillan.

Mehan, H. (1979). *Learning lessons: Social organization in the classroom.* Cambridge, MA: Harvard University Press.

Mehler, J., Jusczyk, P.W., Lambertz, G., Halsted, N., Bertoncini, J., & Amiel-Tison, C. (1988). A precursor of language acquisition in young infants. *Cognition, 29,* 143–178.

Meier, D. (1995). *The power of their ideas: Lessons for America from a small school in Harlem.* Boston: Beacon Press.

Merton, R. K. (1972). Insiders and outsiders: A chapter in the sociology of knowledge. *American Journal of Sociology, 78,* 9–47.

Metge, J. (1984). *Learning and teaching: He tikanga Maori.* Wellington: New Zealand Ministry of Education.

Meyer, J., Ramirez, J., & Soysal, Y. (1992). World expansion of mass education, 1870–1980. *Sociology of Education, 65,* 128–149.

Meyer, M. (1908). The grading of students. *Science, 28,* 243–250.

Michaels, S., & Cazden, C. B. (1986). Teacher/child collaboration as oral preparation for literacy. In B. B. Schieffelin & P. Gilmore (Eds.), *The acquisition of literacy: Ethnographic perspectives* (pp. 132–154). Norwood, NJ: Ablex.

Miller, B. D. (1995). Precepts and practices: Researching identity formation among Indian Hindu adolescents in the United States. In J. J. Goodnow, P. J. Miller, & F. Kessel (Eds.), *Cultural practices as contexts for development* (pp. 71–85). San Francisco: Jossey-Bass.

Miller, G. A., & Keller, J. (2000). Psychology and neuroscience: Making peace. *Current Directions in Psychological Science, 9,* 212–215.

Miller, K. F., Smith, C. M., Zhu, J., & Zhang, H. (1995). Preschool origins of cross-national differences in mathematical competence: The role of number-naming systems. *Psychological Science, 6,* 56–60.

Miller, P. (1982). *Amy, Wendy, & Beth: Learning language in South Baltimore.* Austin: University of Texas Press.

Miller, P. J., & Goodnow, J. J. (1995). Cultural practices: Toward an integration of culture and development. In J. J. Goodnow, P. J. Miller, & F. Kessel (Eds.), *Cultural practices as contexts for development* (pp. 5–16). San Francisco: Jossey-Bass.

Miller, P. J., & Hoogstra, L. (1992). Language as a tool in the socialization and apprehension of cultural meanings. In T. Schwartz, G. White, & C. Lutz (Eds.), *New directions in psychological anthropology.* Cambridge, England: Cambridge University Press.

Milton, O., Pollio, H.R., & Eison, J. A. (1986). *Making sense of college grades.* K. E. Eble (Consulting Ed.). San Francisco: Jossey–Bass.

Minami, M., & McCabe, A. (1995). Rice balls and bear hunts: Japanese and North American family narrative patterns. *Journal of Child Language, 22,* 423–445.

Minami, M., & McCabe, A. (1996). Compressed collections of experiences: Some Asian American traditions. In A. McCabe (Ed.), *Chameleon readers: Some problems cultural differences in narrative structure pose for multicultural literacy programs* (pp. 72–97). New York: McGraw-Hill.

Mindel, C. H., Habenstein, R. W., & Wright, R. Jr. (1988). (Eds.), *Ethnic families in America* (3rd ed.). New York: Elsevier.

Mintz, S., & Kellogg, S. (1988). *Domestic revolutions: A social history of American family life.* New York: Free Press.

Mistry, J. (1993a). Cultural context in the development of children's narratives. In J. Altarriba (Ed.), *Cognition and culture: A cross-cultural approach to psychology* (pp. 207–228). North-Holland: Elsevier Science Publishers.

Mistry, J. (1993b). Guided participation in Dhol-Ki-Patti. In B. Rogoff, J. Mistry, A. Göncü, & C. Mosier, (1993). *Guided participation in cultural activity by toddlers and caregivers. Monographs of the Society for Research in Child Development, 58* (7, Serial no. 236, pp. 102–125).

Mistry, J., Göncü, A., & Rogoff, B. (1988, April). *Cultural variations in role relations in the socialization of toddlers.* Paper presented at the International Conference of Infant Studies, Washington, DC.

Miura, I. T., Okamoto, Y., Kim, C. C., Chang, C.-M., Steere, M., & Fayol, M. (1994). Comparisons of children's cognitive representation of number: China, France, Japan, Korea, Sweden, and the United States. *International Journal of Behavioral Development, 17,* 401–411.

Miyake, K., Chen, S. J., & Campos, J. J. (1985). Infant temperament, mother's mode of interaction, and attachment in Japan: An interim report. In I. Bretherton & E. Waters (Eds.), *Growing points of attachment theory and research. Monographs of the Society for Research in Child Development, 50* (1–2, Serial no. 209), 276–297.

Moll, L. C., & Greenberg, J. B. (1990). Creating zones of possibilities: Combining social contexts for instruction. In L. C. Moll (Ed.), *Vygotsky and education: Instructional implications and applications of sociohistorical psychology.* Cambridge, England: Cambridge University Press.

Moll, L, C., Tapia, J., & Whitmore, K. F. (1993). Living knowledge: The social distribution of cultural sources for thinking. In G. Salomon (Ed.), *Distributed cognitions* (pp. 139–163). Cambridge, England: Cambridge University Press.

Moran, G. F., & Vinovskis, M. A. (1985). The great care of godly parents: Early childhood in Puritan New England. In A. B. Smuts & J. W. Hagen (Eds.), *History and research in child development. Monographs of the Society for Research in Child Development, 50* (4–5, Serial no. 211, pp. 24–37).

Morelli, G., Rogoff, B., & Angelillo, C. (2002, in press). Cultural variation in young children's access to worker involvement in specialized child-focused activities. *International Journal of Behavorial Development.*

Morelli, G. A., Rogoff, B., Oppenheim, D., & Goldsmith, D. (1992). Cultural variation in infants' sleeping arrangements: Questions of independence. *Developmental Psychology, 28,* 604–613.

Morelli, G. A., & Tronick, E. (1991). Parenting and child development in the Efe foragers and Lese farmers of Zaire. In M. H. Bornstein (Ed.), *Cultural approaches to parenting* (pp. 91–113). Hillsdale, NJ: Erlbaum.

Morelli, G. A., & Tronick, E. Z. (1992). Efe fathers: One among many? A comparison of forager children's involvement with fathers and other males. *Social Development, 1,* 36–54.

Moreno, R. P. (1991). Maternal teaching of preschool children in minority and low-status families: A critical review. *Early Childhood Research Quarterly, 6,* 395–410.

Morgan, E. S. (1944). *The Puritan family: Essays on religion and domestic relations in seventeenth-century New England.* Boston: Trustees of the Public Library.

Mosier, C. E., & Rogoff, B. (2002). *Privileged treatment of toddlers: Cultural aspects of autonomy and responsibility.* Manuscript submitted for publication.

Munroe, R. H., & Munroe, R. L. (1971). Household density and infant care in an East African society. *Journal of Social Psychology, 83,* 3–13.

Munroe, R. H., & Munroe, R. L. (1975a). *Infant care and childhood performance in East Africa.* Paper presented at the meetings of the Society for Research in Child Development, Denver, CO.

Munroe, R. L., & Munroe, R. H. (1975b). *Cross-cultural human development.* Monterey, CA: Brooks-Cole.

Munroe, R. L., & Munroe, R. H. (1997). Logoli childhood and the cultural reproduction of sex differentiation. In T. S. Weisner, C. Bradley, & P. L. Kilbride (Eds.), *African families and the crisis of social change* (pp. 299–314). Westport, CT: Bergin & Garvey.

Munroe, R. L., Munroe, R. H., Nerlove, S. B., Koel, A., Rogoff, B., Bolton, C., Michelson, C., & Bolton, R. (1977). *Sociobehavioral features of children's environments: Sex differences.* Unpublished manuscript, Harvard University.

Munroe, R. H., Munroe, R. L., & Whiting, B. B. (1981). *Handbook of cross-cultural human development.* New York: Garland.

Musick, J. S. (1994, Fall). Capturing the childrearing context. *SRCD Newsletter: A Publication of the Society for Research in Child Development.*

Myers, M. (1984). Shifting standards of literacy—the teacher's catch-22. *English Journal, 73,* 26–32.

Myers, M. (1996). *Changing our minds: Negotiating English and literacy.* Urbana, IL: National Council of Teachers of English.

Nagel, J. (1994). Constructing ethnicity: Creating and recreating ethnic identity and culture. *Social Problems, 41,* 152–176.

Nash, M. (1967). *Machine age Maya.* Chicago: University of Chicago Press.

Neisser, U. (1976). General, academic, and artificial intelligence. In L. B. Resnick (Ed.), *The nature of intelligence.* Hillsdale, NJ: Erlbaum.

Neisser, U. (Ed.). (1982). *Memory observed: Remembering in natural contexts.* San Francisco: Freeman.

Nerlove, S. B., Roberts, J. M., Klein, R. E., Yarbrough, C., & Habicht, J.-P. (1974). Natural indicators of cognitive development: An observational study of rural Guatemalan children. *Ethos, 2,* 265–295.

New, R. (1994). Child's play—una cosa naturale: An Italian perspective. In J. L. Roopnarine, J. E. Johnson, & F. H. Hooper (Eds.), *Children's play in diverse cultures* (pp. 123–147). Albany: State University of New York Press.

New, R., & Richman, A. L. (1996). Maternal beliefs and infant care practices in Italy and the United States. In S. Harkness & C. M. Super (Eds.), *Parents' cultural belief systems: Their origins, expressions, and consequences.* New York: Guilford.

Newman, D., Griffin, P., & Cole, M. (1984). Social constraints in laboratory and classroom tasks. In B. Rogoff & J. Lave (Eds.), *Everyday cognition: Its development in social context* (pp. 172–193). Cambridge, MA: Harvard University Press.

Newman, D., Griffin, P., & Cole, M. (1989). *The construction zone: Working for cognitive change in school.* Cambridge, England: Cambridge University Press.

Newman, K. (1998). Place and race: Midlife experience in Harlem. In R. A. Shweder (Ed.), *Welcome to middle age! (and other cultural fictions).* Chicago: University of Chicago Press.

Nicolopoulou, A. (1993). Play, cognitive development, and the social world: Piaget, Vygotsky, and beyond. *Human Development, 36,* 1–23.

Nicolopoulou, A. (1997). The invention of writing and the development of numerical concepts in Sumeria: Some implications for developmental psychology. In M. Cole, Y. Engeström, & O. Vasquez (Eds.), *Mind, culture, and activity: Seminal papers from the Laboratory of Comparative Human Cognition* (pp. 205–225). New York: Cambridge University Press.

Niehardt, J. G. (1932). *Black Elk speaks.* New York: Pocket.

Nieuwenhuys, O. (2000). The household economy and the commercial exploitation of children's work: The case of Kerala. In B. Schlemmer (Ed.), *The exploited child* (pp. 278–291). London: Zed Books.

Nsamenang, A. B. (1992). *Human development in cultural context: A third-world perspective.* Newbury Park, CA: Sage.

Nunes, T. (1995). Cultural practices and the conception of individual differences: Theoretical and empirical considerations. In J. J. Goodnow, P. J. Miller, & F. Kessel (Eds.), *Cultural practices as contexts for development* (pp. 91–103). San Francisco: Jossey-Bass.

Nunes, T. (1999). Mathematics learning as the socialization of the mind. *Mind, Culture, and Activity, 6,* 33–52.

Nunes, T., Schliemann, A. D., & Carraher, D. W. (1993). *Street mathematics and school mathematics.* Cambridge, England: Cambridge University Press.

Nyiti, R. M. (1976). The development of conservation in the Meru children of Tanzania. *Child Development, 47,* 1122–1129.

Oakeshott, M. J. (1962). *Rationalism in politics, and other essays.* New York: Basic Books.

Ochs, E. (1982). Talking to children in Western Samoa. *Language and Society, 11,* 77–104.

Ochs, E. (1988). *Culture and language development: Language acquisition and language socialization in a Samoan village.* Cambridge, England: Cambridge University Press.

Ochs, E. (1996). Linguistic resources for socializing humanity. In J. Gumperz & S. Levinson (Eds.), *Rethinking linguistic relativity* (pp. 407–438) Cambridge, England: Cambridge University Press.

Ochs, E., Jacoby, S., & Gonzales, P. (1994). Interpretive journeys: How physicists talk and travel through graphic space. *Configurations, 1,* 151–171.

Ochs, E., & Schieffelin, B. B. (1984). Language acquisition and socialization: Three developmental stories and their implications. In R. Schweder & R. LeVine (Eds.), *Culture and its acquisition.* Chicago: University of Chicago Press.

Ochs, E., Schieffelin, B. B., & Platt, M. (1979). Propositions across utterances and speakers. In E. Ochs & B. B. Schieffelin (Eds.), *Developmental pragmatics.* New York: Academic.

Ochs, E., Taylor, C., Rudolph, D., & Smith, R. (1992). Storytelling as a theory-building activity. *Discourse Processes, 15,* 37–72.

O'Connor, M.C., & Michaels, S. (1996). Shifting participant frameworks: Orchestrating thinking practices in group discussions. In D. Hicks (Ed.), *Discourse, learning, and schooling* (pp. 63–103). New York: Cambridge University Press.

Ogbu, J. U. (1982). Socialization: A cultural ecological approach. In K. M. Borman (Ed.), *The social life of children in a changing society* (pp. 253–267). Hillsdale, NJ: Erlbaum.

Ogbu, J. U. (1990). Cultural model, identity, and literacy. In J. W. Stigler, R. A. Shweder, & G. Herdt (Eds.), *Cultural psychology: Essays on comparative human development* (pp. 520–541). New York: Cambridge University Press.

Ogburn, W. F., & Nimkoff, M. F. (1955). *Technology and the changing family.* Boston: Houghton Mifflin.

Ogunnaike, O. A., & Houser, R. F., Jr. (2002). Yoruba toddlers' engagement in errands and cognitive performance on the Yoruba Mental Subscale. *International Journal of Behavioral Development, 26,* 145–153.

Okonji, M. O. (1971). The effects of familiarity on classification. *Journal of Cross-Cultural Psychology, 2,* 39–49.

Olson, D. R. (1976). Culture, technology, and intellect. In L. B. Resnick (Ed.), *The nature of intelligence.* Hillsdale, NJ: Erlbaum.

Oppenheim, D. (1998). Perspectives on infant mental health from Israel: The case of changes in collective sleeping on the kibbutz. *Infant Mental Health Journal, 19,* 76–86.

Orellana, M. F. (2001). The work kids do: Mexican and Central American immigrant children's contributions to households and schools in California. *Harvard Educational Review, 71,* 366–389.

Osberg, S. (1994, Fall). Letter from the executive director. *Back in Touch, 10,* 1.

Ottenberg, S. (1994). Initiations. In P. H. Bock (Ed.), *Handbook of psychological anthropology* (pp. 351–377). Westport, CT: Greenwood Press.

Page, H. W. (1973). Concepts of length and distance in a study of Zulu youths. *Journal of Social Psychology, 90,* 9–16.

Panel on Youth of the President's Science Advisory Committee. (1974). *Youth: Transition to adulthood.* Chicago: University of Chicago Press.

Papousek, M., Papousek, H., & Bornstein, M. H. (1985). The naturalistic vocal environment of young infants. In T. M. Field & N. Fox (Eds.), *Social perception in infants* (pp. 269–298). Norwood, NJ: Ablex.

Paradise, R. (1987). *Learning through social interaction: The experience and development of the Mazahua self in the context of the market.* Unpublished doctoral dissertation, University of Pennsylvania.

Paradise, R. (1991). El conocimiento cultural en el aula: Niños indígenas y su orientación hacia la observación [Cultural knowledge in the classroom: Indigenous children and their orientation toward observation]. *Infancia y Aprendizaje, 55,* 73–85.

Paradise, R. (1994). Interactional style and nonverbal meaning: Mazahua children learning how to be separate-but-together. *Anthropology & Education Quarterly, 25,* 156–172.

Parker, S., & Parker, H. (1979). The myth of male superiority: Rise and demise. *American Anthropologist, 81,* 289–309.

Paul, B. D. (1953). Interview techniques and field relationships. In A. L. Kroeber (Ed.), *Anthropology today.* Chicago: University of Chicago Press.

Pea, R. D. (1993). Practices of distributed intelligence and designs for education. In G. Salomon (Ed.), *Distributed cognitions* (pp. 47–87). Cambridge, England: Cambridge University Press.

Pea, R. D., & Gomez, L. M. (1992). Distributed multimedia learning environments: Why and how? *Interactive Learning Environments, 2,* 73–109.

Peak, L. (1986). Training learning skills and attitudes in Japanese early educational settings. In W. Fowler (Ed.), *Early experience and the development of competence.* San Francisco: Jossey-Bass.

Pelletier, W. (1970). Childhood in an Indian village. In S. Repo (Ed.), *This book is about schools* (pp. 18–31). New York: Pantheon Books.

Pepper, S. C. (1942). *World hypotheses: A study in evidence.* Berkeley: University of California Press.

Perry, P. (2001). White means never having to say you're ethnic. *Journal of Contemporary Ethnography, 30,* 56–91.

Pettigrew, T. F. (1998). Intergroup contact theory. *Annual Review of Psychology, 49,* 65–85.

Pewewardy, C., & Bushey, M. (1992). A family of learners and storytellers. *Native Peoples, 5,* 56–60.

Philips, S. U. (1972). Participant structure and communicative competence: Warm Springs children in community and classroom. In C. B. Cazden, V. P. John, & D. Hymes (Eds.), *Functions of language in the classroom* (pp. 370–394). New York: Teachers College Press.

Philips, S. U. (1983). *The invisible culture: Communication in classroom and community on the Warm Springs Indian Reservation.* Prospect Heights, IL: Waveland.

Philp, H., & Kelly, M. (1974). Product and process in cognitive development: Some comparative data on the performance of school age children in different cultures. *British Journal of Educational Psychology, 44,* 248–265.

Phinney, J. S. (1996). When we talk about American ethnic groups, what do we mean? *American Psychologist, 51,* 918–927.

Phinney, J. S., & Alipuria, L. L. (1996). At the interface of cultures: Multiethnic/multiracial high school and college students. *Journal of Social Psychology, 136,* 139–158.

Phinney, J. S., & Rotheram, M. J. (Eds.). (1987). *Children's ethnic socialization: Pluralism and development.* Newbury Park, CA: Sage.

Piaget, J. (1926). *The language and thought of the child.* New York: Harcourt, Brace.

Piaget, J. (1971). The theory of stages in cognitive development. In D. R. Green, M. P. Ford, & G. P. Flamer (Eds.), *Measurement and Piaget.* New York: McGraw-Hill.

Piaget, J. (1972). Intellectual evolution from adolescence to adulthood. *Human Development, 15,* 1–12.

Plank, G. A. (1994). What silence means for educators of American Indian children. *Journal of American Indian Education, 34,* 3–19.

Posner, J. K. (1982). The development of mathematical knowledge in two West African societies. *Child Development, 53,* 200–208.

Potts, M., & Short, R. (1999). *Ever since Adam and Eve: The evolution of human sexuality.* Cambridge, England: Cambridge University Press.

Pratt, C. (1948). *I learn from children: An adventure in progressive education.* New York: Simon & Schuster.

Price-Williams, D. R. (1975). *Explorations in cross-cultural psychology.* San Francisco: Chandler and Sharp.

Price-Williams, D. R. (1980). Anthropological approaches to cognition and their relevance to psychology. In H. C. Triandis & W. Lonner (Eds.), *Handbook of cross-cultural psychology* (Vol. 3). Boston: Allyn & Bacon.

Price-Williams, D. R., Gordon, W., & Ramirez, M., III. (1969). Skill and conservation: A study of pottery-making children. *Developmental Psychology, 1,* 769.

Rabain Jamin, J. (1994). Language and socialization of the child in African families living in France. In P. M. Greenfield & R. R. Cocking (Eds.), *Cross-cultural roots of minority child development* (pp. 147–166). Hillsdale, NJ: Erlbaum.

Read, M. (1968). *Children of their fathers: Growing up among the Ngoni of Malawi.* New York: Holt, Rinehart & Winston.

Reed, I. (Ed.). (1997). *Multi-America: Essays on cultural wars and cultural peace.* New York: Viking.

Reese, L. (2002). Parental strategies in contrasting cultural settings: Families in México and "El Norte." *Anthropology & Education Quarterly, 33,* 30–59.

Reser, J. P. (1982). Cultural relativity or cultural bias: A response to Hippler. *American Anthropologist, 84,* 399–404.

Resnick, D. P., & Resnick, L. B. (1977). The nature of literacy: An historical exploration. *Harvard Educational Review, 47,* 370–385.

Rheingold, H. L. (1982). Little children's participation in the work of adults: A nascent prosocial behavior. *Child Development, 53,* 114–125.

Richman, A. L., LeVine, R. A., New, R. S., Howrigan, G. A., Welles-Nystrom, B., & LeVine, S. E. (1988). Maternal behavior to infants in five cultures. In R. A. LeVine, P. M. Miller, & M. M. West (Eds.), *Parental behavior in diverse societies.* San Francisco: Jossey-Bass.

Richman, A. L., Miller, P. M., & Solomon, M. J. (1988). The socialization of infants in suburban Boston. In R. A. LeVine, P. M. Miller, & M. M. West (Eds.), *Parental behavior in diverse societies* (pp. 65–74). San Francisco: Jossey-Bass.

Riegel, K. F. (1973). Developmental psychology and society: Some historical and ethical considerations. In J. R. Nesselroade & H. W. Reese (Eds.), *Life-span developmental psychology: Methodological issues.* New York: Academic.

Riet, M. van der. (1998, June). *Socialization through story-telling.* Paper presented at the meetings of the International Society for Cultural Research and Activity Theory, Aarhus, Denmark.

Rogoff, B. (1978). *Companions and activities of Highland Maya children.* Paper presented at the meetings of the Society for Cross-Cultural Research, New Haven, CT.

Rogoff, B. (1981a). Adults and peers as agents of socialization: A highland Guatemalan profile. *Ethos, 9,* 18–36.

Rogoff, B. (1981b). The relation of age and sex to experiences during childhood in a highland community. *Anthropology UCLA, 11,* 25–41.

Rogoff, B. (1981c). Schooling and the development of cognitive skills. In H. C. Triandis & A. Heron (Eds.), *Handbook of cross-cultural psychology* (Vol. 4, pp. 233–294). Rockleigh, NJ: Allyn & Bacon.

Rogoff, B. (1982a). Integrating context and cognitive development. In M. E. Lamb & A. L. Brown (Eds.), *Advances in developmental psychology* (Vol. 2). Hillsdale, NJ: Erlbaum.

Rogoff, B. (1982b). Mode of instruction and memory test performance. *International Journal of Behavioral Development, 5,* 33–48.

Rogoff, B. (1986). Adult assistance of children's learning. In T. E. Raphael (Ed.), *The contexts of school based literacy.* New York: Random.

Rogoff, B. (1990). *Apprenticeship in thinking: Cognitive development in social context.* New York: Oxford University Press.

Rogoff, B. (1994). Developing understanding of the idea of communities of learners. *Mind, Culture, and Activity, 1,* 209–229.

Rogoff, B. (1996). Developmental transitions in children's participation in sociocultural activities. In A. J. Sameroff & M. M. Haith (Eds.), *The five to seven year shift: The age of reason and responsibility.* Chicago: University of Chicago Press.

Rogoff, B. (1997). Evaluating development in the process of participation: Theory, methods, and practice building on each other. In E. Amsel & A. Renninger (Eds.), *Change and development: Issues of theory, application, and method* (pp. 265–285). Hillsdale, NJ: Erlbaum.

Rogoff, B. (1998). Cognition as a collaborative process. In W. Damon (Series Ed.) & D. Kuhn & R.S. Siegler (Vol. Eds.), *Cognition, perception and language: Vol. 2. Handbook of Child Psychology* (5th ed.). New York: Wiley.

Rogoff, B., & Angelillo, C. (2002). Investigating the coordinated functioning of multifaceted cultural practices in human development. *Human Development, 45,* 211–225.

Rogoff, B., Baker-Sennett, J., Lacasa, P., & Goldsmith, D. (1995). Development through participation in sociocultural activity. In J. Goodnow, P. Miller, & F. Kessel (Eds.), *Cultural practices as contexts for development.* San Francisco: Jossey-Bass.

Rogoff, B., Baker-Sennett, J., & Matusov, E. (1994). Considering the concept of planning. In M. M. Haith, J. B. Benson, R. J. Roberts, Jr., & B. F. Pennington (Eds.), *The development of future-oriented processes* (pp. 353–373). Chicago: University of Chicago Press.

Rogoff, B., & Chavajay, P. (1995). What's become of research on the cultural basis of cognitive development? *American Psychologist, 50,* 859–877.

Rogoff, B., Goodman Turkanis, C., & Bartlett, L. (2001). *Learning together: Children and adults in a school community.* New York: Oxford University Press.

Rogoff, B., & Lave, J. (1984). *Everyday cognition.* Cambridge, MA: Harvard University Press.

Rogoff, B., & Mistry, J. J. (1985). Memory development in cultural context. In M. Pressley & C. Brainerd (Eds.), *Cognitive learning and memory in children.* New York: Springer-Verlag.

Rogoff, B., Mistry, J., Göncü, A., & Mosier, C. (1991). Cultural variation in the role relations of toddlers and their families. In M. H. Bornstein (Ed.), *Cultural approaches to parenting* (pp. 173–183). Hillsdale, NJ: Erlbaum.

Rogoff, B., Mistry, J., Göncü, A., & Mosier, C. (1993). *Guided participation in cultural activity by toddlers and caregivers. Monographs of the Society for Research in Child Development, 58* (7, Serial no. 236).

Rogoff, B., & Mosier, C. (1993). Guided participation in San Pedro and Salt Lake. In B. Rogoff, J. Mistry, A. Göncü, & C. Mosier, *Guided participation in cultural activity by toddlers and caregivers. Monographs of the Society for Research in Child Development, 58* (7, Serial No. 236, pp. 59–101).

Rogoff, B., Paradise, R., Mejía Arauz, R. Correa-Chávez, M., & Angelillo, C. (2003). Firsthand learning through intent participation. *Annual Review of Psychology, 54.*

Rogoff, B., Sellers, M. J., Pirotta, S., Fox, N., & White, S. H. (1975). Age of assignment of roles and responsibilities to children: A cross-cultural survey. *Human Development, 18,* 353–369.

Rogoff, B., & Toma, C. (1997). Shared thinking: Cultural and institutional variations. *Discourse Processes, 23,* 471–497.

Rogoff, B., Topping, K., Baker-Sennett, J., & Lacasa, P. (2002). Mutual contributions of individuals, partners, and institutions: Planning to remember in Girl Scout cookie sales. *Social Development, 11*, 266–289.

Rogoff, B., & Waddell, K. J. (1982). Memory for information organized in a scene by children from two cultures. *Child Development, U53*, 1224–1228.

Rohner, R. P. (1994). Patterns of parenting: The warmth dimension in worldwide perspective. In W. J. Lonner & R. Malpass (Eds.), *Psychology and culture* (pp. 113–120). Boston: Allyn and Bacon.

Rohner, R. P., & Chaki-Sirkar, M. (1988). *Women and children in a Bengali village.* Hanover, NH: University Press of New England.

Rohner, R. P., & Pettengill, S. M. (1985). Perceived parental acceptance-rejection and parental control among Korean adolescents. *Child Development, 56*, 524–528.

Rosenthal, M. K. (1992). Nonparental child care in Israel: A cultural and historical perspective. In M. E. Lamb, K. J. Sternberg, C.-P. Hwang, & A. G. Broberg (Eds.), *Child care in context* (pp. 305–330). Hillsdale, NJ: Erlbaum.

Rosenthal, M. K. (1999). Out-of-home child care research: A cultural perspective. *International Journal of Behavioral Development, 23*, 477–518.

Ross, B. M., & Millsom, C. (1970). Repeated memory of oral prose in Ghana and New York. *International Journal of Psychology, 5*, 173–181.

Rothbaum, F., Pott, M., Azuma, H., Miyake, K., & Weisz, J. (2000). The development of close relationships in Japan and the United States: Paths of symbiotic harmony and generative tension. *Child Development, 71*, 1121–1142.

Ruddle, K., & Chesterfield, R. (1978). Traditional skill training and labor in rural societies. *Journal of Developing Areas, 12*, 389–398.

Ruffy, M. (1981). Influence of social factors in the development of the young child's moral judgments. *European Journal of Social Psychology, 11*, 61–75.

Sagi, A. (1990). Attachment theory and research from a cross-cultural perspective. *Human Development, 33*, 10–22.

Sagi, A., van Ijzendoorn, M. H., Aviezer, O., Donnell, F., & Mayseless, O. (1994). Sleeping out of home in a kibbutz communal arrangement: It makes a difference for infant-mother attachment. *Child Development, 65*, 992–1004.

Saraswathi, T. S. (2000). Adult-child continuity in India: Is adolescence a myth or an emerging reality? In A. L. Comunian & U. Gielen (Eds.), *International perspectives on human development* (pp. 431–448). Lengerich, Germany: Pabst Science Publishers.

Saraswathi, T. S., & Dutta, R. (1988). *Invisible boundaries: Grooming for adult roles.* New Delhi: Northern Book Center.

Saxe, G. B. (1981). Body parts as numerals: A developmental analysis of numeration among the Oksapmin in Papua New Guinea. *Child Development, 52*, 306–316.

Saxe, G. B. (1988a). Candy selling and math learning. *Educational Researcher, 17*, 14–21.

Saxe, G. B. (1988b). The mathematics of street vendors. *Child Development, 59*, 1415–1425.

Saxe, G. B. (1991). *Culture and cognitive development: Studies in mathematical understanding.* Hillsdale, NJ: Erlbaum.

Scaife, M., & Bruner, J. (1975). The capacity for joint visual attention in the infant. *Nature, 253*, 265–266.

Schaffer, H. R. (1977). *Mothering.* London: Fontana/Open Books.

Schaffer, H. R. (1984). *The child's entry into the social world.* London: Academic Press.

Scheper-Hughes, N. (1985). Culture, scarcity, and maternal thinking: Maternal detachment and infant survival in a Brazilian shantytown. *Ethos, 13*, 291–317.

Schieffelin, B. B. (1986). Teasing and shaming in Kaluli children's interactions. In

B. B. Schieffelin & E. Ochs (Eds.), *Language socialization across cultures* (pp. 165–181). Cambridge, England: Cambridge University Press.

Schieffelin, B. B. (1991). *The give and take of everyday life: Language socialization of Kaluli children.* Cambridge, England: Cambridge University Press.

Schieffelin, B. B., & Eisenberg, A. R. (1984). Cultural variation in children's conversations. In R. Schiefelbusch & J. Pickar (Eds.), *The acquisition of communicative competence* (pp. 377–420). Baltimore: University Park Press.

Schiffrin, D. (1984). Jewish argument as sociability. *Language in Society, 13,* 311–335.

Schlegel, A. (1995). A cross-cultural approach to adolescence. *Ethos, 23,* 15–32.

Schlegel, A., & Barry, H., III. (1991). *Adolescence: An anthropological inquiry.* New York: Free Press.

Schliemann, A. D., Carraher, D. W., & Ceci, S. J. (1997). Everyday cognition. In J. W. Berry, P. R. Dasen, & T. S. Saraswathi (Eds.), *Handbook of cross-cultural psychology: Vol. 2. Basic processes and human development* (pp. 188–216). Boston: Allyn and Bacon.

Schoenfeld, A. H. (1989). Ideas in the air: Speculations on small group learning, environmental and cultural influences on cognition, and epistemology. *International Journal of Educational Research, 13,* 71–88.

Schrage, M. (1990). *Shared minds.* New York: Random House.

Schwartz, D., Dodge, K.A., Pettit, G.S., & Bates, J.E. (1997). The early socialization of aggressive victims of bullying. *Child Development, 68,* 665–675.

Scollon, R. (1976). *Conversations with a one-year-old.* Honolulu: University of Hawaii Press.

Scollon, R., & Scollon, S. (1981). *Narrative, literacy, and face in interethnic communication.* Norwood, NJ: Ablex.

Scribner, S. (1974). Developmental aspects of categorized recall in a West African society. *Cognitive Psychology, 6,* 475–494.

Scribner, S. (1975). Recall of classical syllogisms: A cross-cultural investigation of error on logical problems. In R. J. Falmagne (Ed.), *Reasoning: Representation and process in children and adults.* New York: Wiley.

Scribner, S. (1976). Situating the experiment in cross-cultural research. In K. F. Riegel & J. A. Meacham (Eds.), *The developing individual in a changing world* (Vol. 1, pp. 310–321). Chicago: Aldine.

Scribner, S. (1977). Modes of thinking and ways of speaking: Culture and logic reconsidered. In P. N. Johnson-Laird & P. C. Wason (Eds.), *Thinking.* Cambridge, England: Cambridge University Press.

Scribner, S. (1984). Studying working intelligence. In B. Rogoff & J. Lave (Eds.), *Everyday cognition: Its development in social context* (pp. 9–40). Cambridge, MA: Harvard University Press.

Scribner, S. (1985). Vygotsky's uses of history. In J. V. Wertsch (Ed.), *Culture, communication, and cognition: Vygotskian perspectives* (pp. 119–145). Cambridge, England: Cambridge University Press.

Scribner, S. (1997). A sociocultural approach to the study of mind. In E. Tobach, R. J. Falmagne, M. B. Parlee, L. M. W. Martin, & A. S. Kapelman (Eds.), *Mind and social practice: Selected writings of Sylvia Scribner* (pp. 266–280). Cambridge, UK: Cambridge University Press.

Scribner, S., & Cole, M. (1973). Cognitive consequences of formal and informal education. *Science, 182,* 553–559.

Scribner, S., & Cole, M. (1981). *The psychology of literacy.* Cambridge, MA: Harvard University Press.

Seagrim, G. N. (1977). Caveat interventor. In P. Dasen (Ed.), *Piagetian psychology: Cross-cultural contributions* (pp. 359–376). New York: Gardner.

Sears, R. (1961). Transcultural variables and conceptual equivalence. In B. Kaplan (Ed.), *Studying personality cross-culturally*. Evanston, IL: Row, Peterson & Company.

Segall, M. H., Ember, C. R., & Ember, M. (1997). Aggression, crime, and warfare. In J. W. Berry, M H. Segall, & Ç. Kagitçibasi (Eds.), *Handbook of cross-cultural psychology: Vol. 3. Social behavior and applications* (2nd ed., pp. 226–229). Needham Heights, MA: Allyn & Bacon.

Seligman, K. (2001, September 7). 5.6% of California homes multigenerational. *San Francisco Chronicle*, p. A12.

Sellers, M. J. (1975). *The first ten years of childhood in rural communities of Mexico and Guatemala*. Unpublished manuscript, Harvard University.

Sénéchal, M. & LeFevre J.-A. (2002). Parental involvement in the development of children's reading skill: A five-year longitudinal study. *Child Development, 73,* 445–460.

Senungetuk, V., & Tiulana, P. (1987). *A place for winter: Paul Tiulana's story*. Anchorage, AK: The Ciri Foundation.

Serpell, R. (1976). *Culture's influence on behaviour*. London: Methuen.

Serpell, R. (1977). Strategies for investigating intelligence in its cultural context. *Quarterly Newsletter of the Institute for Comparative Human Development, 1,* 11–15.

Serpell, R. (1979). How specific are perceptual skills? A cross-cultural study of pattern reproduction. *British Journal of Psychology, 70,* 365–380.

Serpell, R. (1982). Measures of perception, skills and intelligence. In W. W. Hartup (Ed.), *Review of child development research* (Vol. 6, pp. 392–440). Chicago: University of Chicago Press.

Serpell, R. (1993). *The significance of schooling: Life-journeys in an African society*. Cambridge, England: Cambridge University Press.

Serpell, R., & Hatano, G. (1997). Education, schooling, and literacy. In J. W. Berry, P. R. Dasen, & T. S. Saraswathi (Eds.), *Handbook of cross-cultural psychology: Vol. 2. Basic processes and human development* (pp. 339–376). Boston: Allyn and Bacon.

Seymour, S. C. (1999). *Women, family, and child care in India*. Cambridge, England: Cambridge University Press.

Shachar, H., & Sharan, S. (1994). Talking, relating, and achieving: Effects of cooperative learning and whole-class instruction. *Cognition and Instruction, 12,* 313–353.

Shapira, A., & Madsen, M. C. (1969). Cooperative and competitive behavior of kibbutz and urban children in Israel. *Child Development, 40,* 609–617.

Sharan, Y., & Sharan, S. (1992). *Expanding cooperative learning through group investigation*. New York: Teachers College Press.

Sharp, D., & Cole, M. (1972). Patterns of responding in the word associations of West African children. *Child Development, 43,* 55–65.

Sharp, D., Cole, M., & Lave, J. (1979). Education and cognitive development: The evidence from experimental research. *Monographs of the Society for Research in Child Development, 44* (Serial no. 178).

Shatz, M. (1987). Bootstrapping operations in child language. In K. E. Nelson & A. van Kleeck (Eds.), *Children's language* (Vol. 6, pp. 1–22). Hillsdale, NJ: Erlbaum.

Sherif, M., Harvey, O.J., White, B. J., Hood, W. R., & Sherif, C. W. (1961). *Intergroup conflict and cooperation: The Robbers Cave experiment*. Norman: Institute of Group Relations, University of Oklahoma.

Sherif, M., & Sherif, C. W. (1969). *Social psychology*. New York: Harper & Row.

Shore, B. (1988, November). *Interpretation under fire.* Paper presented at the meetings of the American Anthropological Association, Phoenix, AZ.

Shore, B. (1996). *Culture in mind: Cognition, culture, and the problem of meaning.* New York: Oxford University Press.

Shotter, J. (1978). The cultural context of communication studies: Theoretical and methodological issues. In A. Lock (Ed.), *Action, gesture, and symbol: The emergence of language* (pp. 43–78). London: Academic Press.

Shwalb, D. W., Shwalb, B. J., Sukemune, S., & Tatsumoto, S. (1992). Japanese non-maternal child care: Past, present, and future. In M. E. Lamb, K. J. Sternberg, C.-P. Hwang, & A. G. Broberg (Eds.), *Child care in context* (pp. 331–353). Hillsdale, NJ: Erlbaum.

Shweder, R. A. (1979). Rethinking culture and personality theory, part II: A critical examination of two more classical postulates. *Ethos, 7,* 279–311.

Shweder, R. A. (Ed.). (1998) *Welcome to middle age! (and other cultural fictions).* Chicago: University of Chicago Press.

Shweder, R. (1991). *Thinking through cultures: Expeditions in cultural psychology.* Cambridge, MA: Harvard University Press.

Shweder, R. A., Goodnow, J., Hatano, G., LeVine, R. A., Markus, H., & Miller, P. (1998). The cultural psychology of development: One mind, many mentalities. In W. Damon (Ed.-in-chief) & R. M. Lerner (Ed.), *Theoretical models of human development* (Vol. 1: pp. 865–937) of *Handbook of child psychology* (5th ed.). New York: Wiley.

Shweder, R. A., Mahapatra, M., & Miller, J. G. (1990). Culture and moral development. In J. W. Stigler, R. A. Shweder, & G. Herdt (Eds.), *Cultural psychology: Essays on comparative human development.* Cambridge, England: Cambridge University Press.

Skeat, W. W. (1974). *An etymological dictionary of the English language.* Oxford: Clarendon Press.

Slaughter, D. T., & Dombrowski, J. (1989). Cultural continuities and discontinuities: Impact on social and pretend play. In M. N. Bloch & A. D. Pellegrini (Eds.), *The ecological context of children's play.* Norwood, NJ: Ablex.

Slobin, D. I. (1973). Cognitive prerequisites for the development of grammar. In C. A. Ferguson & D. I. Slobin (Eds.), *Studies of child language development.* New York: Holt, Rinehart & Winston.

Smitherman, G. (1977). *Talkin and testifyin: The language of Black America.* Boston: Houghton Mifflin.

Snow, C. E. (1984). Parent-child interaction and the development of communicative ability. In R. Schiefelbusch & J. Pickar (Eds.), *The acquisition of communicative competence.* Baltimore, MD: University Park Press.

Solomon, D., Watson, M., Schaps, E., Battistich, V., & Solomon, J. (1990). Cooperative learning as part of a comprehensive classroom program designed to promote prosocial development. In S. Sharan (Ed.), *Cooperative learning: Theory and research* (pp. 231–260). New York: Praeger.

Sorce, J. F., Emde, R. N., Campos, J., & Klinnert, M. D. (1985). Maternal emotional signaling: Its effect on the visual cliff behavior of 1-year-olds. *Developmental Psychology, 21,* 195–200.

Sorenson, E. R. (1979). Early tactile communication and the patterning of human organization: A New Guinea case study. In M. Bullowa (Ed.), *Before speech: The beginning of interpersonal communication* (pp. 289–305). Cambridge, England: Cambridge University Press.

Sostek, A. M., Vietze, P., Zaslow, M., Kreiss, L., van der Waals, F., & Rubinstein, D. (1981). Social context in caregiver-infant interaction: A film study of Fais and the United States. In T. M. Field, A. M. Sostek, P. Vietze, & P. H. Leiderman (Eds.), *Culture and early interactions*. Hillsdale, NJ: Erlbaum.

Spicher, C. H., & Hudak, M. A. (1997, August). *Gender role portrayal on Saturday morning cartoons: An update*. Paper presented at the American Psychological Association meetings, Chicago.

Spock, B. J. (1945). *The common sense book of child and baby care*. New York: Duell, Sloan, & Pearce.

Spring, J. H. (1996). *The cultural transformation of a Native American family and its tribe, 1763–1995*. Mahwah, NJ: Erlbaum.

Stairs, A. (1996). Human development as cultural negotiation: Indigenous lessons on becoming a teacher. *Journal of Educational Thought, 30*, 219–237.

Sternberg, R., Conway, B., Ketron, J., & Bernstein, M. (1981). People's conceptions of intelligence. *Journal of Personality and Social Psychology, 4*, 37–55.

Stevenson, H. W., Lee, S-Y., & Stigler, J. W. (1986). Mathematics achievement of Chinese, Japanese, and American children. *Science, 231*, 693–699.

Stevenson, H. W., Parker, T., Wilkinson, A., Bonnevaux, B., & Gonzalez, M. (1978). Schooling, environment, and cognitive development: A cross-cultural study. *Monographs of the Society for Research in Child Development, 43* (3, Serial no. 175).

Stevenson, H. W., Stigler, J. W., Lucker, G. W., Lee, S., Hsu, C., & Kitamura, K. (1987). Classroom behavior and achievement of Japanese, Chinese, and American children. In R. Glaser (Ed.), *Advances in instructional psychology* (Vol. 3, pp. 153–204). Hillsdale, NJ: Erlbaum.

Stewart, S. M., Bond, M. H., Zaman, R. M., McBride-Chang, C., Rao, N., Ho, L. M., & Fielding, R. (1999). Functional parenting in Pakistan. *International Journal of Behavioral Development, 23*, 747–770.

Stigler, J. W., Barclay, C., & Aiello, P. (1982). Motor and mental abacus skill: A preliminary look at an expert. *Quarterly Newsletter of the Laboratory of Comparative Human Cognition, 4*, 12–14.

Stipek, D. J. (1993). Is child-centered early childhood education really better? In S. Reifel (Ed.), *Advances in early education and day care*. Greenwich, CT: JAI Press.

Strauss, C. (2000). The culture concept and the individualism-collectivism debate: Dominant and alternative attributions for class in the United States. In L. P. Nucci, G. B. Saxe, & E. Turiel (Eds.), *Culture, thought, and development* (pp. 85–114). Mahwah, NJ: Erlbaum.

Strauss, S., Ankori, M., Orpaz, N., & Stavy, R. (1977). Schooling effects on the development of proportional reasoning. In Y. H. Poortinga (Ed.), *Basic problems in cross-cultural psychology*. Amsterdam: Swets.

Subbotskii, E. V. (1987). Communicative style and the genesis of personality in preschoolers. *Soviet Psychology, 25*, 38–58.

Subbotsky, E. (1995). The development of pragmatic and non-pragmatic motivation. *Human Development, 38*, 217–234.

Suina, J. H., & Smolkin, L. B. (1994). From natal culture to school culture to dominant society culture: Supporting transitions for Pueblo Indian students. In P. M. Greenfield & R. R. Cocking (Eds.), *Cross-cultural roots of minority child development* (pp. 115–130). Hillsdale, NJ: Erlbaum.

Super, C. M. (1979). *A cultural perspective on theories of cognitive development*. Paper presented at the meeting of the Society for Research in Child Development, San Francisco.

Super, C. M. (1981). Behavioral development in infancy. In R. H. Munroe, R. L. Munroe, & B. B. Whiting (Eds.), *Handbook of cross-cultural human development*. New York: Garland.

Super, C. M., & Harkness, S. (1982). The infant's niche in rural Kenya and metropolitan America. In L. L. Adler (Ed.), *Cross-cultural research at issue* (pp. 47–55). San Diego, CA: Academic Press.

Super, C. M., & Harkness, S. (1983). *Looking across at growing up: The cultural expression of cognitive development in middle childhood*. Unpublished manuscript, Harvard University.

Super, C. M., & Harkness, S. (1997). The cultural structuring of child development. In J. W. Berry, P. R. Dasen, & T. S. Saraswathi (Eds.), *Handbook of cross-cultural psychology: Vol. 2. Basic processes and human development* (pp. 1–39). Boston: Allyn and Bacon.

Sutter, B. & Grensjo, B. (1988). Explorative learning in the school? Experiences of local historical research by pupils. *Quarterly Newsletter of the Laboratory of Comparative Human Cognition, 10*, 39–54.

Swetz, F. (1987). *Capitalism and arithmetic: The new math of the 15th century*. La Salle, IL: Open Court.

Swisher, K. (1990). Cooperative learning and the education of American Indian/Alaskan Native students: A review of the literature and suggestions for implementation. *Journal of American Indian Education, 29*, 36–43.

Swisher, K., & Deyhle, D. (1989). The styles of learning are different, but the teaching is just the same: Suggestions for teachers of American Indian youth. *Journal of American Indian Education, 21*, 1–14.

Sylva, K., Bruner, J. S., & Genova, P. (1976). The role of play in the problem–solving of children 3–5 years old. In J. S. Bruner, A. Jolly, & K. Sylva (Eds.), *Play: Its role in development and evolution* (pp. 244–257). New York: Basic Books.

Tafoya, T. (1989). Coyote's eyes: Native cognition styles. *Journal of American Indian Education, 21*, 29–42.

Takahashi, K. (1990). Are the key assumptions of the "Strange Situation" procedure universal? A view from Japanese research. *Human Development, 33*, 23–30.

Taylor, D. (1983). *Family literacy*. Exeter, NH: Heinemann.

Tharp, R. G. (1989). Psychocultural variables and constants: Effects on teaching and learning in schools. *American Psychologist, 44*, 349–359.

Tharp, R. G., & Gallimore, R. (1988). *Rousing minds to life: Teaching, learning, and schooling in social context*. Cambridge, England: Cambridge University Press.

Thomas, D. R. (1975). Cooperation and competition among Polynesian and European children. *Child Development, 46*, 948–953.

Thomas, W. I., & Znaniecki, F. (1984). The peasant letter. In E. Zaretsky (Ed.), *The Polish peasant in Europe and America* (pp. 143–156). Urbana: University of Illinois Press.

Timm, P., & Borman, K. (1997). The soup pot don't stretch that far no more: Intergenerational patterns of school leaving in an urban Appalachian neighborhood. In M. Seller & L. Weis (Eds.), *Beyond black and white: New faces and voices in U.S. schools*. Albany: State University of New York Press.

Tizard, B., & Hughes, M. (1984). *Young children learning*. Cambridge, MA: Harvard University Press.

Tobin, J. J., Wu, D. Y., & Davidson, D. H. (1989). *Preschool in three cultures*. New Haven: Yale University Press.

Tobin, J. J., Wu, D. Y. H., & Davidson, D. H. (1991). Forming groups. In B. Finkel-
stein, A. E. Imamura, & J. J. Tobin (Eds.), *Transcending stereotypes: Discovering
Japanese culture and education* (pp. 109–117). Yarmouth, ME: Intercultural Press.

Tomasello, M. (1992). The social bases of language acquisition. *Social Development, 1*,
67–87.

Tomasello, M. (in press). The cultural roots of language. In B. Velichkovsky & D.
Rumbaugh (Eds.), *Naturally human: Origins and destiny of language*. Princeton:
Princeton University Press.

Trawick-Smith, J. W. (1997). *Early childhood development: A multicultural perspective.*
Upper Saddle River, NJ: Prentice Hall.

Trevarthen, C. (1988). Universal co–operative motives: How infants begin to know
the language and culture of their parents. In G. Jahoda & I. M. Lewis (Eds.),
Acquiring culture: Cross–cultural studies in child development. London: Croom
Helm.

Trevarthen, C., & Hubley, P. (1978). Secondary intersubjectivity: Confidence, confid-
ing and acts of meaning in the first year. In A. Lock (Ed.), *Action, gesture and
symbol: The emergence of language* (pp. 183–229). London: Academic.

Trevathan, W. R., & McKenna, J. J. (1994). Evolutionary environments of human
birth and infancy: Insights to apply to contemporary life. *Children's
Environments, 11*, 88–104.

Tronick, E., Morelli, G. A., & Winn, S. (1987). Multiple caretaking of Efe (Pygmy)
infants. *American Anthropologist, 89*, 96–106.

True, M. M., Pisani, L., & Oumar, F. (2001). Infant–mother attachment among the
Dogon of Mali. *Child Development, 72*, 1451–1466.

Tudge, J. R. H. (1992). Processes and consequences of peer collaboration: A Vygotskian analysis. *Child Development, 63*, 1364–1379.

Tudge, J. R. H., & Winterhoff, P. (1993). Can young children benefit from collaborative problem solving? Tracing the effects of partner competence and feedback.
Social Development, 2, 242–259.

Tulviste, P. (1991). *The cultural–historical development of verbal thinking.* Commack,
New York: Nova Science Publishers.

Ueno, N., & Saito, S. (1995, April). *Historical transformations of math as artifacts for
socio–economic distribution in a Nepalese bazaar.* Paper presented at the meetings
of the American Educational Research Association, San Francisco.

United States Census Bureau. (2000). *Statistical abstract of the United States.* Washington, DC: U.S. Government Printing Office.

Utley, R. M. (Ed.). (1964). *Battlefield and classroom: Four decades with the American
Indian 1867–1904 [The memoirs of Richard Henry Pratt].* New Haven, CT: Yale
University Press.

Valdés, G. (2002). *Expanding definitions of giftedness: The case of young interpreters of
immigrant communities.* Mahwah, NJ: Erlbaum.

Valentine, C. A. (1971). Deficit, difference, and bicultural models of Afro–American
behavior. *Harvard Educational Review, 41*, 137–157.

Valsiner, J. (1984). Construction of the zone of proximal development in adult–child
joint action: The socialization of meals. In B. Rogoff & J. V. Wertsch (Eds.),
Children's learning in the "zone of proximal development" (pp. 65–76). San Francisco: Jossey–Bass.

Valsiner, J. (1987). *Culture and the development of children's action.* Chichester, England: Wiley.

Valsiner, J. (1994). *Comparative–cultural and constructivist perspectives.* Norwood, NJ: Ablex.

Valsiner, J. (2000). *Culture and human development: An introduction.* London: Sage.

Valsiner, J., & Lawrence, J. A. (1997). Human development in culture across the life span. In J. W. Berry, P. R. Dasen, & T. S. Saraswathi (Eds.), *Handbook of cross-cultural psychology: Vol. 2. Basic processes and human development* (pp. 69–106). Boston: Allyn and Bacon.

van der Veer, R., & Valsiner, J. (1991). *Understanding Vygotsky.* Oxford: Blackwell.

Velazquez, J. (1999). Pulp nonfiction: The story of paper. *Exploratorium Magazine, 23,* 4–9.

Verba, M. (1994). The beginnings of collaboration in peer interaction. *Human Development, 37,* 125–139.

Verdery, K. (1994). Ethnicity, nationalism, and state–making. In H. Vermeulen & C. Govers (Eds.), *The anthropology of ethnicity: Beyond "Ethnic groups and boundaries"* (pp. 33–58). Amsterdam: Het Spinhuis.

Vigil, J. D. (1988). Group processes and street identity: Adolescent Chicano gang members. *Ethos, 16,* 421–444.

Vivero, V. N., & Jenkins, S. R. (1999). Existential hazards of the multicultural individual: Defining and understanding "cultural homelessness." *Cultural Diversity and Ethnic Minority Psychology, 5,* 6–26.

Vogt, L. A., Jordan, C., & Tharp, R. G. (1987). Explaining school failure, producing school success: Two cases. *Anthropology and Education Quarterly, 18,* 276–286.

Vygotsky, L. S. (1967). Play and its role in the mental development of the child. *Soviet Psychology, 5,* 6–18.

Vygotsky, L. S. (1978). *Mind in society: The development of higher psychological processes.* Cambridge, MA: Harvard University Press.

Vygotsky, L. S. (1987). *Thinking and speech.* In R. W. Rieber & A. S. Carton (Eds.), *The collected works of L. S. Vygotsky* (N. Minick, Trans.) (pp. 37–285). New York: Plenum.

Wagner, D. A., & Spratt, J. E. (1987). Cognitive consequences of contrasting pedagogies: The effects of Quranic preschooling in Morocco. *Child Development, 58,* 1207–1219.

Waldron, J. (1996). Multiculturalism and mélange. In R. K. Fullinwider (Ed.), *Public education in a multicultural society: Policy, theory, critique* (pp. 90–118). New York: Cambridge University Press.

Walker, S. S. (2001). Are you hip to the jive? (Re)writing/righting the pan-American discourse. In S. S. Walker (Ed.), *African roots/American cultures: Africa in the creation of the Americas* (pp. 1–44). Lanham, MD: Rowman & Littlefield.

Ward, M. C. (1971). *Them children: A study in language learning.* New York: Holt, Rinehart & Winston.

Watson-Gegeo, K. A. (1990). The social transfer of cognitive skills in Kwara'ae. *Quarterly Newsletter of the Laboratory of Comparative Human Cognition, 12,* 86–90.

Watson-Gegeo, K. A., & Gegeo, D. W. (1986a). *Communicative routines in Kwara'ae children's language socialization (Final report).* Washington, DC: National Science Foundation.

Watson-Gegeo, K. A., & Gegeo, D. W. (1986b). The social world of Kwara'ae children: Acquisition of language and values. In J. Cook–Gumperz, W. Corsaro, & J. Streeck (Eds.), *Children's worlds and children's language.* The Hague: Mouton.

Watson-Gegeo, K. A., & Gegeo, D. W. (1989). The role of sibling interaction in child socialization. In P. Zukow (Ed.), *Sibling interaction across cultures: Theoretical and methodological issues*. New York: Springer–Verlag.

Waxman, S.,& Gelman, R. (1986). Preschoolers' use of superordinate relations in classification and language. *Cognitive Development, 1*, 139–156.

Weatherford, J. (1988). *Indian givers: How the Indians of the Americas transformed the world*. New York: Crown.

Weisner, T. S. (1989). Cultural and universal aspects of social support for children: Evidence from the Abaluyia of Kenya. In D. Belle (Ed.), *Children's social networks and social supports* (pp. 70–90). New York: Wiley.

Weisner, T. S. (1997). Support for children and the African family crisis. In T. S. Weisner, C. Bradley, & P. L. Kilbride (Eds.), *African families and the crisis of social change*. Westport, CT: Greenwood Press/Bergin & Garvey.

Weisner, T. S., & Bernheimer, L. P. (1998). Children of the 1960s at midlife: Generational identity and the family adaptive project. In R. A. Shweder (Ed.), *Welcome to middle age! (and other cultural fictions)*. Chicago: University of Chicago Press.

Weisner, T. S, Bradley, C., & Kilbride, P. L. (Eds.). (1997). *African families and the crisis of social change*. Westport, CT: Greenwood Press/Bergin & Garvey.

Weisner, T. S., & Gallimore, R. (1977). My brother's keeper: Child and sibling caretaking. *Current Anthropology, 18*, 169–190.

Weisner, T. S., Gallimore, R., & Jordan, C. (1988). Unpackaging cultural effects on classroom learning: Native Hawaiian peer assistance and child–generated activity. *Anthropology and Education Quarterly, 19*, 327–351.

Wells, G., Chang, G. L. M., & Maher, A. (1990). Creating classroom communities of literate thinkers. In S. Sharan (Ed.), *Cooperative learning: Theory and research*. New York: Praeger.

Wenar, C. (1982). On negativism. *Human Development, 25*, 1–23.

Wenger, E. (1999). *Communities of practice*. New York: Cambridge University Press.

Wenger, M. (1983). *Gender role socialization in an East African community: Social inter action between 2- to 3-year-olds and older children in social ecological perspective*. Unpublished doctoral dissertation, Harvard University.

Werker, J. F., & Desjardins, R. N. (1995). Listening to speech in the 1st year of life: Experiential influences on phoneme perception. *Current Directions in Psychological Science, 4*, 76–81.

Werner, E. E. (1979). *Cross-cultural child development: A view from the Planet Earth*. Monterey, CA: Brooks/Cole.

Wertsch, J. V. (1979). From social interaction to higher psychological processes. *Human Development, 22*, 1–22.

Wertsch, J. V. (1984). The zone of proximal development: Some conceptual issues. In B. Rogoff & J. V. Wertsch (Eds.), *Children's learning in the "zone of proximal development"* (pp. 7–18). San Francisco: Jossey–Bass.

Wertsch, J. V. (1985). *Vygotsky and the social formation of mind*. Cambridge, MA: Harvard University Press.

Wertsch, J. V. (1991). *Voices of the mind: A sociocultural approach to mediated action*. Cambridge, MA: Harvard University Press.

Wertsch, J. V. (1998). *Mind as action*. New York: Oxford University Press.

Whaley, A. L. (2000). Sociocultural differences in the developmental consequences of the use of physical discipline during childhood for African Americans. *Cultural Diversity and Ethnic Minority Psychology, 6*, 5–12.

White, M. (1987). *The Japanese educational challenge: A commitment to children.* New York: Free Press.

White, M. I., & LeVine, R. A. (1986). What is an Ii Ko (good child)? In H. Stevenson, H. Azuma, & K. Hakuta (Eds.), *Child development and education in Japan* (pp. 55–62). New York: Freeman.

White, S. H. (1965). Evidence for a hierarchical arrangement of learning processes. In L. P. Lipsitt & C. C. Spiker (Eds.), *Advances in child development and behavior* (Vol. 2, pp. 187–220). New York: Academic Press.

White, S. H. (1976). Socialization and education: For what and by what means? In N. B. Talbot (Ed.), *Raising children in modern America.* Boston: Little, Brown.

Whitehead, H. (1981). The bow and the burden strap. In S. B. Ortner & H. Whitehead (Eds.), *Sexual meanings: The cultural construction of gender and sexuality* (pp. 80–115). Cambridge, England: Cambridge University Press.

Whitehurst, G. J., Arnold, D. S., Epstein, J. N., Angell, A. L., Smith, M., & Fischel, J. E. (1994). A picture book reading intervention in day care and home for children from low–income families. *Developmental Psychology, 30,* 679–689.

Whiting, B. B. (1974). Folk wisdom and child rearing. *Merrill–Palmer Quarterly, 20,* 9–19.

Whiting, B. B. (1976). The problem of the packaged variable. In K. F. Riegel & J. A. Meacham (Eds.), *The developing individual in a changing world.* Chicago: Aldine.

Whiting, B. B. (1979). *Maternal behavior in cross-cultural perspective.* Paper presented at the meeting of the Society for Cross-Cultural Research, Charlottesville, VA.

Whiting, B. B. (1980). Culture and social behavior: A model for the development of social behavior. *Ethos, 8,* 95–116.

Whiting, B. B. (1996). The effect of social change on concepts of the good child and good mothering: A study of families in Kenya. *Ethos, 24,* 3–35.

Whiting, B. B., & Edwards, C. (1973). A cross–cultural analysis of sex differences in the behavior of children aged 3 to 11. *Journal of Social Psychology, 91,* 171–188.

Whiting, B. B., & Edwards, C. P. (1988). *Children of different worlds: The formation of social behavior.* Cambridge, MA: Harvard University Press.

Whiting, B. B., & Whiting, J. W. M. (1975). *Children of six cultures: A psycho–cultural analysis.* Cambridge, MA: Harvard University Press.

Whiting, J. W. M. (1964). The effects of climate on certain cultural practices. In W. H. Goodenough (Ed.), *Explorations in cultural anthropology: Essays in honor of George Peter Murdock* (pp. 511–544). New York: McGraw–Hill.

Whiting, J. W. M. (1981). Environmental constraints on infant care practices. In R. H. Munroe, R. L. Munroe, & B. B. Whiting (Eds.), *Handbook of cross–cultural human development.* New York: Garland.

Whiting, J. W. M., & Child, I. L. (1953). *Child training and personality.* New Haven, CT: Yale University Press.

Wierzbicka, A. (1996). Japanese cultural scripts: Cultural psychology and "cultural grammar." *Ethos, 24,* 527–555.

Willinsky, J. (1998). *Learning to divide the world: Education at empire's end.* Minneapolis: University of Minnesota Press.

Wilson, W. J. (1974). The new Black sociology: Reflections on the "insiders" and "outsiders" controversy. In J. E. Blackwell & M. Janowitz (Eds.), *Black sociologists: Historical and contemporary perspectives* (pp. 322–338). Chicago: University of Chicago Press.

Wilson-Oyelaran, E. (1989). Towards contextual sensitivity in developmental psychology: A Nigerian perspective. In J. Valsiner (Ed.), *Child development in cultural context* (pp. 51–66) Toronto: Hogrefe & Huber.

Witmer, S. (1996). Making peace, the Navajo way. *Tribal College Journal, 8,* 24–27.

Wober, M. (1972). Culture and the concept of intelligence: A case in Uganda. *Journal of Cross-Cultural Psychology, 3,* 327–328.

Wohlwill, J. F. (1970). The age variable in psychological research. *Psychological Review, 77,* 49–64.

Wolf, D. P. (1988). Becoming literate: One reader reading. *Academic Connections* 1–4.

Wolf, E. R. (1994). Perilous ideas: Race, culture, people. *Current Anthropology, 35,* 1–12.

Wolf, E. R. (1997). *Europe and the people without history.* Berkeley: University of California Press.

Wolf, S. A., & Heath, S. B. (1992). *The braid of literature: Children's world of reading.* Cambridge, MA: Harvard University Press.

Wolfenstein, M. (1955). French parents take their children to the park. In M. Mead & M. Wolfenstein (Eds.), *Childhood in contemporary cultures.* Chicago: University of Chicago Press.

Wood, D. (1986). Aspects of teaching and learning. In M. Richards & P. Light (Eds.), *Children of social worlds* (pp. 191–212). Cambridge, England: Polity Press.

Wozniak, R. H. (1993). *Worlds of childhood.* New York: HarperCollins.

Yamauchi, L. A., & Tharp, R. G. (1994, April). Policy and the development of effective education for Native Americans. Paper presented at the meetings of the American Educational Research Association, New Orleans.

Young, V. H. (1970). Family and childhood in a Southern Negro community. *American Anthropology, 72,* 269–288.

Zborowski, M. (1955). The place of book-learning in traditional Jewish culture. In M. Mead & M. Wolfenstein (Eds.), *Childhood in contemporary cultures.* Chicago: University of Chicago Press.

Zellermayer, M., Salomon, G., Globerson, T., & Givon, H. (1991). Enhancing writing-related metacognitions through a computerized writing partner. *American Educational Research Journal, 28,* 373–391.

Zihlman, A. (1989). Woman the gatherer: The role of women in early hominid evolution. In S. Morgen (Ed.), *Gender and anthropology* (pp. 21–36). Washington, DC: American Anthropological Association.

Zinchenko, V. P. (1985). Vygotsky's ideas about units for the analysis of mind. In J. V. Wertsch (Ed.), *Culture, communication and cognition: Vygotskian perspectives* (pp. 94–118). Cambridge, England: Cambridge University Press.

Zukow, P. G., Reilly, J., & Greenfield, P. M. (1982). Making the absent present: Facilitating the transition from sensorimotor to linguistic communication. In K. E. Nelson (Ed.), *Children's language* (Vol. 3, pp. 1–90). New York: Gardner Press.

Figure Credits

1.2, 6.2 David Wilkie. 1.3 From Zborowski, 1955. Courtesy of YIVO. 1.4, 3.1, 3.5, 4.1a, 5.1, 5.2, 5.3, 5.4, 5.7, 7.7, 8.7, 9.1 Shades of L.A. Archives/ Los Angeles Public Library. 1.5, 4.8, 7.3, 7.4 Photographs by John Collier, Jr., courtesy of the Collier Family Collection. 2.1 Reprinted by permission of the publisher from *Children of Six Cultures: A Psycho-Cultural Analysis* by Beatrice B. Whiting and John W.M. Whiting, Cambridge, MA: Harvard University Press, Copyright ©1975 by the President and Fellows of Harvard College. 2.2b Cole & Cole, 1996. 3.3 Photo by Joe Steinmetz, Sarasota, FL, ca. 1950, courtesy of the Fogg Art Museum, Harvard University Art Museums, on deposit from the Carpenter Center for the Visual Arts. 3.4 The Metropolitan Museum of Art, Catharine Lorillard Wolfe Collection, Wolfe Fund, 1907. (07.122). All rights reserved, The Metropolitan Museum of Art. 4.1b Courtesy of Strong Museum, Rochester, NY, copyright 1992. 4.1c Historical Collections and Labor Archives, Penn State. 4.1d Irwin J. Weinfeld and the Centering Corporation. 4.2 Documentary Educational Resources. 4.4 Stephen Koester. 4.5 Photograph by Ed Tronick. Courtesy of Anthro-Photo File. 4.6 Regional Museum of Drenthe, Assen. 4.7 Brown Brothers. 5.5 Lorenzo D. Creel Collection, Special Collections, University of Nevada-Reno Library. 5.8 Reprinted with permission from *America's Children: Resources from Family, Government, and the Economy*, by Donald J. Hernandez. © 1993, Russell Sage Foundation, 112 East 64th Street, NY, 10021. 5.9 Library of Congress. 6.1 Oscar Magarian. 6.3, 6.5 Courtesy of Museum of New Mexico, #50786, #1036. 6.4 The Metropolitan Museum of Art (13.288.7). All rights reserved, The Metropolitan Museum of Art. 7.1 Photograph by Patrik Dasen. Reprinted from *Human Behavior in Global Perspective*, p. 71, by M.H. Segall, P.R. Dasen, J.W. Berry & Y.H. Poortinga (Eds.), Boston, MA: Allyn & Bacon, copyright 1999,1990. 7.5 Geoffrey Saxe. 7.6 Robert Serpell, 1993. 7.8 Courtesy of Marc Hauss. Thanks to Micah Lubensky. 8.2, 8.5a-d Film Study Center, Harvard University. 8.3 Copyright 2002 Bob Sacha. 8.4 Copyright 1990 Marjorie Goodwin. 8.8 The Metropolitan Museum of Art, Rogers Fund, 1922. (JP 1278). All rights reserved, The Metropolitan Museum of Art. 9.2 Courtesy of O.J. Harvey. 9.3a,b Photos by J.N. Choate, courtesy of Museum of New Mexico, #2113 and 2112. Cover photo, 2.3a-g Copyright 2002 Barbara Rogoff. 1.1, 5.6, 8.6, 9.4 Copyright 1975 Barbara Rogoff. 3.2 Copyright 1989 Barbara Rogoff. 4.3, 7.2, 8.1 Copyright 1976 Barbara Rogoff. 6.6 Copyright 1994 Barbara Rogoff.

Quotation Credits

Ch 3 Haley (1976): From *Roots* by Alex Haley, copyright © 1976 by Alex Haley. Used by permission of Doubleday, a division of Random House, Inc.

Ch 4, 7 Kingsolver (1995): Excerpts [453 words] from pp. 77 & 100–1 from *High tide in Tucson: Essays from now or never* by Barbara Kingsolver. Copyright © 1995 by Barbara Kingsolver. Reprinted by permission of HarperCollins Publishers Inc.

Ch 4 Scheper-Hughes (1985): Reproduced by permission of the American Anthropological Association from *Ethos 13*(4). Not for sale or further reproduction.

Ch 5, 6 Shweder, Mahapatra, & Miller (1990): Reprinted by permission from University of Chicago Press from: *The emergence of morality in young children* / edited by J. Kagan and S. Lamb. Chicago : University of Chicago Press, 1987.

INDEX

Page numbers in italics indicate illustrations.